In this study, Steven Botterill explores the intellectual relationship between the greatest poet of the fourteenth century, Dante, and the greatest spiritual writer of the twelfth century, Bernard of Clairvaux. Botterill analyses the narrative episode involving Bernard as a character in the closing cantos of the *Paradiso*, against the background of his medieval reputation as a contemplative mystic, devotee of Mary, and, above all, a preacher of outstanding eloquence. Botterill draws on a wide range of materials to establish and illustrate the connections between Bernard's reputation and his portrayal in Dante's poem. He examines in detail two areas in which a direct intellectual influence of Bernard on Dante has recently been posited: the portrayal of Mary in the *Commedia*, and the concept of 'trasumanar' (*Paradiso*, I. 70). Botterill proposes a fresh approach to the analysis of the whole episode, re-evaluating its significance and its implications.

CAMBRIDGE STUDIES IN MEDIEVAL LITERATURE 22

# DANTE AND THE MYSTICAL TRADITION BERNARD OF CLAIRVAUX IN THE *COMMEDIA*

This series of critical books seeks to cover the whole area of literature written
in the major medieval languages – the main European vernaculars, and
medieval Latin and Greek – during the period *c.* 1100–*c.* 1500. Its chief aim
is to publish and stimulate fresh scholarship and criticism on medieval
literature, special emphasis being placed on understanding major works of
poetry, prose and drama in relation to the contemporary culture and
learning which fostered them.

*Recent titles in the series*
10 *The Book of Memory: A study of memory in medieval culture*, by Mary J.
Carruthers
11 *Rhetoric, Hermeneutics and Translation in the Middle Ages: Academic
traditions and vernacular texts*, by Rita Copeland
12 *The Arthurian Romances of Chrétien de Troyes: Once and future fictions*, by
Donald Maddox
13 *Richard Rolle and the Invention of Authority*, by Nicholas Watson
14 *Dreaming in the Middle Ages*, by Steven F. Kruger
15 *Chaucer and the Tradition of the 'Roman Antique'*, by Barbara Nolan
16 *The 'Romance of the Rose' and its Medieval Readers: Interpretation,
reception, manuscript transmission*, by Sylvia Huot
17 *Women and Literature in Britain, 1150–1500*, edited by Carol M. Meale
18 *Ideas and Forms of Tragedy from Aristotle to the Middle Ages*, by Henry
Ansgar Kelly
19 *The Making of Textual Culture: Grammatica and literary theory,
350–1100*, by Martin Irvine
20 *Narrative Authority, and Power: The medieval exemplum and the Chaucerian
tradition*, by Larry Scanlon
21 *Medieval Dutch Literature in its European Context*, edited by Erik
Kooper
22 *Dante and the Mystical Tradition: Bernard of Clairvaux in the
'Commedia'*, by Steven Botterill

*A complete list of titles in the series is given at the end of this volume*

# DANTE AND THE MYSTICAL TRADITION BERNARD OF CLAIRVAUX IN THE *COMMEDIA*

STEVEN BOTTERILL

*Associate Professor of Italian, University of California at Berkeley*

CAMBRIDGE
UNIVERSITY PRESS

Published by the Press Syndicate of the University of Cambridge
The Pitt Building, Trumpington Street, Cambridge, CB2 1RP
40 West 20th Street, New York, NY 10011-4211, USA
10 Stamford Road, Oakleigh, Melbourne 3166, Australia

First published 1994

Printed in Great Britain at the University Press, Cambridge

Chapter 4, 'Bernard in the Trecento commentaries on the *Commedia*' has been reprinted
from *Dante Studies, Vol. CIX* by permission of the State University of New York Press.

*A catalogue record for this book is available from the British Library*

*Library of Congress cataloguing in publication data*
Botterill, Steven.
Dante and the mystical tradition: the figure of St. Bernard in Dante's Commedia, / by
Steven Botterill.
p.   cm. – (Cambridge studies in medieval literature; 22)
Originally presented as the author's thesis (doctoral – Cambridge).
Includes bibliographical references and index.
ISBN 0 521 43454 8 (hardback)
1. Dante Alighieri, 1265–1321. Paradiso. Canto 31–33.   2. Bernard, of Clairvaux, Saint
1090 or 91–1153, in fiction, drama, poetry, etc.   3. Mysticism in literature.   4. Bernard,
of Clairvaux, Saint, 1090 or 91–1153 – Influence.   5. Dante Alighieri, 1265–1321. Divina
commedia.   I. Title.   II. Series.
PQ4410.B55B67   1994
851'.1 – dc20   93-26480   CIP

ISBN 0 521 43454 8 hardback

*For my parents, Jeanne and Peter Botterill*
*and my grandmother, Alice Stone*
con amore

If we could get the hang of it entirely
    It would take too long;
All we know is the splash of words in passing
    And falling twigs of song,
And when we try to eavesdrop on the great
    Presences it is rarely
That by a stroke of luck we can appropriate
    Even a phrase entirely.

Louis MacNeice

# Contents

*Acknowledgements*                                                  page x

1  (Re-)reading Dante: an unscientific preface                          1

PART I   READING

2  The image of St Bernard in medieval culture                        13

3  Bernard of Clairvaux in the *Commedia*                             64
   Life after Beatrice (*Paradiso* XXXI)                              64
   Mellifluous Doctor (*Paradiso* XXXII)                              86
   Faithful Bernard (*Paradiso* XXXIII)                              108

PART II   RE-READING

4  Bernard in the Trecento commentaries on the *Commedia*            119

5  Dante, Bernard, and the Virgin Mary                               148

6  From *deificari* to *trasumanar*? Dante's *Paradiso* and
   Bernard's *De diligendo Deo*                                      194

7  Eloquence – and its limits                                        242

*Bibliography*                                                       254
*Index*                                                              264

# Acknowledgements

This book owes most of whatever merit it may possess to the teaching and scholarship of three remarkable individuals in the Italian Department at the University of Cambridge: Patrick Boyde, Robin Kirkpatrick, and the much-missed Kenelm Foster. These three have shaped my thinking about Dante, and much else, for many years now, and my constant, if no doubt unavailing, concern has been to make my own work worthy of their example. Many other friends and colleagues, at Cambridge, Berkeley, and elsewhere, have been generous with practical help, sound advice, warm encouragement, and, above all, trenchant criticism: I am especially grateful (more so, perhaps, than they realize) to Peter Armour, Zygmunt G. Barański, John Barnes, Alastair Minnis, Lino Pertile, Ruggero Stefanini, David Wallace, and Tibor Wlassics.

To Kate Brett, Joanna West, and Rosemary Morris, of Cambridge University Press, I owe thanks for the speed, skill and tact with which they guided both book and author through the editorial process.

Translations are mine unless otherwise stated. Chapter 4 was first published independently in *Dante Studies*, 109 (1991), 89–118, and I wish to thank that journal's publishers, the State University of New York Press, and its editor, Christopher Kleinhenz, for permission to reprint it here. The first two sections of chapter 3 draw some of their arguments and phrasing from two earlier articles of mine: 'Life after Beatrice: Bernard of Clairvaux in *Paradiso* XXXI', *Texas Studies in Literature and Language*, 32 (1990), 120–36, and 'Doctrine, Doubt and Certainty: *Paradiso* XXXII. 40–84', *Italian Studies*, 42 (1987), 20–36. The lines from Louis MacNeice's poem 'Entirely' which appear at the beginning of this volume are quoted from *The Collected Poems of Louis MacNeice* edited by E. R. Dodds, by permission of Faber and Faber Ltd.

By pure coincidence, if there is such a thing, I am writing these words on my thirty-fifth birthday, truly 'nel mezzo del cammin di nostra vita'. It is thus not only pleasant, but peculiarly appropriate, to recall how much I owe to the three people who were with me at my journey's beginning, and who have sustained me with their love, unstinting and unquestioning, ever since. Because it is mine, this book is also theirs; and to them it is dedicated.

# CHAPTER I

# (Re-)reading Dante: an unscientific preface

Reflect a little, if you will, on exactly what it is that you are doing at this moment. I have, of course, no way of knowing who you are, or where you are, or when this moment is – whether a day, a month, a year, or (I flatter myself) a century after these words first see the light of print – but I can still affirm, with absolute certainty, what activity you are currently engaged in. You are reading; your eye is scanning a page on which are printed certain symbols whose arrangement forms patterns to which you are able to assign meaning on the basis of your acquaintance with the semiotic system we call the English language. In so doing, you are participating in a remarkably complex and demanding enterprise whose nature is still by no means fully understood. This book begins from the recognition that what is involved in reading requires very careful consideration indeed from those of us who claim to do it well enough to wish to share the results of our reading with others.

The actions and processes that constitute the enterprise of reading, which the vast majority of people (at least in the Western world) are happily able to take for granted and, I suspect, rarely if ever pause to consider, have provoked a good deal of interest in various branches of the academic community in recent decades. Much of this has been directed towards the production of studies whose strictly scientific basis and assumptions carry them far beyond the scope of this book's preoccupations (or its author's competence). But, even within the comparatively circumscribed arena of the scholarly criticism of literature, extensive attention has been paid, especially in the last thirty years or so, to the ways in which the reader of a text may become actively involved in the production or delineation of that text's meaning. The schools of criticism and theory that have developed around the several approaches to the phenomenon of the reader and readerly activity are numerous, prolific, and more than

occasionally combative; and it is no part of my present undertaking
to assess the extent or value of their contributions to critical debate.[1]
It is, none the less, in the broad realm of a criticism informed by an
interest in the role of the reader and the process of reading that this
study aspires to find its place – a place whose marginal location will
perhaps be guaranteed as much by the tentativeness of my conclusions as by the specificity of my project.

The subject of this book is a brief episode that occurs very near the
end of Dante's *Commedia*: the intervention in the narrative of St
Bernard of Clairvaux, and his subsequent exchanges with, and
actions on behalf of, the character Dante. It may be seen primarily as
a close reading of that episode, which aims both to analyse this part
of *Paradiso* more thoroughly than has been attempted before, and to
identify some of the thematic principles that appear to underlie the
episode and to condition the details of its textual fabric. But this
double approach – exposition of the text and definition of the
concepts presumed to have affected its formulation – is further
modified by a broader set of ideas about the act of reading itself.
These ideas seem to me to bear with particular force on the reading
of the *Commedia* (as a poetic narrative, but also as a landmark in
intellectual history), and could thus, perhaps, usefully be brought
into play during the study of any part or parts of the poem – or, best
yet, when studying the whole vast verbal edifice as a single unit.

Briefly, my argument is that the *Commedia* is a Heraclitean river,
into which no reader can ever step twice and find it unaltered. Less
poetically, I would contend that there is a crucial difference between
a *first* reading of the poem and any or all subsequent reading(s); and,
equally, that no matter how many times a reader opens a copy of
*Inferno* at those mysteriously thrilling words 'Nel mezzo del cammin
di nostra vita / mi ritrovai in una selva oscura / ché la diritta via era
smarrita' (*Inf.*, I. 1–3), he or she is never setting out again on the same

---

[1] The work of the major figures in what is now a crowded field – Wolfgang Iser, Stanley Fish,
Hans-Robert Jauss – is voluminous and familiar enough to have inspired not only a large
number of epigones but also a good deal of metacritical writing about theories of readers and
reading. Useful introductions, from a variety of perspectives, include Robert C. Holub,
*Reception Theory: A Critical Introduction* (London and New York, 1984); Ian Maclean,
'Reading and Interpretation', in *Modern Literary Theory: A Comparative Introduction*, edited by
Ann Jefferson and David Robey, 2nd edition (London, 1986), pp. 122–44; and Elizabeth
Freund, *The Return of the Reader: Reader-Response Criticism* (London and New York, 1987). All
these include detailed guides to further reading. In connection with this chapter's interest in
*re*-reading, see François Roustang, 'On Reading Again', in *The Limits of Theory*, edited by
Thomas M. Kavanagh (Stanford, 1989), pp. 121–38; Matei Calinescu, *Rereading* (New
Haven and London, 1993).

journey, never beginning to read again the same poem. Reading and re-reading the *Commedia* are very different propositions; and it is a serious flaw in modern Dante criticism that this fact has been so inadequately recognized.

The reason for this is intimately connected with the status and activities of the poem's readers. Any reader of any text, I would argue, enters into what is essentially an eternal triangle (no less titillating, at least intellectually, than its better-known, more carnal counterpart). This triangle's three corners are the text, its author, and its reader; and the subtle interplay among these three (which often becomes a more or less well-concealed struggle to establish authority) is the process we call the production of meaning.

Sometimes, of course, the triangle turns out to be defective, or the conditions for its successful accomplishment seem to be absent; texts can be corrupt, authors unknown, readers ill-equipped. In such cases, the triangle's failure to operate effectively has to be admitted, and the critic must be content with what fragments of meaning can be salvaged from the wreckage. Where text or author or reader cannot be clearly defined as an element in the interpretative situation, the finally provisional nature of all critical judgements is brought home to criticism's practitioners with unaccustomed bluntness. But the *Commedia* is not such a case. It exists in a reliable and formally complete textual version (the small number of cruces and variants that remain unresolved after Giorgio Petrocchi's monumental labours, though naturally important in their specific contexts, do not substantially affect the coherence of the poem as a whole);[2] its author is all too well known, and his authorial presence all too blatant; and its readers, provided that they have a reasonable grasp of medieval Italian (without which they cannot become readers in the first place), should find no invincible obstacles to a productive engagement with it. Dante's 'poema sacro' thus offers a more than suitable testing-ground for theories of reading and, by extension, of re-reading.

When speaking of the eternal triangle created in reading a text, I mean to stress the active involvement of all three participants (another point of contact, no doubt, with alternative versions of the metaphor). The author is responsible for the text's formulation,

---

[2] *La 'Commedia' secondo l'antica vulgata*, edited by Giorgio Petrocchi, 4 vols. (Milan, 1966–7). Petrocchi's edition, which seems to come as close to perfection as is imaginable in this world, has been used for all quotations from the *Commedia* in this book.

according to designs which it *may*, up to a point, be possible for readers to recover and assess (though the use they then make of their conclusions remains variable and, indeed, controversial). The text, meanwhile, exists as a combination of words on a page that offers both material for interpretation and (implicit or explicit) guidance for that interpretation; and the reader brings to the relationship his or her individual personality, linguistic expertise, cultural formation, aesthetic sensibility, and investigative enthusiasm (or lack of same). All three elements co-exist and co-operate in a tremulous balance, constantly subject to oscillation as a consequence of alterations in one or other of the triangle's corners (new facts about the author, new emendations of the text, new experiences for the reader) – a balance that issues in the generation of meaning(s) and the establishment of (an) interpretation. However, because at least one of the corners is, in theory, terrifyingly unstable – there is a theoretically infinite number of potential readers of any given text – there can, in the end, be no unitary, definitive meaning, at which all readers will arrive and which then excludes all possibility of dissent or the formulation of alternatives. You have as much right to your interpretation of the *Commedia* as I do to mine; and, if we try to convince each other that our reading is more accurate, more plausible, or more satisfactory than any other, we are perhaps doing our duty as critics, but we are exceeding our mandate as readers. Diversity in interpretation is an inescapable consequence of the nature of reading itself.

But the diversity among readers as individuals is more readily comprehended, perhaps, than the equally significant diversity among an individual reader's separate readings. This is the issue with which this book attempts to deal. I would argue, returning to my particular concern with the *Commedia*, that reading and re-reading the poem need to be distinguished, in theory if not always in practice, if we are to achieve anything even remotely resembling an understanding of how the *Commedia* 'works', of how its narrative, language, thematics, and symbolism combine and interact to form a meaningful textual artefact. For any 'meaning' the *Commedia* may be said to possess, whether in the tenacious conviction of an individual reader or the blander consensus of a community of scholars, will vary in startlingly significant ways according, quite simply, to whether or not the reader involved has read the poem before.

Readers come to a first reading of the *Commedia* equipped with some degree of linguistic capability and some kind of intellectual prehistory, but no concrete knowledge of precisely what textual experiences the poem has in store for them. (They may, of course, know something *about* the poem, and thus have a rough idea of what to expect – but between rough idea and direct acquaintance there is a great gulf fixed.) Such readers are thus guided in their reading – wherever they start and wherever they stop – by signals, structures, and strategies built into the text itself; and their derivation of meaning from the words they identify and interpret will also be affected by such information and preconceptions (whether about the poem itself or matters arising from it) as they may have managed to acquire, from immersion in or study of the cultural setting to which the *Commedia* can be seen to belong. 'Immersion', of course, was only possible for Dante's immediate contemporaries; it is replaced by 'study', in the sense of recuperation of a culture that has substantially or totally ceased to exist, very early in the poem's critical history – arguably as early as Boccaccio's commentary (1373–4) and certainly by the time of Landino's (1481).[3]

First-time readers, then, advancing more or less timidly in their notably demanding exegetical adventure, are able to produce for themselves a cumulative interpretation of what they read, which is continually subject to revision in the light of their expanding experience of the poem. Not until the last word of *Paradiso* XXXIII has faded into the vacuum that replaces every text when the reading of it comes to an end can the first-time reader's interpretation be said to be complete; and, by then, every line that precedes *Paradiso*, XXXIII. 142 will, to a greater or lesser degree, look different from the way it did when it was first deciphered.

But the adventure does not end there, at least for those who, sooner or later, find themselves impelled to begin all over again in the 'selva oscura' – or, indeed, anywhere else in the Dantean afterlife. When they do so, they undertake a *re*-reading, and find themselves, therefore, on radically altered terms with the *Commedia*, both conceptually and hermeneutically. The prior knowledge of the text gained from a first reading now itself becomes one (and by no means the least important) of the exegetical instruments that re-readers are able to employ; and it helps them, among other things, to devise a static and internally consistent account of the poem's meaning, as a substitute for the dynamic and sometimes inevitably contradictory

---

[3] On this, see my article on the Trecento commentaries in the forthcoming second volume of *The Cambridge History of Literary Criticism*, edited by A. J. Minnis.

version generated during, and constantly modified by, the initial reading. Now they know how the story is going to end, so to speak, they can never again look at either that story or its characters as they did in the days of their interpretative innocence, when everything still remained to be discovered. So readers familiar with the text almost invariably begin to read prospectively as well as retrospectively, interpreting this or that feature of the poem not only in the light of what has preceded it in the linear unfolding of the *Commedia*'s narrative, but also in that of what they already know is going to happen further along.

And so it continues: each successive re-reading alters – let us hope, deepens – the reader's understanding of the poem as an entity, by modifying his or her interpretation of its (verbal, thematic, narrative) details. The poem comes, then, to exist not just in the temporal present of a particular occasion of reading, but also in the cumulative past created on earlier occasions; its very narrative comes to seem proleptic of itself, apparently announcing in advance what is, in fact, being supplied by the experienced reader's memory. Nor is it just the re-reading of the *Commedia* itself that contributes to this development: in between re-readings, readers are constantly changing, acquiring new experiences, encountering other texts, coining fresh ideas – and they then come back to the *Commedia* with eyes that make of it each time a subtly but unmistakably different text. This is why I spoke of the poem as a Heraclitean river: though it may seem to be always and reassuringly the same, as it sits snug on the shelf in its trinity of leather-bound or paperback volumes, this seeming constancy of the *Commedia*'s textual nature (and thus of its meaning) is exposed as an illusion as soon as one of those volumes is opened and a reader begins to read. The poem is actually, while being read, in a state of motion as rapid and unstoppable as the flow of water downhill to the sea.

In this book, therefore, I posit a crucial (and sadly neglected) distinction between a first reading of the *Commedia* (which I call 'reading'), and any or all later approaches by the 'same' reader ('re-reading'). Ancillary to this basic dichotomy is the potentially endless subdivision of re-readings according to their number, frequency, and so on; but that way lies, if not madness, at least an unnecessarily severe methodological headache. For the purpose of the present study I shall restrict myself to basing my argument on the fundamental difference between first and later readings.

My argument, then, is that 'reading' and 're-reading' are different exercises, capable of producing – indeed, destined to produce – different kinds of interpretation; and moreover that, while both have much to tell us about Dante's *Commedia*, the former – which I take to be an indispensable preliminary to any serious consideration of the poem – has all too often been disdained, omitted, or misperformed by modern Dante scholars. Our century knows too much about the *Commedia* for its own good: many of those who write about the poem in the 1990s begin with acts of 're-reading', taking mere 'reading' for granted (as though it were easy!), and thereby, in effect, asking their audience to join them in the literally preposterous exercise of trying to run before they have learned to walk.

There are, incidentally, a number of more elaborate exegetical schemes that might – with due and heartfelt protestations of modesty – be assimilated to the distinction between 'reading' and 're-reading'. One is the separation, characteristic of late medieval traditions of textual commentary, between the literal and allegorical levels of a text. This is observed, to varying degrees, by almost all the fourteenth-century commentators on the *Commedia*, and is given its most memorable form in the *Esposizioni* of Giovanni Boccaccio, where each canto examined is read first literally and then allegorically, the results of each reading being presented even as formally distinct (there are two separate chapters of analysis of each canto, except those – *Inferno* x and xi – that Boccaccio deems to have no allegorical significance).[4] In this context, 'reading' could be seen as related, conceptually if not historically, to the Trecento notion of literal analysis, being centred on the decoding of the letter of the text; while 're-reading', which takes that letter as its point of departure and then permits the free play of allegorical speculation, would belong to the general sphere of analysis of the letter's symbolic connotations.

At the other end of the historical spectrum, there is also the (distant) possibility of a correlation between the 'reading'/'re-reading' distinction and E. D. Hirsch's account of the difference between 'meaning' and 'significance' (though I am less anxious to restore the prestige of authorial intention, as a validating principle, than is the Hirsch of *Validity in Interpretation*).[5] Here too occurs the idea of the text as possessing – in some (disputable) sense – a (literal) 'meaning' on which all reasonable readers can agree, as well as an

---

[4] Giovanni Boccaccio, *Esposizioni sopra la 'Comedia' di Dante*, edited by Giorgio Padoan (Verona, 1965).

[5] E. D. Hirsch, Jr, *Validity in Interpretation* (New Haven and London, 1967).

(allegorical) 'significance', in which individual emphases and interpretations can be given freer rein, so as to be judged by different standards of evidence and validation. *Si parva licet componere magnis*, I would tentatively propose that the former is akin to what is involved in my notion of 'reading', the latter to what emerges from 're-reading'.

Mention of two approaches as historically far apart as those of the Trecento commentators and E. D. Hirsch raises another issue that should not be overlooked when it comes to thinking about how we read the *Commedia*: the danger of anachronism. It is sometimes claimed, in fact, that a fundamental and insoluble incompatibility afflicts any approach to a fourteenth-century text in the twentieth century: that the attempt to re-create Dante's own cultural horizon as a way of furthering our understanding of the poem, or to propound any particular response to it as being in tune with the presumed or documented response of its contemporaries, can no longer be reconciled with the awareness that we ourselves are inescapably conditioned by our own historical situation. On this view, it is impossible to see the *Commedia* – or any cultural phenomenon of the more than recent past, from the *Epic of Gilgamesh* to *The Waste Land* – with eyes other than those of the late twentieth century. Alterity, in a word, is assumed to preclude identification.

As the use of the 'horizon' metaphor in the previous paragraph implies, the work of Hans-Georg Gadamer is obviously indispensable to any effort to comprehend and overcome – or at least learn to live with – this problem.[6] But, again without wishing to make inflated claims for my own work, I would suggest that the distinction between 'reading' and 're-reading' can also be helpful and relevant in this case. 'Reading' offers an opportunity to come as close as is conceivably possible to an engagement with the poem on its own, medieval, terms (since it is based on the one thing we do have in common with the *Commedia*'s first readers, the letter of its text, and is guided by the indications supplied by that text itself); while 're-reading' not only makes possible the historical consideration of medieval reactions to the poem, and of the nature of the cultural

---

[6] Gadamer's extraordinary *magnum opus*, *Wahrheit und Methode* (Tübingen, 1960; 2nd edition, 1965), remains a necessary, if daunting, point of departure; an English translation, *Truth and Method* (London, 1975; revised edition, New York, 1989) is available. Several of the articles by Gadamer collected in *The Relevance of the Beautiful and Other Essays*, edited by Robert Bernasconi (Cambridge, 1986) also illuminate the possibilities for applying Gadamer's thinking to literary-critical and aesthetic questions.

matrix in which it is embedded, but also encourages fresh acts of interpretation, inspired by intellectual and critical developments that have taken place since the early fourteenth century. In short, while I am aware that there is no such person as the wholly innocent reader, who can occupy an Archimedean point outside history and come to the *Commedia* as a *tabula rasa* on which the poem can inscribe its meaning for itself – thus making our modern interpretations somehow 'authentic' – I suggest that 'reading' offers us the (potentially fruitful) chance to act as if there were. 'Re-reading', meanwhile, is free to stimulate the proliferation of interpretative hypotheses to an extent limited only by our (supposedly) healthy distrust of the arbitrary and the absurd.

What this book proposes, then, is both a 'reading' and a 're-reading' of the episode involving Bernard of Clairvaux in the closing cantos of *Paradiso*. My aim is to demonstrate that reading the letter of Dante's text – expounding its literal meaning and analyzing the narrative and formal structures and patterns that direct, from within the text itself, the production and definition of that meaning – prepares the way for the fullest possible appreciation of the episode's symbolic connotations, cultural background, and exegetical difficulties, all of which are also involved in the establishment of meaning and the activity of interpretation. I do not claim, on the other hand, to have escaped any of the obvious traps of subjectivity or historicity built into the situation I have been describing; the essential instability of the eternal hermeneutic triangle eliminates any such possibility. I do think it feasible, however, at least where the literal level of the *Commedia*'s text is concerned, to arrive at a measure of agreement among readers that may serve as a shared basis for more individually characterized essays in interpretation; and it is as a contribution to the development of such a consensus that this book is chiefly intended.

You, as both Dante's and – I trust – my reader, have, of course, the right and the power to silence my argument at any moment, by closing this book and replacing it wherever seems most appropriate at the time. However, I hope that, even if you do choose such a course, you will not give up the effort to make your own contribution to the reading – and re-reading – of this endlessly absorbing, endlessly frustrating, yet endlessly rewarding text that is Dante's *Commedia*.

# PART I

*Reading*

# CHAPTER 2

# The image of St Bernard in medieval culture

Almost midway through canto XXXI of *Paradiso*, Dante-character turns once again to his guide Beatrice, confident, as ever, that she will be able to resolve his intellectual perplexity – which has been inspired, on this occasion, by the astonishing sight of 'la forma general di paradiso' (*Par.*, XXXI. 51–7). She is no longer there. Instead Dante finds himself in the presence of a saintly old man (58–60), who smiles cheerfully at him (61–3), reassures him that Beatrice has only left his side to take her place 'nel trono che suoi merti le sortiro' (65–9), stands by him while he pays moving tribute to her in prayer (79–90), and only then, after this extensive preamble, declares his own identity and the purpose of his unexpected intervention in Dante's celestial pilgrimage. He has come, he announces, to ensure that Dante's journey reaches its destined and perfect conclusion in a vision of God under the auspices of the Virgin Mary; and he promises that the grace necessary for this altogether exceptional experience will be granted – because he is the Queen of Heaven's faithful subject, 'Bernardo' (94–102).

Dante's response to this revelation is as remarkable as the events that provoke it. An extended simile in the poem's narrating voice (103–11) compares the wonderment he feels, gazing at his interlocutor, to that of a traveller from some unimaginably wild and distant land – perhaps Croatia (103) – who has come to Rome to see the visage of Christ miraculously imprinted on St Veronica's sudarium. So absorbed, indeed, does Dante become, as he studies the newcomer's 'sembianza' (108), that he has to be reminded (112–17) that he will not fully understand the reality of the heavenly condition unless he directs his gaze upwards, through all the many tiers of the Empyrean, to the throne of Mary herself, 'cui questo regno è suddito e devoto' (117). Obedient as always, Dante looks up (118); but, as he does so, there is a strong sense that he is tearing himself away from an object of no less fascination to him, the features and person of 'colui che'n questo mondo, / contemplando, gustò di quella pace' (110–11).

This phrase is, among other things, a hint provided by the poem's narrator for the benefit of those who have not been as quick to identify the new arrival as Dante himself is. For him, this Bernard's self-proclaimed fidelity to Mary is enough, by itself, to mark him out instantly, among the many holy individuals of that name whom he might have anticipated meeting in Paradise; but the descriptive periphrasis that invokes the character's contemplative talents serves to confirm, for the reader with even a minimal knowledge of Christian history, that Dante is dealing here with St Bernard of Clairvaux, the twelfth-century mystic, monastic reformer, and spiritual writer. The narrative audacity of Bernard's arrival on the scene, the intensity of Dante-character's reaction to it, and the care taken by Dante-poet to establish Bernard's identity and stature, all combine to guarantee that this startling development, so close to the climax of the *Commedia*'s action and the culmination of Dante's journey, will be pushed to the very forefront of the reader's attention.

Once there, it can scarcely fail to provoke a number of pertinent questions. Why has Beatrice been replaced? Why at this particular juncture? What is her replacement going to do, to justify his intervention? How will Dante-character fare without his beloved guide, in the hands of an apparent usurper? And, most immediately pressing of all, just who is this Bernard who has taken Beatrice's place, on what grounds has he done so, and why is Dante-character so profoundly impressed by the sight of him?

The more concrete of these questions (those reducible to 'what happens now?') are answered in the course of the few remaining cantos of the poem; the more abstract ('what does it all mean?') have been debated by readers and commentators since the dawn of the *Commedia*'s critical history, and remain substantially unresolved to this day. This book is, in part, both a survey of the solutions put forward by others to the questions raised by Bernard's appearance, and an attempt to propose some additions and refinements to the interpretative consensus that has developed, through the centuries, around the figure of Dante's Bernard and the episode in which he is so centrally involved. But useful discussion of these issues depends on first reading onwards, to the last line of *Paradiso* XXXIII, and then reflecting, with informed hindsight and sharpened sensibility, on the episode as a whole, and on Bernard's place in it. It requires, that is, a *retrospective* view of Bernard, based on the process defined in chapter 1 as 're-reading'.

Before embarking on that very necessary enterprise, however, I would like to interrupt the linear unwinding of the *Commedia*'s narrative, to freeze the frame, as it were, at line 102 of *Paradiso* XXXI, and to try to re-create – in full awareness of the theoretical limitations inherent in the exercise – the reaction of a contemporary of Dante, encountering the poem and Bernard as a character in it for the first time. For it seems to me that the shock and bafflement felt by Dante-character in *Paradiso* XXXI are an image of what the poem's readers may be expected to feel, when they find their basic narrative assumptions, elaborately developed through the course of *Paradiso*, so radically subverted by Beatrice's disappearance; and, likewise, the sense of reassurance and almost passionate interest that Dante begins to feel, when he learns that he has before him none other than Bernard of Clairvaux, seem clearly intended to represent, if not to govern, the reader's reaction to the same discovery. We are, in a word, expected to be as excited by Bernard as Dante *personaggio* is.

We are also, it appears, expected to recognize him. Unlike many other characters in the *Commedia*, from Virgil onwards (*Inf.*, I. 67–75), Bernard offers no lengthy autobiography as a means of clarifying his identity; nor are his life-story and praises put in the mouth of any other character as a formal introduction (as are, for instance, those of St Francis and St Dominic in *Paradiso* XI and XII). Only Bernard's name, lacking even the precise geographical reference that would distinguish him unequivocally from all the other saintly Bernards (of Chartres, Cluny, Aosta, Quintavalle), along with a few scraps of allusion, cast in vague and general terms, to his earthly activities, accompany his entry into, and subsequent involvement in, the poem. Doubtless Dante judged that this would be enough: that his text itself supplied sufficient information about Bernard to make further explanation or justification of his replacement of Beatrice superfluous. But here again, the garnering of this information must be cumulative; it depends on sequential reading of the entire episode, and on assessing Dante's Bernard in retrospect. At this point, I am interested only in the moment of initial encounter in line 102, and in the recognition and understanding of Bernard triggered immediately, in both Dante-character and the reader, by the use of that evocative name.

Dante does not need to have Bernard's identity, or his importance in the Christian scheme of things, spelled out; these are things he already knows. The reader too, participating in Dante's experience and sharing his surprise and pleasure in the meeting with Bernard, is apparently supposed to make a connection between Bernard's presentation in the poem and some pre-constituted image or set of connotations originating outside it. Only thus can the announcement in line 102 make its full dramatic impact (it must inevitably fall flat for a reader whose response is 'Bernard *who?*'); and only thus can Bernard's historical specificity begin to cast the fullest possible light on his speeches and actions in the *Commedia*. As always, the poem's text provides the essentials; a reader wholly ignorant of Bernard's career would still, as we shall see, be able to find adequate guidance towards a valid reading of this episode in *Paradiso* itself. But the reader for whom Bernard is more than an unadorned name will be better placed, even on a first reading, to appreciate the meaning of his presence in the poem to the full; and it is just such a reader that the *Commedia* itself seems to envisage.

Any effort to read this episode 'as if for the first time' must, then, begin with some consideration of the intellectual baggage that the *Commedia* assumes that its readers will bring along on their journey; in this case, it must start by asking what a Trecento reader of *Paradiso* XXXI might reasonably have been expected to know or believe about Bernard of Clairvaux. For the *Commedia*'s characters do not spring fully formed and imaginatively autonomous from their author's pen. With the possible exception of Matelda – and even she has been tentatively identified with several historical women of that name – there is not a single character in the poem who did not enjoy some kind of existence in Western history or culture before Dante decided to incorporate him or her (or it!) into his poetic construct. That existence may have been historical fact (Julius Caesar, Saladin) or literary fiction (Achilles, Dido); it may have been mythological (Cerberus, Geryon) or Biblical (Adam, St Peter); the individuals concerned may have been world-famous (Virgil), locally famous (Ugolino), not famous at all (Ciacco), or of pressing importance only to Dante (Geri del Bello). But, in every case, Dante populated his narrative with individuals whose cultural reality was already attested in some other form. Whether they were chosen from among his Florentine contemporaries, the luminaries of recent history, the mythical avatars of the distant past, or the familiar personalities of classical and medieval literature, Dante's characters are figures about whom his readers might be expected to have some kind of opinion, however nebulous, long before they sat down to read the *Commedia*.

The entire personnel of the *Commedia*, in other words, can – or could – be met with elsewhere: in other texts, other stories, other lifetimes, other literary and documentary guises. According to the depth and extent of their experience or study, readers bring to their encounters with these characters an expectation formed by earlier contact. (Obviously this varies immensely in detail, not just among individuals but between generations: it is a rare twentieth-century reader who has heard of Jacopo Rusticucci, say, before meeting him in *Inferno* XVI; but this would not have been true in fourteenth-century Florence.) The characters of the *Commedia* are not, therefore, like those of the nineteenth-century European novel and the fictional forms descended from it, called into being by a particular text and known only in the form given them by that text (or, in the case of recurrent characters from Plantagenet Palliser to Biggles, texts). This difference has crucial consequences for the reader's response to the poem.

Readers of *Madame Bovary*, for example, know nothing more about its heroine than what the novel chooses to tell them, because Emma's reality is textually circumscribed; she did not exist in culture before Flaubert's novel was written, and she never did exist, as such, in history. As a result, to speak of 'Emma Bovary' is, inevitably, to speak of one character in the specific circumstances of one novel; and all discussion of her nature, motives, significance, and so on, is necessarily bounded by the text of that novel. Readers of the *Commedia*, on the other hand, have (or had) access to other versions of the characters they find there, and, as a result, can have a whole range of independent opinions, beliefs, and information about them, precisely because those characters are not circumscribed by the poem's text, not being Dante's 'invention' in the way that Emma Bovary is Flaubert's. A reader's impression of Dante's Bernard will undoubtedly – and perhaps fruitfully – be conditioned, to some extent, by that reader's acquaintance with the Bernard of history, in a way that is simply not available to readers of *Madame Bovary*, because there is no Emma apart from that conjured into being by Flaubert – and there never was.[1]

---

[1] It may be objected that the modern genre of historical fiction using 'real' characters – Robert Graves's *I, Claudius* or Gore Vidal's *Lincoln*, for instance (though the tradition

Underlying my concern with the reader's possible foreknowledge of Bernard of Clairvaux, and the nature of possible reactions to his appearance in *Paradiso* XXXI, is the contention that one of Dante's most characteristic narrative techniques is, precisely, to exploit his reader's prior familiarity with the *Commedia*'s characters for purposes of moral analysis, either by reinforcing it or, more often, by revising or contradicting it. The latter process, a 'defamiliarization' achieved by drawing attention to the disparity between the cultural consensus about a character and his or her portrayal in the poem, is usually given dramatic form, especially in *Inferno* and *Purgatorio*, where Dante-character repeatedly makes surprising discoveries as to who has been damned and who saved (Brunetto Latini, Guido da Montefeltro, Manfred); or it can, less dramatically, merely be a matter of allowing a character to correct, in his or her speech, an erroneous or uncomplimentary impression that still prevails on earth (Buonconte da Montefeltro succeeds in this; Ugolino, arguably, fails).

Even in *Paradiso* a character's true significance (for Dante, at least) is often brought out through some unforeseeable modification of his or her familiar lineaments, or by placing him or her in some unexpected configuration or company (Trajan and Ripheus, redeemed pagans, in canto XX; Siger of Brabant, surrounded by his intellectual rivals and opponents, in canto X). But in the third *cantica*, concerned as it is with the expression of truth in images of order, familiar aspects of the various characters are less often revised than confirmed, as the major figures of Christian history are successively depicted in ways fully consecrated by precedent. According to need and circumstances, then, Dante both defines and distorts the reader's horizon of expectations, taking his characters from the common stock of cultural experience and giving them back, in his poem, still recognizable, still attached to Christian or classical tradition, but always appropriated for his own ends, and sometimes significantly altered.

From this interplay between the historical reality and traditional

extends back at least as far as Balzac and Manzoni) – is akin to the *Commedia* in its treatment of individuals taken from history; but here too there is a crucial difference. Authors in this genre seek to recreate their characters' experience 'as it happened', and depict them in the context of their historically attested activity. The *Commedia*, of course, *removes* its characters from that context by showing them in the afterlife; at most, they are seen evoking or reflecting on their personal history, but they do not, within the narrative of the *Commedia* itself, re-enact it.

perception of a character, on the one hand, and that character's words and deeds in the *Commedia*, on the other, emerges each individual's significance in Dante's comprehensive vision of the past, critique of the present, and prophecy for the future. This is one reason why the poem must be read intertextually as well as intrinsically: the *Commedia* itself certainly furnishes all the information genuinely necessary for the interpretation and evaluation of its message(s) to the world, but understanding of that message and the form of its expression can only be deepened by studying them in their relations with the other texts and cultural phenomena (in the broadest possible sense) by which the poem, at least in part, is generated. Medieval culture as a whole thus forms a kind of echo-chamber, within which the sound of the *Commedia* must be allowed to reverberate, if it is to produce its richest possible effect, even before the more strident tones produced in post-medieval centuries are worked into the interpretative texture. In order, then, to explore more thoroughly what Bernard of Clairvaux says and does in *Paradiso*, and what his meaning may be in the total symbolic and thematic economy of the poem – which is the twofold project of the rest of this book – we must begin by seeing what Bernard *already* means at the moment of his appearance in *Paradiso* XXXI; that is, what he meant to the audience whom the *Commedia* addresses, and for whose benefit (*Purg.* XXXII. 103) it was undertaken – Dante's contemporaries.

The establishment of an individual's reputation within a given culture, and the dissemination of information about his or her achievement and personality to the point where certain aspects of that reputation become common knowledge, is a complex and fascinating process. It has been greatly facilitated, in our own day, by technological advances and the worldwide expansion of mass communications: in 1993, images (especially visual ones) of the Pope or the President of the United States are likely to be as familiar to the farmhand in Nebraska as to the shepherd in furthest Patagonia. But it would be a mistake to think of this as a purely twentieth-century phenomenon, even if the availability and efficiency of channels of cultural diffusion are greater today than ever before (and their products, it might be added, arguably more ephemeral). Nor would it be accurate to tie the emergence of the possibility of moulding a widespread, shared perception of a given individual too closely to any particular technological innovation, be it television, radio, the cinema, or even the printing-press. For all that they did not enjoy the sometimes debatable benefits of the printed – let alone the electronic – media, Dante's contemporaries participated in a network of cultural transmission whose range and sophistication were considerable, and which exploited many material forms, social institutions, and artistic practices, functioning simultaneously on a variety of levels and in several languages. In attempting to define 'the' – or even 'an' – image of Bernard of Clairvaux that was available to fourteenth-century readers of *Paradiso*, some account must be taken of the diversity of sources, representations, audiences, and ulterior motives involved in its formation.

This diversity is perhaps most readily perceived through the recognition of a number of structuring factors within medieval culture itself, factors whose relationships are usually expressed as oppositions or polarities: literate versus oral, Latin versus vernacular, ecclesiastical versus secular, textual versus visual, learned versus popular, aristocratic versus plebeian, urban versus rural, and, probably most fundamental and least clearly understood of all, male versus female. The intersection of these factors, any or all of which can be operative in any particular case, forms a kind of grid on which individuals and cultural artefacts can be located, as a preliminary to more specific enquiries. Though we should be careful not to employ any of these interpretative categories (for, in the end, that is all that they are) unthinkingly or rigidly, their usefulness lies in reminding us that there never was just one, all-encompassing, 'medieval mind', and that profoundly significant differences of outlook among individuals and groups could be, and were, inspired by their relationships to these categories, or, if you prefer, their location on the grid.

To take a concrete example: a literate male cleric reading a Latin biography of Bernard of Clairvaux in an Italian city is likely to have had a very different idea of him from that entertained by an illiterate laywoman venerating an icon of Bernard painted on the wall of a country church; but both perceptions are equally valid, in the context of the process through which Bernard's medieval reputation began to take shape. (There is also, of course, room for variation within the categories: as we shall see, much might depend on whether our putative clerical reader was a Franciscan or a Dominican.) Even though it is, obviously, not possible to exhaust the range of potential responses to Bernard among the *Commedia*'s earliest audiences (a range which is, after all, ultimately coterminous with the number of individuals making up that audience), and despite the fact that such evidence as survives is overwhelmingly weighted towards the literate, learned, ecclesiastical, Latinate perception of Bernard, we still need to strive to recover what we can of all the views of the saint that were, or may have been, current in the early fourteenth century – because each of them played a part, however trivial or fleeting, in determining the response of readers (as a group) to his appearance in *Paradiso* XXXI.

As used here, then, 'reputation' means the whole body of knowledge, gossip, fact, fiction, prejudice, and propaganda that gathers, in written, spoken, and pictorial form, around any figure of historical or cultural importance. Erudite biographies and flippant anecdotes, the tributes of admirers and the denunciations of opponents, chronicles, commentaries, panegyrics, invectives, and lampoons may all contribute to it in equal measure; certified truth and scurrilous hearsay may find themselves in startling juxtaposition. The point is not what is true, but what is believed. This is as much the case with Dante himself as with his readers: it is less important to decide how 'correct' his view of Bernard was, in terms of its conformity to the historical record, than it is to consider its particular orientation and its consequences for Dante's own thought and poetry, in the light of the multitude of potential interpretations of Bernard offered by late medieval culture. Even so, for all that it eventually becomes a matter of interpretation by posterity, a reputation begins to be fashioned while its subject is still alive and active on the stage of history; and the development of Dante's image of Bernard, as well as his readers' response to it, was thus already under way when Bernard himself died, on 20 August 1153.

Bernard of Clairvaux is unusual among medieval saints, in that materials for his biography began to be assembled by those close to him long before his death. The first substantial account of his life and works, now known as the *Vita prima*, was begun in the 1140s by Bernard's great friend William of St Thierry, and was to form the basis of the majority of later biographies, medieval and modern alike.[2] Although William died before Bernard, in 1148, his work was continued by Arnald of Bonneval, who added a second book to the *Vita*; and Arnald was followed by another Cistercian monk,

<hr />

[2] Jean Leclercq, *Bernard of Clairvaux and the Cistercian Spirit*, translated by Claire Lavoie (Kalamazoo, 1976; originally *Saint Bernard et l'esprit cistercien*, Paris, 1966), pp. 95–118, gives a sketchy account of the growth of Bernard's reputation.

Gaufridus (or Geoffrey) of Auxerre, who was responsible for Book III.[3] With Geoffrey the line of reliable biographers comes to an end. The later books of the *Vita prima* consist of little more than a stereotyped catalogue of miracles; they offer nothing tangible in the way of documentation of Bernard's activities, and are generally agreed to have only slight value for the historian.

The first three books, however, provide a rare glimpse, if not directly into the mind of a saint, at least into the preoccupations of some of his closest followers. William of St Thierry knew Bernard intimately; Arnald and Geoffrey, if they could not claim quite the same degree of personal acquaintance (though Geoffrey had been Bernard's secretary), were his younger contemporaries, moved in the same Cistercian circles, and were steeped in the atmosphere of an Order still rich in recent memories of its most celebrated abbot. Their versions of Bernard's life thus had a central role in defining the official view of him, which the Cistercian Order sought to promulgate as an ideal, both to its own members and to the outside world. They were helped – especially William – by a vivacity of style and a keenness of insight not always associated with medieval hagiographers. The popularity which the *Vita prima* soon acquired is owed, at least in part, to the conviction it carries, as a lively, authentic-sounding, and readable account of the life of a highly unusual man who happened also to be a saint.

This air of authenticity and stylistic verve are not, on the whole, shared by later twelfth-century Cistercian biographies, such as the *Vita secunda* of Alan of Auxerre, various other *Vitae* collected in volume 185 of Migne's *Patrologia latina*, and the definitive official history of the Cistercian Order's founding and early years, the *Exordium magnum cisterciense*.[4] All these draw heavily on the evidence of the *Vita prima*, to supplement their authors' own lack of direct contact with Bernard, and in all of them the tendency towards narrative stereotyping and conscious myth-making, already perceptible in the later books of the *Vita prima*, is accentuated. They frequently turn into a lengthy and eventually monotonous recitation

[3] The *Vita prima* is in the *Patrologia latina* (henceforth *PL*), 185, cols. 225–68 (Book I), 267–302 (Book II), 301–22 (Book III), and 321–466 (Books IV–VII).

[4] All these can also be found in *PL*, 185: the *Vita secunda* at cols. 469–524, the other *Vitae* at cols. 523–620, and the *Exordium* at cols. 995–1198 (Books I–VI) and 415–54 (Book VII, a redaction of the Bernardine material from the earlier books that was eventually incorporated into the *Vita prima*).

of the more or less improbable feats miraculously performed by Bernard on his extensive European travels, rather than chronicling the course of those travels or explaining the purposes (Church politics, preaching the Crusade) for which they were undertaken. In some cases, this tendency may stem from a desire to ensure the availability of enough evidence to secure Bernard's canonization (which was opposed by some elements within the Church, and which the Cistercian Order was naturally anxious to bring about); but it may also be a tacit admission that the mundane specificities of Bernard's ecclesiastical career were of less interest to these authors – and hence, perhaps, to their readers – than his more glamorous thaumaturgical activity.

By the end of the twelfth century, Bernard was already ceasing to be a mere historical personage, and was entering the realm of cultural iconography. Biographers had lost interest in his worldly operations – monastic reform, preaching, writing, involvement in theological controversy and papal schism – and the desire to record such details had largely given way to the impulse to portray Bernard purely as a worker of miracles, a figure of supernatural rather than human resonance, who is, therefore, increasingly distanced from the individual reality of Bernard of Clairvaux, and from any context that later generations would recognize as historical. (This is not to say, of course, that the authors of these later lives believed themselves to be doing anything other than writing history; merely that they were less concerned – unlike, surely, the majority of late twentieth-century readers – with Bernard the man than with Bernard the saint.)

The canonical status which the *Vita prima* enjoyed from the beginning is also reflected in the widespread circulation of its manuscripts. Detailed research by A. H. Bredero has revealed that, although these are to be found all over Western Europe, they are especially numerous – as might be expected – in France and Germany, where there was a strong Cistercian presence from the twelfth century onwards, centred on famous abbeys such as Clairvaux itself, Himmelrode, and Morimond.[5] However, Bredero also lists a number of thirteenth-century manuscripts of Italian provenance (at least two of which are Florentine), and several others from the fourteenth and fifteenth centuries. The *Vita prima* was, then, known in Dante's Italy,

---

[5] A. H. Bredero, 'Etudes sur la *Vita Prima* de saint Bernard', *Analecta Sacri Ordinis Cisterciensis*, 17 (1961), 3–72, 215–60; 18 (1962), 3–59.

and it is not beyond the bounds of possibility that Dante himself read it. It would certainly have been the first work to which anyone interested in learning about Bernard's life would have turned. (It remains so today, as a glance at any modern biography will reveal.)[6] In contrast, the *Vita secunda* and the other *Vitae* have nothing like so rich a manuscript tradition, and are therefore unlikely to have played so significant a role in the circulation of information about Bernard in the late Middle Ages.

The chief aim of the authors of the *Vita prima*, especially those of its first three books, seems to have been to produce an accurate and authoritative history of Bernard's public life, which would reflect credit on the Cistercian Order as a whole, and thus be suitable both for the Order's institutional purposes and for public consumption. This was not always the case with later biographers, especially those who lived and wrote outside the confines of the Cistercian Order, and were thus less familiar with its values and less committed to its objectives. That the narrative tradition which grew up around Bernard was long free from the gaudier excesses of the hagiographical imagination was due, in no small degree, to the authority enjoyed by the *Vita prima*; but even that was not an absolute guarantee against the proliferation of other, unlicensed, images of the saint. However, it is worth noting that many of the most famous (and most obviously spurious) legends about Bernard – such as that of the Lactation of the Virgin Mary, so dear to Spanish painters of the Counter-Reformation – did not appear until well after Dante's time, and can, therefore, safely be ignored for our purposes. The later medieval tradition of Bernardine biography was still strongly influenced by twelfth-century precedent, and that meant, above all, the *Vita prima*. Even so, departure from the *Vita prima*'s historical interest in Bernard's earthly achievements, and concentration on his more spectacular super-natural performances, are increasingly noticeable in the thirteenth- and fourteenth-century sources.

A telling instance, the more so because it emerges from a Cistercian setting, is the treatment of Bernard in Caesarius of Heisterbach's *Dialogus miraculorum*, which dates from about 1220–35. As its title implies, the book as a whole is chiefly concerned with miracles,

---

[6] See, for example, Elphège Vacandard, *Vie de saint Bernard, Abbé de Clairvaux*, 2 vols. (Paris, 1895); Ailbé J. Luddy, *Life and Teaching of St Bernard* (Dublin, 1927); Watkin Wynn Williams, *St Bernard of Clairvaux* (Manchester, 1935; second edition, 1953); Bruno Scott James, *St Bernard of Clairvaux: An Essay in Biography* (London, 1957).

especially those for which Cistercians might take the credit, and it duly deals with Bernard from that viewpoint exclusively, taking practically no interest in other aspects of his career.[7] It has, for example, nothing to say about him as an author; and it shares this trait with most of the later *Vitae*. This is, perhaps, both a sign of the development of a legendary, rather than a historical, approach to Bernard, and an indication of the extent to which texts like these were aimed at a non-scholarly (though not, of course, non-literate) audience, uninterested in formal study of Bernard's works. Where William of St Thierry wrote for followers of a monastic leader, Caesarius and others like him write, rather, for devotees of a canonized saint. The *Dialogus*, accordingly, transmits the image of Bernard the miracle-worker at the expense of that of Bernard the thinker or Bernard the monastic reformer; but it should be noted that the miracles it recounts are almost all taken from the *Vita prima* itself. To that extent, the *Dialogus* is still closely attached to an existing, and specifically Cistercian, tradition.

For all their greater independence and diversity of intention, even non-Cistercian biographers of Bernard remain largely under the spell of the *Vita prima* between the twelfth and fourteenth centuries. Jacobus a Voragine's classic compilation of saints' lives, the *Legenda aurea*, dating from the middle of the thirteenth century, takes most of its Bernardine anecdotes from the *Vita prima* (though some do appear to come from other sources, perhaps including a nascent popular tradition).[8] Jacobus also refers, occasionally and superficially, to Bernard's writings. These are dealt with in more detail in the early fourteenth-century *Legendae de sanctis* of Pietro Calò (who died in 1348), another compilation heavily reliant, for its discussion of Bernard, on the *Vita prima*. This text includes a list of Bernard's works, which is interesting both as an exception to the trend in the later biographies to eschew description of Bernard's scholarly activities and, perhaps more so, as evidence of exactly what at least one medieval intellectual thought Bernard had written.[9] The authentic writings of Bernard named by Calò include *Ad clericos de conversione, De gratia et libero arbitrio, De gradibus humilitatis et superbiae,*

---

[7] Caesarius of Heisterbach, *Dialogus miraculorum*, edited by Josephus Strange, 2 vols. (Cologne, 1851), I, 12, 26–7, 84–6, 120, 171–3, 179–80.

[8] Jacobus a Voragine, *Legenda aurea*, edited by Th. Graesse (Dresden, 1890; photographic reprint, Osnabrück, 1969), pp. 527–38.

[9] Pietro Calò's (unedited) work is substantially reproduced in Petrus de Natalibus, *Catalogus sanctorum* (Venice, 1506).

*De praecepto et dispensatione*, the *Apologia ad Guillelmum*, 'innumerable sermons' (including those *In Cantica canticorum, De psalmo 'Qui habitat'*, and *Super 'Missus est'*, also known as *In laudibus Virginis Matris*), and *De consideratione* – all in all, a substantial sampling of Bernard's major treatises and sermons. Apparently spurious works also attributed here to Bernard include a treatise on the *Magnificat*, a book written 'to Hugh of Saint Victor' (though this may well be a reference to Bernard's famous letter to Hugh, usually known as *De baptismo*), and an *exhortatorium* on Christ's passion and resurrection. Intriguingly, the obviously knowledgeable compiler of this list thought that Bernard's best-known work, the collection *In Cantica canticorum*, consisted of only seventy-three sermons, rather than eighty-six.

The *Legendae de sanctis* are unusual for the scope and extent of their knowledge of Bernard. More revealing of the conventional approach to Bernardine hagiography in the late Middle Ages is the *Sanctuarium* of Boninus Mombritius, which, although compiled in the fifteenth century, is a recension of various texts dating from considerably earlier.[10] This work presents an account of Bernard which is no more than a verbatim reproduction of the first three books of the *Vita prima*. From the 1140s to the end of the medieval period, the wheel has come full circle: the *Vita prima* is still recognized as the basic and most authoritative source for Bernard's biography, the equivalent of W. H. Auden's 'shilling life' that will 'give you all the facts'.[11]

The facts of Bernard's life were of comparatively little concern to another important group of late medieval writers with a deep interest in the abbot of Clairvaux. From the middle of the twelfth century onwards, theologians and spiritual writers drew extensively on Bernard's written legacy; and, as noted above, the extent of that legacy seemed larger to them than it does to us, because many texts circulated under Bernard's name, and were unquestioningly accepted as his, which modern scholarship has shown to be the work of other hands. Thanks to his writings, Bernard became posthumously involved in the vast outpouring of philosophical and theological commentary generated by developments in educational structures throughout Europe between the twelfth and fourteenth centuries, which is conveniently, if reductively, labelled 'scholasticism'.

[10] Boninus Mombritius, *Sanctuarium seu vitae sanctorum*, edited by 'duo monachi solesmenses', 2 vols. (Paris, 1910).

[11] W. H. Auden, 'Who's Who', in *Collected Poems*, edited by Edward Mendelson (London, 1976), p. 109.

The scholastics' approach to Bernard, unlike that of the hagiographers, was in no way biographical. To them he was simply an
*auctor*, a name attached to a body of written work from which they
might draw material, in the form of apposite quotations, to compare
or contrast with their own conclusions, or to bolster their own
arguments. The connection of that material with the personal reality
of a human individual was of no concern to them. But, although their
views need not have been at all affected by knowledge of Bernard's
life, their use of his writings, involving as it did the evaluation of his
thought and the estimation of his standing relative to other thinkers
in Christian history, was still an influence on the overall development
of Bernard's medieval reputation.

Bernard's impact on scholastic thought has been studied in some
detail, but usually by scholars more concerned with the niceties of
doctrine than with broader questions of the perception of Bernard
as a figure in medieval culture.[12] J. Chatillon, for instance, sees
Bernard's influence as beginning early, at the time of the polemics
arising from his bitter controversy with Peter Abelard in the 1140s;
continuing through the work of near-contemporaries such as Hugh of
St Victor and Peter Lombard (who, curiously, never quotes Bernard
outright, though the influence is unmistakable); extending to
numerous minor authors of the late twelfth century; and finally
reaching its full flowering in the scholastic thought of the thirteenth
century, especially that produced in a Franciscan setting.

It may, at first sight, seem remarkable that Cistercians are not
much involved in the absorption of Bernard's thinking into the
scholastic tradition, but there are good reasons for this. As a rule,
Cistercian authors of the twelfth and thirteenth centuries remained
isolated from the mainstream of scholastic activity, in keeping with
the generally anti-intellectual tenets of the Order's founders (Bernard
himself prominent among them); and they also tended to keep their
distance from the emergent universities (Paris, Bologna, Oxford) –
not least because these were an urban phenomenon, and Cistercian
practice, ever since the foundation of Cîteaux itself in a remote and
almost inaccessible wilderness, had discouraged any too close contact
or association with the sinful urban milieu. Moreover, Cistercian
writers in the later medieval period were bound, if only by natural

---

[12] J. Chatillon, 'L'Influence de saint Bernard sur la pensée scolastique au XIIe et au XIIIe
siècle', in *Saint Bernard théologien* (Dijon, 1953; *Analecta Sacri Ordinis Cisterciensis*, 9, 1953,
fascicules 3–4), pp. 268–88.

loyalty to their Order, to adopt the quasi-official standpoint of the *Vita prima*, and to cultivate the hagiographical approach to Bernard as an object of veneration rather than the analytical approach to his writings as text. For this reason, Cistercian houses became focal points for the dissemination of hagiographical writing about Bernard and copies of his own *ipsissima verba*, but not for any significant amount of commentary on, or doctrinal elaboration of, those works. (Such Cistercian writers as did follow directly in Bernard's footsteps – Isaac of Stella, Guerric of Igny – remained more famous within the Order than outside it.) It is thus more profitable to look for substantive evidence of scholastic attitudes towards Bernard elsewhere.

Bernard's position as an *auctor* in scholastic thought was always equivocal. His own approach to theology, coupled with his low opinion of the value of unaided human reason, was not guaranteed to earn him sympathy among the scholastics, founded as it was on a tradition more mystical than rational, a staunch doctrinal conservatism suspicious of novelty, and a sound measure of scorn for anything smacking of 'pagan' learning. It is not surprising, therefore, that Bernard should be far from the most respected of writers in the eyes of scholastic thinkers. Though he certainly belonged to the select company of authorities whom theological writers in the scholastic era were willing to consult, those who did so tended to be thinkers of a conservative disposition, as anxious as Bernard himself to defend the time-honoured teachings of the Church against the dangerously innovative doctrines propounded by more radical writers.[13] Other scholastics seem, at times, even to display a certain scepticism about the value of Bernard's intellectual achievements; and the foremost among these is Thomas Aquinas.

Aquinas was, however, by no means the first scholastic, or indeed the first Dominican, to quote Bernard: his teacher Albert the Great does so frequently. Modern understanding of Albert's indebtedness to Bernard has been seriously affected by the discovery that the *Mariale* formerly attributed to Albert is not, in fact, genuine. It quotes Bernard's Marian writings extensively, and is clearly the work of an author for whom – as for others discussed below – these constituted the most attractive portion of Bernard's considerable output.[14] The

---

[13] Ibid., p. 281.

[14] *Excellentissimi et sanctissimi viri domini Alberti Magni episcopi Ratisponensis ordinis praedicatorum in evangelium Missus est Gabriel angelus* (Milan, 1488).

tenor of Albert's own work, no longer distorted by the presence of this spurious tract, is rather different.[15] Though he refers to many of Bernard's writings, some of them comparatively little known, he quotes two works far more often than all the others put together: *De consideratione* and the sermons *In Cantica canticorum*. In Albert's commentary *Super Isaiam*, for example, the sermons *In Cantica canticorum* are quoted six times, *De consideratione* three times, and *De gradibus humilitatis et superbiae* once. In the treatise *De bono*, there are nine quotations from *In Cantica canticorum*, eleven from *De consideratione*, and two from *De praecepto et dispensatione*. Albert's commentary on the *Mystical Theology* of pseudo-Dionysius the Areopagite has four quotations from *In Cantica canticorum*, five from *De consideratione*, and one each from the *Epistolae*, *De gradibus*, and *De diligendo Deo*. The pattern remains constant throughout Albert's corpus of theological writing and Biblical commentary: a handful of quotations from Bernard (far fewer, indeed, than from many other authors), in which selections from *De consideratione* and the sermons *In Cantica canticorum* predominate. In revealing contrast, Bernard is not mentioned at all in most of Albert's strictly philosophical texts. Bernard is useful to him only as a theologian, and, as Albert's predilection for those two particular works strongly indicates, principally as a theologian of mystical experience. For all the scantiness and indirection of his contribution, Albert may be seen as one of the chief propagators, within scholasticism, of the view of Bernard as an outstanding contemplative.

Albert's quotations from Bernard take the form that remains familiar in all scholastic writing: only the author's name, and occasionally a title, are given as source for the quotation. Sometimes, though by no means always, an honorific epithet, (usually 'beatus' in Bernard's case) is added to the name, to strengthen still further the quoted writer's claims to *auctoritas*. There is, however, no attempt to provide any biographical detail or overall assessment of the writer concerned, and the reader is left to supply the background as best he may.

Thomas Aquinas uses the same method in his treatment of the abbot of Clairvaux. He quotes Bernard rarely in his major works (some twenty times in the *Summa theologiae*), but uses him more

---

[15] The statistical details in what follows are derived from the indexes in the various volumes of Albertus Magnus, *Opera omnia*, edited by B. Geyer and others (Münster, 1951– ).

readily in other texts, notably *De humanitate Jesu Christi domini nostri*.[16] His attitude towards the great Cistercian is, on the whole, cautious, even cool; respecting Bernard as a mystic and an exemplar of saintliness, he is reluctant to accept whole-heartedly his authority as a thinker. Bernard is very frequently quoted in the *argumenta* of an article (thirteen times in the *Summa theologiae*, nine of the seventeen quotations in *De veritate*), or the *sed contra* (the eight remaining quotations in *De veritate*). This proportion suggests that, in general, Aquinas is more interested in contesting Bernard's ideas than in affirming their validity, since he tends to use his work as a source of erroneous theses which are mentioned only to be contradicted, rather than taking from it reliable arguments to be used for the confutation of error. Yet Aquinas had a high opinion of Bernard's personal holiness and his abilities outside the strictly theological sphere. The most striking illustration of this occurs in a sermon: Aquinas takes as his text a verse from Proverbs 20 ('There is gold, and a multitude of rubies: but the lips of knowledge are a precious jewel'), and uses it as a means of praising Bernard 'for the humility of his preaching', in a welter of imagery based on the mystical properties of various precious stones.[17]

Even here, however, Aquinas does not compliment Bernard on his qualities as an intellectual or a theologian, and the abiding impression left by his references to his Cistercian predecessor is that Bernard's achievement in that area was of less lasting importance than his contribution as a preacher. As we shall see, this estimate of Bernard's abilities was to gain considerable currency in the late Middle Ages.

A very different impression of Bernard's place in Christian intellectual history would be gained from another work by a thirteenth-century Dominican, John of Paris's *De potestate regia et papali*.[18] Nothing of Bernard the mystic or the preacher survives in this exercise in political controversy. Bernard is quoted sixteen times, all the extracts being taken from *De consideratione* (which John calls *Liber ad Eugenium*); but, unlike his predecessor Albert, John does not value that work for the mystical doctrine contained in Book v. His quotations, all drawn from the manual of eminently practical advice

---

[16] M. B. Pennington, 'The Influence of Bernard of Clairvaux on Thomas Aquinas', *Studia Monastica*, 16 (1974), 281–91.

[17] *D. Thomae de Aquino doctoris angelici sermones* etc. (Rome, 1571), f. 134v.

[18] See the text in Jean Leclercq, *Jean de Paris et l'ecclésiologie du XIIIe siècle* (Paris, 1942), pp. 171–260.

to Pope Eugenius III that composes the first four books of the treatise, are used exclusively in the framework of an argument in political theory: they furnish support for the anti-papal thesis of John's book, in a way which contrasts interestingly with Boniface VIII's later use of some of the same texts on the other side of the dispute between the papacy and the increasingly assertive secular monarchy of Philippe le Bel, in his notorious bull *Unam sanctam* (1302).[19] Although Bernard is one of his most important sources, John seems a little ambivalent about the value of the evidence that *De consideratione* provides (perhaps because he was aware that his use of Bernard's text to oppose papal authority would have been profoundly unwelcome to Bernard himself).

In Chapter x, for example, discussing the well-worn Biblical image of the 'two swords' and its various interpretations during the conflict between papacy and monarchy, John remarks that Bernard's (papalist) reading 'is of no great authority'; but in Chapter xviii, returning to the same subject, his conclusion is that 'the authority of Bernard, mentioned above, is on our side'.[20] John prefers, then, to use Bernard pragmatically, invoking his *auctoritas* when it suits him and disparaging it otherwise; but, in any case, his main contribution to the growth of Bernard's reputation was to stress the political aspect of Bernard's thought, and to remind at least the informed reader that this mystical theologian and connoisseur of the unseen world had also been the counsellor of a pope, and a man deeply enmeshed in the political and ecclesiastical power-struggles of his time.

Other notable Dominicans influenced by Bernard included the English prelates Robert Kilwardby and Richard Fishacre; but Chatillon's overall assessment leads inexorably to the conclusion that the relatively infrequent citation of Bernard by Dominican writers (Siger of Brabant, for example, never mentions him at all) only becomes the more revealing when compared with the liberal and enthusiastic use made of Bernard's writings by their Franciscan counterparts.[21]

The Franciscan treatment of Bernard was certainly very different in scope and nature from the Dominican. According to J. G. Bougerol, for instance, the voluminous works of Bonaventure contain

---

[19] The relevant extracts from *Unam sanctam* are in *Enchiridion symbolorum*, edited by Heinrich Denzinger and Adolf Schönmetzer, 32nd edition (Barcelona, 1963), pp. 279–81 (especially p. 280, item 873).    [20] John of Paris, in Leclercq, *Jean de Paris*, pp. 200, 233.
[21] Chatillon, 'L'Influence', p. 283.

well over four hundred references to Bernard, the great majority of which are direct quotations.[22] Like Aquinas before him and many another after him, Bonaventure esteems Bernard above all as a preacher, an evaluation reflected in his choice of sources. One hundred and two of his quotations of Bernard come from the sermons *In Cantica canticorum*, 99 from those *De tempore* and *De sanctis*, 49 from those *In laudibus Virginis Matris*, and 21 from those *De diversis*. More than half of Bonaventure's Bernardine citations, then, are taken from sermons.

Furthermore, Bonaventure explicitly names Bernard as a master among preachers, excelled only by Gregory the Great. He does not neglect the treatises, however: *De consideratione* is quoted 52 times, and Bonaventure shows a characteristically Franciscan fondness for *De gratia et libero arbitrio*, which he cites on 32 occasions. There are also 47 quotations from Bernard's letters in Bonaventure, and nine other individual works are quoted more sporadically. In short, Bonaventure shows himself to be deeply affected by Bernard's writings, especially the sermons on mystical and Marian themes and the treatises on the theology of grace; and it is these aspects of Bernard's work that are most readily taken up by other Franciscans.

They had, indeed, already been important to Franciscans writing before Bonaventure himself. The mid thirteenth-century *Summa theologica* begun (though not completed) by Alexander of Hales, a fundamental textbook of Franciscan theology, contains 287 direct quotations from Bernard, of which no fewer than 105 are taken from *De gratia et libero arbitrio*.[23] *De consideratione* and the sermons *In Cantica canticorum* seem as congenial to Alexander as to other scholastics, being accorded 40 and 43 quotations respectively. (The remainder come from *De diligendo Deo*, *De praecepto et dispensatione*, and the letters.) Although this may look like an impressive tally, it should be seen in contrast with still higher scores by still more favoured writers. Peter Lombard (321), Boethius (324), Jerome (336), and Gregory the Great (715) are all quoted more often than Bernard in Alexander's *Summa*, and all of them are clearly far less influential on it than Augustine, who is quoted a staggering 4814 times. None the less, Bernard is a presence to be reckoned with in this Franciscan *Summa*, and he is treated there as an author to be agreed with, rather

---

[22] J. G. Bougerol, 'Saint Bonaventure et saint Bernard', *Antonianum*, 46 (1971), 3–79.
[23] Alexander of Hales, *Summa theologica*, 4 vols. (Ad Claras Aquas, 1924–47).

than challenged, much more often than in Aquinas's analogous Dominican work.[24]

A contemporary of Alexander's who, though never himself formally a Franciscan, was sympathetic to the Order and influenced by its thought, was the great English scholar and bishop Robert Grosseteste.[25] Like John of Paris in the Dominican context, Grosseteste was most keenly interested in Bernard's political ideas, as expressed in *De consideratione*, a work for which, according to Sir Richard Southern, Grosseteste 'had a high regard'; although, unlike John, he was more concerned with the Church's internal self-government than with its external relations with any secular power.[26] (These were, of course, a much more urgent problem in John of Paris's time than in Grosseteste's.) As well as *De consideratione*, Grosseteste was familiar with some of Bernard's letters; but he seems not to have known the most celebrated of all Bernard's writings, the sermons *In Cantica canticorum*, in any depth. An index of his reading drawn up by Grosseteste himself in the 1220s quotes Bernard on seventy-five different subjects, and Southern calculates the total number of Grosseteste's references to Bernard as 244 – a figure exceeded only by Augustine, Gregory, Jerome, John Damascene, and, strikingly enough, Seneca.[27]

To return to fully-fledged Franciscans: the interests already identified in Bonaventure and Alexander of Hales are shared by a late thirteenth-century Franciscan cardinal, Matthew of Aquasparta. He quotes Bernard occasionally in his various sets of *quaestiones*, and, like his more illustrious predecessors, has a predilection for the teaching on grace found in *De gratia et libero arbitrio*.[28] He also refers, in passing, to several other treatises (*De consideratione*, *De diligendo Deo*, *De praecepto et dispensatione*), and to the sermons *In*

---

[24] Another, earlier, work of Alexander's, the *Quaestiones disputatae antequam esset frater* (Ad Claras Aquas, 1960), reveals a similar distribution of quotations from Bernard: of a total of 101 references, 54 are to *De gratia et libero arbitrio*, fourteen to *De consideratione*, twelve to *In Cantica canticorum*, and the rest to *De baptismo, De diligendo Deo, De gradibus humilitatis et superbiae, De praecepto et dispensatione*, the letters, and various other sermons.

[25] For Grosseteste and Bernard, see R. W. Southern, *Robert Grosseteste: The Growth of an English Mind in Medieval Europe* (Oxford, 1986). [26] Ibid., pp. 262–3.

[27] For the relevant statistics and the conclusions to be drawn from them, see ibid., pp. 195 and 198–9.

[28] There are nine quotations from *De gratia et libero arbitrio* in Matthew's *De gratia*, edited by V. Doucet (Ad Claras Aquas, 1935); two in *De productione rerum et de providentia*, edited by G. Gal (Florence, 1956); one in *De anima beata* (Florence, 1959); and one in *De anima*, edited by A. J. Gondras (Paris, 1961). Bernard is also quoted once in the *Quaestiones de fide et de cognitione* (Ad Claras Aquas, 1903); and five times in *De Christo* (Ad Claras Aquas, 1914).

*Cantica canticorum.* One theme of particular significance to Matthew is Bernard's Mariology: this is reflected in a score of references, direct and indirect, in Matthew's own sermons *De beata Maria virgine.*[29] Most of these are to Bernard's Marian sermons and to his letter on the Immaculate Conception to the canons of Lyon (*Epistola* 174), but *De consideratione* is also cited, unusually, in this context.

Bernard's reputation as a devotee of Mary is also crucial for Conrad of Saxony, in whose *Speculum beatae Mariae virginis* Bernard is easily the most favoured authority on a variety of themes connected with the Virgin.[30] Conrad cites Bernard on more than eighty occasions, taking his quotations only from the specifically Marian writings. Unsurprisingly, given his topic, he shows no interest in any other feature of Bernard's life or thought; even the typical Franciscan concern with the workings of grace appears only in relation to the role of the Virgin in helping to obtain it. Conrad's is, clearly, a narrowly concentrated view of Bernard's cultural importance; but the area on which it concentrates is one that was widely recognized in the Middle Ages, especially by Franciscans, as central to Bernard's reputation.

The Franciscan authors examined so far all belonged to the mainstream of Franciscan thought and practice in the thirteenth century. It is, of course, well known that there was a strong undercurrent of more extreme ideas in thirteenth-century Franciscanism, which existed alongside and in polemic with the officially sanctioned thinking and activity of the Franciscan Order, and found its expression in the sometimes violently subversive offshoot of that Order known as the Spiritual movement. It has been suggested that Dante was influenced, to some degree, by the attitudes of the Spiritual Franciscans; and, for that reason, the treatment of Bernard by certain authors more or less closely connected with the movement becomes unusually interesting in the present context.[31] Moreover, because they were to some extent alienated from mainstream Franciscanism intellectually as well as organizationally, the Spirituals did not observe the technical decorum of scholastic writing, its conventions of *quaestio* and *articulus, argumenta* and *sed contra,* as faithfully as did a Bonaventure or an Alexander of Hales. As a result, Spiritual writers show themselves more willing to interpret Bernard

---

[29]  Matthew of Aquasparta, *De beata Maria virgine,* edited by C. Piana (Florence, 1962).
[30]  Conrad of Saxony, *Speculum beatae Mariae Virginis* (Ad Claras Aquas, 1904).
[31]  An extensive bibliography on this subject is provided by Arsenio Frugoni in the *Enciclopedia dantesca,* III (1971), 167.

as a figure of cultural resonance, rather than merely exploiting his writings as a treasure trove filled with nuggets of doctrine and argumentative ammunition.

The unwitting patron of the Spiritual Franciscans was Joachim of Fiore, who was himself a Cistercian of a slightly later generation than Bernard, being in his early twenties when the saint died. He subsequently became something of a renegade, leaving the Order to found a monastery of his own in Calabria, where he lived until 1202. The imprint of Joachim's Cistercian training is clear, however, in his lifelong interest in, and extensive knowledge of, the work of Bernard of Clairvaux; and this formed no small part of the inheritance he unknowingly bequeathed to the Spiritual movement.

Bernard is not mentioned in all of Joachim's many works, but each of his three major prose texts (*Liber concordie novi ac veteris testamenti*, *Psalterium decem chordarum*, and *Expositio in Apocalipsim*) includes brief but pertinent references to the abbot of Clairvaux. Joachim was not, of course, either temperamentally or chronologically close to the scholastics, and his method is very different from theirs. He has no time for the collection of quotations, the evaluation of arguments, and the assessment of *auctores*. Instead, he proceeds, by means of a highly idiosyncratic brand of typology, to establish thematic connections between various Biblical and historical personages, to show how these are integrated into the divine order, and thus eventually to achieve the concord between the Old and New Testaments that gives its name to one of his books. These arguments, the characteristic symbols through which they are expressed (the Tree, the Eagle, the Ten-stringed Psaltery), and a strong dose of the 'spirito profetico' which Dante saw as Joachim's supreme attribute (*Par.*, XII. 140–1) – and which pervades his every page – together form an eccentric but mesmerizing vision of Christian history.

The essence of Joachim's view of Bernard appears in one of his lesser works, the *Tractatus de vita Sancti Benedicti*.[32] Discussing the condition of the Benedictine Order after its founder's death, Joachim speaks of the encouragement offered it by 'futuri ... signum muneris, quod erat omnipotens Deus ... collaturus' ('the sign of a future gift which Almighty God would bestow upon [it]'). This gift was to be the birth of a 'doctor precipuus, qui esset quasi alter Moyses' ('a man of great learning, who would be like another Moses'). This turned

[32] Joachim of Fiore, *Tractatus de vita sancti Benedicti*, edited by Cipriano Baraút, *Analecta Sacra Tarraconiensia*, 24 (1951), 33–122 (quotations from 54, 86, 117).

out to be Bernard. The Mosaic analogy recurs, accompanied by still more exalted comparisons: Bernard was sent 'in spiritu Moysi' ('in the spirit of Moses'), just as John the Baptist was, with the same mission of gathering a multitude of disciples through his preaching. He was to preach another who would come after him, and, in his case as in John the Baptist's, this other was Christ. Here, Joachim is drawing Bernard into a millenarian tradition of the impending Second Coming. But the most extravagant image of all is reserved for the treatise's last reference to Bernard. No longer merely linked with Moses or John the Baptist, Bernard is now worthy of comparison with Christ himself. As Christ received the Holy Spirit after he emerged from Mary's womb, in order that he might baptize, spread his disciples throughout the world, and fulfil his destiny of death, resurrection, and ascension, so the Spirit caused the womb of the Cistercian Order to swell, and eventually descended upon its sons, of whom the first was Bernard, in order that they might follow Christ in his ministry and preaching, and so be led through suffering to eternal glory. The expression of this parallel is somewhat confused – as is not uncommon with Joachim – but the analogy of Christ and Bernard is clear enough, as is that of Bernard and Moses; and, of course, Moses himself was often represented, in medieval exegesis, as a type prefiguring Christ.

The theme of Bernard as 'alter Moyses' is further developed in Joachim's *Liber concordie*.[33] Here he gives a brief account of the foundation of Clairvaux that suggests some familiarity with a reliable biographical source (almost certainly the *Vita prima*), and then promptly begins to devise more analogies. Bernard is another Levi, because his mother had six sons and a daughter, as did Leah, the wife of Jacob. The third of these was Levi, while Bernard was the third son of Tescelin and Aleth. More important, he was another Moses, because he was guided by the Spirit and the hand of the Lord was with him; and, as Moses led his people out of slavery, so Bernard led countless souls out of the slavery of the world and into Clairvaux. Furthermore, he had by his side another Aaron, Pope Eugenius III, to whom he gave another Leviticus, *De consideratione*. Finally, just as the children of Israel murmured against Moses and Aaron after their deliverance from bondage, so there was criticism of Bernard and Eugenius after the failure of the Second Crusade.

[33] Joachim of Fiore, *Liber concordie novi ac veteris testamenti* (Venice, 1519), IV. 38.

Joachim's skilful synthesis here reveals a thorough knowledge of Bernard's biography, and a more than adequate familiarity with his writings, as well as profound respect for him as a historical figure. *De consideratione* is mentioned again later in the *Liber concordie*, and again called 'alter Leviticus', as part of a shorter discussion of Bernard as one of the saintly men sent to the leaders of the Church 'qui securi de charitate et simplicitate sua in libertate spiritus loquerentur ad eos' ('who, emboldened by their charity and simplicity, would speak to them freely in the Spirit').[34] Clearly it is *De consideratione*, with its connotations of ecclesiastical reform, that makes the deepest impression on the Joachim of the *Liber concordie*, but his emphasis on Bernard's powers as a preacher 'in libertate spiritus' is also interesting and suggestive.

A more technically theological use of *De consideratione* is made in Joachim's *Psalterium decem chordarum*, where it is quoted in support of the argument that the Trinity consists of three persons *secundum substantiam*. The quotation is accompanied by a description of Bernard as 'sanctus ac venerabilis pater' ('a holy and venerable father').[35] Still more respectful of Bernard's sanctity is Joachim's only reference to him in the *Expositio in Apocalipsim*: here he is 'beatus Bernardus abbas clarevallis, qui vita miraculis et scientia singulariter in diebus nostris illustravit ecclesiam' ('blessed Bernard, abbot of Clairvaux, who by his life, miracles, and learning has singularly adorned the Church in our day)'.[36]

Joachim of Fiore is an intriguing figure in the development of Bernard's medieval reputation because he relates the details of Bernard's life to a complex typological system, and attempts to show that that life has a meaning beyond any which could be written down in the purely biographical terms of the *Vita prima*. This is clearly a move away from the narrative literalism of the hagiographers, towards an effort to understand what the historical reality that was Bernard might mean, in a perspective that is more than merely historical, and indeed more than merely human. It is, in fact, an approach not unlike that which governs Dante's conception of personality in *Paradiso*; for both authors suggest that 'life' is more than 'biography', and that mortal men may not, after all, be in the best position to understand the meaning of their own or their

---

[34] Joachim of Fiore, *Liber concordie*, v. 64.
[35] Joachim of Fiore, *Psalterium decem chordarum* (Venice, 1527), ff. 232r., 234v.
[36] Joachim of Fiore, *Expositio in Apocalipsim* (Venice, 1527), I. 3 (f. 87v.).

contemporaries' individual existence. But the work of Joachim's that has been most closely (and most controversially) associated with Dante, the *Liber figurarum*, contains no reference to Bernard.[37] This may be because, in the end, Bernard did not fit into Joachim's scheme as neatly as he had once thought; it may suggest that Joachim's interest in Bernard was not uniformly strong throughout his life. However, such references to Bernard as do appear in Joachim's work are sufficiently concrete and laudatory to suggest that they must have impressed Joachim's followers, if only with their powerful sincerity, and that Joachim's works therefore played a part in the moulding of a view of Bernard, as a cultural icon, that was less relentlessly cerebral than that of the scholastics.

Traces of this view are also discernible in two Spiritual Franciscans writing a century after Joachim, in a climate much more strongly influenced by scholastic assumptions: Pietro di Giovanni Olivi and Ubertino da Casale. Both were intellectual celebrities in the Florence of Dante's youth, and he may have had some direct contact with either or both of them.[38] Olivi quotes Bernard in several of his works, rather less abruptly than do most scholastic writers; most of his quotations are lengthy and clearly attributed, and his conclusions usually agree with Bernard's.[39] Yet many other patristic sources are quoted far more often, and, on the whole, Bernard does not appear to be among Olivi's preferred authorities. (Interestingly, considering the use made of Bernard's Marian writings by other Franciscans, Olivi does not quote him at all in his *Quaestiones quatuor de Domina*.)[40]

---

[37] Joachim of Fiore, *Liber figurarum*, edited by Luigi Tondelli, Marjorie Reeves, and Beatrice Hirsch-Reich (Turin, 1953). See the entry 'Gioachino da Fiore' in the *Enciclopedia dantesca*, III (1971), 165–7, for the putative connections between this book, Joachim's other writings, and Dante.

[38] Olivi was at Santa Croce from the spring of 1287 until 1289; Ubertino seems to have arrived shortly after him, and to have stayed a year or two longer. See Raoul Manselli, 'Dante e l'"Ecclesia Spiritualis"', in *Dante e Roma* (Florence, 1965), pp. 115–35; David Burr, *Olivi and Franciscan Poverty: The Origins of the 'Usus Pauper' Controversy* (Philadelphia, 1989), pp. 107–8, 172.

[39] There are seven quotations attributed to Bernard (in two cases wrongly) in Olivi's *Quaestiones in secundum librum Sententiarum*, edited by B. Jansen, 3 vols. (Ad Claras Aquas, 1922–26). Most of them are from *De praecepto et dispensatione*. There are also two such quotations in the *Quodlibeta* (Venice, c. 1510), and a reference, apparently to *De consideratione*, in the *Expositio super regulam fratrum minorum*; see *Peter Olivi's Rule Commentary*, edited by David Flood (Wiesbaden, 1972), IV. ii. Bernard is not, however, included in the list of Olivi's preferred authorities given by Raoul Manselli, *La 'Lectura super Apocalipsim' di Pietro di Giovanni Olivi* (Rome, 1955), p. 145.

[40] Pietro di Giovanni Olivi, *Quaestiones quatuor de Domina*, edited by Domenico Pacetti (Florence, 1954).

Thus, although Olivi evidently respects Bernard and is prepared to turn to him from time to time, he seems not to find his work outstandingly useful.

Ubertino da Casale takes a markedly different view. He quotes or refers to Bernard on some sixty occasions in his *Arbor vite crucifixe Jesu*, and clearly regards him as one of the richest sources of support for his ideas (only Augustine and Jerome can compete in number of citations).[41] About twenty of these references are passing allusions that name no specific text; but in those where an exact source is cited, the division of Ubertino's interests appears significant. There are fourteen quotations from Marian writings, and eight from other sermons; six from the sermons *In Cantica canticorum*; four from those *De psalmo ' Qui habitat'*; two from the letters; and one each from *De gratia et libero arbitrio*, *De praecepto et dispensatione*, *De consideratione*, and the (apocryphal) letter *Ad fratres de monte Dei*. The balance is thus heavily weighted in favour of sermons, and several major treatises by Bernard are not mentioned at all; those that do appear are the ones traditionally found appealing by Franciscan writers. This is the work of a man much inspired by Bernard's preaching, especially on Marian themes, and admiring him for that rather than for the more systematic theology of the treatises. Ubertino, in fact, pays several brief tributes to Bernard's preaching skills, and, at one point, he launches into an extended panegyric on his unparalleled eloquence in glorifying the Virgin:

Et de ... sacratissima virgine Maria iudicio meo nullus locutus est devotius; nullus ferventius; nullus copiosius; nullus sublimius; nullus iocundius; nullus fecundius; nullus dulcius; nullus ad movendum peccatores et iustos ad ipsius matris devotionem efficatius.[42]

This fervent effusion is immensely revealing of Ubertino's attitude towards Bernard. Theologian, contemplative, devotee of Mary are all subsumed, for Ubertino, in Bernard the preacher. In this light, his regular use of formulas such as 'ut ait Bernardus' ('as Bernard says'), 'ut dicit Bernardus' ('as Bernard says'), 'secundum verbum beati Bernardi' ('according to the word of blessed Bernard') takes on a

---

[41] Ubertino da Casale, *Arbor vite crucifixe Jesu* (Venice, 1485).

[42] Ubertino, *Arbor*, IV. xxxviii: 'And, in my opinion, no one has spoken of the most holy virgin Mary more devotedly; no one more fervently; no one more copiously; no one more sublimely; no one more joyfully; no one more fruitfully; no one more sweetly; no one, in inspiring sinners and the righteous alike to devotion to the Mother, more effectively.'

new depth of meaning: for, as Ubertino sees it, it is above all the *word* that is Bernard's gift to posterity.

This is also the view of Robert of Basevorn, English author of an early fourteenth-century manual on the rhetoric of preaching, the *Forma praedicandi*.[43] He names Augustine, Gregory, and Bernard as the three greatest preachers since Biblical times, and claims that they, along with Christ himself and St Paul, are the best models for anyone aspiring to be a preacher nowadays. When he comes to Bernard in particular, he gives what is perhaps the earliest technical analysis of his oratorical style, praising it in the highest terms.[44]

For Robert of Basevorn, Bernard is a preacher pure and simple, and one of the best in Christian history. Yet this is by no means the only estimation of Bernard's cultural significance that was current in the early fourteenth century, even among the learned, Latinate clerics who produced and consumed all the texts we have discussed so far. From the mass of evidence available to them, late medieval readers of theological writing might gain many distinct impressions of Bernard of Clairvaux. They would find some authors concentrating on a single aspect of Bernard's activity, such as John of Paris on his political thought or Conrad of Saxony on his Mariology. In other works, such as those of Thomas Aquinas or Albert the Great, Bernard figures as just one *auctor* among many, and one whose arguments are often contested. From Alexander of Hales or Matthew of Aquasparta, readers might learn that Bernard was a major theologian of grace. Bonaventure and Robert of Basevorn see him, as had John of Salisbury as early as the twelfth century, as the best preacher since Gregory, 'vir potens in opere et sermone coram Deo ut creditur, et uti publice notum est coram hominibus' ('a man mighty in deed and word in the presence of God, as we believe, and also, as is well known, in that of men').[45] Joachim of Fiore would suggest that he was another Moses, another John the Baptist, perhaps another Christ. Siger of Brabant says nothing about him at all. The theological and spiritual literature of the period forms a chorus of voices, each isolating a different aspect of Bernard or stressing it to a different degree, but uniting to create the complex whole that is his reputation.

---

[43] Robert of Basevorn, *Forma praedicandi*, in Th. M. Charland, *Artes praedicandi: contribution à l'histoire de la rhétorique au Moyen Age* (Paris and Ottawa, 1936), pp. 231–323.

[44] Robert of Basevorn, in Charland, *Artes praedicandi*, p. 247.

[45] John of Salisbury, *Historia pontificalis*, edited by Reginald L. Poole (Oxford, 1927), pp. 27, 21. See also pp. 16 and 18 for other tributes by John to Bernard's eloquence, and pp. 26–27 for his knowledge of *De consideratione* and the sermons *In Cantica canticorum*.

It follows that any individual reader's perception of Bernard must have been affected by whichever texts he or she happened to have selected, for motives that may well have had nothing to do with Bernard himself, from the vast amount of material available. Even then, the diversity of responses to Bernard in scholastic and other late medieval thought must have ensured that no one image was transmitted unchallenged; and a reader of more than ordinary intellectual curiosity – Dante, for instance – will have encountered an almost bewildering variety of presentations of Bernard of Clairvaux in contemporary theology and spirituality. (There are good grounds for thinking that Dante was acquainted with at least some of the writings of Aquinas, Siger, John of Paris, Ubertino, Albert, Bonaventure, Olivi, and Joachim of Fiore; no picture of Bernard emerging from that combination could have been banal or uncomplicated.) But if there was one factor that linked the disparate perceptions of Bernard in late medieval culture – contemplative, Mariologist, ecclesiastical reformer, theologian of grace – it was the recognition of his uniquely efficacious use of language, especially in his preaching. It was not only a rhetorician like Robert of Basevorn who saw Bernard as, supremely, a man committed to using words to convey the Word, or who expressed admiration for the beauty and emotive power of his innumerable sermons. Aquinas, Bonaventure, Ubertino, Joachim, despite the diversity of their backgrounds, assumptions, and commitments, are all agreed on this crucial fact. We shall consider below whether their agreement can have been shared by Dante and the early readers of the *Commedia*.

Whatever their individual characteristics or particular angle on Bernard, none of the texts discussed so far can have exerted any influence outside a narrow social and intellectual stratum. They were all written in the language of the academically educated, Latin, for close study by a learned minority of professionally interested readers, by far the majority of whom must have been clerics. The accidents of history and the material realities of cultural conservation have ensured that many more texts originating at this point on the 'grid' evoked above have survived to the present day than have less prestigious writings or, inevitably, texts, images, and traditions that were never recorded in concrete form in the first place. Our appreciation of medieval culture is thus necessarily skewed by the partiality – in both senses – of most of our sources. But, in the particular case of Bernard, there is still some evidence for perceptions of him that, even if originating in learned, Latinate form, were either modified or even deliberately intended for the benefit of a wider audience, one that could not read Latin or, perhaps, could not read at all. The movement from the Latin tomes in the monastic library to vernacular texts accessible to a larger readership, or to hymns, paintings, and statuary depicting Bernard of Clairvaux and used for devotional purposes, is also a move on our grid, from technical theology to popular religion, from intellectual aristocracy to the public at large (or some part of it), and even from the literate in the general direction of the non-literate.

One text in particular exemplifies this movement, starting life as a Latin manual written for the edification of Franciscan friars and eventually, through a process of translation and divulgation, reaching an enormous audience throughout Western Europe and leaving its traces on numerous devotional, artistic, and literary productions. This was the *Meditationes vitae Christi*, traditionally attributed to Bonaventure, but nowadays more plausibly seen as the work of another thirteenth-century Italian Franciscan, Giovanni de' Cauli (Johannes de Caulibus), a native of San Gimignano in Tuscany. The manuscript history of the *Meditationes* is confused but interesting, and it has some relevance for our concern with its portrayal of Bernard, and with that portrayal's subsequent effect on Bernard's reputation – extending, possibly, even as far as his appearance in *Paradiso*.[46]

Briefly, the *Meditationes vitae Christi* exists in three versions of different lengths. The longest of these consists of ninety-five chapters, which recount the nativity, childhood, baptism, ministry, passion, resurrection, and ascension of Christ, and end with the descent of the Holy Spirit on the disciples at Pentecost. Within this simple narrative structure (taken wholesale, of course, from the Gospels and the Acts of the Apostles) is inserted a substantial treatise on the nature and relative merits of the active and contemplative lives. The second version, however, abbreviates the prologue (four chapters in the longest version), omits much of the narrative of Christ's ministry (including several very familiar episodes), ignores the treatise on action and contemplation altogether, and, with the exception of a

---

[46] For the *Meditationes vitae Christi*, see the entry by Columban Fischer in the *Dictionnaire de spiritualité*, edited by Marcel Viller and others (Paris, 1932– ), I, 1848–53. A more detailed study of the problems of its authorship, compositional history, and date, which revises many of Fischer's conclusions, is Giorgio Petrocchi, 'Sulla composizione e data delle *Meditationes Vitae Christi*', *Convivium*, Sept.–Oct. 1952, 757–78.

couple of minor incidents, jumps straight from the baptism of Christ to the events leading up to the crucifixion. A third version, sometimes known as the *Meditationes passionis Christi*, begins with the Last Supper, and is essentially a reproduction of the closing chapters of the other two versions.

The chronological order in which the various versions were composed, and the primacy of the Latin text or its Italian *volgarizzamento*, the *Meditazioni della vita di Cristo*, have been as keenly debated as the question of their authorship.[47] The painstaking researches and persuasive arguments of Giorgio Petrocchi, foremost among the several scholars who have tackled the problem, have convinced many that the Latin text preceded the *volgarizzamento*, and that the longest and most narratologically satisfying version of that text preceded both the shorter ones. (Neither of these conclusions is really contrary to expectations, but both have been strenuously disputed in the past.) Thus all the hundreds of manuscripts of the various forms of the *Meditationes vitae Christi*, and of its translations into several European languages, derive from the ninety-five chapters of the Latin text, which Petrocchi assigns to Giovanni de' Cauli and to the years between 1256 and 1263.[48]

Our concern with the *Meditationes* (and even more with the Italian *Meditazioni*) is inspired and justified by the fact that both the Latin original and the (remarkably faithful) *volgarizzamento* are hugely indebted to Bernard of Clairvaux.[49] There are more than a hundred direct quotations from his works in the longest version of the text, and the large majority of these are of considerable length, sometimes consisting of whole paragraphs rather than mere sentences or phrases. No other author enjoys anything like so extensive or respectful a treatment in the *Meditationes*. But the disposition of these quotations in the text is not uniform, and, consequently, it has something to tell us about the perception of Bernard that motivates his presence in the *Meditationes*; as do the selection of Bernardine texts for quotation and

---

[47] For the *volgarizzamento*, see Petrocchi, 'Sulla composizione', 777–8, and Alberto Vaccari, 'Le *Meditazioni della vita di Cristo* in volgare', in *Scritti di erudizione e di filologia, I: Filologia biblica e patristica* (Rome, 1952), pp. 341–78.

[48] Petrocchi, 'Sulla composizione', 772–6.

[49] Because of its socio-cultural importance as a non-Latin version of Bernard's thought and image, I have relied on, and quoted in what follows, the long version of the *volgarizzamento*, as found in *Cento meditazioni di S. Bonaventura sulla vita di Gesù Cristo: volgarizzamento antico toscano*, edited by Bartolommeo Sorio (Rome, 1847). The manuscript basis of this edition is discussed by Vaccari, 'Le *Meditazioni*', pp. 349–50; though far from perfect philologically, it is adequate for our purposes.

the occasional explanatory comments that introduce or link the quotations.

As we have seen, the full version of the *Meditationes* falls into three clearly defined sections, the first and third of which (chapters I–XLI and LVI–LXXXXIV) are mainly narrative, while the second (chapters XLII–LV) is a self-contained devotional treatise on the active and contemplative lives. All but five of the one hundred-odd Bernardine quotations occur in the first two sections, perhaps because the third deals with events in Christ's earthly life – his later ministry, passion, and resurrection – about which Bernard has comparatively little to say. Indeed, the second section, the treatise, is little more than a *florilegium* of appropriate selections from Bernard, strung together with a minimum of connecting narrative or authorial comment. The first section too, that describing Christ's birth, childhood, and early ministry, quotes Bernard frequently and copiously, including one extended commentary on the exchange between Jesus and his mother at the wedding at Cana (chapter XIX), and another long extract, rather vaguely attributed, which recounts a dispute between the allegorized figures of Mercy and Truth (chapter III). This chapter also includes the narrator's first explicit statement of intent regarding his use of Bernard's work: 'a questo modo fu tra loro gran discordia, secondo che narra santo Bernardo in uno lungo e bello sermone. Ma dirottene la somma il più brevemente ch'io potrò. Ed ho intendimento d'allegare, e spesse volte, li suoi detti dolcissimi, lo più breve ch'io potrò'.[50]

Giovanni de' Cauli perhaps failed to live up to his own express intention of quoting Bernard briefly, but that he did so frequently nobody will wish to deny. His choice of sources is also revealing: nearly half the quotations come from the sermons *In Cantica canticorum*, and, with a handful of exceptions (mostly from the spurious letter *Ad fratres de Monte Dei*), the rest are all taken from other sermons.[51] None of the major treatises is mentioned at all. The overwhelming impression to be gained from this selection of authoritative texts is of Bernard's importance as a preacher; and this is reinforced by overt

---

[50] *Meditazioni*, ed. Sorio, p. 40.
[51] The sermons quoted include those on *Qui habitat* and those for a number of liturgical feasts (Epiphany, Ascension Day, Advent, the Circumcision, Septuagesima, the Assumption, and St Peter and St Paul). The only treatise mentioned is, remarkably enough, *De laudibus nove militie*, written by Bernard for the founders of the Order of Knights Templar, a text seldom alluded to by Bernard's medieval biographers.

narratorial comment within the text itself. The author of the *Meditationes* has, in fact, a strong sense of Bernard's achievement as a user of words, which enables him to describe Bernard himself as 'facondioso', and his utterances as 'parole molto belle', 'detti dolcissimi', and 'melate cose'.[52] And these 'melate cose' are directed above all, in Giovanni de' Cauli's view, towards the discussion of two topics: the Virgin Mary and contemplation.

Bernard's importance as a preacher about Mary emerges from the frequent use of his Marian sermons in the *Meditationes*, and from the equally frequent use of other sermons in evoking Biblical episodes of which the Virgin herself is a protagonist (the Nativity, the wedding at Cana). It is also reflected in incidental comments not directly connected with Mary at all, as in chapter LI: 'E sopra ciò odi san Bernardo nel III sermone dell'Assunzione della Donna nostra, parlando abbondevilmente di lei come è usato'.[53] His corresponding importance as a contemplative is clear from the fact that his works provide the sole doctrinal basis for the treatise on action and contemplation in chapters XLII–LV, as well as from more explicit references, such as this one from the introduction to that treatise (chapter XLII). The narrator is explaining the allegorical significance of the two sisters, Martha and Mary:

E dei sapere che per queste doi sorelle, come dicono li santi, s'intendono doi vite, cioè l'attiva e la contemplativa, delle quali voler parlare saria lunga materia. Ma perché credo ch'a te non bisogni lungo tratto, alcuna cosa di ciò ti scriverò. E però che santo Bernardo in diversi luoghi parla di ciò copiosamente, e sì anco che a te sarà più utile, e più spirituale e più necessario.[54]

But the longest and most detailed of the *Meditationes*' references to Bernard, and the one that best encapsulates the vision of him held by the book's author, comes in chapter XXXIII. The narrator is expounding the nature and meaning of prayer ('orazione'), and its importance as the first, and indispensable, stage in the preparation of the soul for contemplation of the divine. The best way of learning to pray, he asserts, is to listen to Bernard: 'Acciò che tu t'ausi d'essere migliore oratore, odi melate cose che narra santo Bernardo'.[55] And, having given his audience ample opportunity to do just that, by

[52] *Meditazioni*, ed. Sorio, pp. 99, 96, 40, 94.     [53] Ibid., p. 132.     [54] Ibid., p. 114.
[55] Ibid., p. 94.

supplying apposite quotations which extend over two large pages of
the printed edition, he sums up, in a remarkable paragraph that
throws a clear and brilliant light on the essential late medieval
perception of Bernard as a figure distinguished above all for his
eloquence:

Avete dunque udito parole molto belle d'altissimo contemplatore, et
assaggiaste dolcezza del barone santo Bernardo. Rugumale, se tu vuoli che
ti sieno saporose. Però pongo voluntiere in questo libro le parole sue, e ce le
adduco, imperò che sono non solamente spirituali e che passano il core; anco
perché sono piene di decoro e di bellezza, e che molto inducono al servizio
di Dio. Esso santo Bernardo fu bellissimo parladore, e fu pieno di spirito di
sapienzia, e chiaro di santità, il quale tu con desiderio seguita; li suoi
ammonimenti e le parole e fatti adopera; per la qual cosa spesso lui ti porrò
per esempio.[56]

Without wishing to anticipate the conclusions of the reading of
*Paradiso* that awaits us, it none the less seems clear already that the
image of a Bernard of Clairvaux notable as much for the power of his
eloquence as for the depth of his contemplative mysticism and
devotion to the Virgin Mary is one that anyone coming to the
*Commedia* after reading the *Meditazioni* (or the *Meditationes*) would
have no difficulty whatever in recognizing.

The specific importance of the *Meditationes vitae Christi* for Dante
studies lies in the existence, and enormous popularity, of its
*volgarizzamento*, the *Meditazioni della vita di Cristo*. This must have
considerably increased the extent of the work's penetration into early
Trecento culture, by opening it up to those unfamiliar with Latin,
and thereby liberating it from the exclusive embrace of clerical
intellectuals. Its Tuscan origins and linguistic form will also have
ensured comparatively easy diffusion in the region where the
*Commedia* first circulated. It follows that the image of St Bernard
presented in the *Meditationes* will also have become more widely
available as a result of the work's translation, and may thus have
helped to condition readers' expectations of another vernacular work,
the *Commedia*, when they found in it a character bearing the name,
and corresponding to the historical lineaments, of St Bernard himself.
In their stress on eloquence, contemplation, and Marian devotion as
the key elements of Bernard's cultural significance, the *Meditationes*

[56] Ibid., p. 96.

are consonant with the theological tradition preserved in the writings of the scholastics; but, at least in the vernacular form of the *Meditazioni*, they must have brought that picture of Bernard to an infinitely larger audience.

Questions of audience also predominate in certain other cultural categories relevant to our enquiry into Bernard's overall reputation in the early Trecento. The texts considered so far have all been, to a greater or lesser extent, instruments of study, even when that study was aimed at increasing the student's expertise in prayer or devotion rather than in intellectual debate (as is the case of the *Meditationes vitae Christi*). The images to be discussed in the rest of this chapter all derive from forms whose definition is broadly artistic, and which were apparently destined for use in inspiring or sustaining religious enthusiasm among the faithful at large, rather than in instructing the clergy or even the educated laity (though this may have been an ancillary or incidental benefit, especially with material produced by Cistercians). We shall thus examine the poetic images of Bernard found in late medieval hymns and liturgical texts, as well as the visual ones found in manuscript illustrations, paintings, and statuary.

Bernard is not well represented in medieval hymnology. Of more than 28,000 hymns in the *Analecta hymnica medii aevi*, a mere nine appear under the rubric 'de sancto Bernardo Claraevallensi'.[57] Nor is the Breviary rich in specifically Bernardine material. But, although the (surviving) hymns about Bernard are few in number, they were very widely diffused. The editors of the *Analecta* list dozens of manuscript occurrences of most of them, coming chiefly from Cistercian houses in various parts of Europe. Predictably, these follow the Order itself in being strongly concentrated in France and Germany, but they are found in Italy as well, and it is reasonable to assume that there was some knowledge of them (or of others, now lost, akin to them) in the Italy of Dante's time.

The hymns in the *Analecta* vary considerably in their treatment of Bernard. Some are so general in conception and expression that they might equally well refer to any other saint whose name happened to fit in their metrical scheme, while others are clearly based on hagiographical sources. One at least, as its editors point out, is practically incomprehensible without some knowledge of the saint's

[57] *Analecta hymnica medii aevi* (henceforth *AHMA*), edited by Guido Maria Dreves, Clemens Blume, and H. M. Bannister, 58 vols. (Leipzig, 1886–1922), LII (1909), nos. 136–42 (pp. 131–8); LV (1922), nos. 92–3 (pp. 110–12).

biography.[58] The features on which the hymn-writers dwell turn out
to be those familiar from our analysis of prose sources. Bernard is a
renowned man of learning, well versed in the science of contemplation, a devotee of Mary, the author of learned books, a
preacher of marvellous eloquence. The imagery in which these
praises are sung is peculiarly suitable for their subject, much of it
being drawn from the Song of Songs, the Biblical text of most
importance in Bernard's own work. One hymn plays skilfully on the
pretended etymological link between 'Bernardus' and 'nardus' (first
mentioned in the *Legenda aurea*), in a cluster of images of sweetness,
perfume, and sensuous pleasure;[59] another, albeit rather later in date
than the others, uses imagery based on the legendary powers of
numerous precious stones (and thus, even though there appears to be
no direct filiation, compares interestingly with the sermon of Aquinas
mentioned above, p. 30).[60] The notion of sweetness, as applied to
Bernard's eloquence, was to earn him from posterity the most famous
of his honorific titles, 'Doctor mellifluus'; and the germ of this is
already to be seen in hymns which refer to Bernard's 'dulcor eloquii'
and 'eloquium mellifluum' – as well, of course, as in the 'melate
cose' of the *Meditazioni della vita di Cristo*. As if in open tribute to his
powers, there are a few occasions on which the hymn-writer seems
deliberately to quote or paraphrase one of Bernard's own more
distinctive expressions.[61]

On the whole, these hymns do not tell the reader of their texts
much about the life of the saint whom they honour; that was not their
purpose. Instead, they take a few salient aspects of his reputation –
the basic reasons *why* he is honoured – and give them a lapidary,
poetic form, as a means of fixing them in the reader's (or singer's)
memory. This, of course, is one reason why they were produced in
Cistercian abbeys: in order to further the immersion of the monks in
the traditions of their Order, and in devotion to its greatest
representative. But they are a channel of communication as well as an
aid to devotion, and they consequently played some part, however
small, in the creation of Bernard's reputation outside the strictly
monastic context.

---

[58] *AHMA*, LII (1909), no. 138 (pp. 134–5).
[59] *AHMA*, LII (1909), no. 137 (pp. 133–4); *Legenda aurea*, ed. Graesse, p. 527.
[60] *AHMA*, LV (1922), no. 92 (p. 110).
[61] For eloquence, see *AHMA*, LII (1909), nos. 136 (pp. 131–2), 138 (p. 135), and 140 (pp.
136–7). For paraphrases, see *AHMA*, LII (1909), no. 137 (p. 133); LV (1922), no. 93 (pp.
111–12).

Other liturgical material associated with Bernard conforms to this general pattern: the same facets of his life and achievement are treated in concise poetic form. One celebrated extract from the Breviary stresses Bernard the contemplative ('contemplationi sic addictus erat, ut vix sensibus, nisi ad officia pietatis, uteretur'); and, as a result, it has found favour with some commentators on *Paradiso*, even though it is not certain that it was composed before Dante's time.[62] Another, related, factor is the attribution to Bernard of several famous hymns and liturgical texts, foremost among them the *Salve Regina* and the beautiful hymn *Dulcis Jesu memoria*; although these attributions have no basis in fact, they were widely accepted in the Middle Ages (and, indeed, down to the twentieth century), and must also, therefore, have contributed to the esteem in which Bernard was held. It is no coincidence that the texts believed to be Bernard's could all be defined as either Marian (*Salve Regina*) or, broadly speaking, contemplative (*Dulcis Jesu memoria*); or that, as these two instances show, they are, in themselves, notable examples of poetic eloquence.[63]

The representation of St Bernard in visual form is also intimately connected with the development of his reputation in late medieval culture, and moves us to yet another position on our grid. Since written sources, by their very nature, were accessible to so few members of a largely non-literate society, the importance of visual representation and iconographical languages, available to anyone with eyes to see, was correspondingly greater than in our own print-addicted world. But even here some distinctions need to be made. The earliest pictorial representations of Bernard of Clairvaux still appeared in the context of the literate approach to his life, since they were designed as illustrations in manuscripts of his own writings and of hagiographies. Their impact on non-readers must, therefore, have been limited, since such people would have been unlikely to have occasion to consult a manuscript in the first place. Only later, with the appearance of paintings and statues used for the decoration of churches and monasteries, do we find a tradition of depictions of Bernard entirely divorced from the presumption of literacy.

---

[62] 'He was so devoted to contemplation that he scarcely used his senses except for the purposes of piety'; see the *Commedia* commentaries of Manfredi Porena, 3 vols. (Bologna, 1953), III, 300, and Natalino Sapegno (Milan and Naples, 1957), p. 1170.

[63] These well-known texts may be found in *The Oxford Book of Medieval Latin Verse*, second edition, edited by F. J. E. Raby (Oxford, 1959), pp. 196 and 347–53.

As yet, there is no detailed iconographical catalogue of manuscripts of Bernard, still less one that also deals with portrayals of him in manuscripts of works by other writers. However, the doyen of modern students of Bernard, Jean Leclercq, has published a reasonably comprehensive list of examples encountered during his work on the text of Bernard's *opera omnia*, and this provides enough material for some tentative conclusions to be essayed.[64]

From Leclercq's descriptions of individual images, it is obvious that there was a definite iconographical tradition in the portrayal of Bernard from the earliest times. This seems to have been based on the description of Bernard's physical appearance given by Geoffrey of Auxerre in the *Vita prima* (Book III, chapter 1), whose main features it reproduces almost exactly. Bernard is generally depicted in monastic dress (though not always that of the Cistercians), with tonsure and beard. Manuscripts dating from after 1174 usually give him the halo of sainthood, conferred on him in that year. He is shown in a variety of postures: usually standing, sometimes holding a crozier or a book (or both). The book may be closed, or it may be open at some appropriate text, in which case Bernard may be pointing to it with his free hand. (The texts used include the *incipit* of *De consideratione*, and extracts from *De praecepto et dispensatione* and other works.) In some instances Bernard is seen writing, at his devotions, or preaching; in manuscripts from the fourteenth century onwards he is often shown praying to the Virgin or in some more dramatic form of action, casting out demons or slaying a dragon (a popular image of Bernard in the fifteenth century). Notwithstanding these later developments, the facets of his activity that most often catch the illustrators' imagination are those which have already been identified as central to his traditional reputation: prayerful contemplation, devotion to the Virgin, and preaching.

The iconographical tradition is, by and large, homogeneous throughout Europe, but there are a few slight national variations. Most of the illustrated Italian manuscripts are fairly late, although they do include one Florentine example which Leclercq dates to 1293. It seems that, in Italy, the *Vita prima*-based iconography was largely, though not universally, adhered to: two Paduan manuscripts show Bernard preaching, while one from Rome shows him writing

---

[64] Jean Leclercq, 'Pour l'iconographie de saint Bernard', *Analecta Sacri Ordinis Cisterciensis*, 9 (1953), fascicule 1, 40–5, 226–8.

and receiving a vision of the Virgin. This, however, is fifteenth-century, and may have been influenced by developments in painting at around that time. One fourteenth-century manuscript of the sermons *In Cantica canticorum* depicts Bernard preaching to his monks. Otherwise, most Italian manuscripts settle for a simple portrait, generally in accordance with Geoffrey of Auxerre's description.

The iconography of Bernard in painting was clearly affected by that of the manuscript illustrations, which almost certainly pre-dates it. Maria Chiara Celletti's account shows the evident points of contact with the manuscript tradition.[65] The image of the saint is austere and emaciated; he is shown in a posture of prayer or contemplation, tonsured and wearing the monastic habit. The 'props' which decorate this image vary, including a white dog (from a story in the *Vita prima*), a mitre at Bernard's feet (symbolizing his repeated rejection of offers of bishoprics), a bee-hive (for the 'doctor mellifluus'), and a sacramental wafer. Especially in later images, Bernard is seen in various narrative scenes, exorcising, performing miracles, enjoying visions of Christ and Mary, and, from the fourteenth century onwards (especially in Spain), participating in the Lactation of the Virgin. But these are mostly late additions to the stock representations of Bernard, reflecting the embroideries of popular legend; none is at all common before the fourteenth century. The basis of the tradition is both older and simpler than the more outlandish imaginings of the fifteenth-century painters.

In a fascinating article, Pierre Quarré has shown that the iconographical tradition of St Bernard can, in fact, be traced back to Clairvaux itself, and to a *vera effigies* or standard likeness established there in the later Middle Ages – though not to the official portrait said to have been painted at Rome shortly after Bernard's death (Quarré is of the opinion that this never existed).[66] The standard image of Bernard seems, instead, to be based on two specific artefacts: an early fourteenth-century silver bust made for the abbey, which was to serve as a model for many later copies, and a late fourteenth-century statue placed on Bernard's tomb. These two works founded a tradition to which the vast majority of later portrayals of Bernard conform. Since this *vera effigies* is also closely related to Geoffrey of

---

[65] Maria Chiara Celletti, 'Iconografia', s.v. 'Bernardo di Chiaravalle', in *Bibliotheca Sanctorum*, 12 vols. (Rome, 1961–9), III (1963), cols. 37–41.

[66] Pierre Quarré, 'L'Iconographie de saint Bernard à Clairvaux et les origines de la *vera effigies*', in *Mélanges saint Bernard* (Dijon, 1953), pp. 342–9.

Auxerre's description in the *Vita prima*, it seems reasonable to assume that images produced before the early fourteenth century were in this same tradition, which is also, of course, that of the manuscript illustrations. In short, the line of iconography sanctioned by Clairvaux itself appears to stem directly from Geoffrey's account, and this is probably the principal reason for its remarkable consistency through the centuries.

The logical conclusion to be drawn from Quarré's evidence is that early portraits of Bernard will tend to be in broad conformity with the iconographical tradition regardless of their date; and this assumption helps to fill the gap between Bernard's death and Dante's time, from which period very few paintings, as such, survive. George Kaftal, however, gives a thorough account of Tuscan iconography of Bernard, which provides more evidence of the kind of portrayal with which Dante and his readers were probably familiar.[67]

In the later fourteenth century and thereafter, the usual depiction of Bernard was as a young (or youngish), clean-shaven monk, wearing the white habit of the Cistercians. As Kaftal makes clear, this is a departure from convention: abbots are generally shown as old and bearded.[68] It is also inconsistent with the *vera effigies* and the *Vita prima* account, as well as with the manuscript tradition. All these show Bernard bearded (with a very few exceptions among manuscripts), and in late middle or old age. The youthful, beardless Bernard of the later Trecento images is also, of course, the precise opposite of Dante's early fourteenth-century portrayal of Bernard as a 'santo sene' (*Par.*, XXXI. 94).

There are, however, a few exceptions to what otherwise appears to be the rule in Tuscan painting, and at least one of these is, chronologically, closer to Dante than most such images. A slightly ambiguous case is a work of a follower of the Master of the Fabriano Altarpiece, which shows Bernard as elderly and bearded; though this is the usual type of St Benedict in Tuscan painting, this figure holds a book open at a quotation from Bernard. Perhaps more significant is an image in a church at Settimo, outside Florence. Dating from about 1300 and painted on a beam, it shows Bernard (who is named in the painting) as a bearded man, clearly not young, and carrying a closed book and a crozier. It is, therefore, squarely in the tradition of

---

[67] George Kaftal, *Iconography of the Saints in Tuscan Painting* (Florence, 1952).
[68] Ibid., p. xxii.

the *vera effigies*, and indicates that this tradition was not unknown in Tuscany.[69]

The Tuscan paintings listed by Kaftal which show Bernard with an open book are all later than Dante's time, but they do suggest that the main facets of his reputation had remained unchanged over the years. Most of the texts visible on the pages of these books are concerned with the Virgin Mary, some coming from the sermons *In laudibus Virginis Matris*, others from spurious Marian tracts. One quotation ('eloquium tuum dulce', from sermon 34 *In Cantica canticorum*) provides further evidence of Bernard's continuing renown as a preacher.

The iconography of Bernard in the visual arts is closely connected with perhaps the most vital, but certainly the least easily recoverable, factor in the formation of his medieval reputation: common knowledge. By this I mean the mass of legend and superstition, with no rational or factual basis, that to this day tends to gather around the name of any publicly esteemed or well-known figure, and often proves much more tenacious in its hold on the popular memory than the sober formulations of historians and biographers. (A single example: the King Alfred who promoted ecclesiastical reform and the revival of learning in his kingdom is, to put it mildly, less immediately recognizable in England today than the one who burned the cakes.) The vehicles by which such information was transmitted within medieval culture were predominantly oral, and the social circles in which it was disseminated predominantly popular, both of which facts have helped to ensure that, at best, only vague traces of it remain in archival or textual form. None the less, it is possible, especially in fourteenth-century and later sources, to find elements of the *legenda Bernardi* that have no obvious historical or hagiographical precedent, and which may be presumed to have arisen from some kind of popular, non-literate expression of devotion to Bernard's memory.

The connection with iconography depends on the fact that many of the personal traits and narrative episodes that were to become most common in portrayals of Bernard are derived from this background of hearsay, rather than from even remotely authenticated sources. The Lactation is a case in point. This rather unsavoury legend, according to which the Virgin Mary squeezed a few drops of milk

---

[69] For both these paintings, see ibid., p. 146.

from her breast on to the tongue of the praying Bernard, appears in none of the medieval biographies; it seems, instead, to develop as a popular fiction in the fourteenth century, and within a hundred years had become one of the most familiar representations of Bernard in visual form.[70] Obviously it has some relation to the facts, in that Bernard's remarkable devotion to Mary is amply attested in his writings; but in its details it is wholly a product of the popular imagination, based on the prior process in which Bernard's reputation as a Mariologist had been established through the circulation of those writings. Similarly, the tale of Bernard forcing the Devil to mend a wheel on his wagon is a late medieval legend, absent from earlier written sources, which rapidly became widespread in painting. It too is based on facts about Bernard – the extreme holiness of his life and the force of his character, both abundantly clear in the historical record – but, for all its psychological truth, it still arises from popular devotion rather than history or even hagiography.

Unfortunately, common knowledge cannot be exploited to the full in any modern survey of Bernard's medieval reputation. Its inevitably ephemeral nature means that what may well have been the largest and most influential body of cultural material associated with Bernard of Clairvaux in the late Middle Ages has effectively vanished, leaving the picture distorted in favour of the more durable evidence found in the sources we have examined above. As a result, we have no fully reliable way of knowing what, if anything, Bernard's name meant to the man (let alone the woman) in the Florentine piazza in the early Trecento. The man in the Florentine library, however, is a different matter; and this chapter will end with a few words about the material availability of written texts concerned with Bernard in Dante's Italy.

There are two main sources of potentially useful evidence in this area: contemporary library catalogues and information about the production and circulation of manuscripts. The use of both, however, is subject to various abiding difficulties. Library catalogues tell us

---

[70] What appears to be Dom Jean Mabillon's disparaging opinion of this legend is worth preserving: 'In omnibus S. Bernardi miraculorum libris nulla uspiam mentio de miraculoso illo lacte, a beatissima Virgine in Bernardum expresso: quod tamen miraculum prae aliis certissimis a pictoribus et ab incautis sancti Doctoris devotis nunc venditari cernimus' ('In none of the books of St Bernard's miracles is there the slightest mention of this miraculous milk, squeezed out by the Blessed Virgin for Bernard's benefit: and yet we now see this miracle bandied about, at the expense of others whose authenticity is assured, by painters and imprudent devotees of that holy Doctor'). See *PL*, 185, col. 466, n. 141.

that a given book was in a given place at a given time, but not how or when it got there, what became of it later, or under what conditions it was used. Catalogues of manuscripts list those that are still extant today, but cannot always tell us where they were six centuries ago, or where they were produced; and, of course, they are also silent about the (far larger) quantity of manuscripts that have not survived into the present. The result is that proof of a particular text's objective availability in a particular situation is often of only limited value, especially when trying to connect that text with any individual reader or group of readers. (Thus, for example, the mere existence of copies of Bernard's works in the Florentine libraries of the 1290s, say, tells us nothing whatever about Dante's putative interest in or access to them.) Such evidence can, however, be useful in indicating possibilities, trends, or a general cultural climate; and that is the sense in which it will be considered here.

By far the richest cache of evidence about medieval Italian libraries comes from late Duecento and early Trecento Florence. Catalogues from all the major religious houses there have been published, and together these form an impressively detailed account of the character of the various institutional collections. The difficulty of using these catalogues for our purposes becomes apparent, however, on closer inspection. Most of them date from substantially after Dante's death in 1321; and, more important, they hardly ever contain any indication of the date when any individual volume arrived in the library. The consequences will be obvious. It is not possible to state with certainty that all the books in a fifteenth-century catalogue had always been in the library, even if they are themselves thirteenth- or fourteenth-century in date; and it is equally impossible to determine which volumes may have disappeared from the library in the course of time. Catalogue evidence is thus nothing like conclusive, in determining the extent to which Bernard's works were available in Dante's Florence; it can be suggestive, and occasionally intriguing, but no more.

Some of the minor Florentine catalogues can be dismissed almost out of hand. A fifteenth-century list of books belonging to Santa Maria del Fiore is erratically compiled, and too distant in date from Dante, with no indication that the collection had been in even rudimentary existence in the early Trecento.[71] It makes no mention

---

[71] The list is reproduced in Giovanni Lami, *Sanctae ecclesiae Florentinae monumenta etc.* (Florence, 1758).

of Bernard. Slightly more substantial is the (late fifteenth-century) catalogue of the Medici library, which includes annotations identifying the books taken from the suppressed convent of San Marco, which was still functioning in Dante's time.[72] Three works by Bernard (*De consideratione, In Cantica canticorum,* and the *Epistolae*) are each represented by a single copy; but there is no clue to their date or provenance.

The library of the Cistercian Badia in Florence is something of a disappointment in this regard.[73] As might be expected, its late fifteenth-century catalogue contains a generous selection of Bernard's works, but some of the volumes are clearly later than is useful for us (one at least is printed). The crucial difficulty, however, is connected with the history of the library itself. Although the Badia was founded (by Benedictines) in 978, there appears to have been no library worthy of the name in the first four centuries of its existence. The library as catalogued thus dates from the middle of the fourteenth century at the earliest, and its value as evidence for the late Duecento and early Trecento is correspondingly diminished.

More solid evidence is available from the three major monastic establishments of Trecento Florence: the Dominican house at Santa Maria Novella, its Franciscan counterpart at Santa Croce, and the Augustinian community of Santo Spirito. The oldest of these libraries seems to be that of Santo Spirito, begun as soon as the convent was founded in 1250; it was declared a *studium generale* in 1287.[74] Unfortunately, the first attempts at cataloguing the library's holdings date from 1357, and the comprehensive catalogue was not drawn up until 1450. It must, therefore, be used with caution, as it ranges far beyond the limits of any cultural context that Dante might have known; but it is legitimate to see the fifteenth-century library as the culmination of an intellectual tradition that had been developing at Santo Spirito since 1250, and thus to consider Bernard's place in that tradition.

The catalogue of the *libraria maior* at Santo Spirito includes eleven entries relating to Bernard, which refer to about two dozen texts in all. (It is hard to be more precise, as one book is simply called *opera Bernardi.*) A few of these are spurious, and at least two are *florilegia*;

---

[72] E. Piccolomini, 'Inventario della libreria Medicea privata compilata nel 1495', *Archivio storico italiano*, third series, 20 (1874), 51–94.

[73] Rudolf Blum, *La biblioteca della Badia fiorentina e i codici di A. Corbinelli* (Vatican City, 1951).

[74] David Gutiérrez, 'La biblioteca di Santo Spirito di Firenze nella metà del secolo XV', *Analecta Augustiniana*, 25 (1962), 5–88.

but the remainder includes many of Bernard's best-known works (*In Cantica canticorum, De gratia et libero arbitrio, De consideratione, De gradibus humilitatis et superbiae, Apologia ad Guillelmum*), as well as some of his less familiar ones (*De praecepto et dispensatione, De laudibus nove militie*). It is a substantial collection, which would give any attentive reader a perfectly adequate conspectus of Bernard's work as a whole. We know, then, that such a conspectus was available to a Florentine readership in the middle of the fifteenth century; it may well be that some part of it at least was accessible to earlier generations.

Bernard is not, by any means, the most popular author in the library of Santo Spirito – at least if we judge by the number of copies of his writings held there. His eleven entries in the catalogue are exceeded by Cicero (12), Jerome (12), Gregory the Great (15), Aristotle (18), Giles of Rome (24), Thomas Aquinas (25), and the inevitable Augustine (42). Again, this represents a fifteenth-century distribution, but there is no evidence for any radical shift in the community's priorities over the preceding 150 years. Predictably, the authors best represented in this Augustinian house include Augustine himself and the Augustinian friar Giles of Rome, along with the Dominican – but enormously influential – Thomas Aquinas. In this library, then, Bernard seems to occupy the respectably second-rate position among theological and philosophical *auctores* to which he is allocated by a number of the scholastic thinkers discussed above.

The oldest catalogue of the library at Santa Maria Novella dates from the first half of the fourteenth century, and is thus more valuable from our point of view than that of Santo Spirito.[75] It records that the library possessed seven books of Bernard's writings, four of which were apparently *florilegia* (*Dicta Bernardi, Exempla Bernardi*, and two volumes of *Originalia Bernardi*). Apart from these, there are two copies of the sermons *In Cantica canticorum* and a volume of letters. This would imply that, if Bernard's work figured at all in the courses of instruction given at Santa Maria Novella, it cannot have played a very important part in them; and this implication is only reinforced by the provision of other authors in the library. Almost inevitably, in a Dominican establishment, Thomas Aquinas leads the field, with ninety entries in the catalogue; but Bernard also trails behind Aristotle (58), Augustine (21), Albert the Great (12), Jacobus a Voragine (11), and Gregory the Great (8). The intellectual atmosphere at Santa Maria

---

[75] Stefano Orlandi, *La biblioteca di S. Maria Novella in Firenze dal sec. XIV al sec. XIX* (Florence, 1952).

Novella seems, then, to have been overwhelmingly Dominican (with the *Legenda aurea* perhaps offering light relief from the sterner diet of commentaries on Aristotle and the Bible), and opportunities for reading Bernard there, as at Santo Spirito, were probably limited, at least in comparison with the ready availability of the works of Aquinas or Augustine.

There remains the library of the Franciscan community at Santa Croce. It has already been suggested, in these pages, that the Franciscan Order and its tradition were more important than their Dominican rivals in the diffusion of Bernard's influence through the literary and theological culture of the Italian Duecento and Trecento; and it may thus be more rewarding to look to Santa Croce, rather than to any other institution in late medieval Florence, for clear signs of the possibility of direct contact with the work of Bernard of Clairvaux.

It is fortunate that a good deal is known about the composition of the library at the end of the thirteenth century, its contemporary catalogue having been reconstructed in considerable detail and with a high degree of plausibility.[76] There appear, however – perhaps contrary to expectations – to have been only two works of Bernardine interest at Santa Croce in the late Duecento. One is a composite volume, of the twelfth and thirteenth centuries, made up mostly of works by Hugh of St Victor, but also including the so-called *De tribus osculis*, a conflation of Bernard's sermons *De diversis* 87 and 90. The other is a large twelfth-century folio of nearly four hundred leaves, which contains 258 of Bernard's letters, numerous sermons (both genuine and misattributed), a *Planctus Mariae* ascribed (wrongly) to Bernard, and, perhaps most significant of all, an unusually extensive collection of hagiographical material. This includes the first three books of the *Vita prima*, Geoffrey of Auxerre's sermon on the anniversary of Bernard's death, and the letters written by Pope Alexander III at the time of Bernard's canonization.[77] This volume's presence in the catalogue indicates that the most reliable biography

[76] Charles T. Davis, 'The Early Collection of Books of S. Croce in Florence', *Proceedings of the American Philosophical Society*, 107 (1963), 399–414. Also useful are two other articles by Davis: 'Education in Dante's Florence', *Speculum*, 40 (1965), 415–35 (revised and reprinted in *Dante's Italy and Other Essays*, Philadelphia, 1984, pp. 137–65); and 'The Florentine *Studia* and Dante's "Library"', in *The 'Divine Comedy' and the Encyclopedia of Arts and Sciences*, edited by Giuseppe Di Scipio and Aldo Scaglione (Amsterdam and Philadelphia, 1988), pp. 339–66.

[77] The sermon and the letters can be found in *PL*, 185, cols. 573–88 and 619–26.

of Bernard was readily available for study at Santa Croce; but it is noteworthy that it does not seem to have been accompanied by any of his major works.

The picture of the availability of Bernard's writings in Florence at the end of the thirteenth century is thus a little more complicated than might have been foreseen. The most extensive collection of his work appears to have been that at Santo Spirito, one of the less important religious centres in the city at that time (and one with which Dante himself, incidentally, seems not to have had any dealings worthy of record). The most likely of all the religious houses to have offered a focal point for the study of Bernard, Santa Croce, seems not to have owned many actual copies of his works, at least according to the earliest extant catalogue sources. Even Santa Maria Novella, the most active of the *studia generalia* (and the one with which Dante was most closely associated), seems to have possessed only Bernard's most famous work and a handful of *florilegia*.[78] There must, of course, have been other sources where texts of Bernard's could have been obtained – private collections, volumes unrecorded in surviving catalogues, individual copyists; but, on the evidence to hand, it seems that easy access to them in Dante's Florence should not be too readily taken for granted.

The evidence from libraries elsewhere in Italy is too sketchy and unenlightening to be worth dealing with at length, so it may be more helpful to pass on to the question of the production and circulation of manuscripts of Bernard's (authentic) works in late medieval Italy. The most comprehensive modern bibliography lists nearly two hundred extant Bernardine manuscripts as being either currently located in Italy or definitely of Italian origin.[79] The latter group poses no problem: a manuscript now in Cracow, say, or even Washington DC, can safely be assumed to have been involved in the transmission of Bernard's writings in Italy at some time during its career. Manuscripts of uncertain provenance presently located in Italy require more cautious treatment. That there is a large number of such manuscripts in Rome, for instance, need not mean that they are all of Roman origin; they may well have been acquired from a variety of sources and have migrated, as it were, to the cultural and

[78] See Giorgio Petrocchi, *Vita di Dante* (Bari, 1983), p. 32, on Dante and Santa Maria Novella.
[79] The information in what follows has been garnered from *Bibliographie générale de l'Ordre cistercien*, 'Saint Bernard', edited by H. Rochais and E. Manning, 12 fascicules *hors série* (Brussels, 1979–82).

antiquarian focus of Catholicism. In contrast, a single manuscript in, say, Vicenza, is more than likely (even when this cannot be proven) to have originated locally; Vicenza and towns like it will normally have exerted their cultural magnetism over a relatively small area. It follows, then, that the evidence needs to be handled carefully, with close attention to the cultural characteristics of the particular town or region under consideration.

Small Italian towns with twelfth-, thirteenth-, or fourteenth-century manuscripts of uncertain provenance – which can be assumed, without undue temerity, to be local – include Alessandria, Assisi, Bergamo, Bologna, Cesena, Cortona, Modena, Monte Cassino, Ravenna, Todi, and Vicenza. Similar towns with manuscripts of demonstrable origin are Bergamo (from Vercelli), Bologna (local), Cava (from its abbey), Cremona (from Sant'Agostino in the town), Mantua (no fewer than eleven specimens, from the abbey at Padolirone), Novacella (from the abbey there), Padua (mostly from Santa Giustina in the town), Pavia (from Padua), Perugia (from the Badia San Pietro there), Pisa (from Rome), Siena (from the abbey of Monteoliveto), and Vercelli (local). There are also a few oddities among such manuscripts. A fourteenth-century example from Lucca is now in Berlin; conversely, a manuscript from the Cistercian abbey at Morimond in Austria has found its way to the Seminario Maggiore at Como. An early example from Chiaravalle di Milano is to be seen in the Fitzwilliam Museum in Cambridge.

These manuscripts form a group, though only in so far as their geographical origin is known, or can be posited on the basis of the cultural tranquillity of their present location. There remain the large collections in cities where other factors may have come into play. The cities in question are Florence, Milan, Naples, Rome, Turin, and Venice, and the position in each is worth considering individually.

Fifteen manuscripts of Bernard's works survive in Florence, and half of these can be reliably attributed to the scriptorium at Santa Croce. These seven are all thirteenth-century, include all Bernard's major works (one alone containing several of his principal texts), and go some way towards redressing the imbalance in the perception of Santa Croce's importance as a Bernardine centre that was caused by the minimal presence of his works in the community's library. Whatever proportion this may be of the Santa Croce scriptorium's total output – and it is no doubt a tiny one – it at least suggests that Bernard's writings were copied there in more than negligible quantities. There is no evidence for the origin of the other eight manuscripts now in Florence, and it is not altogether permissible to assume that they are local, especially as some of them seem to have been purchased by collectors in the fifteenth century.

The Biblioteca Ambrosiana in Milan holds fourteen manuscripts of Bernard, three of which are known to be from Padua, two from Milan itself, and one from Engelberg in Germany. For the rest there is no confirmed provenance, and again the Ambrosiana's renown as a collection makes it inadvisable to assume that they are all local, or even, necessarily, Italian. In contrast, the manuscripts in the Biblioteca Nazionale in Naples all come from the city itself, two from the Benedictine abbey of San Severino and one from a Franciscan convent.

The Vatican Library is pre-eminent among collections of Bernardine manuscripts in Italy, accounting for more than half of the seventy-nine examples now to be found in Rome, and for far more than any other Italian library. But precisely because it enjoys the status of an international cultural repository, its evidence in the case of strictly Italian manuscripts becomes more than somewhat ambiguous. Some of the Bernardine material in the Vatican is known to come from France, Germany, and England; and there is no guarantee that all or any of the manuscripts of unknown provenance originated in Italy. Those few manuscripts of Bernard in Rome that are definitely Italian all come from Cistercian abbeys: Acquafredda in Lombardy, Casamari and Trisulti in the far south, Rivalta di Torino in Piedmont.

The collections in Turin and Venice are both much smaller. There are five manuscripts in various Turin libraries, three of them from the Cistercian foundation at Staffarda in Piedmont; and two of possibly local, certainly Italian, origin in Venice.

At first sight, this evidence may seem to encourage no very solid conclusions. Certainly, the difficulty of determining the place or date of origin of so many manuscripts makes it hard to draw any such conclusions from those that do survive in Italy. But there are clues to be found, at least among those manuscripts that can be assigned a definite place of origin. First, they come from all over the peninsula, the majority from northern and central Italy (Piedmont to Campania), with a few from further south. Second, they are most often produced in Cistercian religious houses (Staffarda, Casamari, Acquafredda, Chiaravalle di Milano, among others); the most outstanding exceptions are the Franciscan house at Santa Croce in Florence and the Benedictine abbeys at Padolirone and Padua. It is, thus, not unreasonable to suggest both that possibilities for reading Bernard's work in late medieval Italy were not significantly limited by geography (however much they may have been by social factors), and that the Cistercian Order itself must have been prominently involved in the transmission and distribution of texts of Bernard's writings in Italy. For that reason, it is worth briefly considering the Order's history south of the Alps.[80]

The Cistercians appeared in Italy very early in their institutional career, well within St Bernard's own lifetime. The first foundation was at Tiglieto in Liguria (1120); four years later Locedio was founded, near Vercelli; and in the 1130s, under the impact of a number of visits made to northern Italy by Bernard himself, the Order gained ground rapidly. Casamari, south of Rome, was taken over from the Benedictines in 1140, and made a major contribution to the Order's growth in central and southern Italy. By the early fifteenth century, when the last foundation took place, there were eighty-eight Cistercian houses in various parts of the Italian peninsula. Roughly a quarter of these were in the north, mostly in Piedmont, Lombardy, and Liguria (there were very few in the Veneto, Emilia-Romagna, or the Marche), and there were about a dozen in Tuscany. The other large concentration was around Rome, and the remaining abbeys were scattered throughout the south, Sicily, and Sardinia. No region of Italy was entirely devoid of the Cistercian presence, and it therefore seems likely enough that no region lacked a monastery where manuscripts of Bernard's works were being produced at some time during the Middle Ages.

The Cistercian Order's influence on Italian life is regarded as considerable by the leading historian of Italian monasticism, Gregorio Penco – but only in its application to particular fields, such as economic and social structures and the visual arts.[81] Penco expresses reservations about the Cistercians' general importance for culture, claiming that they engaged in 'no intellectual activity worthy of being remembered'. Moreover, he describes Cistercian libraries, at least during the Order's early years, as 'rigidly closed to classical or secular authors' and 'admitting only Biblical and patristic texts'.[82]

---

[80] For the Cistercians in Italy, see Gregorio Penco, *Storia del monachesimo in Italia* (Rome, 1961), pp. 258–67, and Louis J. Lekai, *The Cistercians: Ideals and Reality* (Kent, USA, 1977), pp. 36–7.    [81] Penco, *Storia del monachesimo*, p. 266.    [82] Ibid., p. 267.

This culturally purist conservatism may, in itself, be a pointer to the role played by the Cistercian Order in the formation of Bernard of Clairvaux's reputation: the Cistercians' lack of interest in texts originating outside the Biblical and patristic canon, coupled with the Order's general tendency to look inwards, holding itself aloof from the secular world and even from other monastic and ecclesiastical institutions, must have encouraged concentration on the works of their own most distinguished author – and, in turn, the production of copies of those works, in Cistercian scriptoria, for the embellishment of Cistercian libraries.

There is, however, another interesting aspect of Cistercian history in Italy that may have helped to modify the Order's narcissistic concern with Bernard as, above all, a Cistercian, and thus to bring Cistercian influence to bear on the process in which images of Bernard were diffused through Italian culture as a whole. After the first stages of the Order's penetration into Italy, in the twelfth century, the supply of missionary monks from France began to dry up. As a result, Cistercian abbeys in Italy filled with Italians, who, in Gregorio Penco's view, were more closely aligned with a native tradition of mendicant spirituality (best exemplified, of course, in Francis of Assisi) than with the primitive Cistercian tradition embodied in Bernard. This apparent fusion of related, but essentially different, ideals may well have inspired a new synthesis in perceptions of Bernard, as the official Cistercian line laid down in the *Vita prima*, the orthodox Franciscanism of a Bonaventure, and the radical symbolic interpretations of a Joachim of Fiore (to cite only three possible positions on the spectrum) combined to create a richer and more complex image, indebted as much to Franciscan as to Cistercian spirituality and devotion.

At any rate, that image retained a central place in early Trecento Italian culture, where it was refracted, as we have seen, through a multiplicity of intellectual interests, personal commitments, textual forms, and social institutions. Bernard of Clairvaux was, culturally speaking, very much alive in Dante's Italy. It is now our task to see whether the character who bears his name in the closing cantos of the *Commedia* resembles, to any perceptible or revealing degree, the figure whom several generations of cultural history would have prepared the poem's first readers to encounter.

# CHAPTER 3

# Bernard of Clairvaux in the Commedia

## LIFE AFTER BEATRICE (*PARADISO* XXXI)

The narrator of *Northanger Abbey* famously remarks, in that novel's final chapter, that the 'tell-tale compression' of its pages reveals how little of her story remains to be recounted, and that she, her characters, and her reader are 'all hastening together to perfect felicity'.[1] Unseasoned readers of *Paradiso* XXXI very probably approach that canto in a similar frame of mind. At this point the mighty narrative edifice that is Dante's *Commedia* seems, in fact, to be almost ready for topping-out; all the expectations created by the poem itself, beginning with Virgil's own explanation of his mission and its inspiration (*Inf.*, II. 49–74), seem to have been fulfilled, or at least to be self-evidently on the verge of fulfilment.

Virgil has led his timorous admirer, Dante *personaggio*, down to the lowest point of Hell, and up again through Purgatory to the Earthly Paradise, only to be supplanted there by the noisy, colourful, and psychologically shattering advent of Beatrice; and Beatrice herself has then accompanied Dante upwards, through the nine concentric spheres that make up the heaven of Christian–Ptolemaic cosmology, to arrive (*Par.*, XXX. 38–45) 'al ciel ch'è pura luce' (39), in a place that is really no place, a realm that exists beyond the spatial and temporal limits of the universe, and thus offers access to unmediated experience of divine reality – the Empyrean. From here there is, literally and allegorically, nowhere else to go; the journey seems to be over, the traveller to have reached his destination, Beatrice to have kept her promise. As Dante gazes in wonderment at 'la forma general di paradiso' (*Par.*, XXXI. 52), he and we seem indeed to be hastening

---

[1] Jane Austen, '*Northanger Abbey*' and '*Persuasion*', edited by John Davie (London, 1971), p. 222.

towards a felicity far more literally perfect than anything envisaged in the fiction of Jane Austen.

And yet the comparatively few remaining pages of the *Commedia* hold in store an event unmatched for sheer dramatic effect by anything in the poem since the disappearance of Virgil in *Purgatorio* xxx. In canto xxxi of *Paradiso*, for all its evident proximity to the climax of the *Commedia*'s narrative, the course of that narrative shifts radically, in a way that not only introduces a new and wholly unanticipated element into the poem, but also, thereby, makes possible – or rather, *imposes* – a thoroughgoing reassessment of everything that has happened in the ninety-seven preceding cantos of the poem. Readers are thus required to come to terms immediately with the new event, by adjusting their – by now well-established – interpretations of the 'poema sacro' as a (near-)whole.

This profoundly unsettling occurrence, thrown like a spanner into the outwardly smooth functioning of *Paradiso*'s narrative machinery, is, of course, the removal of Beatrice from Dante's side and the appearance in her stead of 'un sene / vestito con le genti gloriose' (*Par.*, xxxi. 59–60) – a figure whom the text will soon (though not, it must be remembered, straight away) reveal to be St Bernard of Clairvaux. It is ultimately through his intervention, rendered concrete in words and action, that Dante will obtain the intercession of the Virgin Mary, and then proceed to the vision of God that sets the seal on poem and pilgrimage alike. For all that Beatrice inspires Bernard as she had inspired Virgil (*Par.*, xxxi. 65–6; *Inf.*, ii. 52–74), from the middle of canto xxxi to the end of the poem she ceases to be a presence and becomes a memory.

The first thing to be said about Bernard's involvement in the *Commedia* is simple enough: it comes as a surprise. Nothing in the poem prepares the reader for it; nothing overtly justifies it. The episode is well under way before Bernard's identity is ever made manifest, and over almost before the full extent of its baffling complexity has had time to sink in. It raises a whole host of questions about the poem's narrative design, theological implications, and cultural underpinnings, and inflicts them on readers still reeling, like Dante himself, from the shock of Beatrice's departure. It thus calls for especially attentive reading, since it constitutes a devastating subversion, at the eleventh narrative hour, of a whole set of assumptions on which readers of the *Commedia* thus far may, quite legitimately, have come to rely; and it throws doubt on the idea, often treated as axiomatic, that the poem's narrative organization, in itself, represents its author's underlying commitment to a belief in linear, ordered progress towards perfection. Readers of *Paradiso*, XXXI. 58–60 should, in short, be as startled by these lines as Dante *personaggio* himself is by the experience they recount; and they should also, perhaps, share some of his perplexity about the proper response.

Yet, all too often, 'professional' readers of *Paradiso* XXXI, and indeed of the whole Bernard episode, have overlooked this fundamental truth, and have treated Bernard's arrival on the scene as though it were no more than a natural, or at least unremarkable, development of the situation created by the rest of the poem.[2] Taking Bernard's appearance as a familiar textual fact (which it can only become, however, after the *Commedia* has been read *in extenso*), they underestimate its immediate impact on an unprepared reader – which is to astonish. Such 'professionals' have, in a sense, forgotten that they ever did *not* know that this event was going to take place, and have lost the ability to react to it as ordinary readers – the kind to whom the *Commedia* is addressed – surely must.[3] This is, of course, because scholars and critics are inevitably *re*-readers of their texts, in the sense established in chapter 1 above, and normally think and write as such; knowing from past experience that Bernard of Clairvaux is due to pop up (and I use the colloquialism advisedly) in *Paradiso* XXXI, they come to that startling moment fully prepared, even if only subconsciously, to swallow it without complaint, and to integrate it at once into a coherent overall scheme of reading the poem. The difficulty, the unexpectedness, even the seemingly random

[2]　As well as the standard medieval and modern commentaries, the following *lecturae* of *Paradiso* XXXI are of special interest: Alessandro Chiappelli, *Il canto XXXI del 'Paradiso'* (Florence, 1904); Luigi Valli, *Il canto XXXI del 'Paradiso'* (Rome, 1914); Giuseppe Cavazzuti, 'Nel tempio del suo voto (*Paradiso* XXXI)', in *Letture dantesche* (Modena, 1957), pp. 213–35; Giovanni Fallani, *Il canto XXXI del 'Paradiso'* (Rome, 1957); Dorothy L. Sayers, 'The Beatrician Vision in Dante and Other Poets', *Nottingham Medieval Studies*, 2 (1958), 3–23; Francesco Maggini, 'Il canto XXXI del *Paradiso*', in *Letture dantesche: 'Paradiso'*, edited by Giovanni Getto (Florence, 1961), pp. 641–51; Alberto Chiari, 'Il canto XXXI del *Paradiso*', *Ateneo Veneto*, fascicolo speciale (1965), 327–50; Francesco Gabrieli, *Il canto XXXI del 'Paradiso'* (Turin, 1965); Carmine Jannaco, 'Il canto XXXI del *Paradiso*', *Letture classensi*, 1 (1966), 109–20; Francesco T. Roffarè, 'Canto XXXI', in *Lectura Dantis Scaligera: 'Paradiso'* (Florence, 1968), pp. 1097–134; Giorgio Petrocchi, 'Il canto XXXI del *Paradiso*', *Nuove letture dantesche*, 7 (1974), 235–53; Francesco Sisinni, 'Il canto di San Bernardo', *L'Alighieri*, 25 (1984), no. 2, 18–31.

[3]　I am aware, of course, that *Paradiso* is explicitly addressed to a select few, the 'altri pochi' (*Par.*, II. 10–15) who travel in Dante's wake; but even these must begin their textual voyage as 'ordinary', uninstructed, first-time readers, and it is for these that the *Commedia* as a whole plainly seems to be intended.

quality of Bernard's presence, can thus be elided, and critics are able to write as if nothing could be more natural than that the *Commedia* should jettison one of its principal characters within sight of its conclusion, in favour of a personage whose advent is entirely unforeseeable, and who is not recognized, at first, even by the poem's protagonist.

This is another defect of the 're-reading' approach to the Bernard episode: it blurs the distinctions among the different sections of that episode, by ignoring the fact that for nearly forty lines neither Dante-character nor the first-time reader has any idea who this mysterious 'sene' is. As we shall see, there are reasons for the delay in identifying Bernard, reasons that help, in the end, to account for his presence in the *Commedia* and to establish his full significance to it; and it is, accordingly, most unwise to counteract the poem's own reticence by writing as if Bernard's identity were instantly obvious (which it is not now and, surely, was not even in the Trecento) – or, as many modern editions do, by furnishing an explanatory footnote at the point of Bernard's entry into the text (*Par.*, XXXI. 58–60), rather than waiting until the character declares himself (XXXI. 102).[4] The poem's own rhythm, in short, requires that Bernard remain temporarily anonymous; and readings or commentaries that overlook this requirement, based as they must be on the exegete's prior familiarity with the text and not on the way in which that text is actually encountered by readers, are false to the real workings of the *Commedia*.

In this chapter I shall attempt to read the episode involving Bernard of Clairvaux (*Par.*, XXXI. 58 – XXXIII. 54) in a way that respects the careful articulation of the episode's construction, and thus attempts to trace the subtle process through which the text of the poem creates an image of Bernard that both justifies his (outwardly anomalous) insertion into the narrative and, simultaneously, points towards a broader definition of his significance in cultural history (and therefore of his particular significance in the *Commedia*). To do so, it will be necessary to try to recreate the condition of (comparative) innocence in which any reader approaches the poem for the first time, a condition in which engagement with the text alone, unsupported by previously developed knowledge or interpretation, is the sole guide to his or her progressive opening-up of the *Commedia*'s

---

[4] Two recent and authoritative editions that make this mistake are *La 'Divina Commedia'*, edited by Natalino Sapegno (Florence, 1978; first edition, 1955), III, 393, and *La 'Divina Commedia'*, edited by Umberto Bosco and Giovanni Reggio, 3 vols. (Florence, 1979), III, 515.

meaning(s). Of course, this textual virginity can never be fully recovered once lost; but the effort to do so, or at least to establish, for practical purposes, a convincing pretence that we have done so, seems to me worthwhile – if only because it may enable us to appreciate what is actually happening on the *Commedia*'s literal and narrative levels, rather than settling for what our own past readings, and our absorption of the wisdom handed down by our predecessors, have conditioned us lazily to think (or rather, to know in advance) is happening.

Bernard of Clairvaux's involvement in the Empyrean cantos begins in an atmosphere of misapprehension. As Dante-character contemplates the stunning spectacle of Paradise spread out before him, he is understandably possessed by the desire to question Beatrice, so often heretofore his amiably omniscient guide. But this time, as he turns 'con voglia rïaccesa / per domandar la mia donna di cose / di che la mente mia era sospesa' (*Par.*, xxxi. 55–7), Dante discovers that things are no longer what he – and we – had become accustomed to thinking they were, and had assumed they would remain:

> Uno intendëa, e altro mi rispuose:
> credea veder Beatrice e vidi un sene
> vestito con le genti glorïose.
> Diffuso era per li occhi e per le gene
> di benigna letizia, in atto pio
> quale a tenero padre si convene.
> E 'Ov'è ella?' subito diss'io. (xxxi. 58–64)

The pivotal importance of this brief passage can scarcely be over-estimated. As we have already seen, it marks the end of a narrative epoch in the poem and the inauguration of a new and, as yet, inexplicable phase in its development, with the departure of Beatrice and the arrival of the unidentified 'sene'. It inevitably – and, beyond question, deliberately – recalls the only *coup de théâtre* of comparable audacity elsewhere in the *Commedia*, Virgil's equally sudden disappearance in *Purgatorio* xxx, and thereby establishes (or, better, reinforces) a parallel between the two guides on the narrative plane (since their involvement in the poem ends in identical fashion), while driving home the crucial difference between them on the symbolic one (since their ultimate destinations, Limbo and the 'candida rosa', lie at opposite ends of the otherworldly spectrum, and hence represent, with stark clarity, the eternal destinies between which the individual must choose). Perhaps most telling of all, the passage indirectly but effectively underlines a vital, yet easily disregarded, feature of all the Empyrean cantos: the utter novelty of Dante's experiences there, a novelty which consists in the fact that now, for the first time in Paradise, he is able to interact with the blessed on equal terms – and thus to begin to prepare himself to participate, to the fullest possible degree, in their condition of blessedness (which he will do in the visionary accord of wills described in the poem's final lines – and not before).[5] All this is made plain in *Paradiso*, xxxi. 58–64 by those lines' implicit dependence on a single, novel fact: that Dante-character can *see*.

The keenness of eyesight that Dante enjoys in the Empyrean is, in fact, unprecedented in Paradise, and, as we shall see in a moment, concentration on it is one of the major thematic features that define the Empyrean cantos. What is important at this stage, however, is that the as yet unnamed Bernard appears first of all as an object of Dante's vision, as something *seen*, and that Dante sees him, as he has not seen any other individual character in *Paradiso* except Beatrice herself, face to face and in every detail (59–63). (At *Paradiso*, xxxi. 49–51 Dante had indeed seen 'visi a carità süadi, / d'altrui lume fregiati e di suo riso, / e atti ornati di tutte onestadi', but these faces are in no way personalized; Bernard is the first – indeed, the only – individual to emerge from the massed ranks of the newly visible blessed.) Instead of the glittering lights that form majestic patterns in other spheres, and from which issue the authoritative voices of Dante's many paradisiacal interlocutors, instead even of the faintly perceptible outlines of Piccarda Donati and her companions in *Paradiso* iii, Dante now sees before him a (glorified) human being whose age, clothing, facial expression and demeanour can all be accurately registered and conveyed in visual terms. This newfound clarity of vision suffices to set the encounter with Bernard apart from any other in the third *cantica*; because Dante (and, by extension, the reader) can *see* Bernard as well as hear him, he is the only character in *Paradiso* – apart from the always and wholly exceptional Beatrice – in whom beatitude becomes manifest on a recognizably human scale.

The Bernard episode's uniqueness in this respect derives from the particular nature of the Empyrean itself, not from that of Bernard as a character: Dante can see Bernard because Bernard is *where* he is, not

---

[5] I return to this point, at some length, in chapter 6.

because he is *who* he is. Untrammelled powers of vision in the Empyrean had been promised to Dante by St Benedict as long ago as *Paradiso* xxii, when Dante had asked that he might see the saint 'con imagine scoverta' (60), receiving in reply the admonition '"Frate, il tuo alto disio / s'adempierà in su l'ultima spera, / ove s'adempion tutti li altri e'l mio' (61–3). Accordingly, when Dante at last arrives in that 'ultima spera', in canto xxx, the text begins at once to insist on the concomitant strengthening of his visual faculty. At first he is dazzled by the overwhelming splendour of the 'luce intellettüal, piena d'amore' (40) that shines in, indeed constitutes, this most sublime of heavenly regions:

> Come subito lampo che discetti
> li spiriti visivi, sì che priva
> dall'atto l'occhio di più forti obietti,
> così mi circunfulse luce viva;
> e lasciommi fasciato di tal velo
> del suo fulgor, che nulla m'appariva.         (46–51)

But this blindness (like its Biblical precedent, Saul's affliction on the road to Damascus)[6] is no more than temporary, and Dante swiftly recovers, finding himself able now to see as never before:

> Non fur più tosto dentro a me venute
> queste parole brievi, ch'io compresi
> me sormontar di sopr'a mia virtute;
> e di novella vista mi raccesi
> tale, che nulla luce è tanto mera,
> che li occhi miei non si fosser difesi.         (55–60)

Immediately thereafter begins an astonishing series of richly detailed visual evocations of Paradise, punctuated by direct references to Dante's eyes and their powers: 'come fec'io, per far migliori spegli / ancor delli occhi' (xxx. 85–6); 'O isplendor di Dio, per cu'io vidi / l'alto triunfo del regno verace, / dammi virtù a dir com'ïo il vidi!' (xxx. 97–9); 'La vista mia ne l'ampio e ne l'altezza / non si smarriva, ma tutto prendeva / il quanto e'l quale di quella allegrezza' (xxx. 118–20); 'su per la viva luce passeggiando, / menava ïo li occhi per li gradi, / mo su, mo giù e mo recirculando' (xxxi. 46–48). The

---

[6] The parallel with Saul is confirmed by the verbal resemblance between line 49 and Acts 9.3: 'And as he journeyed, he came near Damascus: and suddenly there shined round about him a light (*circumfulsit eum lux*) from heaven.' The key phrase recurs in the two re-tellings of the incident, at Acts 22.6 and 26.13. The *circunfulse* of *Par.*, xxxi. 49 is, significantly, a *hapax legomenon*.

series culminates in a triumphant assertion that now Dante has seen all that there is to see in the heavens ('La forma general di paradiso / già tutto mïo sguardo avea compresa', XXXI. 52–3) – an assertion whose confidence is promptly undercut by Dante's realization that what he now sees is not, in fact, exactly what he had expected ('*credea veder Beatrice, e vidi un sene*', XXXI. 59).

The *sight* of Bernard is thus crucial to Dante's perception of him from the very beginning of their encounter, more so indeed than his name or his history, neither of which is yet known to Dante *personaggio* or has been explained by Dante *poeta*. It functions both as a concrete illustration of the utterly new conditions prevailing in the Empyrean and, more specifically, as a means of devising a comprehensive portrait of Bernard as a character (because in his case, unlike that of his many counterparts in *Paradiso*, physical description is used as a point of departure for his characterization). But it should be repeated that it is the first alone of these functions that is dominant at the moment of the reader's initial encounter with *Paradiso*, XXXI. 58–64; the details of Bernard's portrayal only acquire their personal significance with readerly hindsight, once it has become clear with whom we have to deal in this episode. Only after Bernard's identity is known does it become possible to see that the visual aspects recorded here are historically appropriate to him as an individual; for the moment they remain generic, indicative more of Dante-character's rekindled ability to see than of his interest in what – or whom – it is that he sees.[7] For Dante himself – as his startled, abrupt, almost discourteous question in line 64 clearly reveals – is still, at this juncture, totally preoccupied with and committed to Beatrice, and is, as yet, unable to concern himself even minimally with the newcomer: hence his failure even to respond directly ('sanza risponder', 70) to Bernard's polite explanation (65–9) of his own role and Beatrice's whereabouts.

From the outset, then, the encounter between Dante and Bernard is pervaded by the connected motifs of eyes and sight. Bernard's opening gambit, in which he explains that he comes not of his own volition but at Beatrice's request ('A terminar lo tuo disiro / mosse Beatrice me del loco mio', 65–6), clearly a *captatio benevolentiae* aimed

---

[7] For this reason I am unconvinced by A. J. Butler's attempt to relate the description of Bernard in *Paradiso* XXXI directly to a source in the *Vita prima*; there is, in any case, no close verbal similarity between the two texts. See A. J. Butler, *The Paradise of Dante* (London, 1885), p. 400; Paget Toynbee, *A Dictionary of Proper Names and Notable Matters in the Works of Dante*, revised by Charles S. Singleton (Oxford, 1968), p. 94.

at reconciling Beatrice's deserted lover to the new state of affairs by placing it under her auspices, is followed at once by instruction in the use of Dante's eyes and explanation of the potential benefits to be gained thereby:

> e se riguardi sù nel terzo giro
> dal sommo grado, tu la rivedrai
> nel trono che suoi merti le sortiro.     (67–9)

Dante's obedient reaction introduces another extended reference to the 'novella vista' (58) that is the gift of the Empyrean, and which now enables him to see Beatrice in all her glory:

> Sanza risponder, li occhi sù levai,
> e vidi lei che si facea corona
> reflettendo da sé li etterni rai.
> Da quella regïon che più sù tona
> occhio mortale alcun tanto dista,
> qualunque in mare più giù s'abbandona,
> quanto lì da Beatrice la mia vista;
> ma nulla mi facea, ché süa effige
> non discendëa a me per mezzo mista.     (70–8)

And with this passage the encounter begins to come into sharper focus, as it becomes clear exactly what narrative purpose has been served by the effacement of Beatrice and the introduction of her substitute. It is, in fact, a purpose intimately connected with the power to see, both in the strict sense in which Dante *personaggio* literally beholds Beatrice's 'effige' (77), and in the deeper sense in which removal from her immediate presence and the intervention of a third party make possible a spiritual re-vision of Beatrice herself.[8]

Only through Bernard's intervention can Dante see Beatrice 'nel trono che suoi merti le sortiro' (69), which is as if he were seeing her for the first time. Only now that another invites him to contemplate her as if she were an icon rather than a person (71–2; and the later use of 'effige' is also highly significant in this regard) can Dante comprehend the reality of Beatrice's existence and his situation in respect to her: namely, that the personal meaning she formerly held for him must now yield, both to her need to identify with the heavenly court, and to Dante's need to move beyond his present understanding of her so as to become worthy to be identified with the heavenly court himself.

[8] In what follows I draw to some extent on an earlier article, 'Life after Beatrice: Bernard of Clairvaux in *Paradiso* XXXI', *Texas Studies in Literature and Language*, 32 (1990), 120–36.

Up to now, in fact, Dante has seen Beatrice and her actions and powers only in relation to himself and his own salvation; now he sees her in her true place in the universal order, a place that is not defined only by her relationship to him, and he realizes that he too has a place in that order which, likewise, is not exclusively dependent on her. Bernard's interposition of himself between Dante and his beloved guide makes plain, in short, that Beatrice herself is not the terminal point of Dante's pilgrimage; he must go beyond her, even outgrow her, and, as part of that process, both see her in her proper (Empyrean) setting and learn how to bid her farewell. This is the opportunity that Bernard's intervention offers Dante *personaggio*: to step back from Beatrice, to see her more clearly, and to appreciate more fully the part she has played (and, though only implicitly, will continue to play) in his salvation. Bernard's appearance thus provides the necessary distance (and note the stress on precisely that in lines 73–6) from which Dante can apply his 'novella vista' to the object of his adoration, and therefore also makes possible the new understanding that informs the solemn prayer of leave-taking that follows (79–90).

This aspect of Bernard's role in *Paradiso* connects him with a small but distinguished sub-group among the personnel of the *Commedia*, other members of which include Sordello, Statius, Matelda, and Cacciaguida. These characters are set apart from the majority of their counterparts in various functional ways. In their encounters they enter into a peculiarly intimate relationship with Dante-character, or one of his guides (Virgil and Beatrice), or both. (Consider Statius, linked to Virgil by religious and poetic vocation, or Sordello, Virgil's fellow-citizen and fellow-poet, or Cacciaguida, Dante's ancestor and partaker of his civic ideal.) Partly for this reason, their encounters usually extend over more than one canto. None is to be found in Hell, where intimacy of this kind is impossible (though there may be frustrated traces of it in the meeting with Brunetto Latini). As well as telling their personal tales, they take on some of the functions of the guides, providing information, answering questions, allaying doubts, expounding theology. Finally, what all these characters have in common is that, whatever the ostensible subject of their discourse, they are used to re-define Dante's attitude towards a subject of particular and personal importance to him. Each of them takes one of the cornerstones of the intellectual, moral, or religious structure that has sustained Dante's thinking, and shows it to him in a completely fresh light. These 'cornerstones' are objects, ideas, and persons that Dante had thought he had understood, had fully absorbed into his scheme of things, and which he now, during and after the experience of his pilgrimage, needs to make his own again in a wholly new way.

In the meeting with Statius, it is Virgil who is held up for renewed consideration; in that with Cacciaguida, Florence and its history; in that with Matelda, the active life of the world. In each case, Dante is forced to re-evaluate something he has long held dear, and the basic premises of his journey have to be revised as a result. It is with this group that the Bernard of *Paradiso* XXXI belongs. In the early stages of his activity in the poem, before he has even acquired a name or an identity, the primary significance of his role is clearly the pretext it offers for Dante to arrive at an objective view of Beatrice; and it is to that view that the prayer of *Paradiso*, XXXI. 79–90 gives such memorable expression.

Bernard himself, of course, is absent from the text for the duration of the prayer, although, within the terms of Dante-poet's fiction, he is obviously to be imagined as listening to and approving of it. It is worth noting, however, that this last and perhaps greatest of Dante's love-songs to Beatrice is characterized by its focus, similar to that identified above, on the double nature of sight. Dante has seen, in the literal sense, many things in the course of his journey ('tante cose quant' i' ho vedute', 82); but only now does he seem them in a richer sense, that of insight rather than physical sight alone ('di tante cose quant' i' ho vedute / ... / riconosco la grazia e la virtute', 82–4). This insight is achieved primarily, of course, through the operation of Beatrice's qualities of 'podere' and 'bontate' (83); but it is Bernard's arrival that enables Dante to understand this, and thus to embark on his re-vision of Beatrice. And that re-vision ends with a single *terzina* that, in a characteristic marvel of Dantean economy, pulls together all the threads that make up the textual fabric of this crucial event in the *Commedia*'s narrative: Dante's prayerful devotion to Beatrice ('Così orai', 91), the distance now established between them ('quella, sì lontana / come parea', 91–2), Beatrice's benevolence towards her 'fedele' ('sorrise', 92), their mutual contemplation ('riguardommi', 92), and, finally, the knowledge that it is time for them to part, and for both to turn to fresh and worthier objects of contemplation ('poi si tornò a l'etterna fontana', 93). It is by no means without significance, in fact, that Beatrice's response to Dante's prayer takes the form not of words but of almost hieratic gesture, nor that this gesture is an unmistakable, if affectionate, sign of dismissal.

The first phase of the encounter between Dante and Bernard ends at this point, with Beatrice's disappearance from the narrative and the completion of Bernard's vital role as inspirer and guarantor of Dante's spiritual re-vision of his beloved. But it needs to be pointed out that, so far, nothing has been done or said that indicates any specific or individual importance in Bernard himself; to put it bluntly, anyone else might have done as much. We readers – like Dante *personaggio* – still do not know who he is, or what, if any, particular qualifications he may have for the (still partly mysterious) role he has begun to play in the poem; and the three dozen lines since his appearance have been so thoroughly dominated by Beatrice as to inhibit the growth of any independent interest in the 'santo sene' who replaces her, and who only now, in line 94, begins to assume full authority over her erstwhile protégé.

This, in fact, is why the naming of Bernard has been so long delayed; no personal details or biographical baggage connected with him have been allowed to distract Dante – or the reader – from the supreme moment of concentration on Beatrice. Now that she is gone, however, Dante's attention is free to apply itself to a new object. From this point onwards, the tenor of *Paradiso* XXXI shifts decisively; Bernard comes to the forefront, more than adequately filling the void left by Beatrice's departure. The first step in this process, which also initiates the second phase of the Dante–Bernard encounter, is that in which Bernard himself dispels the growing mystery by revealing his own identity.

Some idea of this shift in tenor is perhaps conveyed by the abruptness of the transition from line 93 to line 94. The former is wholly occupied by Beatrice and her actions ('poi si tornò a l'etterna fontana'); but the beginning of the latter ('E 'l santo sene'), thanks to the blunt connective (its bluntness visually reinforced by capitalization in modern editions), jerks the reader's attention sharply away from her towards Bernard, whose presence has gone unremarked since Dante ignored him in line 70, and it is he who dominates the remainder of the canto (not to mention the whole of the next one and the first third of the one after that). This abruptness seems to be a conscious narrative effect, enacting at the verbal and rhythmic level the separation from Beatrice that is taking place in this episode; and the descriptive phrase 'santo sene' is also carefully chosen. It reminds us, through the repetition of 'sene', of the terms in which Bernard was initially presented (59), and it accentuates, in both noun and adjective, his holiness and venerable stature – both of which are seemingly obvious to Dante *personaggio*, even though he does not yet know Bernard's name.

Any doubt that might have lingered as to this apparent usurper's fitness to replace Beatrice is soon resolved by his words. He begins by repeating that his purpose is to bring Dante to the fulfilment of his journey, and that he does so at Beatrice's command ('"Acciò che tu assommi / perfettamente," disse, "il tuo cammino, / a che priego e amor santo mandommi"', 94–6, reproducing the sense of 65–6); but he then moves to exert the authority over Dante that he has inherited from his predecessor. It should come as no surprise by now that his first injunction to his pupil is connected with the use of his eyes, and with the refinement of his 'novella vista' to make it adequate for the ultimate vision of the Godhead:

> vola con gli occhi per questo giardino;
> ché veder lui t'acconcerà lo sguardo
> più al montar per lo raggio divino. (97–9)

But this speech does not limit itself to the exertion of authority over Dante-character; Bernard is at last ready to justify his actions by declaring himself, and he does so in terms that not only put an end to his anonymity but also begin to lay bare the cultural, historical, and symbolic bases for his involvement in the *Commedia*:

> E la regina del cielo, ond' ïo ardo
> tutto d'amor, ne farà ogni grazia,
> però ch'i' sono il suo fedel Bernardo. (100–2)

These are the most important words that Bernard has yet spoken. They mark the point at which he comes into his own as a fully rounded character, possessing not just lineaments (61–3) but a name, and therefore a history. They also throw new light on everything that has taken place and been said since Bernard's début in line 59; for now that the 'sene' is no longer anonymous, it becomes feasible to look afresh at the opening description of his 'benigna letizia' and 'atto pio' (62), and to decide, for instance, that the evocation of a 'tenero padre' in line 63 has a peculiar aptness, given Bernard of Clairvaux's renown as an abbot and the evidence, in his and others' writings, of his concern for the monks committed to his charge.

But even here we may be getting ahead of ourselves. Bernard's monastic celebrity is nowhere explicitly referred to in the text of the *Commedia*, and so an image that seems to allude to it, like this one, can only bear that particular meaning for a reader already armed with the requisite knowledge. It is thus useful, but not indispensable, to the interpretation of the episode. Meanwhile, we should rather be asking ourselves just how the poem itself conveys that this is Bernard of Clairvaux (since the toponymic is never added to his – common – personal name), and exactly what aspects of the historical Bernard's achievement it chooses to highlight. This alone is the information genuinely necessary for a valid reading of the episode, since it is provided by the *Commedia* itself; anything else, exegetically speaking, is gravy.

It is the connection with the Virgin Mary that both makes the identification of Bernard unequivocal and begins to make it possible to understand his symbolic function in the *Commedia*. Bernard's relationship with Mary is to be the single most crucial element in his involvement in Dante's journey, since it is the necessary precondition for the successful obtaining of Mary's intercession on Dante's behalf in *Paradiso* XXXIII; and that, in turn, is necessary before Dante can advance to the final vision of God. It is for this reason that, when Bernard finally comes to occupy centre stage, after Beatrice's exit, he does so with a ringing declaration of his fidelity to the 'regina del cielo'. And this declaration alone suffices to make his identity plain: of all the celebrated Bernards in Christian history, only one – as we saw in chapter 2 – was universally recognized in Dante's culture as being intimately linked with the Virgin to the degree that Bernard of Clairvaux was. No other candidates need apply: 'fedel Bernardo' is instantly recognized by Dante *personaggio* (and thus, we can assume, by a Trecento audience) as the author of the sermons *In laudibus Virginis Matris*. As Bernard, no longer nameless, first enters into the fulness of his role in *Paradiso*, he does so above all as a devotee of Mary.

The exact terms in which Bernard makes his declaration also deserve scrutiny, though they will not, perhaps, sustain the full weight of symbolic interpretation that has sometimes been brought to bear on them. The key words are 'ardo' and 'fedel'. Both of these are not infrequently attested elsewhere in Dante's corpus, in a variety of contexts, but with broadly consistent semantic values.[9] Most

---

[9] See the respective entries in the *Enciclopedia dantesca* (I, 354–5 and II, 822) for admirably full accounts.

pertinent to their usage in *Paradiso* XXXI is the fact that both are staples of the standard diction of secular love-poetry in the Italian Duecento and its Provençal antecedents, being expressive of feelings (passionate desire and devoted loyalty) that often ground the psychological construction of the lover-figure in that poetry. The transfer of both narrative situation and lexical particulars from a secular to a religious setting is not, in itself, very remarkable, since it is one of the mainstays of medieval religious poetry throughout Europe; but, in the specific context of the *Commedia*, Bernard's self-description as an ardent and faithful lover acquires notably individual resonance.

In the first place, it establishes a parallel between Bernard's situation vis-à-vis Mary and Dante's vis-à-vis Beatrice, since both may now be seen as men intensely dedicated to beloved women; in the second, it helps to suggest that the worldly metaphor of love-service that has underpinned Dante's relationship with Beatrice since the earliest stages of the *Vita nuova* may also operate as a valid way of expressing an essentially spiritual devotion, beyond the limits of Florentine society or even life on Earth, while retaining just a whiff of the flavour that it possesses in its secular context.[10] But a certain amount of caution is advisable at this point.

Although 'fedel Bernardo' clearly offers an analogue to the Dante who is Beatrice's 'fedele' (*Purg.*, XXXI. 134), his position is not necessarily identical in all respects. In particular, quite apart from the difference in spiritual stature between the two lovers (and indeed the two beloveds), it is worth noting that 'fedel' in *Paradiso*, XXXI. 102 is an adjective pure and simple, rather than an 'aggettivo sostantivato' (as it is in *Purgatorio*); and this apparently trivial distinction is not, in fact, without significance.[11] The adjectival usage implies that Bernard's faithfulness to Mary is one among many attributes of his personality, albeit the one of most relevance at this point (since success in obtaining Mary's intercession is the matter at issue); but 'fedel' here is not used antonomastically, to define the essence of Bernard's nature or the exclusiveness of his relationship with the Virgin. It is an accident rather than a substance. When Dante is

[10] Ibid., II, 822.
[11] The practice of inserting a comma after 'fedel' in *Par.*, XXXI. 102, and thus converting it into an 'aggettivo sostantivato' ('però ch'i' sono il suo fedel, Bernardo') seems to have died out after the appearance of the Società Dantesca Italiana's standard text of the poem in 1921, but before that it was not unknown: see, for instance, the edition of G. A. Scartazzini (Leipzig, 1874–90), the eighth edition of which (revised by Giuseppe Vandelli, Milan, 1922) still retained this detail of punctuation (III, 959).

called Beatrice's 'fedele' (or indeed Lucia's – *Inferno*, II. 98), however, these are precisely the connotations evoked by the substantive usage. 'Il tuo fedele', addressed to Beatrice, can only mean Dante; 'fedel Bernardo', in the sight of the Virgin, is one among millions.

If only for this reason, it is better to avoid pushing the Dante–Bernard parallel too far, and, in particular, to refrain from equating the Dante-character of the *Vita nuova*, the 'fedele d'Amore' in the strict sense, with the Dante-character of the Empyrean, or, *a fortiori*, with the *Commedia*'s version of Bernard.[12] That way lies a perilous confusion of understanding, in which semantically and conceptually distinct uses of 'fedele', 'amore', and related terms are compounded into anachronistic meaninglessness. Briefly put, the 'amor' with which Bernard burns for Mary and the fidelity with which he serves her are not identical with those of Dante for Beatrice in either the *Vita nuova* or the *Commedia*, and the verbal continuity between the several texts expresses both similarity and difference between the relationships and experiences involved.

Dante-character's reaction to the long-delayed announcement of his new companion's identity is expressed in a complex extended simile that both pulls together some of the themes already detected in the Bernard episode and continues to propel the episode forwards:

> Qual è colui che forse di Croazia
>  viene a veder la Veronica nostra,
>  che per l'antica fame non sen sazia,
> ma dice nel pensier, fin che si mostra:
>  'Signor mio Iesù Cristo, Dio verace,
>  or fu sì fatta la sembianza vostra?';
> tal era io mirando la vivace
>  carità di colui che'n questo mondo,
>  contemplando, gustò di quella pace.      (103–11)

It will at once be apparent that the simile, like much else in Dante's encounter with Bernard so far, is based on the use of sight. Bernard is

---

[12] The temptation is made all the greater for some by the acknowledged connection between the historical Bernard's writings and the development of the ethical conventions of courtly love-poetry; see Etienne Gilson, *La Théologie mystique de saint Bernard* (Paris, 1947), pp. 193–215. On the meaning of 'fedele d'Amore' and the various quasi-mystical interpretations of the phrase, see Antonio Viscardi's trenchant summary in the *Enciclopedia dantesca* (IV, 822–4). Bernard's affiliation with the Order of Knights Templar has also been seen as relevant in this context; see William Anderson, *Dante the Maker* (London, 1980), p. 414. Most readings of this kind seem to me to depend on reading far more into the word 'fedel' than its actual usage in the *Commedia* will justify.

depicted as an image to be contemplated with religious awe ('mirando'), like that of the face of Christ miraculously preserved on St Veronica's sudarium. The comparison of Dante himself to a pilgrim from some farflung, alien territory ('forse di Croazia'), arriving at his journey's end and rejoicing in the satisfaction of his 'antica fame' to behold the sacred object of his pilgrimage, is also, clearly, appropriate to the character's narrative situation at this stage in the *Commedia*. But there are also other aspects of the simile that make it particularly suggestive of Dante-poet's view and presentation of Bernard of Clairvaux.

The first of these is the implicit parallel between Bernard and Christ himself. The 'sembianza' seen by the putative Croatian pilgrim is that of Jesus, 'Dio verace' (and note here the play on veracity and semblance, made concrete in the vocabulary of lines 107–8, that underlies the simile as a whole); that seen by Dante *personaggio* is Bernard's, which seems no less capable than Christ's of inspiring wonder and satisfying a longing that goes far beyond mere curiosity. This remarkable tribute to Bernard could in itself be taken, at least by readers with biographical inclinations, as evidence for a particularly exalted view of Bernard on Dante-poet's part. But more substantially interesting, perhaps, is the *terzina* dedicated entirely to 'la vivace / carità di colui che'n questo mondo, / contemplando, gustò di quella pace' (109–11).

These lines form, of course, an extended periphrasis on the name 'Bernardo', one that reveals, through the voice of the narrator, aspects of Bernard's importance not so far expressed (overtly or otherwise) by Bernard himself. The first of these is the unusual phrase 'vivace / carità'. Commentators rightly explain this as meaning, in Sapegno's formulation, 'l'ardore di carità che si manifestava nell'aspetto del santo', the outward and visible sign, so to speak, of Bernard's inward spiritual grace;[13] but they have not remarked that the phrase is also an explanatory gloss on Bernard's earlier declaration of devotion to the Virgin Mary. The use of 'carità' in line 110, in fact, makes it clear that this is the 'amor' of which Bernard himself spoke (101), a purely spiritual *caritas* that can be compared to, but not equated with, other, more secular varieties of love (as has just been argued). Bernard's being is so completely possessed by spiritual love as to make him its very embodiment, *caritas* in person as

---

[13] Sapegno, '*Divina Commedia*', III, 396.

it were; and as such he provides a model towards which Dante, as he grows beyond Beatrice and out of feelings for her that were rooted in *eros*, can legitimately aspire. But the *terzina* also introduces the second keynote of the *Commedia*'s presentation of Bernard: his fame as a contemplative.

The description of Bernard as 'colui che'n questo mondo, / contemplando, gustò di quella pace' is intriguing from several points of view. Firstly, it confirms the identity of 'Bernardo' as Bernard of Clairvaux, for anyone who had not recognized him on the basis of the Marian allusion alone: equal distinction in devotion to Mary and contemplative mysticism could, in the early Trecento, be claimed by no other individual of that name. Second, it extends the foundations for Bernard's participation in the poem's narrative, and retrospectively contributes to the justification of his replacement of Beatrice: only someone equally qualified in precisely these two areas could, as part of the *Commedia*'s *fictio*, act on Dante's behalf in the way required in the closing cantos of *Paradiso*. By drawing attention to these well-known features of the historical Bernard's reputation, the text of *Paradiso* XXXI thus provides its own explanation of the fictive Bernard's presence in the Empyrean, and, therefore, its own commentary as well; it is enough, for the purposes of the *Commedia*, that Bernard be recognized on the twofold basis that the poem itself sets out.

There is, however, another significant aspect of the presentation of Bernard in these lines, lying dormant in the apparently inoffensive adjectives 'questo' (110) and 'quella' (111). *This* world, *that* peace; the narrator is clearly speaking from an earthly perspective, stressing the extraordinary nature of Bernard's contemplative achievement by pointing out that he managed, while still in the body, to attain heights of spiritual ecstasy normally reserved for the souls in beatitude. This does more than simply reinforce the tribute being paid to Bernard throughout this passage; it supplies another allusion to one of the vital subtexts of the Empyrean cantos (and arguably of the entire *Paradiso*) – the mystical experience of St Paul.

Paul's celebrated description of what is surely his own experience, in his second letter to the Corinthians, is, for all its fervour, hedged about with uncertainties:

It is not expedient for me doubtless to glory. I will come to visions and revelations of the Lord.

I knew a man in Christ above fourteen years ago, (whether in the body, I cannot tell; or whether out of the body, I cannot tell: God knoweth;) such an one caught up to the third heaven.

And I knew such a man, (whether in the body, or out of the body, I cannot tell: God knoweth;)

How that he was caught up into paradise, and heard unspeakable words, which it is not lawful for a man to utter.[14]

But Paul's nervously reiterated phrase 'whether ... I cannot tell' finds no counterpart in *Paradiso* xxxi: that text's bold assertiveness ("'n questo mondo, / contemplando, *gustò* di quella pace') brooks no debate. Quite apart from their particular applicability to Bernard, these lines are also a resounding declaration of a general principle, namely that full experience of the divine is indeed possible in this life – a principle that subtends the entire plot of the *Commedia*, which recounts, of course, a progress towards precisely that experience. If Bernard did it, Dante can. And the desire to underscore this aspect of Bernard's history perhaps lies behind the fact that it is the narrator who describes Bernard as a contemplative, whereas Bernard himself had chosen to stress his own devotion to Mary: if Bernard is above all a Mariologist in his own eyes, in those of Dante – and thus of the world – it is his contemplation that best defines him. The two functions are obviously complementary, and both will contribute to Bernard's activity in the poem, but the divergent manner of their presentation is revealing. Bernard's fidelity to Mary is chiefly connected with the internal circumstances of the *Commedia* (his characterization and his relationship with Dante *personaggio*); his exemplification of the possibility of supreme contemplative experience in this life is, potentially, of much wider relevance.

What is at stake throughout the unfolding of Bernard's identity and the lengthy simile that follows is, in a word, Bernard's qualifications to exercise authority over Dante; and only at the simile's end is that question resolved. In line 56 Beatrice was still, for Dante, 'la mia donna' (here too the word has the courtly *sfumatura* mentioned above, p. 78), and, as a result, Dante was so absorbed in and concerned with her that he ignored Bernard's intervention (70). By line 111, however, the wondering Dante has adopted a pose of

---

[14] This key passage from 2 Corinthians is also, of course, of considerable importance in the *Letter to Can Grande*; see my '"Quae non licet homini loqui": The Ineffability of Mystical Experience in *Paradiso* I and the Epistle to Can Grande', *Modern Language Review*, 83 (1988), 332–41 (pp. 335–6).

reverent humility towards Bernard analogous to that of the Croatian pilgrim before the 'vera icona' of Christ, and he who was the 'fedele' of Beatrice is now, as part of the process of detachment from and revision of her that Bernard facilitates, to be seen as part of a larger network of relationships and obligations, no longer the lover of a woman but the child of grace (112).

Bernard's cardinal function within this canto, in fact, is precisely to lead Dante away from his narrowly individual devotion to Beatrice towards comprehension of this larger scheme – first by showing him that Beatrice herself is only one element in the providential plan of Dante's salvation and not the object towards which that plan tends, and then by directing him towards the higher principle embodied in the Virgin Mary. Accordingly, as soon as his identity has been announced and Dante-character's awestruck reaction registered, Bernard resumes his course of instruction in the use of Dante's eyes:

> 'Figliuol di grazia, quest'esser giocondo',
>     cominciò elli, 'non ti sarà noto,
>     tenendo li occhi pur qua giù al fondo;
> ma guarda i cerchi infino al più remoto,
>     tanto che veggi seder la regina
>     cui questo regno è suddito e devoto'.          (112–17)

There is an obvious echo here of Bernard's first speech (65–9), in which he urged Dante to look up 'nel terzo giro / dal sommo grado' (67–8), in order to see Beatrice 'nel trono che suoi merti le sortiro' (69); but there are some equally obvious, and more significant, differences.

Bernard is now urging on Dante the necessity of finding a new object for his gaze; one that is neither Beatrice nor, be it noted, Bernard himself. This speech serves, in part, to prevent Dante from becoming so absorbed in the study of Bernard's own 'sembianza' (108), which is what he is now looking at (109), as to mistake that image, or the person behind it, for the true goal of his pilgrimage. (This is one significant way in which Dante *personaggio* and 'colui... di Croazia' (103) differ, since the latter has indeed reached his destination, while Dante still has a little further to go.) Bernard is, in fact, implicitly repeating the warning uttered by Beatrice in *Paradiso* XVIII, to a Dante who there also seemed too taken with the immediate object of his interest to remember his duty to the broader context of Paradise in which he found himself: 'Volgiti ed ascolta; / ché non

pur ne' miei occhi è paradiso' (*Par.*, XVIII. 20–1). Paradise is no more
in Bernard's eyes than it was in Beatrice's; and so, once more, Dante's
gaze must be directed away from his interlocutor, and this time not
just to the 'terzo giro / dal sommo grado' (67–8), but to the 'più
remoto' of the Empyrean's 'cerchi' (115), where sits not Beatrice,
but Mary. So, having inspired the re-vision of Beatrice, Bernard now
inspires the new vision of Mary; and a verbal echo in the depiction of
Dante's response confirms the link that makes Bernard's two speeches
part of one and the same process ('li occhi sù levai', 70; 'Io levai li
occhi', 118).

   The portrayal of Mary that follows (117–35) is, in part, a re-
working – in (fittingly) more elaborate form – of that of Beatrice in
lines 70–8: the 'corona' (71) and 'etterni rai' (72) of the earlier
passage almost pale in comparison with the imagery of sunrise
(124–6), flames (128–9), and 'angeli festanti' (131) in the later, but
both present an essentially visual image to be contemplated by the
onlooker's eyes (on which there is a notable stress in the text: 118,
121–2, 131, 133, 135). But, for all that these half-dozen *terzine* are
fully occupied with Mary, relegating Bernard once more to the
sidelines, they do have a functional role in the construction of the
Bernard–Dante encounter, as the closing lines of the canto reveal.
The narrating voice ends its evocation of Mary's splendour with a
characteristic recourse to the 'ineffability *topos*' ('e s'io avessi in dir
tanta divizia / quanta ad imaginar, non ardirei / lo minimo tentar di
sua delizia', 136–8). After this, attention immediately reverts to
Bernard, whose name appears, for only the second time in the text of
*Paradiso*, at the beginning of line 139 (a position as strongly emphatic
as its terminal position in line 102):

> Bernardo, come vide li occhi miei
>    nel caldo suo caler fissi e attenti,
>    li suoi con tanto affetto volse a lei,
> che ' miei di rimirar fé più ardenti.          (139–42)

   These concluding lines clinch the argument of everything that has
been said so far about the fundamental importance of eyes and sight
in the encounter between Dante and Bernard, since they provide the
clearest illustration yet of the way in which the direction of Dante-
character's gaze is used as a symbol of his emotional and spiritual
attachments. Dante is now completely engrossed in the vision of
Mary ('li occhi miei / nel caldo suo caler fissi e attenti'); Bernard,

perceiving this with his own eyes ('vide'), joins him in contemplation of the spectacular image of the Virgin ('li suoi con tanto affetto volse a lei'), which in turn inspires Dante to intensify the ardour of his own gaze ('che ' miei di rimirar fé più ardenti') – and thus to attach himself ever more profoundly to Mary. The two characters, who at the outset had no common ground on which to meet, are now united in contemplative veneration of the same object, and, as the canto comes to an end, are spurring each other on to greater heights (or depths) of contemplation, through the mutual enthusiasm ('affetto') reflected in their eyes.

But there is more to it than that. Bernard has not only succeeded in directing Dante's gaze towards Mary (as he set out to do in lines 115–17), but, in so doing, has completed the process of Dante's detachment from Beatrice, which began with his appearance in line 59. Indeed, he has brought Dante to what looks very like a state of equality, in devotion to the Virgin, with Bernard himself: the word used earlier to describe Bernard's own feelings towards Mary ('ardo', 100), now recurs, in adjectival form, as a description of the passionate eagerness with which Dante also contemplates her ('ardenti', 142).

By now Dante *personaggio* has, so to speak, been weaned from his attachment to the familiar (and indeed quasi-maternal) figure of Beatrice, and introduced to the new and proper object of his devotion, the Virgin; and the process in which his gaze moves from Beatrice to Bernard to Mary reproduces, figuratively, the progress of his spiritual commitment. Once again, it is clear that Beatrice's departure is the starting-point for a reconsideration, on Dante's part, of her personal implications for him in the light of his wider obligations as a Christian believer, and thus for the development within the narrative of universal, rather than purely personal, themes and concerns. It is equally clear that Bernard's arrival is the indispensable event that helps to set this process in motion.

By the end of *Paradiso* XXXI, then, Bernard of Clairvaux has been fixed in the reader's mind as a devotee of the Virgin (100–2) and a contemplative (110–11), in accordance with the prevailing interpretation of his significance in early Trecento culture; he has helped Dante *personaggio* to arrive at a proper understanding of Beatrice and her place in the scheme of his own salvation; and he has directed Dante's attention and, more important, his spiritual and devotional energies, towards a new object, Mary, whose intercession he has already (100–1) promised to secure. The revolution that Dante has undergone through his agency, in the space of fewer than a hundred lines of narrative, is arguably the most profound of the psychological dislocations to which the protagonist is subjected in the course of the *Commedia*. That fact alone suggests that Bernard should be considered one of the poem's principal characters. But, as we shall see, there are further developments in store, which not only confirm Bernard's stature and the importance of the episode in which he is involved, but also extend the depth and resonance of both character and episode in directions as fascinating as they are unpredictable.

Even at the end of *Paradiso* xxxi, however, the transition from Beatrice to Bernard can already be seen as more than a simple narrative event, a changing of the heavenly guard and transfer of authority over Dante-character; and also as more than merely emblematic of developments in Dante-poet's historical expertise, theological interests, or allegorical intentions. It marks Dante's recognition that the transformed humanity that was Beatrice's gift (*Par.*, I. 70) is not, after all, to be the final goal of his pilgrimage; that he must pass beyond even this, to the peace that only a contemplative like Bernard could taste in this world, to an eternal life of deified beatitude that must inevitably be – and not only in the temporal sense – life after Beatrice.

### MELLIFLUOUS DOCTOR (*PARADISO* XXXII)

The thirty-second canto of *Paradiso* has never received its fair share of critical attention.[15] This may be due, in part, to its position in the *cantica*, bracketed as it is by two much more immediately interesting cantos. In comparison with the dramatic events of canto xxxi or the scintillating sublimity of canto xxxiii, the content of *Paradiso* xxxii is bound to hold a less straightforward appeal for most readers; and the tone of its poetry is also, on the whole, likely to appear somewhat subdued when set against the lyrical exaltation of the cantos that precede and follow it. Unlike these, based as they are on narrative

---

[15] The most substantial modern studies of the canto as a whole are Raffaello Fornaciari, *Il canto XXXII del 'Paradiso'* (Florence, 1904); Guido Di Pino, 'Canto xxxii', in *Letture dantesche: 'Paradiso'*, edited by Giovanni Getto (Florence, 1961), pp. 655–72; Vincenzo Pernicone, *Il canto XXXII del 'Paradiso'* (Turin, 1965); Antonio Russi, 'Canto xxxii', in *Lectura Dantis Scaligera: 'Paradiso'* (Florence, 1968), pp. 1135–90; Fausto Montanari, 'Il canto xxxii del *Paradiso*', *Nuove letture dantesche*, 7 (1974), 255–63; Tommaso Pisanti, 'Il canto xxxii e la poesia del *Paradiso*', in *Filologia e critica dantesca: studi offerti a Aldo Vallone* (Florence, 1989), pp. 329–50; and Maria Luisa Doglio, 'L'"officio di dottore". *Institutio* ed *exempla* nel canto xxxii del *Paradiso*', *Giornale storico della letteratura italiana*, 156 (1989), 321–39.

and verbal exchange, *Paradiso* XXXII consists chiefly of monologic discourse; and, moreover, of discourse intended to instruct, through the exposition of a number of fairly abstruse doctrinal issues. The reader might be forgiven for thinking that at this stage in the poem, with Dante *personaggio* at last about to apprehend the divine reality through the intercession that Bernard has just promised to obtain on his behalf (XXXI. 97–102), this canto's exhaustive description of the arrangement and population of the 'candida rosa' of the Empyrean is ill-timed, not to say superfluous; for a moment, the visionary seems to be elbowed aside by the lecturer.

On grounds such as these, *Paradiso* XXXII has frequently served as a target for critics anxious to illustrate or defend the Crocean distinction between *struttura* and *poesia* in the *Commedia*; for here, if anywhere, the relationship between Dante-poet's artistic aims and powers and his didactic purpose seems to be strained almost to the point of breakdown.[16] Even as sympathetic a reader as Natalino Sapegno can find nothing kinder to say of this 'canto prevalentemente descrittivo ed informativo' than that it stands between cantos XXXI and XXXIII 'a guisa di pausa preparatoria';[17] and most of those, such as Vincenzo Pernicone, who have sought to justify the canto's placement on structural grounds have none the less conceded, tacitly or otherwise, that its 'largo spazio degli intervalli riservato a particolari descrittivi dell'Empireo e ad un discorso dottrinale... ha lasciato alquanto inerte la musa del Poeta'.[18]

A problematic canto, then; one that readers intoxicated by the linguistic bravura on display in the Empyrean cantos up to this point might well concur in finding something of a bromide, not to say a soporific. And yet there is still an unconvincing quality, even a theoretical weakness, about the view that this canto is placed where it is merely as a delaying tactic, its rebarbative material and unexciting style being thus intended, apparently, to sharpen our readerly appetites for the *pièce de résistance* with which the *Commedia* is due to end. This view depends on an anachronistic, if tempting, confusion of what the *Commedia* is with what it ought to be; it forgets that the poem is under no obligation to satisfy a late-twentieth-

---

[16] A representative opinion is that of Salvatore Frascino, who denies that the canto possesses a 'vera poesia d'insieme', but concedes that its 'poesia' can certainly be found 'in parecchi particolari, e talora con grande potenza'. See *La* '*Divina Commedia*', edited by Vittorio Rossi and Salvatore Frascino, 3 vols. (Rome, 1948), III, 433.

[17] Sapegno, '*Divina Commedia*', III, 399.     [18] Pernicone, *Il canto XXXII*, p. 8.

century public. Instead of confining ourselves to the observation that a modern audience, not greatly exercised by doctrinal controversy or expert in the niceties of theology, is likely to find *Paradiso* XXXII tedious (an observation borne out, incidentally, by the experience of many a teacher), it might be more profitable to give the poem the benefit of the doubt, to ask exactly what is going on in this canto and why it may have been of interest to the canto's author and its original readers, and to go on from there to consider just why these particular doctrinal excursuses should appear in this particular place and be allotted to this particular speaker. Even tentative answers to questions like these will probably prove more illuminatory of Dante's poetic practice and the *Commedia*'s inner workings than the banal hypothesis that, after working so hard on *Paradiso* XXXI, his Muse simply felt like taking the day off.

The canto's content is easily summarized. It consists, notoriously, of an extended lecture by Bernard of Clairvaux on the 'candida rosa', the identity of some of the souls who inhabit it, their classification according to historical criteria, and their organization in hierarchical structures that are mirrored in the allocation of 'sedi' (7) within the 'rosa'. (Those who find something faintly comic in the idea of the saints being seated in a flower may find it helpful to think of the Empyrean as an amphitheatre, or even a football stadium.) Within this framework is inserted an explanation (40–84) of the presence in Heaven of baptized infants who died before they could make a free choice of Christian faith for themselves. This explanation in turn involves more general issues of baptism, predestination, and the miraculous operation of grace. The discourse is divided in two by a vision of Mary accompanied by Gabriel and other angels (85–99), and a question about Gabriel that Dante-character puts to Bernard (100–8). Bernard's answer (109–14) leads to further development (115–38) of his descriptive account of the 'rosa' (seen now as an 'imperio giustissimo e pio', 117), until, in conclusion, he urges Dante to join him in prayer to the Virgin (139–52).

Clearly, much of *Paradiso* XXXII is grist to the mill of those with an interest in Dante's thought and its place in the history of Christian doctrine; and a number of studies have explored its content from that angle and in some detail.[19] My own intention in this chapter is

---

[19] As well as Russi, whose *lectura* is the most detailed study of the allocation of places within the heavenly rose, see Bruno Nardi, 'I bambini nella candida rosa dei beati', *Studi danteschi*, 20 (1937), 41–58; G. C. Di Scipio, *The Symbolic Rose in Dante's 'Paradiso'* (Ravenna, 1984),

slightly different. My analysis will be concerned less with what Bernard says in *Paradiso* XXXII than with how (and why) he says it; with the manner rather than the matter of his discourse, therefore, and with the way in which that discourse is constructed and inserted into the framework of the Empyrean cantos and Bernard's encounter with Dante *personaggio*. This is an aspect of the canto that previous readers have tended to overlook, since most have been more eager to explicate Bernard's words than to examine the setting in which those words are spoken; but it seems to me that *Paradiso* XXXII has much to tell us about subjects other than infant baptism and Dante's conception of the heavenly host.

In particular, the allocation of these subjects to Bernard for discussion, as well as the language in which that discussion is carried on, is evidence both for Dante-poet's estimation of the historical Bernard of Clairvaux and for the significance of the fictional Bernard's activities in the *Commedia*. In reading this canto, then, I shall be as attentive to the speaker as to the speech; and, instead of detaching Bernard's doctrinal utterances from their narrative context, and thus treating him simply as a mouthpiece for Dante-poet's theological disquisitions, I shall base my reading on the assumption that the intrinsic nature and external effects of *Paradiso* XXXII are alike conditioned, from beginning to end, by Bernard's presence in the text and by the canto's location within the poem as a whole. *Paradiso* XXXII will be studied, in short, not as a treatise in its own right, but as a contribution to the *Commedia*'s progressive construction of its image of Bernard of Clairvaux, and as testimony to the historical and symbolic importance that Dante *poeta* perceived in him.

To conduct a reading of this kind, it will be necessary (though it may seem perverse) to look more closely than is usually done at the canto's relatively brief non-doctrinal portions: the introductory *terzina* (1–3), the vision of Mary (85–99), Dante's question (100–8), and Bernard's final exhortation (139–52). The reason for this is not only that these are the parts of the canto that have been least fully examined in the past; it is also that they define both the structure of *Paradiso* XXXII and its relationship with surrounding cantos, by giving it a framework into which the doctrinal discourse is fitted, and by connecting it explicitly with themes and expressive vocabularies already adumbrated in earlier cantos (especially and inevitably, as

(especially chapter 2); and Steven Botterill, 'Doctrine, Doubt and Certainty: *Paradiso* XXXII. 40–84', *Italian Studies*, 42 (1987), 20–36.

far as Bernard is concerned, *Paradiso* XXXI). What seem at first sight to be no more than stage-directions and narrative machinery, in short, are really the technical devices by means of which this outwardly anomalous canto is integrated into the Bernard–Dante episode, and therefore into the entire *Commedia*.

*Paradiso* XXXII begins with an apparently innocuous *terzina*, whose ramifications are easily missed by anyone who mistakes it for a mere *didascalia*:

> Affetto al suo piacer, quel contemplante
> libero officio di dottore assunse,
> e cominciò queste parole sante: (1–3)

These lines may seem to do little more than resume the narrative after the end of canto XXXI, which saw Dante and Bernard united in ardent contemplation of the Virgin Mary (XXXI. 139); but in fact they have a function that goes far beyond supplying a bridge across the (narrative and auditory) space between the cantos. They are also a formative element in the characterization of Bernard, and, in particular, in the elucidation of his symbolic significance. The first line highlights the two aspects of Bernard, sanctioned by popular tradition and historical record, that are central to his presentation in *Paradiso* XXXI: Marian devotion and contemplation.[20] The second, however, introduces a major shift in his role within the *Commedia*'s narrative, as he takes on ('assunse'), without prompting ('libero'), the 'officio di dottore' that will, as we are soon to find out, be his principal occupation for the remainder of this canto.

This new pedagogic function is also, of course, justified in the light of the historical Bernard's career and reputation: his learning is amply attested in his voluminous writings and in the chronicles of his activity as an intellectual polemicist (most notably against Abelard), and recognition of his exemplary status among the Doctors of the late medieval Church began well within his own lifetime. (By the end of the twelfth century, that is, within fifty years of his death, he had already earned the honorific title 'Doctor Mellifluus'; although the

---

[20] It will be apparent (a) that I prefer Petrocchi's reading 'affetto' to any of the other possibilities in the manuscript tradition ('refetto', 'l'effetto', and 'l'affetto'), all of which have been defended by reputable editors, and (b) that I interpret 'piacer' as referring to Mary, which some commentators do not. While acknowledging that the claims I make for the line will not stand up if either a different text or a different reading of 'piacer' is adopted, I think I can legitimately claim that my preferences are those that have the most authority behind them and are most widely accepted; and I should also be tempted to argue, from the opposite direction, that the formal neatness of this reading of the line is a supplementary reason for preferring both 'affetto' and the Marian interpretation of 'piacer'.

epithet refers specifically to his expertise as a Biblical commentator rather than to his verbal felicity in general, its broader connotations are obvious, and were widely accepted among his admirers.)[21] By the end of line 2, then, the incipient canto has already reminded its readers of two of Bernard's qualifications for the role he is undertaking in *Paradiso*, and has begun to point towards a new development of that role, in language that recalls yet another aspect of Bernard's medieval reputation. But there is more to come. The canto's third line, seemingly undistinguished by either linguistic vivacity or narrative interest, in fact offers, for the first time since his appearance, the key to Bernard's presence in the *Commedia*: his 'parole sante'.

The phrase, in itself, may not look very revealing. In one sense, indeed, it seems to apply, by definition, to everything said in *Paradiso*; and certainly Bernard's words must of necessity be 'sante', since they are pronounced by a saint in the Empyrean, where other kinds of word are presumably not available. This instance of 'sante' might, then, seem to be a redundant, or at best quasi-Homeric, epithet, devoid of any genuine charge of meaning: the paradisiacal equivalent of the 'wine-dark sea'. But in fact this is the only occurrence of the phrase 'parole sante' in *Paradiso*: Bernard is the only heavenly speaker, among so many, whose words are singled out for designation as holy. This alone should alert us to the possibility of a more wide-ranging significance, in this line, than its unassuming diction might suggest; at the very least, the adjective, in its stressed position at the end of the line, should encourage the reader to attend especially closely to what is to follow. But line 3 does not only serve as a narrative signpost, indicating that at this point Bernard began to speak, and suggesting that readers should, accordingly, pay as much attention as Dante *personaggio* does. It is also, and more importantly, a gloss on its immediate predecessor, which unpacks the portentous but obscure terms in which line 2 is couched.

The syntactic connection between *Paradiso*, xxxii. 2 and 3 makes it clear that the utterance of 'parole sante' is, in fact, precisely that in which Bernard's 'officio di dottore' consists. Bernard takes on his office, and immediately begins to speak; the latter act is the concrete realization of the former. And, in so doing, Bernard both extends his own role in the poem and raises an issue of considerable import for Dante *poeta*. As a 'dottore', Bernard must, by definition, possess

[21] See Leclercq, *Bernard of Clairvaux and the Cistercian Spirit*, p. 100.

doctrine; but by using that doctrine to embark upon his lecture he
shows that the duty ('officio') of the 'dottore' is to *speak*. Mere
possession of doctrine is not sufficient, since it can do no good unless
it be shared: the true 'dottore' must be not only *doctus* (learned) but
*docens* (a teacher). And the means by which the 'dottore' shares his
learning is, of course, communication, achieved through the use of
words.

We are, here, at the roots of Dante's theory of language, expressed
by him as long ago as the second chapter of *De vulgari eloquentia*:
speaking is the exposition of our thinking to others.[22] The essence of
human language, its fundamental purpose and greatest utility, is that
it makes communication possible between individuals (from which
communication, in the long run, all forms of human society develop);
and Bernard's 'parole sante' exemplify this communicative capacity
to the utmost degree, by taking as their subject the highest
conceivable level of human existence, eternal beatitude. His words
are thus holy for their content, for the setting in which they are
spoken, and for the identity of the man who speaks them; but their
deepest significance lies in how they illustrate the power of human
language to be adequate to the description even of the 'candida rosa'
of the Empyrean, and to convey an accurate image of what it
describes to a receptive audience (whether Dante *personaggio* or the
reader of the *Commedia*).

It is for this reason that the text of *Paradiso* XXXII moves so swiftly
to proclaim the importance of Bernard's words: to prevent us from
imagining – as the narrating voice's frequent recourse to the 'ineffability topos' elsewhere in *Paradiso* might well encourage us to – that
human language has altogether outlived its usefulness in Heaven.
The tongues of mankind cannot say everything; but that does not
mean that they can therefore say nothing. So, throughout *Paradiso*
XXXII, Bernard is shown *speaking*, fulfilling his 'officio di dottore' by
handling language, using words to expound truth, refute error, and
resolve his pupil's doubts, asserting in every line the value of human
linguistic activity; and his efficacious use of 'parole sante' – in a
word, his eloquence – is what makes Bernard's teaching so successful
in imparting conviction here (just as it will guarantee his success in

---

[22] *De vulgari eloquentia*, I. ii. 3: 'Si etenim perspicaciter consideramus quid cum loquimur
intendamus, patet quod nichil aliud quam nostre mentis enucleare aliis conceptum' ('Now,
if we wish to define with precision what our intention is when we speak, it is clearly nothing
other than to expound to others the concepts formed in our minds'; my translation).

petitioning the Virgin in *Paradiso* XXXIII). Moreover, as far as Bernard the character is concerned, this linguistic slant to his actions in *Paradiso* XXXII is perfectly consonant with his historical counterpart's contemporary reputation as an eloquent user of words.

The first *terzina* of *Paradiso* XXXII, then, shows Bernard as devoted to Mary ('affetto al suo piacer'), as contemplative ('quel contemplante'), and, for the first but not the last time, as eloquent; and it seems far from unreasonable to conclude that this combination of factors, all three of which the Bernard of Trecento culture and the Bernard of the *Commedia* have in common, goes a very long way indeed towards explaining why Bernard appears in the poem at all, why he appears where he does, and why his words and actions in the text take the form that they do. In turn, the fact that *Paradiso* XXXII offers Bernard the chance to further develop and exemplify these features of his reputation may be one of the more important reasons for its existence and its location in the *Commedia*. It is as much 'about' Bernard himself as it is about any of the topics he discusses.

The first part of Bernard's speech (lines 4–48) is devoted to a description of the seating-plan in the celestial amphitheatre (or rose). The most striking aspect of the conception of Heaven expressed in these lines (and in many ways the most characteristic, both of Dante and of medieval thinking in general) is that it is so ruthlessly based on ideas of classification, distinction, and hierarchy: it is a monarchy – indeed, an empire – and not a republic. The souls of the blessed are divided, first of all, into those who believed in Christ before the Incarnation and those who became his followers after it (22–7), and the two groups occupy opposite sides of the 'rosa': the seats on the 'Old Testament' side are all filled, of course (22–4), whereas there are still a few vacancies on the 'New Testament' side (25–7) – not many, though, because the end of the mortal world is not far off (*Par.*, XXX. 131–2).

Secondly, Bernard's examples of 'quei che credettero in Cristo venturo' (24) and 'quei ch'a Cristo venuto ebber li visi' (27) are also divided on the basis of gender: the former are all women, the latter all men. Although this distinction is merely a feature of Bernard's explanation, rather than a structuring principle in the organization of Heaven – it would be absurd, not to mention hopelessly contradictory of the rest of *Paradiso*, to deduce from it that Dante *poeta* believed gender alone to have any consequences, positive or negative, for one's chances of salvation – its use for aesthetic effect (the creation of an elegant formal symmetry), within the exposition of doctrine, further reflects the fundamental importance of classification in the Empyrean.

Moreover, the 'rosa' also has, necessarily, a vertical dimension: Bernard's descriptions of its occupants begin at the top and continue 'per la rosa *giù* di foglia in foglia' (15), '*fin qua giù* di giro in giro' (36), with the result that some of the souls are placed above others and therefore, in a reductive physical sense, seem 'closer' to God. Although the souls' hierarchical distribution in the various spheres of the universe, witnessed earlier in *Paradiso*, has already been explained as no more than a concession to Dante-character's limited (human) powers of understanding (*Par.*, IV. 28–48), the same principle is now revealed to be permanently operative in the Empyrean itself, in keeping with Piccarda Donati's explanation (*Par.*, III. 70–87) that all the souls do not enjoy the same degree of beatitude (though they are all fully contented with the degree that they do enjoy), and with the narrator's recognition there that 'ogni dove / in cielo è paradiso, *etsi* la grazia / del sommo ben d'un modo non vi piove' (III. 88–90).[23]

Within this scheme of distinctions and hierarchies, the treatment of the two groups of souls is symmetrical: in each case, Bernard lists some representatives of the group (Eve, Rachel, Sarah, Rebecca, Judith and Ruth among the Old Testament 'Ebree' in line 17, John the Baptist, Francis, Benedict, and Augustine among their New Testament and post-Biblical counterparts), and stresses that these are but a few of many in their respective categories (16–18; 36). Finally, like all good taxonomies, this one includes a noteworthy exception to its rules: Beatrice is seated among the Old Testament women, in accordance with *Inferno*, II. 102, presumably because this is as close as she could be placed to Mary without subverting altogether the traditional typology ('Eva–Ave') that requires Eve to be seen as the type of the Virgin and the woman most indissolubly associated with her. Hence it is she who is placed immediately below Mary (4–6); Beatrice is in the row beneath her (7–9).

The same issues of classification and hierarchy underlie the next section of Bernard's speech, in which he draws Dante-character's attention to another group of souls, those seated 'dal grado in giù che fiede / a mezzo il tratto le due discrezioni' (40–1) – that is, below the level at which the lines that divide the souls already mentioned into

---

[23] See the section 'Il Paradiso nella *Commedia*' of the entry *Paradiso* in the *Enciclopedia dantesca* (IV, 286–9, especially 286).

two groups are intersected by a tier running horizontally around the circular structure of the rose.[24] Bernard explains that these are the souls of infants who died after being baptized, but before they could use their free will to accept the faith for themselves; they are saved through the merits of those responsible for their baptism (40–5). They are visibly and audibly recognizable as infants, thanks to the heightening of Dante's perceptive powers in the Empyrean, and Bernard, characteristically, invites Dante *personaggio* to use his eyes (and ears) to identify them as such: 'Ben te ne puoi accorger per li volti / e anche per le voci püerili, / se tu li guardi bene e se li ascolti' (46–8).

So far there is nothing controversial about these infants: Christian tradition had laid down for several centuries that infant baptism, validated by the faith of those who arranged and performed it, was both efficacious and necessary for salvation (in cases where the infant did not live to attain the age of reason); and Dante's distinction between these saved souls and those of the unbaptized infants, who are assigned to Limbo (*Inf.*, IV. 28–36), shows that he had no qualms about accepting the traditional view.[25] But as the implications of Bernard's remarks sink into his hearer's mind, they begin, in the context of what he has just said about the disposition of the other souls on a hierarchical basis, to pose a challenge to conventional wisdom.

Bernard's description of the 'due discrezioni' has confirmed what readers' memories of *Paradiso* III and IV may already have suggested: that in Heaven there is 'più e meno', and that the blessed sit on different levels that correspond to the differing degrees of their blessedness; and it is equally plain that this also applies to the baptized infants, who are distributed in various tiers, higher and lower, and must therefore have been rewarded differently. However, since they all died in the same unreasoning – and therefore equally deserving – state, there can, in their case, logically be none of the distinctions among individuals that justify the hierarchical arrangement of the adult blessed. Since they have no merit of their own (42), they should have no reward of their own either. The apparent

---

[24] In what follows I use some material already treated more extensively in my article cited above (n. 19).

[25] For the history of the doctrine and practice of baptism, see the *Oxford Dictionary of the Christian Church*, edited by F. L. Cross, 2nd edition (Oxford, 1974), pp. 126–8 ('Baptism') and 701–2 ('Infant Baptism'); and the *Dictionnaire de théologie catholique*, edited by A. Vacant, E. Mangenot, and E. Amann, 15 vols. (Paris, 1923–50), II (1923), cols. 167–355 (especially 250–96).

incongruity (or, worse, potential for injustice) in their heavenly destiny provokes in Dante *personaggio* a mildly rebellious response that Bernard is quick to identify and act to deal with:

> Or dubbi tu, e dubitando sili;
> ma io disciogliderò'l forte legame
> in che ti stringon li pensier sottili. (49–51)

The doubt that Bernard detects in Dante-character's unspoken reaction is not really, of course, the sign of any impending defiance of the authority that Bernard has by now come to represent. The state in which Dante finds himself here is used, as similar states of dubiety are used elsewhere in *Paradiso*, as a narrative pretext for the exposition of a difficult or unconventional truth enshrined in 'pensier sottili'.[26] In such instances, the morally dangerous condition of doubt comes to have a positive function, since it calls forth the intellectually healthy response by which it will itself be dispelled. So it is on Dante-character's doubt, seemingly the antithesis of the faith that under-girds the structure of the whole *Commedia* (never more vitally than in the Empyrean cantos), that the doctrinal affirmations of *Paradiso* XXXII come, paradoxically enough, to depend.

Bernard recognizes Dante's doubt as 'forte' (50), thereby ac-knowledging its power and its basis in (human) reason; and doubt is thus presented as a legitimate intellectual response even in Heaven – but only in so far as it affords Bernard the opportunity to demonstrate the authority of his countervailing certainty. Doubt is a constricting force, a 'legame' (50) that limits the free play of Dante-character's mind; Bernard's certainty is the liberating agent that unties the knot and frees his listener for the active contemplation of truth.

It cannot, moreover, be a coincidence – given what we have already seen of Bernard as a user of language ('parole sante') – that doubt is connected with silence ('dubitando *sili*', 49), or that release from it is achieved through speech. Dante's tongue, as well as his mind, is caught in the 'forte legame'; and he can only be freed by the expression, in the language to which he has temporarily lost access, of Bernard's true thoughts. So what follows the recognition of Dante's perplexity over the state of the baptized infants is a notable display of theological eloquence, in which Bernard calls to the full on his

---

[26] See the entry 'dubbio' in the *Enciclopedia dantesca* (II, 601), where Lucia Onder identifies *Paradiso*, IV. 124–32, XI. 22, XIV. 99, and XXIX. 64 as analogous instances.

linguistic resources, in order to assert the truth that Dante is unwilling to admit.

This passage (52–84) is as remarkable for the rigour of its argument as for the pungent economy of its language; but it is worth noting that its argument is not self-contained. Throughout, Bernard relies heavily on external authority for support. First he invokes the 'etterna legge' (55) by which the Empyrean is maintained, to show that nothing there is the product of chance, and that therefore there can be nothing random in the distribution of the baptized infants; as a result ('e però', 58) the differing degrees of their beatitude are neither incidental nor illogical (58–60), but are instead the consequence of a act of divine will, analogous to that by which God preferred Jacob to Esau (61–9). This, says Bernard, with an air of finality worthy of a scholastic *respondeo*, is all that man needs to know in order to be sure that justice has indeed been done ('e qui basti l'effetto', 66).

According to their different degrees of grace, then, the infants are differently blessed, and thus inhabit different levels of the 'candida rosa'. The two *terzine* that make these points (70–2 and 73–5) together form the climax of Bernard's demonstration; significantly, each begins with a firmly conclusive (and again suitably scholastic) conjunction ('però' and 'dunque' respectively), clearly intended to clinch the argument beyond possibility of rebuttal. Having thus quieted Dante's doubt, Bernard ends his discourse on baptism with a brief history of the subject (76–84), which encapsulates the time-hallowed doctrine that in the earliest times the faith of Christian parents sufficed for an infant's salvation (76–8); that later, boys had to be circumcised (79–81); and that after the coming of Christ baptism became indispensable (82–4).

The motive for Bernard's insistence on what might seem to be a comparatively minor detail of theological history, as well as for his fervent invocation of divine authority to buttress his argument, is simple: he is maintaining what was, in the early Trecento, a distinctly heterodox position. None of the major medieval theologians of baptism seems to have agreed with Dante that unequal distribution of grace among baptized infants in Heaven was a normative principle; at best, some (including the most influential, Bonaventure and Aquinas) were prepared to concede that it might, in certain specific and unfathomable cases, be a possibility.[27] Dante clearly goes

---

[27] See Botterill, 'Doctrine', 30–33.

a step (or two) further than this; and, to that extent, the baptismal doctrine expounded by Bernard in *Paradiso* xxxii is perceptibly outside the theological mainstream.

This not only explains the sheer amount of space that the canto devotes to Bernard's remarks on a seemingly peripheral subject; it also lays bare the subtext of those remarks, which is, I would contend, the focal point of the whole canto, and arguably of the whole *Paradiso*. This is the relationship between doctrine and authority, and the manifestations of both in language. Bernard's speech on infant baptism needs to be authoritative precisely because, doctrinally, he is standing on shaky ground; and the canto thus employs a number of devices to reinforce the halo of authority that hangs over Bernard's saintly but theologically audacious pronouncements. These devices fall into two categories. Some are intrinsic to the text, being rooted either in Bernard's own words or in the narrative context established around them, while others are extrinsic to it, having to do with Dante-poet's (or the informed reader's) knowledge and view of the historical Bernard of Clairvaux. It will be apparent that, on a strict interpretation of the principle that the *Commedia* is self-sufficient as its own commentary, only the former category can be admitted as evidence; but the latter is also of interest, since, while it provides the essential minimum of information to all its readers, the *Commedia* is also capable of producing resonances and overtones that will only reach the ears of those equipped to hear them. Thus the devices in our first category will be accessible to any reader of *Paradiso* xxxii, while those in the second will furnish additional satisfaction to those who know something about Bernard – as they may also have done to Dante *poeta*.

Bernard's authority derives in part, then, from a number of contextual features we have noted already: his position in the Empyrean, his replacement of Beatrice, Dante-character's awestruck adulation of him, his manifest intimacy with Mary. To these must now be added the linguistic dimension: the canto itself has assured us that everything Bernard says qualifies as 'parole sante', and it now becomes possible to see, in retrospect, that that suspiciously pallid adjective also guarantees the authenticity of his theological arguments, which might otherwise be open to contest. The 'parole' themselves are also much concerned with the assertion of their own authoritative stature: hence the invocation of 'etterna legge' (55), the imitation of scholastic techniques in the logical progress of the argument and its co-ordinating conjunctions, the blatant Latinisms ('sili', 49; 'sine causa', 59; 'ausa', 63), and, most significant of all, the final, unanswerable ascription of the state of things in the Empyrean directly to God's will (61–6). At this point there can be no further argument, as such ('e qui basti l'effetto'); by playing this rhetorical trump-card, Bernard replaces the silence of doubt with the silence of assent. (Dante-character's failure to react to Bernard's discourse with supplementary questions, or even with comment, may in itself be a sign that Bernard's authority has duly been established and accepted.) The vehicle by which Bernard achieves the recognition of an intellectual authority that extends even to the expression of unorthodox ideas is, then, his efficacious – eloquent – use of language.

There are also, however, external factors, connected with the historical Bernard, which have a part to play here – at least for readers conversant with them – and which may also have affected Dante-poet's perception of the abbot of Clairvaux enough to have influenced his choice of Bernard for the role that is his in *Paradiso*. Foremost among these is the fact that Bernard himself was a theologian of baptism, author of a letter on the subject to his friend Hugh of St Victor that was widely disseminated as a treatise *De baptismo*.[28] If Dante knew, or knew about, Bernard's letter, the potential attraction of allotting a speech on exactly this subject to a fictional version of Bernard will be clear enough; and it may have been all the greater in that the doctrine to be placed in Bernard's mouth was (as we have seen) not entirely orthodox, and thus could only gain in stature by being associated with so impeccable a source.

Dante would no doubt have been untroubled by the fact that nothing resembling *Paradiso* xxxii's account of the variable distribution of grace among the baptized infants appears in *De baptismo* itself; it is not necessary to assume, because a historical figure in the *Commedia* presents certain teaching, that such teaching invariably conforms to the historical figure's real view of the same subject, or even to Dante-poet's acquaintance with it. On the other hand, it seems unduly reductive to assume that Dante's choices of such spokesmen (and women) are arbitrary; that, in this case, he gave the baptism discourse to Bernard with no thought at all for his historical

---

[28] Botterill, 'Doctrine', 25; the text of the letter is in *Sancti Bernardi Opera*, edited by Jean Leclercq, H. Rochais, and C. Talbot (Rome, 1957– ), vii (1974), 184–200.

identity, or that he would just as readily have given it to someone else. Dante's choosing Bernard to make this speech inevitably inspires questions about the poet's view of the saint and the motivation for his choice.

At the most immediate level, the reasons for the allocation of this speech to Bernard are clearly structural. The description of the Empyrean, and of the principles that define and sustain its existence, is appropriate only to the final stage of Dante's pilgrimage, when he actually arrives there; and Bernard has already been chosen, on grounds that have emerged clearly enough by this point in the narrative, as the figure who will unite the three cantos of the Empyrean episode, with their very different concerns, into a coherent whole. But there may also be more personal considerations involved. Bernard is strikingly well-fitted to present an account of baptism and grace that embodies a less than traditional version of the relevant doctrine. Not only was he the author of a *De baptismo* and a *De gratia et libero arbitrio*, he was an *auctor* who habitually proclaimed his adherence to the orthodoxy of his forefathers in religion. At the beginning of *De baptismo* itself he proudly announces that he has no intention of usurping the place of the Fathers of the Church: 'Patrum tantum opponimus sententias et verba proferimus, et non nostra: nec enim sapientiores sumus quam patres nostri.'[29]

Bernard's *De baptismo*, like most of his work, openly claims to belong to a valid doctrinal tradition that is preserved from contamination or error by its very conservatism. In a word, it lays claim to authority. In putting forward what he declares to be the words and opinions of the Fathers, Bernard effaces himself behind his *auctores*, denies any radical or innovative intent, guarantees the soundness of his doctrine by invoking the authority of those from whom it is derived. It is a procedure intriguingly similar to that adopted by his counterpart in the *Commedia*; and it may help to explain why that counterpart exists at all, or at least why he says what he says in *Paradiso* xxxii. Precisely because Dante's doctrine of infant baptism is not wholly conventional, its authoritative nature is tacitly asserted and confirmed by its being expounded by a figure of such unimpeachable theological rectitude as Bernard. The choice of Bernard, in itself, functions as part of the attempt to prevent Dante-character's doubt from gaining a foothold in the mind of the reader.

---

[29] Bernard, *De baptismo*, Prologue; *Opera*, vii (1974), 184.

This was a real danger. Any Trecento reader who knew enough about the subject to realize that the question of the baptized infants' blessedness was, at best, not clearly defined in contemporary theology, and that, as a result, the solution offered by *Paradiso* XXXII was no more than speculative (and might even be a source of error or confusion), would have been in a position similar to Dante-character's: willing to listen, perhaps, but reluctant to be convinced. The very emphasis given to authority in and around this passage may be an indication of Dante-poet's awareness that his characters are not wholly secure in their orthodoxy, and that his reader has reason to be sceptical. So the narrative movement in which Bernard convinces Dante by overcoming his doubt can, perhaps, be read as a representation of the intended effect of the *Commedia* itself; that is, as an analogue *in parvo* of the process through which the poem seeks to establish its claim to truth in its reader's mind.

After the historical paragraph (79–84) that concludes the baptism speech (and whose content, unlike that of the rest of the speech, is wholly traditional, not to say hackneyed),[30] Bernard reverts to the manner of the previous canto, and resumes the direction of Dante's intellectual interests and spiritual desires through the manipulation of his eyes:

> Riguarda omai ne la faccia che a Cristo
> più si somiglia, ché la sua chiarezza
> sola ti può disporre a veder Cristo.     (85–7)

The face most like Christ's is, of course, that of Mary his mother; so that the narrative seems for a moment to have come full circle, and returned to the point it had reached at *Paradiso*, XXXI. 115–17:

> ma guarda i cerchi infino al più remoto,
> tanto che veggi seder la regina
> cui questo regno è suddito e devoto.

But in fact the situations are different, and Dante-character's second contemplation of Mary constitutes a significant advance, in spiritual terms, on his first. In *Paradiso* XXXI, Mary herself was the primary object of contemplation; Dante's reason for looking at her was to see her in all her celestial glory. In canto XXXII, however, looking at Mary has become a way of looking beyond her; contemplative familiarity with her is now a means of preparation to

---

[30] See Botterill, 'Doctrine', 23 (on Aquinas and Bonaventure), and 26 (on Bernard) for the canonical status of these ideas.

contemplate the similar but still more splendid visage of Christ.
Dante has, in fact, made progress in contemplative skill while under
Bernard's tutelage; and the second vision of Mary, while adding
another page to *Paradiso*'s substantial anthology of ecstatic praise of
the Virgin, also makes clear the effects on Dante of his encounter with
Bernard:

> Io vidi sopra lei tanta allegrezza
>   piover, portata ne le menti sante
>   create a trasvolar per quella altezza,
> che quantunque io avea visto davante
>   di tanta ammirazion non mi sospese,
>   né mi mostrò di Dio tanto sembiante.          (88–93)

Dante's visual sense and contemplative capacity – both, surely,
inherent in the word 'vidi' – have been sharpened beyond even the
degree that they had attained in *Paradiso* XXXI; and so nothing
already seen, in either sense, during his journey can compare, as a
source of 'ammirazion', with what he sees now. Nothing, including
Bernard; for the last object of Dante's 'ammirazion' before Mary was
Bernard himself, in the 'veronica' simile of *Paradiso*, XXXI. 103–11.
We noted at the time that Bernard was keen to ensure that Dante
*personaggio* did not mistake his 'sembianza' for the proper object of his
contemplation, and these lines (XXXII. 91–3) show that that peril has
been avoided. Thanks to Bernard's intervention, Dante's spiritual
concentration is now immovably fixed on its rightful object, and he
can, accordingly, now begin to contemplate Mary in the way that
will lead to the vision of Christ and ultimately of God himself.

Mary is accompanied here by Gabriel ('quello amor che primo lì
discese, / cantando "*Ave Maria, gratïa plena*"', 94–5), and the angel's
presence evokes a reaction of unusual interest from Dante *personaggio*:

> 'O santo padre, che per me comporte
>   l'esser qua giù, lasciando il dolce loco
>   nel qual tu siedi per etterna sorte,
> qual è quell'angel che con tanto gioco
>   guarda ne li occhi la nostra regina,
>   innamorato sì che par di foco?'
> Così ricorsi ancora a la dottrina
>   di colui ch'abbelliva di Maria,
>   come del sole stella mattutina.               (100–8)

It is all too easy to overlook the central fact about these lines: that
they include the first speech that Dante has addressed directly to

Bernard since he asked 'Ov'è ella?' at *Paradiso*, XXXI. 64. Indeed, the speech marks the point at which the relationship between the two characters comes most closely to resemble those between Dante and his guides in the earlier stages of his journey. Now, for the first time (and the only one – this is also the *last* speech that Dante addresses to Bernard), Dante actively acknowledges his subordinate status vis-à-vis his interlocutor, addressing him respectfully (the elaborate courtesy of lines 100–2 forms a revealing contrast with the dismissive treatment of Bernard at XXXI. 70), entering willingly into the role of pupil, and seeking from him the 'dottrina' he had so often sought from Virgil and Beatrice. The humility with which Dante now recognizes Bernard's authority does not only lie in the honorific 'santo padre' (though both terms are fully charged with meaning here, not least because the person addressed is, literally, both a saint and a (monastic) father). It is also apparent in the reference to Bernard's condescension – in the older, positive sense – which has brought him down to Dante's level, for Dante's benefit (100–2).

Now that Dante-character has acquired not only knowledge of Bernard's identity but also understanding of his contemplative achievement (through their shared experience at the end of *Paradiso* XXXI), not to mention his linguistic and theological expertise (demonstrated in most of canto XXXII so far), he is in a position to recognize the value of Bernard's 'dottrina', and the appropriateness of seeking to draw on it by eliciting another display of eloquence. It is also noteworthy that, as he does so, the narrating voice reminds us that this possessor of doctrine is also, above all, a follower of Mary (107–8). Once again, an apparently inert passage of stage-direction in fact helps to pull together and underline the major themes of the *Commedia*'s presentation of Bernard in the light of his historical reputation.

Dante's question itself is of some interest, particularly because, unlike almost all the many other questions he asks in the course of the *Commedia*, it is one to which even minimally alert readers will already know the answer. The narrating voice has already identified Gabriel (95–7) in his position of immediate proximity to Mary; and Dante-character's request that Bernard name the angel (103–5) might thus appear supererogatory. In fact it permits a further variation on the motif of Bernard's own devotion to Mary. The inquisitive Dante's description of Gabriel ('che con tanto gioco / guarda ne li occhi la nostra regina, / innamorato sì che par di foco') cannot fail to recall the image of Bernard himself, gazing 'con tanto affetto' at Mary (*Paradiso*, XXXI. 141), or his self-description as aflame with ardent love for her (XXXI. 100–1); and the periphrastic allusion to Bernard as 'colui ch'abbelliva di Maria / come del sole stella mattutina', which closely follows (107–8), seals the connection between Gabriel and Bernard as members of the same tradition, or, if you prefer, devotees of the same cult.

This is also the motivation of Bernard's tribute to Gabriel's 'baldezza e leggiadria' (109–14), which is based, as was the narrator's reference at 94–5, on Gabriel's involvement in the Annunciation: Gabriel was the first created being to honour Mary as Mother of God – in a sense, the first Mariologist – and Bernard is thus recognizing not merely a forerunner in the *cultus* of Mary but its founder. The desire to accentuate still further this perception of 'fedel Bernardo', by giving Bernard himself the opportunity to discuss Gabriel, perhaps helps to explain the canto's otherwise slightly puzzling concern with Gabriel at this point, as well as the curiously inverted order of his presentation: narrator's identification, Dante-character's question, Bernard's repetition of the identification.

Be that as it may, at the beginning of line 115 Bernard seems keen to change the subject. Once again he directs Dante's eyes away from their present object towards a new one:

> Ma vieni omai con li occhi sì com'io
> andrò parlando, e nota i gran patrici
> di questo imperio giusto e pio. (115–17)

At least two things in this *terzina* are worthy of note. One is the effect of the resounding Latinisms 'patrici' and 'imperio', which make of Heaven not only an imperial court but a court that uses the language of the Roman Empire (and the reference to Mary as 'Agusta' in line 119 confirms this figurative association beyond a shadow of a doubt); the other is that the use of Dante's eyes, central to the encounter with Bernard since its earliest phase, is now so closely identified with Bernard's use of words that their physical movement must literally follow that of Bernard's utterance. Bernard's 'parole sante' are again shown to be the indispensable and absolutely reliable guide to the vision of Heaven.

The 'gran patrici' are listed in the next several *terzine*: they are Adam (121–3), Peter (124–6), John (127–30), Moses (130–2), Anna, Mary's mother (133–5), and Dante's patron Lucia (136–8). The painstaking precision with which their seats in the 'fior venusto' (126) are pointed out and related one to another (so that Adam is next to Peter, John on Peter's right, Moses on his left, Anna opposite him, and so on) doubtless represents Dante-poet's understanding of the symbolic relationships among these founding fathers and mothers of the Christian faith – Adam and Peter are both called 'padre' (122; 124), while Anna is literally maternal (134); but it calls forth no detailed explanation from Bernard, who, indeed, is beginning to feel the pressure of time:

> Ma perché il tempo fugge che t'assonna,
> qui farem punto, come buon sartore
> che com'elli ha del panno fa la gonna;
> e drizzeremo li occhi al primo amore,
> sì che, guardando verso lui, penètri
> quant'è possibil per lo suo fulgore.           (139–44)

The first of these lines has been much debated, chiefly because the different possible interpretations of 't'assonna' (physical sleep? ecstatic transport?) have profoundly divergent consequences for our understanding of the strictly mystical aspect of *Paradiso* (which some, indeed, deny that it even possesses); but, in either case, it is the brevity of Dante-character's experience, and the imminence of its ending, that Bernard refers to here.[31] The time has come to proceed to the vision of the 'primo amore'; and so Bernard and Dante, whose eyes were united in contemplation of Mary at the end of *Paradiso* XXXI, will now jointly direct their gaze towards God, bringing the process of Dante's education in the use of his eyes to its climactic fulfilment. This is not to be achieved, however, without help:

> Veramente, *ne* forse tu t'arretri
> movendo l'ali tue, credendo oltrarti,
> orando grazia conven che s'impetri
> grazia da quella che puote aiutarti;
> e tu mi seguirai con l'affezione,
> sì che dal dicer mio lo cor non parti.           (145–50)

---

[31] The classic statement of the terms of this debate is Michele Barbi's, in *Problemi di critica dantesca: prima serie* (Florence, 1934), pp. 294–5; for later contributions and an authoritative response to them, see Ruggiero Stefanini, 'Spunti di esegesi dantesca: due contrappassi (*Inf.* VI e XIX) e due *cruces* (*Purg.* XXVII. 81 e *Par.* XXXII. 139)', in *Forma e parola: studi in memoria di Fredi Chiappelli*, edited by Dennis J. Dutschke, Pier Massimo Forni, and others (Rome, 1992), pp. 45–65.

These lines collect, once again, the major features of Bernard's role in the poem: contemplation, devotion to Mary ('quella che puote aiutarti'), and the fusion of the two in a prayer for the grace that will enable Dante to enjoy the final vision of God. As the Bernard–Dante encounter approaches its end, Bernard's activities continue to be wholly consistent with his presentation in the *Commedia* and his traditional reputation outside it. But this entire closing sequence of *Paradiso* xxxii also shows at work the third crucial feature of both the fictional and the historical Bernard: his eloquence.

Dante's longing for the vision of God is explicitly equated here with Bernard's oratorical powers ('sì che dal *dicer* mio lo *cor* non parti', 150), and the passage as a whole tellingly exemplifies those powers, never more so than in the much-maligned image of the 'buon sartore' (140–1). Commentators of various ideological stamps have been at one in finding this concrete, down-to-earth, almost colloquial simile hopelessly out of place in the celestial regions, and have suggested that it is an unfortunate stylistic *stonatura* in a canto otherwise so formally structured, so lexically demanding, and so rich in stately Latinisms[32] and rhetorical devices.[33] But it is surely possible to argue, on the contrary, that the simile's pointed vivacity and hint of earthiness are its own justification.

This reference to the humble life of the world helps to prove that that life is, ultimately, one with that of the highest reaches of Heaven, since what happens in the one can be evoked in terms of what happens in the other; and, more relevant for us at this point, the use of a 'low' stylistic register and 'unpoetic' vocabulary ('sartore', 'panno', 'gonna') reveals Bernard as a master of *all* forms and levels of human language, equally capable of expressing himself in homely

---

[32] Those already mentioned are only a few of the canto's many obvious Latinisms: others include 'sedi' (7), 'dirimendo' (18), 'semicirculi' (26), 'intercisi' (28), 'cerna' (30), 'cerner' (34), and the syntactic '*ne*' (145). The use of so many words of this kind, as well as conferring solemnity on the canto's diction (and thus reinforcing Bernard's claims to authority), may also be intended to remind us of Bernard's own reputation as a user of Latin in his writings; it is worth remembering that he is introduced into the poem with the Latinism 'sene' (xxxi. 59).

[33] The simile met with general disfavour in the nineteenth and early twentieth centuries: see Scartazzini-Vandelli, (Milan, 1922), iii, 970; Fornaciari, *Il canto XXXII*, p. 28, for instances. Since then it seems to have become more acceptable, and has even found its defenders, such as Russi, 'Canto xxxii', p. 1168, and Mario Fubini, *Critica e poesia* (Bari, 1956), pp. 23–5. But Di Pino still finds it 'ruvida' ('Canto xxxii', p. 671), and as late as 1989 Tommaso Pisanti was prepared to argue that it would become 'un po' stridente' ('Il canto xxxii', p. 349) if 't'assonna' were given the sense of a contemplative rather than a purely physical state. For the reasons outlined in my text, I find that the simile works equally well either way.

proverbs and of undertaking an incisive scholastic exposition or an ornate petition to the Virgin. He is, in fact, able to apprehend and convey the reality of the universe in any way he deems appropriate, and to use language with complete freedom in so doing; and it is this same intellectual and linguistic assurance, this combination of 'dottrina' and 'parole sante', that enables him, when confronted with Dante-character's silent doubt, to speak out with such unruffled certainty ('ma io *discioglierò* 'l forte legame', 50). Bernard's eloquence, in short, is an integral part not only of his being as a character in the *Commedia*, but also of the role he is called on to play there.

And so, at the end of *Paradiso* xxxii, Bernard turns to begin his long-awaited prayer to the Virgin. The language of the narration ('E cominciò questa santa orazione', 151) seems at first to be an echo of that with which Bernard's involvement in the canto began ('e cominciò queste parole sante', 3), and it certainly reiterates the stress on words and their holiness that we have traced throughout this canto. But there is also, of course, a vital difference on this second occasion: the 'parole' have become an 'orazione'. This is more than just a move from the generic to the particular, a specifying of the kind of words in which *Paradiso* xxxiii will deal; it is the definitive statement of Bernard's role in the Empyrean. He is, in the end, not a guide, not even a lecturer, but an orator; and he is required to be so in a double sense, his eloquence and his doctrine joining forces to enable him, in the same words, both to speak and to pray.[34] *Paradiso* xxxii – and indeed the rest of the *Commedia* – have been occupied by other kinds of speech, which in their time and place were appropriate and, for the most part, well performed; but now 'il tempo fugge', and the last human voice to be heard in Dante's poem, the voice of the 'santo sene' Bernard of Clairvaux, is to be uplifted in prayer. The suspense created by the placement of a break between cantos at this point is a measure of the solemn importance of what is about to happen – that is, of the words that the eloquent Bernard is about to speak.

[34] I return to this point when considering Benvenuto da Imola's account of Bernard, in chapter 4.

## FAITHFUL BERNARD (*PARADISO* XXXIII)

The expectant silence artfully created at the end of *Paradiso* XXXII is broken by one of the most striking and justly celebrated *incipit*s of any canto in the *Commedia*:

> Vergine madre, figlia del tuo figlio,
> umile e alta più che creatura,
> termine fisso d'etterno consiglio,
> tu se' colei che l'umana natura
> nobilitasti sì, che 'l suo fattore
> non disdegnò di farsi sua fattura. (1–3)

This jubilant outburst initiates the last and most complex of Bernard's speeches in the poem, a passage whose magnetic attraction has been felt by creative artists as diverse as Geoffrey Chaucer and Giuseppe Verdi, and which, unusually, has evoked a unanimous chorus of approbation from critics of the *Commedia* down the centuries (the only significant dissent being that registered by Benedetto Croce).[35] The speech consists, as is well known, of the prayer to the Virgin that occupies the first thirteen *terzine* of *Paradiso* XXXIII, and which constitutes the last of the rites of passage that Dante *personaggio* must undergo in the course of his journey: when the prayer is finished and Mary's sanction obtained, nothing and no-one can any longer stand between Dante and the accomplishment of his purpose, the achievement of his vision.

This passage thus marks not only the climax of Bernard of Clairvaux's involvement in the *Commedia* – since after this he will be heard from no more – but also the end of any involvement by characters other than Dante himself. The vast dramatic panoply of encounters and exchanges between individuals that has composed the poem's action hitherto is now refined down to an unprecedented intensity of concentration on Dante's personal and unmediated experience of the ultimate reality that is his God. Bernard's words in *Paradiso* XXXIII are the last words spoken in the *Commedia*, just as his is the last (human) face seen in the Empyrean. From this point onwards, Dante is on his own.

---

[35] Chaucer made use of the prayer twice, adapting it in the Prologue to the *Prioress's Tale* and translating it, with remarkable fidelity, in the Prologue to the *Second Nun's Tale* (lines 36–56); see *The Works of Geoffrey Chaucer*, edited by F. N. Robinson, 2nd edition (Oxford, 1966), p. 207. Verdi set it to music, as one of his *Quattro pezzi sacri*. For Croce's dissent, see his *Poesia antica e moderna*, 2nd edition (Bari, 1943), p. 159.

Which does not, however, mean that he is alone. One of the crucial points about these lines is that they show Dante-character to be enmeshed in a network of mutual dependencies, relying on Mary's intercession to secure grace for him, and on Bernard's oratory to secure Mary's intercession; but Bernard, in turn, draws his inspiration from Beatrice (*Par.*, XXXI. 94–6), who herself was encouraged by Lucia and commissioned by the Virgin (*Inf.*, II. 94–114), and who also entrusted the guidance of Dante, in its early, formative stages, to Virgil (*Inf.*, II. 67–72). Nowhere along the way, in fact, has Dante achieved anything unaided; and it would be quite wrong to suggest that those who have presided over his journey and, in a sense, taken responsibility for it and for him, have now abandoned him, merely because their active participation in his 'fatale andare' (*Inf.*, v. 22) has reached its appointed end.

Bringing Dante to a state of grace (and thus, in the long run, making possible his salvation) has been, and remains, a collective effort; and it is no coincidence that the prayer of *Paradiso* XXXIII should end with a reference to the number of blessed who join in it: 'vedi Beatrice con quanti beati / per li miei prieghi ti chiudon le mani!' (38–9). Though speaking on Dante's behalf, Bernard also gives voice to the wishes of the multitudinous occupants of the 'candida rosa', thus making the matter of the individual Dante's spiritual situation one of concern to the entire company of Heaven.

It may seem mildly perverse to begin looking at Bernard's prayer from its conclusion, when the poetic artifice of its opening lines is so dazzling; but, in the context of this chapter's argument, it is the second half of this passage (22–39) that is the more relevant. There are a number of excellent studies of the prayer's content, rhetoric, and putative sources, and I return to these issues in chapter 5, when considering the hypothesis of direct connection between it and the Marian writings of Bernard of Clairvaux;[36] but for the present I am more concerned with the prayer's function as part of the Bernard-Dante episode, and with the extent to which it fits with what we have

---

[36] As well as the studies examined in detail in chapter 5 and the numerous *lecturae* listed in the *Enciclopedia dantesca* (VI, 588), see Eugene Longen, 'The Grammar of Apotheosis: *Paradiso* XXXIII', *Dante Studies*, 93 (1975), 209–14; Enzo Esposito, 'Il canto dell'ultima visione (*Paradiso* XXXIII)', *Letture classensi*, 7 (1979), 13–26; Lino Pertile, '*Paradiso*, XXXIII: l'estremo oltraggio', *Filologia e critica*, 6 (1981), 1–21; Edward Hagman, 'Dante's Vision of God: The End of the *Itinerarium Mentis*', *Dante Studies*, 106 (1988), 1–20; and Piero Boitani, 'The Sibyl's leaves: Reading *Paradiso* xxxiii', in *The Tragic and the Sublime in Medieval Literature* (Cambridge, 1988), pp. 223–49.

already established about Bernard's role and presentation in the closing cantos of the *Commedia*.

For all its (remarkable) beauty, the first half of the prayer remains, from a narrative point of view, static and self-contained; it lacks the functional significance that dominates the (less aesthetically satisfying) second half. For that reason alone, it is less interesting in the present context. Instead of seeing Bernard's prayer as a detachable anthology piece, I shall try to relate it to its narrative setting, by analysing what it *does*, rather than what it says; and I shall also take into account its immediate aftermath (40–54), in which Bernard of Clairvaux – still smiling but suddenly, definitively, silent – finally disappears from the text.

It is, then, generally agreed that the prayer falls into two sections, of which the second, while growing organically out of the first, is stylistically and functionally distinct from it. The obvious dividing line comes between lines 21 and 22. The canto's first seven *terzine* form an extended *captatio benevolentiae*, in which Bernard piles up complimentary epithets and laudatory metaphors as a means of simultaneously praising Mary and asserting the fundamental dogmatic truths about her: her humanity (expressed at once in virginity and motherhood), her divine election, her mediating role in the economy of salvation; but in line 22 the focus shifts from Mary as object of praise to Dante *personaggio* as supplicant, and the remainder of the prayer has a function more practical than celebratory. Lines 1–21 thus provide Bernard with an opportunity to display his credentials as a Mariologist, which he does in a passage as notable for its theological authority as for its verbal bravura; lines 22–39, on the other hand, show that characteristically Bernardine combination of doctrine and eloquence placed at the service of an urgent and specific purpose within the narrative. Bernard has something to ask for; and it is the efficacy of his speech that ensures that he gets it.

Bernard begins the second section of his prayer by reviewing the whole course of Dante's past journey, and sketching the part of it that still remains to be completed. It is of a piece with his preoccupations and linguistic habits earlier in this episode that he does so by centering his description on the metaphorical value and employment of Dante's eyes:

> Or questi, che da l'infima lacuna
> de l'universo infin qui ha vedute
> le vite spiritali ad una ad una,

> supplica a te, per grazia, di virtute
> tanto, che possa con gli occhi levarsi
> più alto verso l'ultima salute.                    (22–7)

Once again, the eyes are posited as the vehicles through which experience is apprehended, even in the (immaterial) other world; but, once again, Dante's sight is not merely the physical registration of phenomena but the comprehension of their innate reality. It is 'vite spiritali', rather than things or people, that Dante has seen; and the object towards which he will now turn his gaze is equally, if more profoundly, abstract, an 'ultima salute' that can clearly not be encompassed by the organs of material sense-perception alone.

Sight, in the Empyrean, is always insight; to see is always to understand; so seeing always turns to contemplation. And thus Bernard can go on to equate himself with Dante, describing the activity in which they are both now engaged simply as 'veder'. This 'veder', first of all, is spiritually rather than physically generated, by the ardour already noted as basic to Bernard's own relationship with Mary (XXXI. 100–1). Moreover, it is only to be perfected by going *beyond* the body and its faculties, so that the obstacles inherent in Dante's human condition may be overcome, and he achieve the unhindered – contemplative – *visio Dei*:

> E io, che mai per mio veder non arsi
> più ch'i' fo per lo suo, tutti miei prieghi
> ti porgo, e priego che non sieno scarsi,
> perché tu ogne nube li disleghi
> di sua mortalità co' prieghi tuoi,
> sì che 'l sommo piacer li si dispieghi.           (28–33)

These lines are important because they finally – and not before time – reveal the essence of Bernard's role in the poem; this is what he has been brought into the *Commedia* to do and to say. The entire Bernard episode so far has, in a sense, been devoted to establishing, in the minds of the reader and Dante *personaggio* alike, Bernard's qualifications to make the request he now makes, and to occupy the position vis-à-vis Dante – and Mary – that he now takes up. By now, these qualifications, in terms of Marian devotion, contemplation, and eloquence, have been amply demonstrated in the text of *Paradiso*; and Bernard's role can thus be seen to be constructed on that basis. He is a spokesman for Dante, expressing the dedication to Mary that Dante had come to feel at the end of *Paradiso* XXXI (139–42). He stands proxy for Dante, saying and doing for him things that mortal limitations or due humility prevent him from saying or doing for himself. He is Dante's sponsor, appearing for him before his patron, beseeching that patron on his behalf, and putting the full weight of his own prestige and abilities behind his petitions, to the point where his emotional commitment to Dante's cause exactly matches that which he would feel on his own account (XXXIII. 28–9). He acts as a spiritual mentor, taking thought even for the future health of his protégé's soul, concerned how it will fare after the (inevitably transient) contemplative experience comes to an end, when Dante's troublesome humanity will re-assert itself:

> Ancor ti priego, regina, che puoi
> ciò che tu vuoli, che conservi sani,
> dopo tanto veder, li affetti suoi.
> Vinca tua guardia i movimenti umani.                    (34–7)

And he is, finally, as we have already seen, the mouthpiece of the court of Heaven, now united in its prayer for Dante, with one particular individual significantly picked out from the crowd:

> vedi Beatrice con quanti beati
> per li miei prieghi ti chiudon le mani!                    (38–9)

It is, perhaps, the last and greatest of the *Commedia*'s tributes to Bernard's oratorical powers that, in the end, his voice alone speaks not only for Beatrice but for the heavenly host, his 'prieghi' also become the utterance of her and their desire for Dante's salvation.

Spokesman, proxy, sponsor, mentor, mouthpiece: Bernard is all of these in relation to Dante, while continuing to be 'fedel Bernardo', 'quel contemplante', and *doctor mellifluus* in himself. What he is not – as was clear even from our reading of *Paradiso* XXXI – is Dante's third guide. Both his character and his actions in the *Commedia* fall within certain well-defined limits – limits that, as we have seen, do not correspond to those assigned to the characters and actions of the undisputed guides, Virgil and Beatrice.[37] The prayer of *Paradiso* XXXIII both sums up and spells out these limits of Bernard's role. In the first section he speaks *in propria persona*, illustrating the three

---

[37] For more on why Bernard is not a guide, see Botterill, 'Life after Beatrice', 129–30. The first to deny that he is a guide in the usual sense seems to have been Scartazzini, in the early version of his *Commedia* commentary (Leipzig, 1874–90), IV, 503. The term 'sponsor' was first used, though not developed, by Helen Flanders Dunbar, in her *Symbolism in Medieval Thought and its Consummation in the 'Divine Comedy'* (New Haven, 1929), p. 92.

salient points of his presentation in the poem (and of his medieval reputation); in the second he speaks for Dante, interceding for him with Mary as Mary herself will intercede for him with God. And this, as the echoes of Bernard's prayer die away, is exactly what she does:

> Li occhi da Dio diletti e venerati,
>     fissi ne l'orator, ne dimostraro
>     quanto i devoti prieghi le son grati;
> indi a l'etterno lume s'addrizzaro,
>     nel qual non si dee creder che s'invii
>     per creatura l'occhio tanto chiaro.          (40–5)

Still harping upon eyes, though now it is Mary's that have sought out an appropriate object for their gaze and become the vehicle for an expression of emotion (40–2), before being themselves employed for contemplative ends (43–5). For our present purpose, however, it is more interesting to notice just how the text defines the object at which Mary here chooses to look. '*Orator*': this is how *Paradiso* XXXIII sees Bernard, just as the previous canto had informed us that his impending speech was to be not only 'parole sante' but a 'santa *orazione*' (XXXII. 152). Moreover, the word is clearly infused here with both its possible sets of connotations, that connected generally with eloquence and that connected specifically with prayer; if we were in any danger of overlooking the latter, the presence, in the preceding dozen lines, of three instances of 'prieghi' (29, 32, 39) and two of 'priego' (30, 34), as well as the reminder (42) that Bernard's speech consists of 'devoti prieghi', would surely suffice to avert it.

This is the poem's last periphrastic reference to Bernard, it is the one that lingers as he slips smiling out of the text, and it is the one that best encapsulates the whole of his activity during the encounter with Dante *personaggio*. That it is demonstrably consonant with a widespread perception of the historical Bernard in Dante's culture only helps to confirm that a truly satisfactory reading of the Bernard episode in the *Commedia* must take his eloquence, both intra- and extra-textual, into account. The next chapter will show that some, at least, of the poem's earliest readers did exactly that – which makes it all the more regrettable that this vital aspect of Dante's Bernard should have been allowed to fade from the collective memory of later generations.

The last trace of Bernard's presence in *Paradiso* shows him still faithful to the thematics of the episode as a unit – still, that is,

directing Dante *personaggio* in the use of his (contemplative) eyes –
and also closes the narrative circle that opened with his appearance
in *Paradiso* XXXI:

> Bernardo m'accennava, e sorridea,
> perch' io guardassi suso; ma io era
> già per me stesso tal qual ei volea.     (49–51)

The smile, the gesture, the encouragement to look upwards,
towards God: it is hard not to think of the farewell of the figure whose
departure was enjoined by Bernard's arrival – Beatrice:

> Così orai; e quella, sì lontana
> come parea, sorrise e riguardommi;
> poi si tornò a l'etterna fontana.     (XXXI. 91–3)

But, as ever with Dante, repetition does not mean replication. In
*Paradiso* XXXI, Dante-character was still in need of a teacher, a
protector, an exemplar; he did not understand his newly bereft
situation, or know how to react to it, and had to be directed by the
paternal wisdom of the all-seeing Bernard. Now, however, he has
learned his lesson, knows how to use his eyes, and understands what
Bernard wants of him even before Bernard himself has had a chance
to express it (50–1). Bernard's intervention has set the seal on the
educative process that Dante has been undergoing throughout the
poem: having learned freedom of the will from his first guide ('libero,
dritto e sano è tuo arbitrio', *Purg.*, XXVII. 140), and that of the soul
from his second ('Tu m'hai di servo tratto a libertate', *Par.*, XXXI. 85),
Dante has now learned, through Bernard's eloquent example, not
just to see but to contemplate, not just to register but to understand.
As a result, he is ready, with the grace procured for him by Mary, to
proceed unaccompanied to the vision of God:

> ché la mia vista, venendo sincera,
> e più e più intrava per lo raggio
> de l'alta luce che da sé è vera.     (52–4)

It is this 'sincerity' of Dante-character's (physical and contemplative) sight that is Bernard's gift, obtained through his
intervention, in accordance with his example, and under his tutelage;
and only Bernard, with his unique, triune, set of historical qualifications, is competent to bestow it.

The foregoing analysis of the three cantos of *Paradiso* in which
Bernard of Clairvaux appears is, of course, partial in both senses of

the word: many other things might have been said about them, many other textual features selected for comment, and the things that were said and the features that were selected enjoyed that privilege because they suited the purposes of a particular argument about Bernard's role in the poem and the perception of the historical Bernard that informs it. It has been my contention throughout, however, that this argument finds its strongest justification in the text of the poem itself, and that it can best be followed through a process of 'reading' rather than 're-reading' that text; and it will be the concern of the next chapter to show that a view of Bernard compatible with that expressed here was also held by the first readers of the *Commedia* of whose reactions we have concrete evidence, the authors of the numerous Trecento commentaries on the poem.

# PART II

*Re-reading*

CHAPTER 4

# Bernard in the Trecento commentaries on the
# Commedia

A number of 'invidïosi veri' (*Par.*, x. 138) confront anyone who tries
to use study of the Trecento commentaries as a means towards fuller
understanding of Dante's *Commedia* – let alone as the principal, or
even exclusive, guide to what is taken, at so vast a remove of time, to
be the poem's authentic cultural context. The most immediate of
these is the unsatisfactory state of the relevant material: several
important commentaries and sets of glosses still exist only in
manuscript (and are thus, sadly but understandably, all too often
neglected by scholars who lack the time and resources needed to
study them *in situ*), while some of those that have been published are
available only in (mainly nineteenth-century) editions whose dis-
astrously unreliable texts are a standing reproach to philological
scholarship.[1]

Another potential difficulty – though this should perhaps be seen
as a source less of frustration than of interest, even excitement – is the
fact that the various commentaries steadfastly refuse to be forced or

---

[1] The availability of the commentaries has been much improved of late by the valuable work
of the Dartmouth Dante Project; but although this enormous computerized database has
made many Trecento commentaries more accessible than ever before, it has not been able
– nor was it intended – to deal with the deficiencies of the editions involved, or to include
manuscripts that remain unedited. Cases in point include the *Ottimo commento*, only one of
whose three redactions exists in print – edited by Alessandro Torri (Pisa, 1827–9) – the
other two still being available only in manuscript. (On this see Giuseppe Vandelli, 'Una
nuova redazione dell'*Ottimo*', *Studi danteschi*, 14 (1930), 93–174; Saverio Bellomo, 'Primi
appunti sull'*Ottimo commento* dantesco', *Giornale storico della letteratura italiana*, 157 (1980),
533–40.) The same is true of the *Commentarium* of Pietro Alighieri, despite the (much-
criticized) recent effort to provide a synoptic edition of at least the three redactions of
*Inferno*: *Il 'Commentarium' di Pietro Alighieri nelle redazioni Ashburnhamiana e Ottoboniana*, edited
by Roberto della Vedova and Maria Teresa Silvotti (Florence, 1978). See also the
commentaries of Graziolo de' Bambaglioli, Jacopo della Lana, and Francesco da Buti, the
nineteenth- and early twentieth-century editions of which have been overtaken by
subsequent philological research. That the difficulties inherent in editing the commentaries
have not diminished with the passage of time is shown by the unfriendly critical reception
accorded Vincenzo Cioffari's edition of Guido da Pisa's *Expositiones* (Albany, NY, 1974).

cajoled by critics into speaking with one voice, or into providing, for the hurried modern reader's convenience, a single, homogenized reading that can safely be treated as the 'official' Trecento view and, very likely, be disregarded thereafter. Quite the contrary, in fact: the commentaries' interpretations of detail are as disparate as their methods of analysis, and their conceptions of even the most basic theoretical issues – the disputed primacy of literal or allegorical reading, the *Commedia*'s status as truth-telling vision or poetical fiction, the technical employment of the *accessus ad auctores* or the *quadruplex sensus* – vary to an alarming, or exhilarating, degree. Indeed, even at the level of simple information (geographical, historical, biographical), the extent of what the commentators know, seem to know, or think they know can often surprise the reader who has preconceived expectations about their authority, whether because it is so much or – the case of Dante's sons Pietro and Jacopo is especially poignant here – because it is so little.

This remarkable exegetical diversity, appearing so early in what has turned out to be the immensely protracted critical history of Dante's poem, clearly reflects the wide range of cultural backgrounds and intellectual formations out of which the individual commentators emerge, from the relatively scanty preparation of a Jacopo Alighieri to the erudite professionalism of a Boccaccio or a Benvenuto da Imola. Until very recently, however, twentieth-century Dante criticism has found it depressingly easy to disparage or patronize the Trecento commentaries, perhaps as a consequence of our instinctive post-Romantic view of ourselves as giants firmly ensconced on the shoulders of dwarves; but the time now seems right to start attending more closely to what these voluminous texts have to say. Taken as a whole, and listened to with an ear attuned to their peculiar accords and discords with later ways of responding to the poem, their critical polyphony offers a uniquely variegated document of a medieval text's reception by its contemporaries; and it may be that now, more than ever, it is worth asking whether the information and analysis contained in the Trecento commentaries may not after all be indispensable, albeit in varying degrees, to the attempt to bridge the constantly growing historical and cultural distance between us and the *Commedia*.[2]

[2] For a summary treatment of the Trecento commentaries, see Bruno Sandkühler, *Die frühen Dantekommentare und ihr Verhältnis zur mittelalterlichen Kommentartradition* (Munich, 1967); *Die italienische Literatur im Zeitalter Dantes und am Übergang vom Mittelalter zur Renaissance (Grundriß*

Adequate treatment of the issues raised by any effort to make use of the Trecento commentaries in the 1990s would, of course, require a stout volume to itself, and this book is not it. However, the present chapter is intended to deal with the substance of the commentaries to the extent that they impinge on the question we have been studying so far, namely the presence of Bernard of Clairvaux as a character in the final cantos of *Paradiso* and what that presence may mean. For, as we have already seen, Bernard's unexpected appearance in *Paradiso* XXXI, seemingly as a replacement for Beatrice in her function as Dante's mentor in the Empyrean, has always been a puzzle, not to say a scandal, to commentators. The comparatively few Trecento commentaries that deal with *Paradiso* (those of Jacopo della Lana, Pietro Alighieri, 'Falso Boccaccio', Benvenuto da Imola, 'Stefano Talice da Ricaldone', Francesco da Buti, and Giovanni Bertoldi da Serravalle) are no exception in this respect; but it is my contention that the Trecento exegetes' efforts to deal with Bernard's discomfiting presence on the basis of their own knowledge of history and understanding of Dante's poetic practice, as well as being valuable documents in themselves, also express ideas and opinions that were widespread and influential enough in the late Middle Ages to cast some light on the cultural conditions in which Dante's image of Bernard was produced and by which it was defined.

The commentators' reactions to Bernard, in short, may give us some clue to the perception of the saint that Dante could have expected his readers to share; and their attempts to account for their own perplexity may be seen as attempts to make Dante's Bernard conform to the nature of that perception, to align the troubling particulars of this text with the familiar generalities of their culture. The issue will be examined here under three headings: the commentators' use of Bernard as an *auctor*, whether or not in the immediate context of *Paradiso* XXXI–XXXIII; their grasp of the facts of Bernard's writings and career, as evidenced in the biographies that most of them supply at the moment of his entry into the narrative; and their interpretations of his symbolic function in *Paradiso*, which usually

*der romanischen Literaturen des Mittelalters*, X/1), edited by August Buck (Heidelberg, 1987), pp. 166–208 (also by Sandkühler); L. Jenaro-MacLennan, *The Trecento Commentaries on the 'Divina Commedia' and the Epistle to Cangrande* (Oxford, 1974); Aldo Vallone, *Storia della critica dantesca dal XIV al XX secolo* (Padua, 1981); Steven Botterill, 'The Trecento Commentaries on Dante's *Commedia*', in vol. II of *The Cambridge History of Literary Criticism*, edited by Alastair Minnis (Cambridge, forthcoming).

take the form of explaining, at greater or lesser length, just why Dante should have chosen Bernard in Beatrice's stead.

Bernard of Clairvaux is a long way from being the most authoritative of the Fathers of the Church in the Trecento commentators' eyes, at least if the extent to which they draw directly on his writings is a valid criterion for assessing their estimate of his stature. Jacopo della Lana, for instance, in the earliest surviving commentary on the whole *Commedia* (1324–8), quotes Bernard only twice outside the cantos in which the character bearing Bernard's name is involved, although his commentary as a whole is rich in illustrative material drawn from the Bible and from theological literature. The first of these quotations comes as Lana is looking for a definition of avarice in his prologue to *Inferno* VII, where the punishment due to that sin is described:

Or per questa tal paura inordinata, che l'anima segue e il corpo, si è peccato: e dice san Bernardo: *avaritia est quarumlibet rerum insatiabilis et inhonesta cupido* ('avarice is an insatiable and dishonourable desire for things of any kind'); e l'Apostolo dice: *avaritia est ydolorum servitus, quia homo avarus exhibet creaturae, quod debet creatori, scilicet fidem spem et dilectionem* ('avarice is enslavement to idols, because the avaricious man gives to the created what he should give to the creator, namely faith, hope, and love').[3]

Although it might be seen as complimentary to Bernard that he is placed here on a level with 'the Apostle' – by whom Lana apparently means St Paul – closer scrutiny encourages some scepticism about this quotation's value as an indication of Lana's intimacy with Bernard's theological writings. It seems, in fact, not to occur, at least in this form, anywhere in that weighty corpus of texts; and the impression that Bernard's name has here become attached, for no clearly discernible reason beyond its prestige, to a commonplace or proverbial saying is only strengthened by Lana's equally trusting ascription of his other quotation to apostolic authority. Though this may be a vague reminiscence or conflation of a number of Pauline passages (the discourse on idolatry in 1 Corinthians 8, the reproach of the unrighteous in Romans 1. 25, even the famous evocation of love in 1 Corinthians 13. 1–13), it is not, in itself, a Biblical text.

Lana's other reference to Bernard outside the Empyrean episode seems to be a little more firmly rooted in textual reality. In his

---

[3] Jacopo della Lana, *La 'Comedia' di Dante degli Allagherii col 'Commento' di Jacopo della Lana bolognese*, edited by Luciano Scarabelli, 3 vols. (Bologna, 1866), I, 170–1.

commentary on *Paradiso* XII, he embarks on a long description of the monastic ideals of St Francis and St Dominic, the two 'campioni' whose achievements are invoked in Dante's Heaven of the Sun by their respective followers St Bonaventure and Thomas Aquinas, each of whom undertakes the eulogy of the founder of the Order to which he himself did not belong. The most crucial aspect of these ideals, according to Lana, was poverty; and he sees this necessary monastic virtue as threatened, in his own day, by the unhealthy fondness of some monks for 'delicate e valevoli vestimenta':

[E] a questo provvideno li detti due campioni quando ordinonno li abiti suoi di vili e non di curiosi panni sì in fermezza come eziandio in colore, li quali panni non debbono avere alcuno colore accidentale. Lo quale freno non solo guarisce l'affezione del tesaurizzare, ma eziandio schifa che vanagloria non dannifichi, imperquello che quando l'uomo è ben vestito, bene intende delicate e preziosamente, elli se l'imprende in quore alcuna vaghezza di essere veduto, e così vanagloriando crede essere stimato grande fatto; e questo è quello che san Bernardo nella sua regola scrisse *vestimenta nostra non sint nota* ('let our clothing not draw attention').[4]

The phrase attributed here to Bernard is certainly very much in the spirit of his thinking about the moral (and sartorial) obligations of the monastic life. In his *Apologia ad Guillelmum*, for example, luxurious clothing is both cited literally, as an instance of a vice to be avoided, and used metaphorically, as a symbol of the dangers that threaten the successful implementation of the monastic ideal.[5] But the phrase as quoted by Lana appears nowhere in this text, which is the closest approach, among Bernard's authentic writings, to the kind of explicit statement of monastic precept and practice that could legitimately be called a 'regola'. Moreover, the idea that fine clothes are inappropriate for monks had, of course, been a commonplace among monastic legislators long before Bernard's time.

The Rule of St Benedict includes a chapter spelling out the need for the monks' clothing to be no more than practical in design and humble in form, and the same intention is expressed in the Augustinian Rule in terms that come notably closer to those of Lana's alleged quotation from Bernard than anything in the *Apologia* ('Non

---

[4] Lana, *Commento*, III, 212.
[5] See Bernard, *Apologia*, I. 1 (*Opera*, III (1963), 81–2; *PL*, 182, cols. 898–9); III. 5–6 (*Opera*, III (1963), 84–7; *PL*, 182, cols. 901–3); VI. 12 (*Opera*, III (1963), 91–2; *PL*, 182, cols. 905–7); and x. 25–6 (*Opera*, III (1963), 102; *PL*, 182, col. 913).

sit notabilis habitus vester').[6] Given the normative value of this idea
in medieval monasticism, it would be unwise to press the connection
with Bernard too far; it seems likely that Lana has in mind one of the
several Rules of the Cistercian Order (which were habitually, though
wrongly, ascribed to Bernard in the Middle Ages), rather than the
*Apologia* itself or any other genuinely Bernardine text. This vagueness
of attribution, coupled with the similarly uncertain status of the
quotation used in the commentary on *Inferno* VII, strongly suggests
that although Lana recognized the prestige of Bernard's name and
had encountered texts to which that name had been appended, he
had not gone out of his way to study Bernard's writings in any depth.
(It is worth noting that when Lana is truly intimate with a text – the
Bible, Thomas Aquinas' two great *Summae* – his references to it are
usually much more precise than these.)

In the commentary on *Paradiso* XXXIII, Lana supplies three
quotations on Marian themes which he assigns to Bernard, thereby
helping to inaugurate the tradition of seeing Bernard's renown as a
devotee of Mary as the determining factor in Dante's allocation to
him of his role in the *Commedia*:

Or quanto siano maravigliosi li suoi atti, appare per la sua umilitade in
prima, della quale scrive santo Bernardo: *Quae est ista tam sublimis humilitas
quae honori cedere non novit, insolescere gloria nescit, Dei mater eligitur et ancillam se
nominat de se dicens: Respexit humilitatem ancillae suae* ('What is this humility, so
sublime that it has not succumbed to pride, does not grow arrogant in its
glory, is chosen as Mother of God and calls itself a handmaid, saying: He
hath regarded the lowliness of his handmaiden?'). Ancora si denota sua
umilitade quando servì Elisabeth in parto, onde santo Bernardo: *In
momentanea confestinatione Maria abivit Elisabeth salutata, eius ministerio quasi
mensibus tribus humiliter stetit, etc.* ('In great haste Mary went there, and,
having greeted Elisabeth, remained humbly in her service for almost three
months'). Ancora si è nostra avvocata dinanzi da Dio, onde santo Bernardo:
*Securum accessum habes, o homo, ad Deum, ubi mater ante filium et filius ante patrem,
mater ostendit filio pectus et ubera, filius patri latus et vulnera, nulla ergo poterit esse
repulsa tibi ubi tot occurrant caritatis insignia, etc.* ('You have secure recourse, o
man, to God, where, the mother before the son and the son before the father,
the mother shows the son her bosom and breasts, the son shows the father his
side and wounds; nothing, therefore, can be denied you where there are so
many signs of love').[7]

---

[6] See *Benedicti Regula*, edited by Rudolf Hanslik, Corpus Scriptorum Ecclesiasticorum
Latinorum, 75 (Vienna, 1960), pp. 127–31; George Lawless, *Augustine of Hippo and his
Monastic Rule* (Oxford, 1987), p. 86.     [7] Lana, *Commento*, III, 497.

Here at last Lana makes textual contact with the authentic Bernard. The first of these quotations is a slightly garbled version of a passage in one of Bernard's sermons *In laudibus Virginis Matris* (IV. 9: 'Quae est haec tam sublimis humilitas, quae cedere non novit honoribus, insolescere gloria nescit? Mater Dei eligitur, et ancillam se nominat' – *Opera*, IV, 55); while the second, less clearly derived from any text of Bernard's, is, in any case, closely modelled on the account, in Luke's Gospel, of Mary's visit to the pregnant Elisabeth (Luke 1. 39: 'abiit ... cum festinatione'; 1. 56: 'Mansit autem Maria cum illa quasi mensibus tribus'). The third quotation, however, presents a case that is both interesting in itself and exemplary of the difficulties and potential for confusion inherent in the use of the Trecento commentaries as cultural source-books for the study of the *Commedia*.

The quotation's relevance to the situation in *Paradiso* XXXIII will be apparent. It urges the penitent to turn to Mary for assistance in obtaining grace, just as Dante himself does at this point in the *Commedia*'s narrative, and it expresses the same confidence in the certain success of this undertaking as Bernard does in his prayer. So apt did the passage seem to later commentators, indeed, that it was taken up enthusiastically (sometimes being slightly modified in the process): first by Pietro Alighieri, later by Francesco da Buti, and eventually by a string of commentators from Cristoforo Landino in the late Quattrocento to Scartazzini, Casini, Gualberto de Marzo, and Poletto at the turn of the nineteenth and twentieth centuries.[8]

All these would no doubt have concurred with Landino's remark that the passage shows *Paradiso*, XXXIII. 1–39 to consist of 'parole ... molto convenienti a Bernardo' – with the possible exception of Pietro Alighieri, since he, while undeniably finding it useful for the purposes of commentary, somewhat perversely attributes it to Augustine. Yet, although so may commentators cite the passage and describe it as Bernard's, none gives any more specific reference that might enable interested readers to track it down for themselves. The

---

[8] Pietro Alighieri, *Petri Allegherii super Dantis ipsius genitoris Comoediam Commentarium*, edited by Vincenzo Nannucci (Florence, 1846), p. 736; Francesco da Buti, *Commento di Francesco da Buti sopra la 'Divina Comedia' di Dante Allighieri*, edited by Crescentino Giannini, 3 vols. (Pisa, 1858–62), III, 858; *La 'Commedia' di Dante Alighieri* [with the commentary of Cristoforo Landino] (Venice, 1491), *ad loc. Paradiso*, XXXIII. 1–39; *La 'Divina Commedia'*, edited by G. A. Scartazzini, 4 vols. (Leipzig, 1874–90), III, 863; *La 'Divina Commedia'*, edited by Tommaso Casini, revised by S. A. Barbi, 3 vols. (Florence, 1955–9), III, 1056; Antonio Gualberto de Marzo, *Studi filosofici, morali, estetici, storici, politici e filologici su la 'Divina Commedia'*, 3 vols. (Florence, 1864–82), III, 727; *La 'Divina Commedia'*, edited by Giacomo Poletto, 3 vols. (Rome, 1894), III, 686.

reason for this suspicious unanimity in silence is, predictably, that the quotation is not to be found anywhere in Bernard's *opera omnia*, nor, indeed (*pace* Pietro Alighieri) in Augustine's. Its origins are, in fact, a little more obscure than that.

The passage actually occurs, in the form in which Lana quotes it, in the *Quaestiones de Assumptione* of Gualterus Cancellarius, a thirteenth-century Franciscan bishop.[9] But Gualterus' version is not absolutely identical with Lana's. It has a significant further refinement, in the form of a gloss: 'Ergo mater ante filium habet pectus et ubera. Aliter non ostenderet. Ergo et in corpore glorificato' ('Therefore the mother before the son has bosom and breasts. Otherwise she could not show them. Therefore she is glorified in the body also'). The effect of this addition is to change the whole sense of the passage. Rather than encouraging the repentant sinner to turn in prayer to Mary when in need of grace, Gualterus is engaged in an entirely separate doctrinal enterprise: he is trying to prove the truth of the Virgin's bodily assumption by showing that even in Heaven she possesses breasts and, therefore, a body.

Clearly this argument, in itself, is not especially relevant to the matter of Bernard's prayer in *Paradiso* XXXIII. So Gualterus too is revealed as a commentator, using the passage as evidence in scholastic debate; and he too ascribes it to Bernard, doubtless in the hope of exploiting Bernard's authority to the full as support for his contentious position. Both the (mis)attribution to Bernard and the quotation's use as powerful reinforcement for a theological argument, then, considerably pre-date the Trecento commentaries; and neither can be taken as demonstrating any independent knowledge of or interest in Bernard on Lana's part. He is merely repeating the received – if slightly addled – wisdom of his predecessors.

Yet there is a connection here both with Bernard and with the theology of grace. Gualterus' proof of the bodily assumption of the Virgin, which was to enjoy so prolonged and ultimately incongruous a career in Dante scholarship, is in fact a corruption of an extract from the *De laudibus beatae Mariae* of Arnald of Bonneval, the twelfth-century Cistercian abbot and biographer of none other than Bernard of Clairvaux. Moreover, Arnald's treatise is often attributed in manuscripts to the saint himself, no doubt because of both the

---

[9] Gualterus Cancellarius and Bartholomaeus de Bononia, OFM, *Quaestiones ineditae de Assumptione BVM*, edited by A. Deneffe and H. Weisweiler, 2nd edition (Münster, 1952), p. 28.

personal connection between the two authors and the similarity of Arnald's title to that of Bernard's own *In laudibus Virginis Matris*. In Arnald, the passage reads as follows:

Securum accessum iam habet homo ad Deum, ubi mediatorem causae suae Filium habet ante Patrem, et ante Filium Matrem. Christus, nudato latere, ostendit Patri latus et vulnera; Maria Christo pectus et ubera; nec potest ullo modo esse repulsa, ubi concurrunt et orant omni lingua disertius haec clementiae monumenta et charitatis insignia.[10]

Now that the passage is restored to its rightful author and context, it can be seen that Lana and the later commentators were indeed justified in using it as they did; for Arnald's concern is clearly that which they identify, namely to demonstrate the central importance of Mary's role in the spiritual economy of grace. But, for all that these words are consonant with those of the prayer to the Virgin in *Paradiso* XXXIII, they are not from the mouth (or the pen) of the historical Bernard of Clairvaux; and the fact that several modern commentators have been misled by Lana and his contemporaries into assuming that they are, and thence into constructing models of the Bernard–Dante relationship in which direct influence is guaranteed by the consensus of the Trecento commentaries, is an object-lesson in how those commentaries should not be used. They are more reliable, in short, as a guide to what Trecento readers believed than to what is or was actually the case; there are gaps and obscurities in their knowledge and interpretation, which are due as much to the practical realities of medieval cultural activity (in particular, the universal distribution of unreliable, misattributed, corrupt, or fragmentary texts), as to the vagaries of a given individual's learning or sensibility.

That Jacopo della Lana believed that Bernard of Clairvaux had written things that were relevant to his figure's involvement in the *Commedia* is, ultimately, more significant for us than the fact that, most of the time, Lana was irritatingly vague or downright wrong in his selection and attribution of texts. Given the all-pervading climate of philological confusion in which even the most authoritative texts circulated in the Middle Ages – to the point where a celebrated name

---

[10] Arnald of Bonneval, *De laudibus Beatae Mariae Virginis*, in *PL*, 189, col. 1726: 'Now man has secure access to God, where as mediator of his cause he has the son before the Father and the mother before the Son. Christ, baring his side, shows his Father his side and his wounds; Mary shows Christ her bosom and her breasts; nor can she be spurned in any way, where these tokens of clemency and signs of love come together and pray more eloquently than any tongue.'

like Bernard's, by virtue of its mere celebrity, could attract all kinds of spurious material to itself like a comet gathering stellar debris on its headlong course among the planets – the definition of textual 'authenticity' often becomes a slippery, time-consuming, and, in the end, not very meaningful process. For late medieval readers, what bore Bernard's name became, for all practical purposes, 'authentic'. As a result, the intrinsic appropriateness of the glosses themselves is a more valid yardstick by which to judge a medieval commentary's quotient of 'cultural literacy' than the accuracy of its ascriptions to *auctores*.

Yet it must be said that, even by this tolerant criterion, Lana seems not to be deeply affected by Bernard. His quotations are few indeed, set against the imposing mass of his commentary and the frequency with which other authors are cited, and Lana's acquaintance with the facts of Bernard's life is as superficial as his familiarity with Bernard's writings. He knows that Bernard was 'molto devoto in contemplazione di nostra Donna' – which he could have deduced from the quotations he uses, wherever he found them (not to mention the text of *Paradiso* itself), so that we need not take this as evidence that he had studied any biographical account of Bernard.[11] On the other hand, his allusions to Bernard's monastic career are no more than fleeting, especially when compared with the attention paid to it by some of his successors; he cites none of Bernard's works by name (except, implicitly, the spurious 'regola'); and he mentions none of the numerous anecdotes about Bernard that were sanctioned by hagiography or recorded in popular tradition. All in all, Lana's commentary cannot be considered either rich or reliable as a source of information about Bernard.

It is, then, all the more interesting that Lana should have so highly developed a concern with Bernard's symbolic meaning in the *Commedia*. Like most of the Trecento commentators on *Paradiso*, he is much exercised by the baffling replacement of Beatrice in *Paradiso* XXXI; and, again like most of his medieval contemporaries, he uses that narrative occurrence as a pretext for a detailed exposition of his own understanding of Bernard's importance to Dante *poeta*:

Alla quarta cosa toccata nel presente capitolo si è da sapere che l'autore introduce santo Bernardo a sua custodia, il quale lo introduce poi a vedere nostra Donna, come apparirà, e ciò fae per due ragioni: la prima si è perché

---

[11] Lana, *Commento*, III, 471.

santo Bernardo fue molto devoto in contemplazione di nostra Donna e
perché questa parte tocca di contemplazione di nostra Donna e visione
d'essa, fue ragionevile ch'esso santo Bernardo fosse lo introduttore; l'altra
ragione si è che la fine a che propose l'autore di consumare sua vita fue ad
essere delli seguaci, e in vestigia e in vita, del predetto santo; per la quale
osservazione ello fosse, all'altro mondo, per santo Bernardo introdotto a
quella beatitudine eterna che è lo Paradiso...[12]

With these two hypotheses, Lana simultaneously hits a critical
bull's-eye and shoots far wide of the target. The first suggestion, that
the historical Bernard's devotion to Mary justifies his presence in this
particular part of the poem (where Mary becomes crucial to the
narrative) is eagerly picked up by the Trecento commentators and
repeated, with varying degrees of emphasis, by the large majority of
their successors down the years. The second, that Dante chose
Bernard here because he planned to end his days as a Cistercian,
disappears without trace. Yet, taken together, Lana's two explanations of Bernard's involvement in the *Commedia* are doubly revealing,
both of his thinking about Bernard specifically and of his overall
approach to Dante's poem. For both are based, above all, on the
evidence offered by the text itself, rather than on certified information
culled from other sources.

This is particularly clear in the case of the presentation of Dante as
a would-be Cistercian. At first sight, this seems to be a concrete fact,
external to the text of the *Commedia*; and when Lana remarks that
'puossi provare per tal modo', the reader naturally anticipates some
biographical or documentary proof of Dante's intentions in this
respect. The only evidence that Lana has, however, is that offered by
the *Commedia* itself:

L'autore mette nell'Inferno e Purgatorio fino a certa parte essere suo duce
Virgilio, lo quale hae a significare solo tutte le scienzie che per intelletto
umano si possano sapere, imperquello che'l vero e'l dritto fino a quella parte
per ragione umana si può procedere e cognoscere, da quella parte innanzi
mette Beatrice essere suo duce, la quale hae a significare la scienzia di
teologìa, sì come più volte è stato detto, per la quale ad intelletto ello seppe
di quello la verità che possiamo sapere per scienzia divine cose. Or fa bisogno
che non solo noi abbiamo la scienzia delle virtudi, ma è bisogno che noi le
adovriamo; per la quale operazione noi conseguiamo poi quella visione, che
è beatitudine eterna; e così fe' bisogno all'autore che non solo elli avesse

Beatrice per duce, che è la scienzia ad intelletto, ma fèlli bisogno Bernardo per duca acciò che avesse l'adovrazione della scienzia, e però se in essa fu scienzia naturale e teologìa, in esso conviene essere religione secondo quello ordine di santo Bernardo, ch' ello si elesse per suo duce, e così si conclude che'l proposito dello autore fue di consumare sua vita in tale ordine.[13]

The intellectual leap of faith in the last sentence is little short of breathtaking, and helps to explain why Lana's belief that Dante intended to follow Bernard 'e in vestigia e in vita' has never found another adherent in the whole long history of Dante commentary. But, on the way to that startling conclusion, Lana touches on another symbolic interpretation of Bernard, one that was, though often subjected to refinement and clarification, to prove as durable in critical history as the notion of a Bernard chosen chiefly as a Mariologist. This is the suggestion that Bernard's role is essentially a development of that of Beatrice, in that where she represented theology as a body of knowledge, Bernard represents the employment of that knowledge in the context of (specifically mystical) experience. The stress thus falls on Bernard as a *user*, rather a mere possessor, of doctrine; as one who shows Dante *personaggio*, by example, what the 'adovrazione della scienzia' (that is, of theology) really is. It seems, in fact, to be closely related, if not actually equivalent, to 'contemplazione' – which is, of course, the specific area of expertise that the poem itself attributes to Bernard (*Par.*, XXXI. 103–11; XXXII. 1).

Once again, Lana's interpretation can be seen to be based directly on the text before him, rather than on any intervening study, intuition, or information of his own. Yet his importance in the development of a critical consensus around the 'Bernard cantos' of *Paradiso* is considerable, and not just because he was first in the field. Leaving aside his colourful but unfounded excursions into Dantean biography, his main contribution was to identify Marian devotion and contemplative activity as factors, common to both the historical and the poetic Bernard, that justify his selection for his part in the *Commedia*; and in this identification he has been followed by nearly every significant commentator on the poem from his own time to ours. That the basis for his reading is the letter of Dante's text and not some more or less nebulous 'cultural background' perhaps only guarantees the soundness of that reading, rather than convicting its formulator of insufficient intellectual enterprise.

[13] Ibid.

Lana's commentary soon acquired considerable influence and enjoyed rapid and widespread diffusion: it survives in more than eighty manuscripts. Moreover, parts of it were taken over wholesale to supply the perceived deficiencies of other commentaries, especially those apparently left unfinished by their original authors: this is the case of the *Ottimo commento*, normally attributed nowadays to Andrea Lancia, a Florentine notary, whose three redactions date from the central decades of the fourteenth century, as well as of the text ascribed to the 'Anonimo Fiorentino', which can reliably be dated to about 1400. Both these commentaries deal with the whole *Commedia*, and therefore seem at first sight pertinent to the present discussion; but in fact, as far as *Paradiso* is concerned, neither does much more than reproduce Lana's text, with minor and largely insignificant verbal and orthographical alterations. (Some independent material is included in the *Ottimo commento*, especially in its – unedited – later redactions, which makes their relative inaccessibility all the more regrettable.) They thus offer little fresh evidence of the Trecento commentators' attitudes towards Bernard, though they do testify to the fact that the interpretation proposed by Lana in the 1320s could still be found useful and convincing by readers as much as seven decades later.

The next commentary to deal with *Paradiso* in original and substantial fashion was that of Dante's son Pietro, the first version of which dates from about 1340. (Two later versions, of 1350–5 and c. 1358, each exist in a single manuscript; neither is yet available *in extenso* in a modern edition.) There are nearly twenty quotations in Pietro's first redaction that are attributed to Bernard, which initially seems an impressive tally; but in fact Bernard enjoys much less authority with Dante's elder son than do several other authors, at least numerically speaking. Augustine is cited by Pietro on no fewer than 160 occasions (at least one of which, as we have seen, involves a text more commonly, though equally wrongly, attributed to Bernard); and Bernard is also outstripped in this particular field by Boethius, Aquinas, Gregory, Isidore, and Jerome.[14] Nor is Pietro's Bernardine scholarship always reliable: most of his quotations are badly mangled or unidentifiable, either because he was using corrupt manuscripts or because he is quoting from memory, and the majority

---

[14] These figures are taken from the index in Nannucci's edition of Pietro's first redaction; more scrupulous attention to Pietro's three texts would probably modify them in detail, though not, I suspect, in proportion.

of those which can be identified come not from Bernard himself but from spurious texts, chief among them the immensely popular *Meditationes piissimae*.[15] However, even with these limitations taken into account (and remembering, on the other hand, that the concept of a 'spurious' text is not a very helpful one anyway, since it depends exclusively on twentieth-century hindsight), it is clear that Bernard is a figure of some resonance for Pietro, whose potential applicability to his father's poem extends beyond the boundaries of the single narrative episode (*Paradiso*, XXXI–XXXIII) of most obvious relevance.

Pietro quotes Bernard (or, more usually, pseudo-Bernard) on many different subjects, ranging from the proper preparation of food ('sufficit ut cibus comestibilis sit, non concupiscibilis' – 'it is enough that food be edible, it need not be desirable') to the nature of mystical union with God (a celebrated passage from the *Meditationes piissimae*, based on the 'oculus non vidit' motif of Isaiah 64. 4 and 1 Corinthians 2. 9, is used twice).[16] It is noteworthy that Bernard's *auctoritas* is invoked by Pietro more often in *Purgatorio* than in *Paradiso*, where he actually appears (eight quotations to six); and the canto with the most references is *Purgatorio* VIII, where Pietro seems to respond especially warmly to what for him is Bernard's (though in fact it seems to be pseudo-Bernard's) view of the nature of prayer, and his trust in the protection afforded by divine providence:

Et Bernardus dicit: quod obsecrationes fiunt affectu verecundo, orationes puro, postulationes amplo, gratiarum actiones devoto. Debet enim oratio esse fidelis, pura, devota, discreta, verecunda et secreta.[17]

It seems, in fact, that Bernard's primary significance for Pietro was that of the theologian of grace and director of the Christian life, since these are the aspects reflected in his choice of quotations outside the Empyrean episode itself; but this impression is hard to document

---

[15] Nannucci identifies seven of Pietro's 'Bernardine' quotations as coming from the *Meditationes piissimae*, the letter *Ad fratres de Monte Dei*, a collection of *Declamationes ex Bernardo*, the Decretals, and two genuine sermons, *In dedicatione Ecclesiae*, IV, and *In festo Pentecoste*, II (see the Appendix to his edition, pp. lviii, lxxi, lxxxi, lxxxiv, c, civ, cxxv, cxxix-cxxx). One that he missed is the quotation used to illustrate the proper attitude towards food in the commentary on *Inferno* VI (p. 92), which is clearly derived from the letter *Ad fratres de Monte Dei*, I. xi. 33 ('De condimentis vero sufficiat, obsecro, ut comestibiles fiant cibi nostri, non etiam concupiscibiles, vel delectabiles' – *PL*, 184, col. 329). This and many other pseudo-Bernardine texts, including the *Meditationes piissimae*, can be found in *PL*, 184.

[16] Pietro, *Commentarium*, ed. Nannucci, pp. 92, 544–5, 729.

[17] Ibid., p. 346: 'And Bernard says, that oaths are to be made in a spirit of truthfulness, prayers in a spirit of purity, requests in a spirit of generosity, thanksgivings in a spirit of devotion. For prayer should be faithful, pure, devout, discreet, truthful, and private.'

further, if only because Pietro makes no reference at all to the facts of the historical Bernard's life, even at the moment, used as a cue for biographical excursus by almost every other commentator on *Paradiso*, of the fictional Bernard's appearance in the poem. For Pietro, instead, this development offers a chance to proceed immediately to the explication of Bernard's symbolic meaning:

... fingendo se reliqui a Beatrice. Figura est, quod per theologiam Deum videre et cognoscere non possumus, sed per gratiam et contemplationem. Ideo mediante sancto Bernardo, idest contemplatione, impetratur a Virgine gratia videndi talia, quae per scripturas percipi non possunt.[18]

The airy confidence of that 'idest contemplatione' might be envied by many of those who have struggled since to find a satisfactory explanation of Bernard's role in the poem; but for Pietro its accuracy is confirmed simply enough, by means of a lengthy quotation which conflates two passages from the first chapter of the *Meditationes piissimae* (which Pietro calls *Liber de interiori homine*):

Unde ipse Bernardus in libro de interiori homine ait: cognoscere Deum est vita aeterna, beatitudo perfecta, summa voluptas. Oculus non vidit, nec auris audivit, nec in cor hominis ascendit, quanta charitas, quanta suavitas et jucunditas maneat in nobis in illa visione. Ad quam recolendam, inspiciendam, ut recordor ejus, ea delector, eam contemplor, intueor quid sit Deus in se ipso, quid in Angelis, quid in sanctis, quid in creaturis. In seipso incomprehensibilis, quia principium et finis, principium sine fine. Ex me intelligo quod incomprehensibilis Deus est, quoniam me ipsum intelligere non possum, quem ipse fecit.[19]

The other two 'Bernardine' quotations that occur in the Empyrean cantos both appear in the context of the prayer to Mary in *Paradiso* XXXIII, and are apparently intended to illustrate Bernard's fitness to perform this duty on Dante's behalf. Curiously, although they fulfil

---

[18] Ibid., p. 729: 'saying that Beatrice left him. And this is a sign, that we cannot see and know God through theology, but through grace and contemplation. Thus by means of St Bernard, that is, contemplation, grace is obtained from the Virgin for the seeing of things that cannot be perceived according to the scriptures.'

[19] Ibid., p. 729: ''Wherefore Bernard himself, in his book On the Inner Man, says: to know God is eternal life, perfect beatitude, the highest pleasure. No eye has seen, no ear heard, nor into any human heart has come, that charity, that delight and happiness that dwell in us during that vision. Which is to be reflected upon and examined, that I may remember it, delight in it, contemplate it, and understand what God is in himself, and what he is in the angels, in the saints, and in his creation. In himself he is incomprehensible, because he is the beginning and the end, the beginning without end. From myself alone I can see that God is incomprehensible, for I cannot understand myself, whom God made.' As far as 'illa visione', the text is from *Meditationes piissimae*, I. 3; thereafter, from *MP*, I. I (*PL*, 184, cols. 487, 485).

that function effectively enough, another author is called upon to sanction the poetic enterprise of *Paradiso* XXXIII, one hailing from a very different neck of the cultural woods:

Item autem Bernardus: coelum ridet, Angeli gaudent, mundus exultat, Daemones fugiunt, cum dico, Ave Maria. Ipsa est virga egressa de Jesse, idest de incendio divini amoris, qui fuit cum dedit in mundo ipsam Mariam ut terminum nostrae damnationis... Unde Bernardus: bene est gratia plena, quia per partes ceteris praestatur. Mariae vero se totam simul infudit gratiae plenitudo. Inde, post orationem circa laudes ejus, petit Bernardus ut sua virtute auctor possit oculos intellectus elevare usque ad ipsam Deitatem, et quod postea suos affectus conservet sanos. Ad hoc Juvenalis ait: Orandum est ut sit mens sana in corpore sano.[20]

There could scarcely be a more potent illustration of the Trecento commentators' fundamental eclecticism, their willingness to appropriate material from any potentially authoritative source when it suits their purpose, than this remarkable juxtaposition of Bernard and Juvenal, Christian saint and pagan moralist. The insouciance with which Pietro passes from the florid vocabulary of Marian devotion and visionary mysticism to the pithy materialism of the famous tag from the *Satires*, without, it seems, troubling himself about the possible discrepancy of significance between the Christian and pagan understanding of such words as 'orandum' and 'sanus', impresses by its sheer audacity. Yet there is a sense in which it is profoundly true to the cultural inclusiveness that animates the poem itself, where Dante's own perennially invigorating fusion of Christian and classical cultures (pre-eminently, of course, the Bible and the *Aeneid*) runs like a thread from the first canto of *Inferno* to the last of *Paradiso*, so that the vision of God, no less, can be evoked through a parallel with Neptune's amazement at the sight of the Argonauts (*Par.*, XXXIII. 94–6). As so often, what seem to be lapses of taste or naivety of judgement in the Trecento commentaries in fact conceal a more vital and heartfelt sympathy with the informing spirit of the *Commedia* than any that is readily available to us.

[20] Ibid., pp. 736–7: 'Thus also Bernard: Heaven laughs, the angels rejoice, the world exults, the devils flee, when I say Ave Maria. She is the rod sprung from Jesse, that is, from the fire of divine love, which was when he gave into the world this Mary as the end of our damnation ... Whence Bernard: indeed she is full of grace, because in every way she excels all others. In truth the fullness of grace is all infused into Mary in a single moment. Then, after the oration in her praise, Bernard requests that, by his power, the author may raise the eyes of his intellect as far as the Deity itself, and that afterwards his spirit may be kept in a state of grace. To this Juvenal says: you should pray to have a healthy mind in a healthy body.'

The invention of the *lectura Dantis* as a formally autonomous approach to the exposition of the *Commedia*, apparently in the aborted series given by Giovanni Boccaccio in Florence in the winter of 1373–4, revolutionized the tradition, and eventually produced the outstanding commentaries of the late Trecento, those of Benvenuto da Imola (based on lectures given at Bologna in 1375) and Francesco da Buti (Pisa, c. 1385). A more immediate reaction, however, seems to have been that of an unknown Florentine glossator, whose painstaking but uninspired observations on the poem are attributed (wrongly, as even the earliest editors recognized) to Boccaccio himself in at least one manuscript. The so-called 'Falso Boccaccio' deals briefly with Bernard while glossing *Paradiso* XXXI, in a way that shows how firmly the tradition founded by Lana and continued by Pietro Alighieri had become established by the 1370s:

In questa seconda parte l'altore introdducie un vecchio venerabile il quale da qui inanzi fingie l'altore che questo tal vecchio il debba ghuidare e menare più in suso e che Beatricie lui abandoni e questo fingie l'altore perché qui non bisognia teologia anzi bisognia l'animo contemplativo. E perché san Bernardo fu huomo al mondo molto contemplativo e più devoto della vergine maria che mai niuno altro però fingie l'altore che san Bernardo gli sia qui apparito e che lui il debba ghuidare da qui inanzi esendosi partita Beatricie.[21]

As for the two lecture-based commentaries of the late Trecento, Francesco da Buti's treatment of Bernard as an *auctor* is the reverse of Pietro Alighieri's: he quotes him directly only once (the text is our old friend beginning 'securum accessum habes', which Buti applies to *Paradiso*, XXXIII. 12),[22] but provides substantially accurate biographical details. He knows that Bernard had been the abbot of a monastery, and therefore finds the epithet 'tenero padre' (*Par.*, XXXI. 63) peculiarly fitting,[23] and he claims some acquaintance with Bernard's Marian writings:

E nessuna creatura è sofficiente ad impetrare la divina grazia, quanto la Vergine Maria; e però finge che santo Bernardo li apparisse ad insegnarli a pregare la Vergine Maria, perché nessuno Dottore ne scrisse mai tante belle meditazioni, quante santo Bernardo, come appare nella sua opera.[24]

[21] *Chiose sopra Dante: testo inedito* ['Falso Boccaccio'], edited by Lord Vernon (Florence, 1846), pp. 696–7. I have silently emended the many unorthodox divisions of words in the original text that make reading Vernon's diplomatic transcription such a wearisome experience.

[22] Buti, *Commento*, III, 858.

[23] Ibid., 815: 'E queste condizioni furno in santo Bernardo, quando fu abbate nel mondo al suo monasterio in verso li suoi monaci; e però finge l'autore che con esse a lui si rappresentasse.'

[24] Ibid., 816.

And Buti does not stop there. He goes on, in the commentary on *Paradiso* XXXII, to argue that Bernard's Marian 'meditazioni', perhaps in conjunction with some other work or works of his, are the sole justification for his exalted office in the narrative of *Paradiso*:

E per questo [*Par.*, XXXIII. 1–3] si può comprendere che, poi che l'autore ebbe letto li trattati che fece santo Bernardo de le Meditazioni, ch'elli ebbe delli atti della Vergine Maria, e della gloria sua, elli leggesse alcuno suo trattato dove trattò dell'ordine de' beati; e però fa questa fizione l'autore ch'elli li parlasse in questa forma: imperò che, se questa cagione non fusse, non so perché l'avesse dato più a santo Bernardo che a li altri Dottori, se non fusse già per inducerlo a fare la preghiera a la Vergine Maria, che seguita nel seguente canto ...[25]

It is worth noting that Buti's rather ingenuous admission of inability to understand Dante's choice of Bernard other than in terms of Marian devotion rests on somewhat vague and hypothetical foundations. Though Buti names a specific title in the area of Mariology ('li trattati ... de le Meditazioni, ch'elli ebbe delli atti della Vergine Maria'), it is far from clear exactly to what text(s) this refers. One's immediate reaction, when confronted with the word 'meditazioni' in a Bernardine context, is to think of the hugely popular *Meditazioni della vita di Cristo*, which, as we have seen, are steeped in Bernard's Marian sermons, and could thus, perhaps, have been taken for a work *by* Bernard; but this identification cannot be conclusive. (The hardly less popular *Meditationes piissimae*, so dear to Pietro Alighieri, are not particularly Marian in theme.) Buti's own phrasing, moreover ('alcuno suo trattato'), lays bare his uncertainty about his second reference, to a work 'dell'ordine de' beati'; he seems to think that some such work must exist, and thus that Dante must have read it, but not to have any particular text in mind himself. In short, although Buti insists not just on Bernard's Marian reputation, but on Dante's personal contact with his Marian texts, as the motivation for his appearance in these cantos, the force of his conviction is not matched by the weight of his evidence.

Yet it is presumably the same conviction that inspires his trenchant denial, in the face of one of his most influential colleagues, that Bernard's 'orazione' was written by anyone other than Dante himself:

---

[25] Ibid., 831.

Questa è lo XXXIII canto de la terza cantica del nostro autore, nel quale fa due cose principalmente: imperò che prima lo nostro autore finge che santo Bernardo, pregando per Dante, componesse questa devotissima orazione, la quale veramente compuose elli...[26]

The contemporary against whom Buti seems to be reacting here is Benvenuto da Imola, whose slightly earlier commentary on *Paradiso* shows him to be equally certain of the opposite conclusion:

Sed antequam descendam ad declarandum literam est evidentialiter praenotandum, quod licet autor noster videatur hic fingere quod Bernardus faciat istam orationem, tamen de rei veritate ista fuit oratio Bernardi antequam autor esset in rerum natura. Oratio ergo Bernardi, de qua autor exscripsit aliqua dicta hic inserta est...[27]

Despite his wholly mistaken insistence on this point, the set of commentaries associated with Benvenuto's Bolognese *lecturae Dantis* of 1375 remains the most interesting body of writing about Bernard of Clairvaux – as about much else – in Trecento criticism of the *Commedia*. As well as the text prepared by Benvenuto himself between 1375 and 1380 – one version of which is extant only in manuscript, while the other formed the basis of Lacaita's 1887 edition, the high point of nineteenth-century textual criticism of the Trecento commentaries – these include a *recollectio* of the original lectures, taken down at the time by a listener and mistaken by its modern editors for an independent commentary by Stefano Talice da Ricaldone, the copyist of the work's unique (but late fifteenth-century) manuscript;[28] and the commentary of Giovanni Bertoldi da Serravalle, commissioned by two English bishops and written between 1415 and 1417, during the (apparently copious) spare time afforded by Serravalle's participation in the Council of Constance. Despite its comparatively late date, this commentary is heavily dependent on

---

[26] Ibid., 856.

[27] Benvenuto da Imola, *Comentum super Dantis Aldigherii Comediam*, edited by G. F. Lacaita, 5 vols. (Florence, 1887), v, 506–7; 'But before I begin to expound the literal meaning it is obviously necessary to state that our author here chooses to pretend that it is Bernard who makes this speech, when in fact it was a speech of Bernard's long before the author had come into the world. This is thus a prayer of Bernard, from which the author has made some extracts, that is inserted here...'

[28] For the background to this convoluted episode in the history of Dante commentary, see the relevant *voci* in the *Enciclopedia dantesca* ('Benvenuto da Imola', I, 593–6, by Francesco Mazzoni; 'Talice, Stefano da Ricaldone', v, 513–4, by Vittorio Russo), with their bibliographies; and two fundamental articles by Michele Barbi: 'Benvenuto da Imola e non Stefano Talice da Ricaldone', in *Problemi di critica dantesca: prima serie* (Florence, 1934), pp. 429–53, and 'La lettura di Benvenuto da Imola e i suoi rapporti con altri commenti', in *Problemi di critica dantesca: seconda serie* (Florence, 1941), pp. 435–70.

both Benvenuto and 'Talice', though in significantly differing degrees. Taken as an interconnected group, these texts reveal both a thorough grounding in Bernard's life and works and a highly developed interpretation of his role in the *Commedia*, neither of which is matched by any other Trecento commentary.

The 'Talice' commentary includes a short biography of Bernard, which shows a sound knowledge of a reliable source – probably, though not necessarily, the *Vita prima*:

Auctor hucusque omnia viderat preter Deum; et non poterat ipsum videre, nisi cum licentia Regine celi, scilicet Marie. Nec poterat impetrare licentiam ab ea, nisi per unum suum familiarem, scilicet Bernardum. Qui fuit de Burgundia, nobilis et pulcher corpore, et ditissimus; et tamen omnia dimisit, et reduxit se ad locum solitudinis. Et secum traxit quinque suos fratres; deinde patrem et sororem. Primo, quando ivit ad contemplationem, nesciebat litteras; nec habuit alios magistros, ut ipse dicit, nisi quercus et fagos. Et evasit maximus doctor, et multos fecit pulcherrimos libros in divina scriptura, et suavibus et dulcibus latinis et dictis. Et sunt forte ducenti anni, quibus fuit; et fuit devotissimus Marie.[29]

There is more accurate information about Bernard in this brief paragraph than in all the other Trecento commentaries put together; and it is supplemented elsewhere in 'Talice' by biographical allusions to Bernard's monastic background. The context for these is the eulogy of St Francis and his Order in *Paradiso* XI: 'Talice' begins by criticizing Bernard and his followers, along with those of Augustine and Benedict, for contributing to the decline in ecclesiastical morality that had reached its nadir in the time of the Emperor Frederick II; but the text goes on to defend Bernard (and others) against the implication (*Paradiso*, XI. 61–6) that no-one before Francis had led a life of true poverty. This seems not to be true, says 'Talice', because Bernard, Utacarius [*sic*; *sc.* Macarius?], Benedict, Anthony, Augustine, and many others had practised poverty.[30] (The solution to this

---

[29] La '*Commedia*' di Dante Alighieri col commento inedito di Stefano Talice da Ricaldone, edited by Vincenzo Promis and Carlo Negroni, 3 vols. (Milan, 1888), III, 388: 'So far the author has seen everything except God; and he could not see him, without the permission of the Queen of Heaven, that is, Mary. Nor could he get permission from her, without going through one of her devotees, namely Bernard. Who was from Burgundy, a nobleman, physically handsome, and very rich; and yet he left all this, and withdrew to a place of solitude. And with him he took five of his brothers; and later his father and sister. When first he started out in contemplation, he was illiterate; nor did he have other teachers, as he himself says, than the oaks and the beeches. And he turned out to be a man of great learning, and wrote many very beautiful books about divine scripture, in a sweet and pleasing Latin style. And it is about two hundred years, since he was alive; and he was very devoted to Mary.'

[30] 'Talice', *Commento*, III, 144, 147.

apparent contradiction is that here Dante's text speaks 'anthono-mastically' – that is, that Francis' poverty was unequalled in degree but not unique in nature.)

Concentration on Bernard as monk is a notably individual feature of the 'Talice' commentary, which, in this respect, goes well beyond the passing references of a Jacopo della Lana or a Francesco da Buti. But its idiosyncrasies do not end there. In the gloss on *Purgatorio*, xxix. 143–4, the 'vecchio solo' who walks in procession 'dormendo, con la faccia arguta', is identified as Bernard, because he was, in life, 'venerabilis senex et solus' ('a venerable and solitary old man'), and therefore often lost in 'immensam speculationem' ('profound speculation').[31] As we shall see, this unusual detail reappears in Benvenuto's own version of the commentary, which seems to guarantee that it originated with Benvenuto himself, rather than with the anonymous editor responsible for the 'Talice' version.[32] Moreover, as if to compensate for this extra appearance by Bernard outside the Empyrean, 'Talice' makes very little of his part in *Paradiso* itself, including no quotation from Bernard, and only scattered references to him, in the commentary on the poem's closing cantos. The most intriguing of these is the explanation of Dante-character's doctrinal question to Bernard at *Paradiso*, xxxii. 100–5:

Nunc autor petit Bernardum. Et non mireris si Dantes facit ei tantum honorem, quia fuit excellentissimus doctor; sed nunquam fuit canonizatus, quia dixit multa mala de pastoribus Ecclesie. Sed merita sua canonizaverunt ipsum per totum orbem.[33]

This striking mixture of insight and inaccuracy – for although Bernard did indeed both say and write 'multa mala' about his ecclesiastical colleagues and superiors, this did not prevent him from being canonized, by Pope Alexander III in 1174 – is followed by a

---

[31] Ibid., ii, 384.

[32] The idea that the 'vecchio solo' is Bernard was also known to 'Falso Boccaccio', though he does not commit himself to it: 'Ancora dicie l'altore che dietro a tutti chostoro veniva un vecchio solo. Alquanti intendono di san bernardo altri di san govanni [*sic*] vangielista ch'essendo addormentato nel genbo [*sic*; *sc.* grembo] di Cristo vide tutta la divinità' (p. 489). It would be interesting to know if the 'alquanti' are Benvenuto and his admirers, or if they are other readers of *Purgatorio* whose ideas went unrecorded or have been lost over time. The commentaries associated with Benvenuto are the only surviving ones to include this detail, apart from 'Falso Boccaccio' itself.

[33] 'Talice', *Commento*, iii, 403: 'Now the author asks Bernard a question. And do not be surprised if Dante pays him such a tribute, because he was a man of enormous learning; but he was never canonized, because he spoke much evil of the pastors of the Church. But his merits canonized him throughout the world.'

fairly lengthy account of a reproof allegedly addressed by Bernard to his erstwhile disciple Pope Eugenius III. 'Talice' appears, however, to be standing at some distance from history here: although his text is certainly similar in spirit to ideas expressed on occasion by Bernard, nothing verbally akin to it occurs either in *De consideratione*, Bernard's handbook on the privileges and perils of being Pope, or in any of his several letters to Eugenius. Both the image of an uncanonized Bernard and this stress on his role as papal mentor remain unique to the 'Talice' commentary.

The commentary which goes under Benvenuto's own name, and which was prepared by his own hand, shows a somewhat different set of preoccupations from those which dominate the picture of Bernard in the 'Talice' version. Bernard is still thought of as 'senex venerabilis et doctor magnus' ('a venerable old man and a great teacher'), 'valde solitarius' ('most solitary'), and 'contemplativus nimis' ('exceedingly contemplative') into the bargain; and these flattering designations are duly applied to the mystically entranced old man of *Purgatorio* xxix, whom Benvenuto, here as in the 'Talice' commentary, resolutely identifies with Bernard.[34] He also supplies a spirited defence of the identification, thereby revealing that he knew it to be contentious; he dismisses St John and St Thomas Aquinas as candidates on the grounds of their relative youth, while the objection that Bernard cannot appear twice in the poem is confronted with the argument that, along with Saints Peter, Paul, and John – whom Benvenuto, though by no means every commentator, also finds in the procession – Bernard has a doubly representative role, appearing here in the Church Militant, in *Paradiso* in the Church Triumphant. (Later readers have remained sternly unconvinced.) The detailed biography in the earlier version has now, however, been reduced to its bare bones:

Ad intelligentiam autem pleniorem huius passus est sciendum, quod iste senex erat beatus Bernardus abbas Clarevallensis, qui fuit luculentus doctor et instituit ordinem etc.[35]

The particular stress in 'Talice' on Bernard's monastic career has also been substantially modified: to the stark phrase just quoted, Benvenuto adds only that the comparison of Bernard to a 'tenero

---

[34] Benvenuto, *Comentum*, IV, 202.

[35] Ibid., v, 474: 'For the fuller understanding of this passage it is necessary to know that this old man was blessed Bernard, abbot of Clairvaux, who was a brilliant man of learning and founded an order, etc.'

padre' is apt because 'fuit enim optimus paterfamilias, qui tot filios spiritualiter genuit et bonam curam gessit familiae' ('for he was an excellent father, who sired so many sons in the spirit and took good care of his family').[36] Thus it would not be correct to say that the Benvenuto of the later version seems to know or care less about Bernard than the Benvenuto of the 'Talice' version: indeed, the addition of the adjective 'beatus' to Bernard's title may suggest that Benvenuto had carried out further research into Bernard's canonization in the interval between giving the lectures and writing the commentary (or else, of course, that it was an unauthorized interpolation by the 'Talice' editor that denied Bernard his saintly status in the first place). It does seem, however, that the ways in which Bernard appealed to Benvenuto's interest have changed, or at least that the commentator himself was keen to highlight and develop them in a way that the listener (or editor) who prepared the 'Talice' commentary was unable or unwilling to do. In the full version of Benvenuto's text, the presentation of Bernard is dominated, to an extent unparalleled in any other Trecento commentary, by the three issues pinpointed above (in chapter 2) as central to the saint's reputation in the Middle Ages: contemplation, Marian devotion, and eloquence.

The first two of these features emerge as Benvenuto, like all commentators on *Paradiso* before and since, is wrestling with the questions raised by Beatrice's startling departure from Dante's side and Bernard's equally unexpected appearance in her place:

Et ad clariorem intelligentiam dicendorum est hic praenotandum, quod auctor ductu Beatricis hucusque vidit omnes ordines beatorum et angelorum, et omnem formam paradisi in generali: nunc autem ascensurus ad tribunal aeterni regis non fidit nec praesumit posse pervenire ad illud nisi mediante intercessione Mariae: ideo elegantissime introducit beatum Bernardum, qui commendat eum isti reginae, ut dignetur eum licet immeritum, gratia sua juvare, ut possit suis intercessionibus ad hoc tribunal attingere; quoniam iste Bernardus fuit inter caeteros devotissimus istius clementissimae dominae. Et bene fingit ipsum Bernardum missum ad se precibus Beatricis, tum quia fuit bonus doctor theologiae, ideo verus alumnus Beatricis; tum quia fuit maxime contemplativus, et Beatrix sedet in sede contemplationis.[37]

---

[36] Ibid.
[37] Ibid., v, 478–9: 'And for a clearer understanding of what must be said it is necessary to state first that the author, guided by Beatrice, has so far seen all the orders of the blessed and the angels, and the whole form of Paradise in general; but now, being about to ascend to the court of the eternal king, he neither believes nor presumes that he can attain that height

So, for Benvenuto, the Bernard who was both learned in the things of the intellect ('bonus doctor theologiae') and skilled in the science of the soul ('maxime contemplativus') is especially fitted to be 'alumnus' of the Beatrice whom Benvenuto consistently identifies as the personification, on the symbolic level, of Theology itself; and thus he acts as her replacement when Dante *personaggio* needs an advocate before the throne of the Virgin, to whom the historical Bernard was, of course, devoted in the superlative degree ('devotissimus istius clementissimae dominae').

Such attribution of Bernard's presence in the poem to these two factors is, as we have seen, familiar in the commentary tradition from Jacopo della Lana onwards, and was to become time-worn indeed through later centuries of exegesis. But Benvenuto has up his sleeve, as it were, a more original contribution to the Trecento commentaries' view of the abbot of Clairvaux, one that clinches the argument about Bernard's selection for his office and justifies the compliment Benvenuto pays to Dante on his choice ('elegantissime introducit beatum Bernardum'). It becomes explicit when Benvenuto turns to gloss the great prayer to the Virgin in *Paradiso* XXXIII (which, as noted above, he believed Bernard himself to have written):

[F]*issi nell'oratore*, idest, Bernardo, qui fuit orator Domini: fuit enim de rei veritate luculentus orator, quia habuit dulcem et claram eloquentiam cum florido et polito stylo, sicut patet intuenti dicta ejus; fuit etiam orator, idest precator devotissimus, sicut patet ex praemissa oratione dulcissima et aliis multis quas vidi. Et vere Bernardus fuit bonus orator, et faciliter et affabiliter dixit bonum et malum, sicut de romanis et praelatis romanae ecclesiae ...[38]

This passage is of unusual interest from a number of points of view. Most significant, perhaps, is the central importance in it of the word

without the intercession of Mary. Therefore he most elegantly introduces blessed Bernard, to commend him to the queen, that she may deign, although he is unworthy, to assist him with her grace, that he may, by her prayers, arrive at that court. For this Bernard was the most devoted of all men to that most merciful lady. And he aptly pretends that Bernard was sent to him by the prayers of Beatrice, first because he was a good scholar of theology, and therefore a true disciple of Beatrice; and second, because he was a very great contemplative, and Beatrice sits on the throne of contemplation.'

[38] Ibid., v, 513–14: '*Fixed on the speaker*, that is, on Bernard, who was the orator of the Lord: for he was in truth a brilliant orator, because he had a sweet and clear eloquence with a polished and colourful style, as is clear to anyone who studies his words; and he was also an orator in that he was most skilled in prayer, as is clear from the oration quoted above and many others that I have seen. And indeed Bernard was a good orator, and with facility and affability he spoke good and evil, as he did of the Romans and the prelates of the Roman church...'

'orator', given by Benvenuto its double sense of both 'one who speaks' and 'one who prays': not only is Bernard an orator because he possesses eloquence and an elegant literary style, but also because he is a 'precator devotissimus'. This fusion of verbal dexterity and spiritual profundity is precisely, in my view, the aspect of the historical Bernard of Clairvaux that appealed to Dante *poeta* and caused him to pick Bernard out from the massed ranks of contemplatives and devotees of Mary who might otherwise have been qualified for this particular role; and Benvenuto was definitely the first commentator to perceive the importance of eloquence as the third element in the equation, linking contemplation and Marian devotion by enabling both experiences to be given powerful expression.

It is also worth remarking that Benvenuto judges Bernard's eloquence to be a matter of writing as well as of speech: all the terms he uses to evoke it ('dulcem et claram eloquentiam', 'florido et polito stylo', 'dicta eius') combine to give the impression of equal expertise in written and spoken delivery, for the benefit of an 'intuens' who may, semantically, be either a reader reading or a listener listening; and, as the present tense of 'patet' twice indicates, the chance to appreciate that eloquence is not confined to those who were able to hear Bernard in the flesh, but is available to anyone who reads his 'orationes' in the present day.

Secondly, the passage raises tantalizing questions about Benvenuto's own access to Bernard's writings. He claims to have studied many of these ('aliis multis quas vidi'), and his reference to Bernard's comments about the Roman people and the prelates of the Church may suggest – as did, however vaguely, the similar but much longer passage in the 'Talice' commentary, examined above – that the text which attracted him the most was *De consideratione*, in which Romans and ecclesiastics alike are soundly lashed by Bernard's scathing tongue (or pen). (Notice, however, that the 'Talice' image of Bernard is somewhat toned down in the Benvenuto version: the 'multa mala' that Bernard there uttered 'de pastoribus Ecclesiae' have not only become 'bonum et malum' – a more even-handed treatment, it would appear – but are delivered 'faciliter et affabiliter', a characterization that may surprise those familiar with Bernard's talent for invective.) Yet neither here nor in the 'Talice' commentary does Benvenuto allude directly to any specific work of Bernard's, and the attribution to him of the prayer in *Paradiso* XXXIII certainly offers some grounds for doubting that Benvenuto was as deeply immersed in Bernard's 'dulcissimae orationes' as he suggests, since he could not, as he implicitly claims, have found it among them.

The only trace of direct reference to a Bernardine title comes, in fact, in the commentary on the description of Bernard as 'colui ch'abbelliva di Maria / come del sole stella mattutina' (*Par.*, XXXII. 107–8):

Et est comparatio propria, quia sicut Venus stella matutina associat solem in cursu suo et illuminatur prae caeteris ab eo; ita Bernardus tamquam stella qui fuit doctor, et doctores figurantur in forma stellarum in corpore solis, sicut ostensum est supra capitulo huius Paradisi, associavit Mariam ex summa devotione et compassione: unde devotissime describit planctum eius, et ideo bene prae caeteris illuminatur ab ea.[39]

Although no authentic *Planctus Mariae* by Bernard is known to exist, the genre was a popular one in the late Middle Ages, and nothing could be more natural than that some such text should have become attached to Bernard's name; in particular, a dramatic lament beginning 'Quis dabit capiti meo aquam?' ('Who will pour water on my head?') is not infrequently attributed to Bernard (though also to Augustine and Anselm), under such titles as *De lamentatione Beatae Mariae Virginis* or *Liber de compassione Beatae Mariae Virginis*, and this, or something very like it, may be the text that Benvenuto has in mind at this point.[40]

Whatever the exact extent of his acquaintance with Bernard's writings, it is at least clear that the great Cistercian was a figure of major significance for Benvenuto, and that the crucial element in the image of Bernard that is adumbrated in 'Talice' and elaborated in the fuller version of Benvenuto's commentary is that Bernard is not merely a contemplative and an ardent follower of Mary, but also a man universally renowned for eloquence. Whether in the polished style of his sermons, the sweetness of his prayers, or the affable facility

[39] Ibid., v, 499: 'And it is a fitting image, because just as Venus the morning star follows the sun in its course and is illuminated by it above all others, so Bernard is like a star because he was a man of learning, and the men of learning are depicted in the form of stars in the body of the sun, as was shown above in another chapter of this Paradise, and he followed Mary out of the highest devotion and fellow-feeling; and so he most devoutly describes her lament, and thus indeed he is illuminated by her above all others.'

[40] See André Wilmart, *Auteurs spirituels et textes dévots du Moyen Age latin* (Paris, 1971; original edition, 1932), pp. 422, 456, 517 n. 1. Mentioning the Song of Songs in his commentary on *Purgatorio* xxx, Benvenuto (*Comentum*, IV, 206) remarks in passing that Bernard 'pulcre scribit super istum librum' ('writes beautifully about that book') – a phrase which, while not involving the actual citation of a title, leaves little room for doubt that Benvenuto knew Bernard's sermons *In Cantica canticorum*.

of his diatribes against errant clerics and feckless Romans, Bernard is always, for Benvenuto, 'luculentus orator' in the fullest possible sense.

This fortunate conjunction of features in a single historical individual explains, in Benvenuto's eyes, Dante's apparently bizarre choice of substitute for Beatrice; and it is in terms derived from these that he interprets Bernard's figural role in the poem: the learned and eloquent theologian, appearing simultaneously as advocate before Mary and as protégé of the Beatrice who has taken her seat 'in sede contemplationis', thus comes to personify both his historical self and the triple basis of his activity in the poem. The successful integration of Bernard of Clairvaux into the narrative and symbolic scheme of the Empyrean cantos, where other commentators (think of Francesco da Buti) had found him problematic and even intrusive, is one of Benvenuto da Imola's greatest gifts to the history of commentary on the *Commedia*.

The main lines of Giovanni da Serravalle's account of Bernard follow those laid down by Benvenuto, as is only to be expected, given the generally backward-looking orientation of his commentary and its consistent reliance on the model that Benvenuto's work offered; but it is noteworthy that Serravalle relies more obviously on the 'Talice' commentary than on Benvenuto's own version. Dealing with *Paradiso* XXXI, he paraphrases the 'Talice' biography of Bernard with some skill, changing many details of vocabulary, but presenting exactly the same material in very nearly the same order.[41] (He is, however, sufficiently conscientious to update his source where necessary: where 'Talice', in 1375, refers to Bernard as having lived 'forte ducenti anni' previously, Serravalle, in 1417, is careful to note that two hundred *and forty* years have passed since Bernard was alive.) So closely does Serravalle follow 'Talice' that it may be doubted whether he had the first-hand knowledge of a biographical source that Benvenuto – or the 'Talice' editor – probably did.

Elsewhere, Serravalle's portrayal conforms to what is now a familiar pattern. Bernard is 'valde contemplativus et solitarius' ('very contemplative and solitary'), 'inter omnes devotos Beatae Virginis ... singularissimus' ('most exceptional among all the devotees of the Blessed Virgin'), 'optimus rethoricus' ('an excellent

---

[41] *Fratris Johannis de Serravalle translatio et comentum totius libri Dantis Aldigherii, cum textu italico Fratris Bartholomaei a Colle*, edited by Marcellino da Civezza and Teofilo Domenichelli (Prato, 1891), p. 1184.

rhetorician').[42] He thus reproduces the three cardinal points of Benvenuto's reading of Bernard, while adding practically nothing of his own except a flair for thinking of synonyms. Indeed, Serravalle's commentary omits the idiosyncratic details of both the 'Talice' version (Bernard's failure to be canonized) and Benvenuto's (his authorship of the prayer to the Virgin), though he is loyal enough to adopt the equally idiosyncratic identification of the 'vecchio' of *Purgatorio* xxix as Bernard. His is a cautious and derivative account, relying on Benvenuto's precedent for its substance, but lacking the confidence to follow its mentor beyond the limits of convention into more speculative interpretation. (A more sympathetic view, of course, might be that Serravalle had decided that the idiosyncrasies of Benvenuto and 'Talice' were unreliable enough to be discarded; in which case, it is a pity that he did not make this putative – and unprecedented – declaration of independence a little more explicit.)

At all events, Serravalle's commentary marks, with exemplary clarity, the end of an exegetical era. Distant by nearly a century from Dante himself, and by more than four decades even from the text in whose footsteps it follows most doggedly, Serravalle's *Comentum*, while it no doubt gladdened the hearts of his episcopal patrons, still embodies, in both its critical assumptions and its analytical methods, the attitudes that had underpinned Dante commentary since the 1320s but were to cease to do so during the fifteenth century. Comparison with Cristoforo Landino's commentary, which appeared just over half a century later, reveals the extent to which Serravalle's work belies its Quattrocento date. Landino, steeped in Platonism and condescending towards his Trecento predecessors, evaluates and interprets the *Commedia* in ways unthinkable to them, while Serravalle, standing unawares on the threshold of the Renaissance, writes a commentary that Jacopo della Lana would have recognized and Benvenuto da Imola might well have called his own.[43] It is no coincidence that serious critical interest in Bernard of Clairvaux also ends with Serravalle, not to resurface until the antiquarian commentators of the nineteenth century came to tackle *Paradiso*, armed with a historical understanding of the Middle Ages,

---

[42] Serravalle, *Translatio*, pp. 768, 1184, 1207.

[43] See Landino's commentary, f. 1r., for his attitude towards his predecessors: even though they had said 'many things worthy of their learning and by no means useless to the listener', they had corrupted the poem with 'the barbarism of many foreign dialects'. Landino, accordingly, wishes 'to examine Dante's mind and intentions from a loftier starting-point, and ... to investigate his more abstruse doctrine.'

not to mention a generally positive estimation of the worth of medieval culture, that the commentators of the Renaissance and the Enlightenment, by and large, did not and could not possess.

As far as their treatment of Bernard goes, the Trecento commentators, from Lana to Serravalle, are – inevitably, no doubt – men of their times. They know about, and duly underscore in their commentaries, those aspects of his achievement that had been consecrated by cultural tradition long before the Trecento: contemplation, monasticism, Mariology, and, in Benvenuto's case at least, eloquence. They have varying degrees of biographical expertise, probably derived from the *Vita prima* or one of the more substantial later hagiographies (Benvenuto, 'Talice', and Serravalle also use material taken from the *Legenda aurea*, such as the fanciful etymology of Bernard's name that connects him with the sweet-smelling nard, *ber-nardus*).[44] They have read, or claim to have read, some, perhaps many, of his writings. They have a profound respect for him as a historical figure which, while not exceeding that paid to the greatest saints of the past (Augustine, Jerome, Gregory), is still deeper than that due to any modern saint except Thomas Aquinas (as the relative frequency of Pietro Alighieri's citations implies). This respect, in turn, inspires their attempts to document and justify his involvement in the poem's narrative, and to provide persuasive explanations for it in terms of symbol. Bernard of Clairvaux, monk, mystic, Mariologist, and, above all, 'orator' of both the written and the spoken word, was evidently a living figure in the culture of their century; and the fascinatingly disparate ways in which they respond to the *Commedia*'s textual simulacrum of him throw revealing light on the particular importance he seems also to have had for Dante.

[44] Benvenuto, *Comentum*, v, 480; for other instances see chapter 2, n. 59, above.

# CHAPTER 5

# Dante, Bernard, and the Virgin Mary

Although, as we have just seen, the attempt to explain Dante's choice of Bernard of Clairvaux as substitute for Beatrice begins with the very earliest commentators on the *Commedia*, they and all their successors face the same difficulty: the paucity of relevant textual material on which to base their analyses. Outside *Paradiso* XXXI–XXXIII, in fact, only one reference to Bernard appears anywhere in the corpus ascribed to Dante; and the reason for what will seem to some an overly cautious turn of phrase is that this unique reference occurs in the *Letter to Can Grande* (*Epistolae*, XIII), whose Dantean paternity has been the object of increasingly frequent – and increasingly persuasive – attacks in recent years.[1]

If the Can Grande letter is 'genuine', as the rhetoric of disputed authorship would have it, its mention of Bernard (*Ep.*, XIII. 80) would show that Dante respected him as an authority in the field of contemplative theology, on a par with Richard of St Victor and Augustine; and it would strongly suggest (though perhaps not quite prove) that Dante had read *De consideratione*, which is cited in the *Letter* on a reading-list of basic mystical texts that also includes Richard's *De contemplatione* and Augustine's *De quantitate animae*.[2] If the *Letter* is not genuine, of course, these things would still be true of some anonymous intellectual of the early 1320s – in itself a useful and

---

[1] Especially substantial contributions to the debate about the *Letter* and its authenticity have been made in recent years by Peter Dronke, *Dante and Medieval Latin Traditions* (Cambridge, 1986), pp. 103–11; Henry Ansgar Kelly, *Tragedy and Comedy from Dante to Pseudo-Dante* (Berkeley and Los Angeles, 1989); Ralph G. Hall and Madison U. Sowell, '*Cursus* in the Can Grande Epistle: A Forger Shows his Hand?', *Lectura Dantis*, 5 (1989), 89–104; and Carlo Paolazzi, 'Nozione di "comedìa" e tradizione retorica nella dantesca *Epistola a Cangrande*', in *Dante e la 'Comedìa' nel Trecento* (Milan, 1989), pp. 3–110.

[2] See my '"Quae non licet homini loqui": The Ineffability of Mystical Experience in *Paradiso* I and the *Epistle to Can Grande*', *Modern Language Review*, 83 (1988), 332–41, for a detailed study of the reference to Bernard in its epistolary context.

worthwhile, though perhaps slightly less glamorous, piece of information.

The element of doubt regarding the *Letter*'s authorship has, in many cases, deterred scholars from leaning too heavily on it as concrete evidence for Dante's own reading, thinking, or belief; and, in the particular case of Bernard, this justifiable circumspection has meant that critical examination of his place in Dante's intellectual and spiritual formation has always started from, and usually been confined to, close reading of the three cantos in which the character bearing his name appears. This is especially true of the Trecento commentators, who, although many of them seem to have known the *Letter* in some form, never (before Filippo Villani in the very early fifteenth century) either mention it directly or attribute it to Dante. Not one of them, when dealing with the Bernard of *Paradiso*, so much as hints at the reference in the Can Grande letter; their Bernard is exclusively that of the *Commedia*.

It follows that speculation about Dante's view of Bernard and its extra-textual ramifications has always found its double focus in the text of *Paradiso*: in the words put into the Bernard character's mouth and in the actions which that character is represented as carrying out. Attention to both these facets of Dante's Bernard – or indeed any other character in the *Commedia* – is indispensable, for it is not only unwise but, in practical terms, impossible to separate the ideas and emotions expressed, or the doctrinal information expounded, by Bernard as an individual, from the part he has to play in the system of universal order that *Paradiso* depicts (and which is, in a urgently real sense, its true subject). The *Commedia*'s characters should not be extracted altogether from their narrative context, nor should the speeches they address to Dante *personaggio* (or anyone else) be considered in isolation from the actions they choose – or are compelled – to perform. (That way lie the Romantic and neo-Romantic readings and misreadings that continue to offer such fertile terrain for anachronism and projection of our own concerns on to Dante and his text.)[3] Every individual in the *Commedia*, in short, even (and perhaps most potently) those who do not actually speak – Paolo

---

[3] This interpretative vice, if such it be, is, of course, usually traced back to Francesco De Sanctis; two more recent studies that exemplify both the genuine strengths and the glaring weaknesses of the (neo-)Romantic approach are Glauco Cambon, 'Dante's Noble Sinners: Abstract Examples or Living Characters?', in *Dante's Craft: Studies in Language and Style* (Minneapolis, 1969), pp. 67–79; and Thomas Goddard Bergin, 'Lectura Dantis: *Inferno* V', *Lectura Dantis*, 1 (1987), 5–24.

Malatesta, Geri del Bello, Archbishop Ruggieri – could make his or her own the words of Gerard Manley Hopkins's kingfisher: 'What I do is me: for that I came.'[4]

For all that they had not read Hopkins, the medieval commentators on *Paradiso* recognized that Bernard's actions in the poem spoke, if not louder than his words, at least at equal volume with them. So throughout their consideration of his puzzling irruption into the narrative of *Paradiso* runs a concern with what Bernard *does*, as well as with what he says. Commentators from Jacopo della Lana onwards were quick to notice that what the Bernard of the *Commedia* does is, essentially, to present Dante to the Virgin Mary, as a supplicant for the grace that will enable him to proceed to the direct and unmediated vision of God; and they were equally quick to connect that role with the historical fact of Bernard of Clairvaux's voluminous production and outstanding reputation as a writer on themes of Marian devotion, and to conclude that this was either the major or the only reason for Dante's choice of his as the last voice (other than the narrator's) to make itself heard in the poem.[5]

Other reasons, of course, can be and have been adduced: Bernard's fame as a contemplative, his commitment to the cause of ecclesiastical and monastic reform, perhaps (as I would contend) his reputation for eloquence in preaching and prayer; and it may be that all these – and more – were operative in qualifying Bernard for his exalted position in Dante's scheme. But dozens of scholars, from the Trecento to the present day, have accepted the basic reasoning outlined above, and have posited the historical Bernard's devotion to Mary as the catalyst for both the fictional Bernard's speeches and his actions in the *Commedia*.[6]

---

[4] See *The Oxford Authors: Gerard Manley Hopkins*, edited by Catherine Phillips (Oxford, 1986), p. 129.

[5] Lana, *Commento*, III, 471; Buti, *Commento*, III, 831; Benvenuto, *Comentum*, V, 478–9; Serravalle, *Translatio*, p. 1184.

[6] See, for example, Edward Moore, *Studies in Dante*, edited by Colin Hardie, 4 vols. (Oxford, 1968; original edition, 1896–1917), II, 62n.; *La 'Divina Commedia' di Dante Alighieri*, edited by Francesco Torraca (Milan, 1920; first edition, 1905), p. 929; Giovanni Busnelli, *Il concetto e l'ordine del 'Paradiso' dantesco*, 2 vols. (Città di Castello, 1911–12), I, 243; *Die 'Göttliche Komödie': Kommentar*, edited by Hermann Gmelin, 3 vols. (Stuttgart, 1954–7), III, 526–7; *The 'Divine Comedy'*, translated with a commentary by Charles S. Singleton, 3 vols. (Princeton, 1971–5), III, part 2, 527; Romano Guardini, 'Bernhard von Clairvaux in Dantes *Göttlicher Komödie*', in *Unterscheidung des Christlichen: Gesammelte Studien 1923–1963* (Mainz, 1963), pp. 558–68 (p. 564); Giorgio Petrocchi, 'Dante e la mistica di san Bernardo', in *Letteratura e critica: studi in onore di Natalino Sapegno*, edited by Walter Binni and others, 4 vols. (Rome, 1974), I, 213–29 (p. 224); Philip McNair, 'Dante's Vision of God: An Exposition of *Paradiso* XXXIII', in *Essays in Honour of John Humphreys Whitfield*, edited by H. C. Davis and others

This, however, was only the initial stage of the enquiry into the relationship between Dante, Bernard, and the Virgin Mary. It was, inevitably and necessarily, followed by attempts to see whether the actual writings on which Bernard's Marian reputation rested, as distinct from the reputation itself, had had, or could have had, any direct or formative influence on Dante's thinking about Mary, or had left any tangible traces in the text of the *Commedia*. The first to suggest that this was so seems to have been Francesco da Buti, as described in chapter 4, but he goes no further than a vague, if confident, assertion that Dante had read Bernard's Marian 'meditazioni' – whatever they may be. It was left to later scholars, equipped with a more rigorously philological attitude towards relationships between texts, to pursue the question more keenly. The first systematic attempt comes from the middle of the nineteenth century; and, as we shall see, since then several scholars have sought to revise or improve on each other's findings, and to add to the list of proposed *riscontri* between Bernard's work and Dante's.

The part of the *Commedia* to which the closest attention has been paid is, naturally enough, the prayer to the Virgin that opens *Paradiso* XXXIII: not only is this Dante's most sustained, effective, and theologically complex piece of writing about Mary, it is also, of course, put in the mouth of Bernard himself. Here, if anywhere, the unspoken assumption runs, contact will have been – nay, must have been – established between Dante and the historical Bernard. In this chapter, however, I shall argue that much of this attention has been misdirected; that the conclusions reached in this area not infrequently owe more to wishful thinking than to common sense or critical acumen; and that those who seek to put Bernard forward as the chief and conscious inspiration of Dante's Mariology have sometimes been led to overestimate his importance at the expense of other, no less relevant, factors. The question of Dante's putative indebtedness to Bernard for his vision of Mary, both in general and in particular, is, in fact, nicely illustrative of the difficulties involved in considering the transmission of 'influence' from one medieval writer to another, and of the ever-present danger of jumping to conclusions that we would like to be true, but which the evidence is not as ready to confirm as we are to accept.

(London, 1975), pp. 13–29 (p. 14). These names are no more than a representative selection of scholars who have considered the question especially closely; many more might have been cited.

There is no shortage of books that examine the several appearances made by the Virgin Mary, as both idea and character, in the various works of Dante. Some of these are no more than manuals of devotion . aimed at the edification of the pious reader, but others, especially those of more recent date, incline towards a more critical view of Dante's Marian writing.[7] It has been pointed out, for instance, that Dante nowhere explores the 'theology of Mary' at any great length: outside cantos XXIII and XXXIII of *Paradiso* – which are largely, though not wholly, devoted to her – references to Mary are scattered and infrequent, and are often no more than nominal allusions. This is especially true of the minor works, where Mary's name appears a handful of times in the *Vita nuova* and the *Convivio*, once in the *Monarchia* and once in the letter *Cardinalibus ytalicis* (*Ep.*, XI). Yet some of these references, incidental though they may seem, still hint at themes that are developed in the *Commedia*, and there become familiar features of Dante's Marian thought. Thus Mary is called 'Virgin Mother' outside *Paradiso*, as at *Monarchia*, II. xi. 6 and *Epistolae*, XI. 3; and other essential characteristics to which Dante will later give more elaborate treatment are also sketched in his early works, such as Mary's humility. Note how the paradoxical combination of that humility with outstanding merit and divine election, eventually to be the motive force of *Paradiso*, XXXIII. 1–3, is here, in *Vita nuova*, XXXIV, already found in germ:

> Era venuta ne la mente mia
> la gentil donna, che per suo valore
> fu posta da l'altissimo Signore
> nel ciel de l'umiltate, ov'è Maria.

The idea that Mary was pre-ordained to her destiny by divine will emerges in *Convivio*, IV. v. 5 ('ordinata fu una progenie santissima, de la quale dopo molti meriti nascesse una femmina ottima di tutte l'altre, la quale fosse camera del Figliuolo di Dio') long before reaching its full flowering in *Paradiso*, XXXIII. 3 ('termine fisso d'etterno consiglio'); and indeed the introduction to this passage from the *Convivio* (IV. v. 1), though not directly concerned with Mary, gives an account of the workings of divine providence, including the phrase 'eterno consiglio', which is to reappear in *Paradiso* XXXIII. But

---

[7] See the comprehensive bibliography appended to the entry 'Maria Vergine' (by Mario Apollonio) in the *Enciclopedia dantesca*, III, 835–9.

these references, for all that they are suggestive of later developments, do not in themselves create, or even supply more than rudimentary foundations for, a substantive Mariology; and it is to the *Commedia* that we must turn to find Dante's mature and fully thought-out view of Mary.

Three major elements combine in the presentation of Mary in the *Commedia*: Dante's personal devotion to her, Mary's function as an exemplar for the faithful, and her glorified status as Queen of Heaven. Each of these is highlighted at a different stage of the poem, and each is characterized by the use of a particular language that carefully distinguishes it from the others; but all three are fused in what thus becomes the culmination of Dante's portrayal of Mary, the prayer in *Paradiso* XXXIII.

Much has been made of Dante's personal devotion to the Virgin, especially by critics of an older generation and a sentimental turn of mind, but it is by no means evident that it was as distinctive as some would like to suggest. It is possible to read too much into lines such as *Paradiso*, XXIII. 88-9, where the narrating voice describes Mary as '[il] bel fior ch'io sempre invoco / e mane e sera'. By identifying that voice with Dante-poet's (which is itself, perhaps, a riskier enterprise than it seems), these lines might be used to demonstrate his fervent attachment to the *cultus* of the Virgin; but they may also be read as expressing no more than the ordinary devotion of any sincere contemporary believer – which Dante certainly was – to the Mother of God. (Although the twice-daily recitation of the Angelus had not yet become universal practice in Dante's time, morning and evening prayer to the Virgin would have been nothing exceptional in the observance of the devout Christian.) Nowhere in his writings, in fact, does Dante *poeta* claim, or even suggest, that his own devotion to Mary is in any way unusual, however marvellous the grace that she grants Dante *personaggio* in Paradise.

Yet this is not to deny that Dante's attachment to Mary is represented as both heartfelt and profound. It is a constant factor throughout the pilgrimage of the poem, where Mary is the prime source of Dante-character's inspiration to break free from the 'selva oscura' and set out on his journey (*Inf.*, II. 94-9), is regularly recalled and invoked along that journey's course, and is at last encountered and venerated in glory, as the channel of the grace that finally permits Dante to enjoy his ultimate vision. Clearly, then, Mary has a pivotal role in the *Commedia*, which loses none of its continuing significance when she herself remains in the background of the poem's action (which is, of course, most of the time). What makes Dante's devotion to her at once striking and wholly individual is not its substance or profundity, but the form of its expression; for his Mary is the creation of one who was not primarily a theologian but a poet, and, at that, an experienced and masterly poet of secular love.

That Dante's Marian devotion is specifically and essentially poetic is apparent from the *Commedia*'s first reference to her, in *Inferno* II. This scene sets the tone for the whole range of Marian allusions that follow in the poem. Virgil is explaining to Dante *personaggio* the reasons for his appearance as rescuer in the dramatic situation depicted in *Inferno* I:

> Donna è gentil nel ciel che si compiange
> di questo 'mpedimento ov'io ti mando,
> sì che duro giudicio là sù frange.
> Questa chiese Lucia in suo dimando
> e disse: – Or ha bisogno il tuo fedele
> di te, ed io a te lo raccomando.          (94–9)

This is the central and most enduring image of Dante's Mariology, the Virgin portrayed as a sympathetic intercessor on behalf of her faithful, a purveyor of grace to the errant soul, actively involved in the salvation of a human individual (though in this case, of course, at one remove, through Lucia). But the image also has a strictly poetic resonance: the Virgin is connected here, through the use of certain vital and highly charged words, to a literary tradition of acute personal significance for Dante. For the portrayal of a 'donna gentil' who 'si compiange / di questo 'mpedimento', and urges Lucia to rescue her 'fedele', inescapably recalls the lyrics of the *Vita nuova*, where it is repeatedly made clear that to be 'gentil' is the peak of human perfection in this life; and behind the *Vita nuova*, as Dante and his first readers were well aware, stands a whole mass of writing on the theme of the 'donna angelicata', with its origins in the courtly love tradition of Provence and Sicily, and its development through the *poesia aulica* of the Italian Duecento as far as the *dolce stil novo* in the Florence of the 1290s – a style of which Dante himself was a leading practitioner. The Mary of these lines from *Inferno* is a poet's Mary, set apart from the Maries of the Bible, the Church Fathers, and popular culture through the use of a language with precise, even technical, connotations in (secular) poetic tradition.

These other images of Mary will find their place in Dante's overall treatment, but at the outset the dominant impression is of a Mary at once the spiritual inspiration and the textual creation of a (love-) poet. At the end of the *Commedia*, where the threads of the Marian tradition are woven together into the great invocation of *Paradiso* XXXIII, the apotheosis of Mary herself is also that of Mary as poetic artefact: for Bernard, preparing to pronounce his 'santa orazione' (*Par.*, XXXII. 151), declares himself 'fedel' to Mary (XXXI. 102), and thus closes the circle of devotion opened in *Inferno* II. Mary in *Paradiso* is thus what she was in *Inferno*, a 'donna gentil' who, through her agents, protects her 'fedele'. From first to last, Dante's devotion to her is marked less by the theological depth of his beliefs than by his passionate commitment to the expression of those beliefs in poetic form. His writing about Mary in the *Commedia* is entirely conditioned by this fact.

Mary is not mentioned again in *Inferno*, and Alexandre Masseron may well be right to suggest that this apparent avoidance of her name is motivated by a respect for holy things that eschews bringing them into (even verbal) contact with Hell.[8] So Christ himself goes unnamed in the underworld. This first reference in *Inferno* II thus establishes the keynote of Dante's Marian writing, while the theme itself is resumed and embellished only in *Purgatorio*.

It is in the second *cantica* that Mary becomes important as a moral and spiritual exemplar, the second of the three major elements in Dante's overall portrayal. References to her and illustrations drawn from the Biblical sources for her life are used to reprove the penitent sinners (and thus, by extension and no less significantly, Dante's readers), and to encourage them in the process of purgation. As is well known, each of the seven purgatorial cornices where a particular sin is expiated is equipped with images (visual, aural, or mental) of the sin itself and its countervailing virtues; and, in every instance, one of the images of virtue is taken from the life of Mary.

The images are, in order: the Annunciation, illustrating humility (*Purg.*, X. 43–5); the Wedding at Cana, where Mary's solicitude for the other guests showed generosity (XIII. 28–30); Mary's reaction to finding Jesus among the Doctors, an expression of meekness (XV. 85–93); her haste to visit Elisabeth, future mother of John the Baptist, a sign of zeal (XV. 100); the birth of Christ in a stable, demonstrating serene acceptance of poverty and thus the refusal of

---

[8] Alexandre Masseron, *Dante et saint Bernard* (Paris, 1953), p. 77.

avarice (xx. 19–24); the Wedding at Cana again, this time because Mary was more anxious that the celebrations be 'orrevoli ed intere' than that they be lavish, thereby displaying temperance (xxII. 142–4); and, finally, the Annunciation again, Mary's words to Gabriel ('Virum non cognosco' – 'I know not a man') being cited directly as an instance of chastity (xxv. 128). Here the exemplary purpose of the depiction of Mary is readily apparent – is, indeed, a structuring principle in the narrative organization of *Purgatorio* – and has been identified as such by all commentators. But it is possible also to detect a refinement of this purpose in the other references to Mary in *Purgatorio*. Brief though many of these are, they too serve an exemplary function, this time for the reader, in a way closely related to that in which visual and aural images of Mary are presented for the benefit of the repentant sinners.

Throughout *Purgatorio*, Mary is seen as intimately and actively concerned with the work of salvation in the individual human soul, even after all hope for its eventual admission to blessedness might seem to have been lost. Perhaps the most memorable example of her salvific intervention is the case of Buonconte da Montefeltro (*Purg.*, v. 100–2), who recounts how, after a lifetime of wrongdoing, he died with a prayer to Mary on his lips ('nel nome di Maria fini'', 101) and was saved. Indeed, the efficacy of prayer to Mary is highlighted by the fact that it does not end after salvation is assured, but continues even in Purgatory: the princes in canto vII (82–4) sing the *Salve Regina* as part of their evening liturgy. Nor does it cease even in Paradise, for Piccarda Donati sings the *Ave Maria* in *Paradiso* III (121–3), and in cantos xv (133) and xvI (34) Cacciaguida remembers the power of prayers to Mary uttered during (or, more precisely, at the beginning of) his life on earth.

These allusions are clearly intended to be exemplary: by illustrating Mary's power to help supplicants, they convey an urgent moral message to the reader, and indeed anticipate another of the major themes of Bernard's 'orazione' in *Paradiso* xxxIII. For in Purgatory Mary is also seen to *answer* prayer: the angels who guard the valley of the princes come 'dal grembo di Maria' (*Purg.*, vIII. 37–9), as if in response to the singing of the *Salve Regina*, and Buonconte himself famously offers concrete and vivid testimony to Mary's mediating powers.

The briefer references to Mary in *Purgatorio* thus share the exemplary function of the more extended illustrations in its central cantos. As we have seen, these are drawn from scripture (often involving direct quotation of the Biblical text), and evoke the most celebrated events of the Virgin's earthly life as instances of active virtue, used in reproof of the vices of which the sinners on the respective cornices are being purged. The purely Biblical basis of these images of Mary deserves to be underlined: Dante seems quite uninterested in the vast undergrowth of non-Biblical legend and anecdote that had grown up around Mary by his time, and, when treating her literally or historically, adheres strictly to Biblical precedent. (Metaphor, as we shall see, is another matter.)

That there was, in the fourteenth century, a pre-existing tradition of using the Virgin as an exemplar in this way has long been established: a century ago, Paget Toynbee quoted (following Paolo Pérez) a comparable passage from the *Speculum Beatae Mariae Virginis* traditionally ascribed to Bonaventure (though in fact by Conrad of Saxony).[9] Conrad's treatment is undoubtedly of interest in this context, and Toynbee goes so far as to claim that it was from his work that 'Dante seems to have derived the idea of representing the Virgin as the type of the several virtues opposed to the seven deadly sins'; but, even if this is true (and it seems unlikely that the idea, as distinct from his expression of it, was original to Conrad), Dante's approach is fundamentally distinguished from Conrad's precise but painfully schematic method, by what has already been identified as the basis of his portrayal of Mary: his view of her as a *poetic* creation, to whose depiction the language of secular love-poetry is as appropriate as that of theological definition.

The Mary of *Purgatorio* is a living being, seen constantly in action, literally an incarnation of the virtues, not merely an ethereal or impossibly idealized perfection (or, as Conrad makes of her, a string of superlative adjectives and abstract nouns). Dante's poetic diction matches this concreteness in vocabulary and imagery. The exemplary Mary of the second *cantica* is marked by the frequent recurrence of blatantly physical language: she is seen to run ('corse'), heard to speak, shown giving birth; she possesses a 'grembo' and a 'bocca', and is even (though this, admittedly, is from an exemplary usage in *Paradiso*) 'fatta ... pregna'.[10] The less concrete imagery used to convey the supreme mystery of the Incarnation still also depicts

[9] Toynbee, *Dictionary*, ed. Singleton, p. 428. The reference is to Paolo Pérez, *I sette cerchi del 'Purgatorio' di Dante: saggio di studi* (Verona, 1867).
[10] Respectively, *Purg.*, XVIII. 100; XV. 85–92; III. 37–9; VIII. 37; XXII. 142–4; and *Par.*, XIII. 82–4.

Mary in terms of physical action or human situation: she turns a key, she comes as the bride of the Holy Spirit.[11] In *Purgatorio* Mary is always human, always the young woman of the Biblical account (so stunningly portrayed, incidentally, in Pasolini's *Il Vangelo secondo Matteo*), with her 'atto / dolce di madre' (*Purg.*, xv. 88-9): the Mary who was to become, in Catholic devotion, the universal mother to whom all may and should turn for succour. (Mention of the Pasolini film, and of the equally stunning performance of the director's own mother as the adult Mary who sees her son crucified, provokes, in passing, the perhaps not entirely irrelevant thought that precisely this episode, the crucifixion and its aftermath, is the one major event of the Biblical Mary's life that is not evoked in the *Commedia*.)

This humanity is what gives Mary her exemplary force for the reader, and makes the manner of her presentation especially appropriate for *Purgatorio*. In this temporal realm, removed alike from eternal torment and eternal bliss, there is still scope for change and amendment in the penitent soul, as there is for the souls of Dante's readers still on Earth – those souls which, according to the *Letter to Can Grande*, it is the poem's intention to rescue from their wretched state and lead to a state of bliss (*Ep.*, XIII. 15). Here, then, Mary is connected with the human condition by evocation of her own earthly experience and the model it offers for every human life, as well as by the use of a poetic language that makes the abstract virtues, necessarily inherent to the supreme degree in the Mother of God, vividly and comprehensibly present in human terms.

The transition from Purgatory to the Earthly Paradise in the final cantos of *Purgatorio* has a transforming effect on many aspects of the *Commedia*: most notably, of course, on the understanding and reactions of Dante *personaggio* himself. But it also signals a transition in the treatment of Mary. As has been noted, her exemplary role continues, to some extent, even in Paradise; but from *Purgatorio* XXIX onwards we begin to see the first signs of the third facet of Dante's portrayal, in which Mary is presented not as a recognizably human individual, but as a dazzling exception to the common lot of humanity, in the full implications of her status as chosen of God and Queen of Heaven. (This move from biography to apotheosis is, perhaps, analogous to that in the *Vita nuova*, from description of Beatrice's involvement in everyday activities to evocation of her

[11] *Purg.*, x. 40-2; xx. 97-8.

mysterious glory, achieved through the development of the *stilo della loda*, in which all other concerns are subordinated to the desire – rather, the need – to praise the beloved.)

The first indication of this transformed poetic mode comes in *Purgatorio* xxix, where the twenty-four elders participating in the symbolic procession join in a version of the oldest and best-known hymn of praise to Mary, the *Ave Maria*:

> Tutti cantavan: '*Benedicta* tue
> ne le figlie d'Adamo, e benedette
> sieno in etterno le bellezze tue!' (85–7)

Although this effusion is clearly intended in praise of the Virgin, and underlines her wholly exceptional status – she alone is picked out from among all the 'figlie d'Adamo', her beauty alone is uniquely, eternally blessed – it is still linked with the earlier, exemplary images in *Purgatorio*. Like them it is closely based on the text of the Bible, and like them it still conceives Mary in fundamentally human terms; for Adam's daughters and their beauty, however blessed, are still necessarily human.[12] The transition to the Marian variety of the *stilo della loda*, the fully fledged apotheosis of Mary as transcendentally – not just objectively – human, only becomes complete in *Paradiso*, where it reaches its climax in canto xxxiii.

It is prepared by a fleeting, but none the less significant, locution at *Paradiso*, xxi. 123, where Peter Damian speaks of Mary as 'nostra Donna' – the only use of that familiar title in the entire *Commedia*. By so doing he simply, but effectively, distances her from the human figure of *Purgatorio*. Although there Mary is 'una donna', the title '*nostra* Donna' has very different connotations, created above all by the possessive pronoun, with its implications of the existence of a community, represented by the speaker, which shares a symbolic relationship with Mary as an individual. In *Paradiso* xxi, Mary is thus more closely associated than in *Purgatorio* with the ideas of sovereignty and loyalty implicit in the Latin 'domina' and, to some extent, in the Provençal 'domna'. The use of 'donna' in *Purgatorio*

---

[12] For this reason, some commentators have suggested that the hymn is addressed to the (as yet unseen) Beatrice; but it also seems perfectly possible that it is intended to evoke both Mary (immediately and inevitably) *and* Beatrice (when she eventually appears). It would thus be a good example of the play between immediate associations and retrospective understanding that informs the concepts of 'reading' and 're-reading' explored in chapter 1.

functions more straightforwardly, as a courteous appellation that defines Mary's gender but is shared with every other woman who ever lived; 'nostra Donna', however, could only be the unique individual that Mary is. This shift of register, and its implied recourse to a vast popular tradition of devotion to 'Our Lady', prepare the way for the still more exalted titles that will be applied to Mary later in *Paradiso*.

The concept of 'titles' is crucial at this point. In *Purgatorio*, Mary was depicted in action, and her nature and attributes were largely defined by the scope and consequences of that action ('What I do is me'). Now, in Paradise, she actually *does* very little; instead she is addressed, invoked, implored, and it is the language of the addresses to her that conveys her qualities and powers. Furthermore, where the vocabulary used of her in *Purgatorio* was strikingly concrete and literal, so as to represent human action and experience most effectively, here it becomes abstract and metaphorical, to embody the numinous meaning of the *Regina celi*. Mary no longer appears as a mother, possessing a human body, performing human actions, and feeling human emotion; in Paradise, she is Queen among the blessed and under God, and human tongues must resort to metaphor to communicate her glory. Thus in *Paradiso* XXIII she becomes 'rosa', 'bel fior', 'stella', 'bel zaffiro', 'donna del cielo', 'Regina celi'; she is one of the 'due luci sole' of *Paradiso*, XXV. 128, and 'bellezza' incarnate at XXXI. 134; and between Bernard's arrival and the prayer of canto XXXIII she is 'regina' twice more, 'donna del cielo' once, 'sole' for the first time and, finally and perhaps (for its classical echo) most remarkably, 'Agusta' (XXXII. 119).[13] This is a figure whose exaltation strains the *stilo della loda* to its expressive limits.

Yet *Paradiso*'s view of Mary is not as coherent as a simple harvesting of its laudatory metaphors might suggest. For at the epicentre of its glorification of the Virgin, in *Paradiso* XXIII, stands an image that seems to invalidate much of what has just been said:

> E come fantolin che 'nver' la mamma
> tende le braccia, poi che'l latte prese,
> per l'animo che 'nfin di fuor s'infiamma;
> ciascun di quei candori in sù si stese
> con la sua cima, sì che l'alto affetto
> ch'elli avieno a Maria mi fu palese.      (121–6)

---

[13] *Par.*, XXIII. 73, 88, 92, 101, 106, 128; XXXI. 100; XXXII. 29, 104, 108.

The image is brilliant and touching, a characteristically earthy and well-observed piece of Dantean realism, employed in simile to describe the essentially indescribable experience of Heaven; but it is also helpful in assessing Dante-poet's comprehensive understanding of Mary. For if what is taking place in *Paradiso* XXIII is the preparatory stage of her enthronement as Queen of Heaven, how, if at all, can this be reconciled with the humble image of instinctive tenderness conveyed in these lines – rendered, indeed, in terms of the most viscerally human affection of all? What can it mean to say that Mary is, or can be seen as, both 'Agusta' and 'mamma'?

It may be useful, at this point, to retreat a little from the details of the text, and to consider the overall development of Mary's portrayal through the latter two *cantiche* of the *Commedia*. Certainly the apparent dissonance created by this simile's placement in its paradisiacal context offers a salutary pretext for such reflection. For, while it is legitimate to suggest, as has been done above, that the text of the *Commedia* concentrates on different aspects of the Virgin at different stages, representing each in turn through the use of language and imagery that vary accordingly, it would be wholly wrong to imagine that the various aspects themselves were at all contradictory of each other. Dante-character's pilgrimage is one of discovery; and this applies as much to his knowledge about Mary as to anything else. As he advances through Hell and Purgatory (always – though this often seems to slip his mind – under Mary's protection), so he learns more and more about her, until now, in Paradise, he is able at last to see her on the throne whence she despatched Lucia and Beatrice to his rescue.

But the meaning of Mary is not *all* in her apotheosis, any more than it is all in her exemplary function for the world or her personal resonance for Dante himself. The real meaning of Mary is not just that she is, but that she *must be* at once 'regina' and 'madre', 'Agusta' and 'mamma', 'zaffiro' and 'donna'; that she must, in short, incorporate every level of human activity into her own transcendent being, because all humanity is (if it chooses to be so) under her protection, a protection which is at once that of a sovereign and that of a parent. Proper devotion to Mary must, then, be founded on recognition of the extraordinary mystery that, by God's grace, a single human being can reconcile in herself what seem to be immeasurably distant modes of being; and this is, of course, precisely the mystery adumbrated in the Annunciation and in Mary's own wondering, fearful question to Gabriel ('How shall this be?') – the mystery of humility and sublimity that is given resounding textual expression in the flagrant paradoxes that open Bernard of Clairvaux's 'orazione' in *Paradiso* XXXIII.

It is in this astonishing prayer that the various themes of Dante's Marian devotion, and the various modes of its expression, are, for the first time, brought into full and indissoluble conjunction. The path is prepared by Bernard's discourse in *Paradiso* XXXII, where meta-phorical praise of Mary and reminiscences of the Annunciation are combined with the more concrete language typical of *Purgatorio*, so that Mary is seen in the act of healing a (metaphorical) wound, possesses a 'faccia', and is presented in a context of intimate human relationships, as the daughter of St Anne (*Par.*, XXXII. 4, 85, 134); but the most profound expression of Dante's perception of Mary is held back until the following canto. The first pair of *terzine* in *Paradiso* XXXIII sums up the fusion that has been achieved in the course of the poem, with its effortless shift from stress on Mary's human and physical nature (1–2), to a metaphor of enormous theological scope (3), and thence to an image of the human Mary in action – but an action that is essentially metaphysical (4–6):

'Vergine Madre, figlia del tuo figlio,
   umile e alta più che creatura,
   termine fisso d'etterno consiglio,
tu se' colei che l'umana natura
   nobilitasti sì, che'l suo fattore
   non disdegnò di farsi sua fattura ...'          (1–6)

The fusion of physical and metaphysical is maintained in a startling metaphor, firmly based on the physical (and Biblical) reality of the Incarnation, but taking a word as semantically concrete as 'ventre' and subjecting it to not one but two metaphorical extensions (the heat imagery of 'raccese' and 'caldo' and the organic imagery of 'germinato' and 'fiore'), to the point where the norms of linguistic realism seem to have been as effectively suspended as those of sublunary existence are in the experience of Paradise:

Nel ventre tuo si raccese l'amore
   per lo cui caldo ne l'etterna pace
   così è germinato questo fiore.          (7–9)

And so throughout the 'orazione', especially as far as line 21, where there is a shift from *elogium* to *supplicatio*, as Bernard presents his petition on Dante's behalf. Mary is described in forcefully meta-phorical terms:

> Qui se' a noi meridïana face
> di caritate, e giuso, intra ' mortali,
> se' di speranza fontana vivace.　　　(10–12)

But she also receives tribute to the sovereignty and liberality befitting the Queen of Heaven:

> Donna, se' tanto grande e tanto vali,
> che qual vuol grazia e a te non ricorre
> sua disïanza vuol volar sanz' ali.
> La tua benignità non pur soccorre
> a chi domanda, ma molte fïate
> liberamente al dimandar precorre.　　　(13–18)

And there is also a potent stress on her role as exemplar of the spiritual perfection of created humanity:

> In te misericordia, in te pietate,
> in te magnificenza, in te s'aduna
> quantunque in creatura è di bontate.　　　(19–21)

Finally, the supplicatory portion of the prayer (22–39) depends wholly on the recognition of her power to assist those who turn to her, and to act on their behalf ('regina, che puoi / ciò che tu vuoli', 34–5). In these lines, then, Mary is seen in her fullness for the first time, because only now, on the threshold of the vision of God and through the intervention of the most famous and best-equipped of her faithful, can Dante *personaggio* fully understand her.

The prayer itself thus deserves to be recognized as the most substantial exposition of Dante's Marian thought, and also as the summation, both stylistic and intellectual, of the ways in which Mary is considered and represented earlier in the *Commedia*. Erich Auerbach, in a detailed analysis of the prayer and its forerunners in Christian literature, makes the essential point that, notwithstanding its poetic form and ecstatic vigour, 'this famous text, in its basic structure, is a rigid composition of dogmatic statements'.[14] This remark is probably aimed in the general direction of Benedetto Croce, the most famous proponent, in the field of Dante studies, of the

---

[14] Erich Auerbach, 'Dante's Prayer to the Virgin and Earlier Eulogies', in *Gesammelte Aufsätze zur romanischen Philologie* (Berne and Munich, 1967), pp. 123–44 (p. 143); originally in *Romance Philology*, 3 (1949–50), 1–26.

view that (as Auerbach puts it) 'didactic matter is incompatible with true poetry'. It comes, indeed, as little surprise to discover that, in his *lectura* of *Paradiso* xxxiii, Croce himself had hardly anything to say about the 'santa orazione', only finding time to dismiss it as 'stilizzata'.[15] For this is a text that might have been designed to irritate Croceans. As Auerbach rightly says, it is basically dogmatic, at least in the opening seven *terzine* (which are more clearly abstracted from the poem's narrative requirements than the *supplicatio* that follows); and yet the manner of the dogma's exposition is undeniably and consummately dictated by the assumptions and conventions of poetry.

The controlled rhythm of the first *terzina*, building up through the titles of the Virgin to the bold assertion of her activity in line 4; the anaphora on 'tu' and 'in te', constantly reiterating the reality of Mary as a person and her involvement in the process of salvation; the alliterative word-play of lines 5–6; the imagery of light, fruitfulness, irrigation, and abundance – all are instances of the forceful use of poetic form and technique to sharpen and concentrate the expression of dogmatic content. What Dante *poeta* is doing in these lines is, in fact, creating a new *kind* of theology. It is not argumentative or analytical, for, as Auerbach stresses, these are essentially dogmatic *statements*; it is not even truly expository, as theological passages elsewhere in *Paradiso* (and as recently as canto xxxii) have been, for no attempt is made to expand upon the meaning of complex ideas such as those conveyed in line 3, and no opportunity is provided for the kind of questioning and expression of perplexity that have so often served before as pretexts for the doctrinal instruction of Dante *personaggio* and, beyond him, the reader. It is, rather, a declarative and consciously poetic theology, in which concepts are given meaning and reality (if, sometimes, a persistently baffling reality) through the use of metaphorically resonant language and the forms of poetry, rather than through lucid analytical definitions and the formal conventions of scholastic argument.

At this stage in *Paradiso*, ratiocination is no longer an issue. Bernard is impelled to address Mary only by the love that consumes him utterly, and the union of poetic and intellectual force in *Paradiso* xxxiii. 1–39 reflects that phase of contemplative experience in which the mind becomes impatient of argument and seeks to communicate

---

[15]  Croce, *Poesia antica e moderna*, p. 159.

by immediate intuition. This may be one reason why Dante *poeta* does not apply himself here to any of the heated Marian controversies of his age, such as the debate about the Immaculate Conception. But the dogmatic statements in the first part of the prayer can have only a limited force, unless they are seen to be operative in the life of the faithful (for 'the letter killeth, but the spirit giveth life', 2 Corinthians 3. 6); and so, in lines 22–39, dogma is converted into praxis, faith into works, and Bernard becomes supplicant for Dante, inspired by the truth of the doctrine he has just so eloquently stated.

In these lines too the poetic charge is unmistakable and powerfully effective, whether in the play of assonances based on the word 'priego' (28–34), or in the skilful use of *enjambement* throughout the passage, which creates a cumulative effect that leads up to the concluding tableau in which the whole court of Heaven joins in Bernard's prayer (38–9). But it cannot and should not be separated from the spiritual charge implicit in the prayer's ideas and indeed in the idea of prayer itself, which is firmly grounded in Dante's understanding of devotion to Mary. The point of these lines is, finally, that poetry and prayer have become indistinguishable, that the poet has found his highest vocation in the act of prayer and that the believer's most profound vehicle of expression is revealed to be poetry. So the poet's Mary of *Inferno* ii, recognizably emerging from a literary tradition of the depiction of an adored and exceptional human being, has now reached an imaginative plane where the poet lets the theologian speak – and finds that the two of them have but one voice.[16]

In recent years scholars have begun to re-evaluate Bernard of Clairvaux's reputation as a writer on the Virgin Mary. That reputation had stood very high for several centuries, and many pious (and doubtless unhistorical) legends had grown up to support it. But when modern scholarship, philological and ideological, came to examine Bernard's Marian writings, with a view to establishing more accurately both their texts and their place in theological and literary history, it became apparent that the received view of Bernard as Mariologist had been distorted to some extent; and the Bernard who has emerged from twentieth-century scrutiny is an altered, though not necessarily a diminished, figure.

---

[16] This point is well made by Aldo Vallone, 'La Preghiera', in *Studi su Dante medievale* (Florence, 1965), pp. 83–109 (pp. 93–4).

In her exhaustive study of the history of devotion to Mary, Hilda Graef discusses Bernard's contribution to the growth of technical Mariology and the formulation of its intellectual basis, and records that his writings on Marian themes form no more than 3.5 % of the whole corpus of his work.[17] Henri Barré provides what is, perhaps, a more immediately useful statistic: according to his researches, there are no more than a score of references to Mary outside Bernard's specifically Marian texts.[18] Those texts themselves are limited to the sermons *In laudibus Virginis Matris*, the sermons on the liturgical feasts of the Virgin (and not all of those: none of the sermons on the Purification, for example, is at all Marian in theme), a few scattered pieces among the sermons *De diversis* (which seem to be sketches or abandoned drafts), and the celebrated letter on the Immaculate Conception addressed *ad canonicos Lugdunenses*. Compared with the several stout volumes of Bernard's *Opera*, this is a small quantity indeed; and however suspicious one may be of the statistical precision of the figure quoted by Graef, it is clear that she is correct in identifying the Marian writings as a tiny proportion of the whole. Even counting spurious texts that may have been taken for Bernard's does not change the picture substantially: volume 185 of the *Patrologia latina*, which gathers most of the works habitually ascribed to Bernard in the Middle Ages and beyond, includes only half a dozen Marian sermons among its nearly eighty items.

Nor, it seems, is Bernard distinguished by any outstanding originality in his Marian thought. Barré calls him a 'traditionalist' rather than an 'innovator', and goes on to describe his Mariology as 'incomplete'.[19] Yet, despite the fact that his works do not seem to match his reputation in either quantity or quality, Bernard still merits the attention he has always received as a Marian writer, partly for his own sake, partly because of the undoubted influence that his writings – or what were believed or assumed to be his writings – had on other writers. As Barré himself suggests, to deny Bernard the name of a theological innovator is to miss the point, unless his importance in another sphere is recognized. Simply by remaining true to the Marian tradition he had absorbed from other authors, and applying to it his own considerable powers of synthesis and expression, Bernard

---

[17] Hilda Graef, *Mary: A History of Doctrine and Devotion*, 2 vols. (London, 1963–5), I, 235.

[18] Henri Barré, 'Saint Bernard docteur marial', in *Saint Bernard théologien* (*Actes du congrès de Dijon*, 15–19 *septembre* 1953), *Analecta Sacri Ordinis Cisterciensis*, 9 (1953), fascicules 3–4, pp. 92–113.        [19] Barré, 'Saint Bernard', p. 113.

came to sum up that tradition, and gave many aspects of it their definitively influential form, as the later development of his reputation shows. In a way connected with, but not exclusively conditioned by, his own actual achievement as a Mariologist, Bernard became the incarnation of Marian theology in his own generation and beyond.

So in Bernard's work we have a body of Marian writing that, without appreciably furthering the development of doctrine, encapsulates a received tradition and passes it on in more memorable, and therefore more durable, textual form: an eloquent conservative, in short. But apart from the question of allotting Bernard a place in the history of Mariology, there is the problem of evaluating his works in themselves, and attempting to account for their indisputable success. Here again Bernard is helped by the very fact that his thinking is not on the cutting edge of academic theology: his writings about Mary are filled with an intense and intensely personal devotion to the Virgin, and aim as much to stir his audience's hearts as to provoke activity in their minds. Here, as in his other sermons, treatises, and letters, Bernard never writes theology for its own sake; his concerns are always immediate, psychological, and, above all, practical.

One basic factor that helps to determine the scope of Bernard's Marian writings is the fact that most of them are sermons. Jean Leclercq has examined the question of whether any or all of Bernard's sermons were ever actually delivered before a congregation.[20] In the case of those *In laudibus Virginis Matris*, as indeed with the better-known sermons *In Cantica canticorum*, it seems unlikely that this was so. (Bernard himself calls the work an *opusculum*, and seems to regard it throughout as a text for private study.)[21] With the liturgical sermons, more closely tied to specific dates in the ecclesiastical calendar and to the everyday needs of a monastic community, the possibility of oral delivery is greater; but, in any case, the underlying purpose with which that particular genre must have been chosen remains the same. The chief intent of any sermon is to edify its hearers; it is a genre that presupposes a collective audience. It is also a genre essentially concerned with the psychological, rather than the intellectual, benefit of its audience; it provides material for meditation rather than a vehicle for the systematic exposition of a body of doctrine. Doctrine

---

[20] Jean Leclercq, 'Les Sermons sur les Cantiques ont-ils été prononcés?', in *Recueil d'études sur saint Bernard et ses écrits*, 3 vols. (Rome, 1962–9), I, 193–212.

[21] Bernard, *Opera*, IV (1966), 58; *PL*, 183, cols. 86–8.

must, of course, be the basis on which any sermon rests; illustrations
of its workings in scripture and the world will make up much of its
content; but the mode of its discourse is quite distinct from that of a
textbook or a *summa*.

Nor, indeed, is that what Bernard supplies. The theological basis of
his Marian sermons emerges by degrees (though seldom in minute
detail), but the expository manner is never allowed to displace the
meditative. In Bernard's sermons there is a close inter-relation
between the lyrical impulse towards doxology (the praise that gives
*In laudibus Virginis Matris* its far from insignificant title) and the
discursive requirement to preach the Word. Bernard's minute
attention to the formal nature and verbal detail of his sermons, the
organization of words on his page, is inseparable from – indeed
becomes the guarantee of – the doctrinal solidity of the ideas that he
is seeking to convey. Christine Mohrmann, who has demonstrated
this double impulse in a close textual analysis of one of Bernard's most
famous passages, is not alone in holding that this approach to the
expression of his Marian thinking makes it legitimate to think of
Bernard as essentially a poet of devotion to Mary.[22]

Much of this is of interest when it comes to the relationship
between Bernard's work and Dante's, for we have seen above that
there is in the *Commedia* a similar fusion of lyrical and doctrinal
elements in the poetic expression of devotion to Mary. So the
treatment that Bernard accords the Virgin in his writings also,
perhaps, merits examination from this point of view.

Bernard habitually treats the figure of Mary from a double
standpoint, reflecting the combination of lyrical and doctrinal
impulses that subtends his Marian thinking. His account is based on
the usual Biblical sources, and the Mary of the Bible is used, as she is
in the *Commedia*, as an exemplar of human perfection. (Here also
appears Bernard's basic concern to edify his audience, by holding
Mary up to them as a model.) Bernard returns constantly to the
Biblical Mary, dwelling especially on the episode of the Incarnation,
which best exemplifies the virtues that occupy the largest place in his
estimation of Mary's exemplary importance: chastity and humility.
Once again the Annunciation, in which Mary's words most effectively demonstrate these virtues ('I know not a man'; 'Behold the

---

[22] Christine Mohrmann, 'Observations sur la langue et le style de St Bernard', in Bernard,
*Opera*, II (1958), ix–xxxiii; see also Masseron, *Dante et saint Bernard*, p. 110.

handmaid of the Lord'), is the key text: the sermons *In laudibus Virginis Matris* take as their starting-point the beginning of that narrative in Luke's Gospel (1. 26), 'the angel Gabriel was sent from God'.

Alongside this exemplary usage, there occurs in Bernard's work, as in Dante's, a more clearly metaphorical language, which is used to praise Mary in her glory and invoke her aid for the faithful still in this life. It is in this area of metaphor, indeed, that Bernard makes his most distinctive contribution to the advancement of Marian thinking; and it is revealing that this should consist of an innovation in vocabulary rather than in idea. This is the image of Mary as aqueduct, a channel of grace overflowing from God and conveyed to earth, like water flowing down from the mountains, which appears in his sermon *In nativitate Virginis* and gives it the title by which it is better known, *De aquaeductu*.[23] The image has not pleased all readers, some finding its vehicle, so to speak, unworthy of its tenor; but it seems to be entirely Bernard's own.

Bernard is very careful, in his treatment of this idea and newly minted metaphor, not to fall into Mariolatry. Grace can only come from God, who alone, in his three persons, is divine. (The boundary between Mary's humanity and the divine nature of the persons of the Trinity, which more enthusiastic Mariologists have often been tempted to blur, is always meticulously observed by Bernard; hence, in part, his objections to the institutionalization of Marian ideas like the Immaculate Conception.)

Bernard's use of the aqueduct metaphor cleverly conveys at once the crucial importance of Mary in the distribution of grace to the world – without the aqueduct, the water would never reach its appropriate destination – but also places her firmly in a subordinate and instrumental position: the aqueduct can never be the source of the water it transports, as Mary cannot be the source of the grace that she purveys. Her mediating activity is thus also subordinated to that of Christ, who shares directly in the divine nature, as she does not. Yet, paradoxically, it is in her subordination that her true power lies: by virtue of being closer to the human plane, she is more approachable by those who have reason to fear, or who cannot comprehend, the ineffable mystery of God or the stern authority of Christ.[24]

---

[23] Bernard, *Opera*, v (1968), 275–99; *PL*, 183, cols. 437–48.
[24] Bernard, *Opera*, v (1968), 279–80; *PL*, 183, cols. 441–2.

There is, of course, little that is new in this doctrine; and we have seen that Bernard has no great claim to be an innovator in Mariology. What is noteworthy in the sermon *De aquaeductu*, however, is the centrality of Mary's role in Bernard's understanding of the nature and workings of grace, coupled with the unusual rhetorical power that he brings to his exposition of doctrine. The invention of the aqueduct metaphor is only the most prominent example of his verbal bravura; this passage is another:

Laudamus virginitatem, humilitatem miramur; sed misericordia miseris sapit dulcius, misericordiam amplectimur charius, recordamur saepius, crebrius invocamus. Haec est enim quae totius mundi reparationem obtinuit, salutem omnium impetravit. Constat enim pro universo genere humano fuisse sollicitam, cui dictum est: 'Ne timeas, Maria, invenisti gratiam' utique quam quaerebas. Quis ergo misericordiae tuae, o benedicta, longitudinem et latitudinem, sublimitatem et profundum queat investigare? Nam longitudo eius usque in diem novissimum invocantibus eam subvenit universis. Latitudo eius replet orbem terrarum, ut tua quoque misericordia plena sit omnis terra. Sic et sublimitas eius civitatis supernae invenit restaurationem, et profundum eius sedentibus in tenebris et in umbra mortis obtinuit redemptionem. Per te enim coelum repletum, infernus evacuatus est, instaurate ruinae coelestis Jerusalem, exspectantibus miseris vita perdita data. Sic potentissima et piissima caritas et affectu compatiendi, et subveniendi abundat effectu, aeque locuples in utroque.

Ad hunc igitur fontem sitibunda properet anima nostra: ad hunc misericordiae cumulum tota sollicitudine miseria nostra recurrat.[25]

There are several reasons why this passage is appropriate to the present discussion, and which justify the length of this quotation.

---

[25] Bernard, *Sermo in Assumptione Beatae Mariae Virginis*, iv. 8–9; *Opera*, v (1968), 249–50; *PL*, 183, cols. 428–30: 'We praise her virginity, we wonder at her humility; but her mercy tastes sweeter to the wretched, it is her mercy that we embrace more dearly, recall more often, invoke more frequently. For it was she who obtained the restoration of the whole world, who successfully implored the salvation of all. It is fitting that she should have been concerned for the whole human race, she to whom was said "Fear not, Mary, you have found favour", just that which you were seeking. Who, therefore, blessed one, could explore the length and breadth, the heights and depths, of your mercy? For its length reaches out to all who call upon it, even unto the last day. Its breadth fills the whole world, so that all the earth may be full of your mercy also. Just as its loftiness has brought about the restoration of the heavenly city, so has its profundity secured the redemption of those who sat in darkness and the shadow of death. For through you is Heaven filled, Hell emptied, the ruined heavenly Jerusalem restored, lost life given back to the wretched who await. Thus this most powerful and holy charity abounds in the force of its compassion and the efficacy of its assistance, and in both with equal richness.

Let our thirsty soul then hasten to this fountain: to this rich source of mercy let our wretchedness be at pains to have recourse.'

Firstly, it is an excellent example of the way in which Bernard's verbal dexterity inspires his exposition of doctrine: the rhythm and balance of the lines, the use of chiasmus, parallelism, internal echoes, and other forms of verbal patterning, both provide aesthetic satisfaction and help to structure the argument. Consider even the first sentence alone: the resounding chiasmus in the opening clause highlights, through its structure, the basic element of Mary's condition ('virginitatem, humilitatem'), while the first-person plural verbs on either side draw the audience into the speaker's relationship with Mary, help to found that relationship on the praise and wonder that are their semantic significance, and, by virtue of their morphological difference ('laudamu*s*', 'miramu*r*') provide a pleasing variation on the clause's otherwise absolute symmetry. The remainder of the sentence, after the structuring adversative 'sed', begins with an internal echo ('misericordia miseris'), and continues with parallel clauses based on a verb and an adverb. Here too, though, the pattern is richly varied (none of the clauses is syntactically identical with any other); and the clearest evidence of Bernard's attention to textual detail is perhaps the way on which the last of these clauses is reversed ('crebrius invocamus'), beginning with its adverb (rather than ending with it, as the others do), in order to provide the sentence with a triumphant *cursus velox* at its end.

Speaking more generally, the passage also illustrates Bernard's treatment of Mary as exemplar (focusing on her chastity, humility, and mercy), and abounds in the figurative language normally used in her praise. It is also – and this, as far as I know, has not been noticed before – a passage of some relevance to Dante's treatment of Marian themes.[26]

As well as the general resemblances (exemplary function, metaphorical language), there are some more specific points of contact. The stress on virginity and humility, underpinning the greater glory of Mary as mediatrix, is bound to recall the prayer of *Paradiso* XXXIII, especially lines 1–3 and 13–18; the notion of Mary 'quae totius mundi reparationem obtinuit, salutem omnium impetravit' recalls both the idea of *Paradiso*, XXXII. 4 ('la piaga che Maria richiuse e unse') and her actions on Dante-character's behalf; the neverfailing abundance of Mary's mercy ('usque in diem novissimum

---

[26] An earlier passage from the same sermon, beginning 'Sileat misericordiam tuam' (IV. 8) is among the parallel passages for *Paradiso* XXXIII suggested by Celestino Cavedoni; see below, pp. 180–9.

invocantibus eam subvenit universis') is also stressed in *Paradiso* XXXIII ('La tua benignità non pur soccorre a chi domanda, ma molte fïate / liberamente al dimandar precorre', 16–18); the references to Heaven, Hell, and the 'exspectantibus miseris' echo the broad structure of the *Commedia*; Mary is the 'fons' and the 'misericordiae cumulum' to which the anxious soul should hasten, as she is 'fontana' at *Paradiso*, XXXIII. 12 and the supreme embodiment of 'misericordia' at XXXIII. 19.

None of this, of course, suffices to prove, or perhaps even to suggest, any closer connection – let alone any direct influence. The concepts are similar largely because they are commonplace, and the diction is identical only at the most basic level of vocabulary, rather than, say, showing complex phrases or locutions from Bernard that are replicated in the *Commedia*. But, for all that, there remain clear affinities of thought and expression between this passage and Dante's Marian writing, especially in *Paradiso* XXXIII. It will be argued below, when we come to deal with the direct parallels between the two authors that have been proposed by commentators, that it is seldom advisable to go far beyond this in connecting Bernard's work with Dante's; that the possibility of a direct intertextual relationship cannot be excluded, but can, equally, not be regarded as confirmed. With this caveat in mind, it still seems worth adding this page of Bernard's to the list of extracts from his Marian works that may have found, consciously or otherwise, an echo in the *Commedia*.

Despite such (potentially) identifiable affinities of theme and approach, there are also ways in which Dante and Bernard differ appreciably and revealingly in their writing about Mary. The most obvious of these is, perhaps, their divergent attitudes towards doctrinal controversy. It was suggested above that the Mariology of *Paradiso* is declarative rather than argumentative, and that this is one reason why Dante avoids becoming embroiled in the disputes that raged over topics such as the Immaculate Conception. No such inhibition restrains Bernard. In his letter to the canons of Lyon he enters the fray with vigour, staunchly upholding traditional practice in the Church's observance, and therefore rejecting the new feast of the Immaculate Conception that the recalcitrant canons had taken to celebrating. In this letter, indeed, he sums up his approach to the doctrinal development of Marian thought: the Virgin already has glories and prerogatives enough, derived from the Bible and established tradition, to provide ample material for those who wish to honour her, and she needs no false or invented title to add to her fame.

This is the true voice of the doctrinal conservative, speaking for and out of an existing tradition, bitterly resentful of any attempt to tamper with that tradition or adapt it to changing intellectual or institutional circumstances: 'Ego vero quod ab illa [ecclesia] accepi securus et teneo, et trado; quod non, scrupulosius, fateor, admiserim' ('As for me, what I have received from her [the Church] I am determined both to hold and to hand on; what I have not, I would only accept, I must admit, with great difficulty').[27] It is also the voice of the practised controversialist that Bernard had become in the course of his political and ecclesiastical career, most notably in his doctrinal squabbles with Peter Abelard and his unyielding resistance to the claims of the anti-pope Anacletus in the 1130s. Dante himself, of course, was by no means averse to engaging in controversy with powerful adversaries, but on the disputed niceties of Marian doctrine he remains silent.

He is, admittedly, writing almost two centuries after Bernard's death, at a time when the debate about the Immaculate Conception had receded somewhat from the initial fervour of the mid-twelfth century; but it was still far from settled (not being officially resolved, indeed, until the promulgation of Pius IX's bull *Ineffabilis Deus*, in 1854). It is, thus, surely not without significance that Dante not only avoids mentioning the subject himself, but refrains even from alluding, in *Paradiso*, to Bernard's notorious opposition to it. The obvious inference is that he was not aware of Bernard's views; but it is difficult to accept that they could have escaped his notice altogether if he knew anything at all about Bernard's life and character – which he self-evidently did. The early *Vitae* mention the dispute (though it is absent from the *Legenda aurea*), and there was already, in the early Trecento, a fund of popular legend along the lines of the (rather later) tale of Bernard appearing in a vision with a blot on his white habit, representing his refusal to countenance the celebration of the feast. Dante's silence on this point may be tactful (since Bernard is chosen at least partly as a Mariologist, it would be unwise to draw attention to anything that might even risk disqualifying him from fulfilling that role); or it may, just possibly, be a sign that, for Dante,

---

[27] Bernard, *Epistolae*, CLXXIV, 2: 'Virgo regia falso non eget honore' ('The royal Virgin needs no false honour'); see *Opera*, VII (1974), 388–9; *PL*, 182, col. 333.

this was not a controversial matter at all: that is, that there was no need to mention Bernard's rejection of the Immaculate Conception because Bernard had been right all along.

As always with the *argumentum e silentio*, a doubt remains – despite Giorgio Petrocchi's authoritative and judicious statement that Dante 'very probably' knew the letter to the canons of Lyon.[28] Perhaps more indicative in this regard is the overall nature of the presentation of Bernard in *Paradiso*: though possessed of doctrine on certain matters (not, be it noted, specifically Marian matters), as instanced in canto XXXII, when dealing with Mary Bernard exchanges his 'officio di dottore' (*Par.*, XXXII. 2) for that of 'fedel Bernardo' (XXXI. 100–1): it is the rhetorical ardour of his devotion to Mary, not its intellectual rigour, that is the lingering impression of Dante's portrait of him, and this is true even of the most intellectually rigorous speech he makes, the first seven *terzine* of *Paradiso* XXXIII – whose conceptual depth and audacity far exceed anything in the (comparatively) mainstream theology expounded in *Paradiso* XXXII. It may be, in the end, that Dante *poeta* felt that any allusion to Bernard's talent for controversy would have been detrimental to the image that the text of *Paradiso* enshrines: that of a Bernard who comes to Mary as a lover, not as a scholar and still less as a polemicist.

As early a commentator as Francesco da Buti was prepared to claim that Dante had read Bernard's writings about Mary (see chapter 4); and, over the years, many other commentators have arrived at the same conclusion, and given more or less tentative voice to it in their commentaries. One who is not tentative in the least is Alexandre Masseron. He bases his argument on what may seem a slightly forced interpretation of *Paradiso*, XXXII. 106–8 – taking 'ancora' to imply that the first time Dante had recourse to Bernard's 'dottrina' was when the *poeta* read his Marian works in life, not when the *personaggio* asked him where Beatrice had gone (*Par.*, XXXI. 64) – and concludes that there can be no possible doubt in the matter. According to Masseron, in fact, we have no right to question whether Dante profited from the study of Bernard's Marian doctrine, because Dante himself unambiguously tells us that he did.[29]

Elsewhere, speaking of Bernard's works in general, Masseron claims that we can be 'certain' that Dante had read them.[30] Other

---

[28] Petrocchi, 'Dante e la mistica', p. 228.     [29] Masseron, *Dante et saint Bernard*, p. 142.
[30] Ibid., p. 67.

scholars more noted for their expertise in Dante studies have been more circumspect, preferring, like Sapegno or Petrocchi, to speak only of probability.[31] However, in view of the strong body of opinion that holds that Dante both knew Bernard's Marian writings and was influenced by them, the rest of this chapter will be given over to an examination of some of the tangible evidence that has been brought forward.

The medieval commentators, especially those of the first half of the Trecento, are not greatly concerned with the idea of 'sources' for the *Commedia*, in the sense that they do not normally trouble to trace lines of filiation from the authors they liberally plunder for illustrations of Dante's text. They approach the *Commedia* as a body of autonomous propositions, whose justice or poetic merit can be confirmed by juxtaposition with authoritative extracts from earlier writers – *auctores*. Bernard of Clairvaux was one of these; and it is natural enough that the Trecento commentators should turn to his writings, especially when analysing those cantos in which a figure bearing his name is involved. But this does not mean that they are necessarily suggesting any direct influence, merely that they are trying to prove the existence of an affinity of thought; they seek to show that a great writer of the past had had a similar idea to Dante's, but not that this, or indeed any, particular formulation of it was the one that inspired him. (This is why Buti's unequivocal assertion that Dante did actually read Bernard on Mary is so important.) The distinction is an immensely meaningful one, and it will be argued here that modern critics, accustomed to a very different, post-Romantic, conception of authors, texts, and the relationships among them, have too frequently been willing to obscure it.

The search for textual evidence of direct Bernardine influence on the *Commedia* began in the middle of the nineteenth century, as part of the process of rediscovery of Dante's work (and application to it of new scholarly techniques) that coincided, not altogether by chance, with the Risorgimento. In 1864 there appeared the first edition of Celestino Cavedoni's *L'orazione di san Bernardo alla beatissima Vergine nell'ultimo canto del 'Paradiso' di Dante esposta co' riscontri di quel santo padre e d'altri*, which a contemporary scholar has called 'remarkable'[32] – not just for its title – and which certainly both provided the

[31] *La 'Divina Commedia'*, edited by Natalino Sapegno (Milan and Naples, 1957), p. 1166; Petrocchi, 'Dante et la mistica', p. 228.

[32] Masseron, *Dante et saint Bernard*, p. 117n.

material and set the agenda for subsequent enquiry along these lines.[33] Cavedoni's researches were limited to passages relevant to the prayer of *Paradiso* XXXIII, but he is justified by the fact that this has continued to prove the most fertile soil for scholars seeking to assimilate Bernard and Dante on the basis of their writings. (Other connections have been made, notably between Bernardine imagery and some of the symbolism of *Paradiso* XXXI, as well as, more recently, between characteristics of the early cantos of *Inferno* and certain treatises and sermons of Bernard's, in particular *De gradibus humilitatis et superbiae* and *De diversis*, III.)[34] The present chapter, concerned as it is with Marian devotion and doctrine, will follow Cavedoni and his various successors by concentrating on *Paradiso* XXXIII.

Cavedoni's essay attracted some attention, and enjoyed several reprints; and, from the late nineteenth century onwards, commentators on the *Commedia* began to suggest parallels between Bernard and Dante more frequently. For the most part, however, they were content to use those propounded by Cavedoni himself, and some of those that were new (such as Giacomo Poletto's lengthy quotations from the spurious sermon *De duodecim stellis*) were, on the whole, unconvincing, and were never absorbed into the critical consensus that was forming around the canto.[35] At the turn of the century also appeared the first signs of reaction by those who found Cavedoni's analysis less than persuasive. One such was Francesco Torraca, whose commentary was first published in 1905: he argues that 'il modello intero ed esatto della preghiera dantesca' is not to be found anywhere in Bernard, and notes both the vagueness of the suggested parallels and the possibility of their derivation from the two writers' use of common sources.[36]

Torraca's assessment was eminently level-headed and plausible, but he was speaking ahead of his time. Commentators remained content to follow Cavedoni until a fresh outbreak of enthusiasm took place after the Second World War, as three scholars of different

---

[33] The article is most readily available in Celestino Cavedoni, *Raffronti tra gli autori biblici e sacri e la 'Divina Commedia'*, edited by Rocco Murari (Città di Castello, 1896), pp. 137–64.

[34] See, especially, Edmund G. Gardner, *Dante and the Mystics* (London, 1913), pp. 342–8. Gardner's edition of Bernard's *De diligendo Deo – The Book of St Bernard on the Love of God* (London, 1916) – lists about a dozen parallels, none very convincing. For Bernard and *Inferno*, see A. Bozzoli, 'Due paragrafi sul prologo della *Divina Commedia*', *Aevum*, 41 (1967), 518–29 (on *De gradibus humilitatis et superbiae*); and Mario Aversano, 'San Bernardo e Dante', *L'Alighieri*, 29 (1988), no. 1, 37–45, and *San Bernardo e Dante: teologia e poesia della conversione* (Salerno, 1990) (on *De diversis*, III).

[35] Poletto, '*Divina Commedia*', III, 688, 692–3.     [36] Torraca, '*Divina Commedia*', p. 941.

nationalities tried to add to the stock of Bernardine *riscontri* for *Paradiso* XXXIII. The first of these was Erich Auerbach, in the article quoted above (p. 163), which was first published in 1949. He provides an exhaustive account of possible precedents for the 'orazione', including quotations both from Bernard's Marian sermons and from those *In Cantica canticorum*. Next came Masseron, whose *Dante et saint Bernard* includes a lengthy (and sadly ill-organized) chapter on Dante, Bernard and Mary that adds little to Cavedoni;[37] and third in line was Aldo Vallone, who took Cavedoni's list as the basis for renewed, if not notably productive, researches of his own.[38]

More recently, Giorgio Petrocchi, while sounding a general note of caution, has named certain instances of apparent influence that he considers probably valid:[39] most of these, however, were already listed by Cavedoni or Masseron, and those that were not are to be found in other commentaries.[40] Reaction against too narrowly Bernardine a reading of the potential sources of *Paradiso* XXXIII has also continued in recent years: Natalino Sapegno describes the prayer only as 'intessuto di calde formule liturgiche', with no mention of Bernard's work at all, and Umberto Bosco, echoing Torraca at a distance, gives one of the most lucid and sensible summaries of the situation yet to appear, commenting that, of the many parallels put forward by more venturesome readers, 'alcune sono probabili, nessuna certa'.[41]

This kind of quest for *riscontri*, if undertaken with a good measure of flexibility, scepticism, and caution, can yield interesting results. But what finally makes it worthwhile is the critical use to which those results are put. Too often in the past, barely perceptible affinities between Bernard's work and Dante's have been used as the fragile foundations for a whole series of strictly unjustifiable deductions; pieces of evidence that do no more than point to possibilities have been bandied about as if they amounted to proof. Instead of using Bernardine *riscontri* to hint at the possibility of Bernard's direct

---

[37] Masseron, *Dante et saint Bernard*, pp. 71–143.

[38] As well as 'La Preghiera' (n. 16 above), see also Aldo Vallone, 'Ancora del "Veltro" e della preghiera di san Bernardo', in *La critica dantesca nel Settecento e altri saggi danteschi* (Florence, 1961), pp. 85–9.    [39] Petrocchi, 'Dante et la mistica', pp. 228–9.

[40] For example, the parallel with *Sermo in Adventu*, II. 4, is pointed out in Casini/Barbi, '*Divina Commedia*', p. 1055.

[41] Sapegno, '*Divina Commedia*' (Florence, 1978), III, 412; Bosco and Reggio, '*Divina Commedia*', III, 507.

influence on Dante, some scholars (Masseron is the chief offender)
start by assuming the existence of such an influence, and then use the
*riscontri* to prove it.

A similar consequence of this widespread wishful thinking is that
passages which, considered objectively, do not appear relevant or are
divorced from their proper context – and thus from their meaning –
are pressed into service on specious grounds, again to prop up a
preconceived notion of the Bernard–Dante relationship. (The whole
process is, in fact, alarmingly reminiscent of the practice of the
Trecento commentators, to whom modern scholarship, unwisely, so
often condescends.) Cavedoni's original batch of quotations, especially those taken from authors other than Bernard, often
exemplifies this fault, as does Vallone's article (again mostly in the
quotations from other authors, as nearly all Vallone's references to
Bernard come straight out of Cavedoni).

Such misuse of textual parallels – or quasi-parallels, such as the
one that Masseron identifies on the basis of his odd belief that
Bernard's phrase 'fecundae Virginis' is 'exactly the same' as Dante's
'Vergine madre'[42] – has an unfortunate effect, since it devalues the
genuine importance of the conceptual affinities that such parallels
may indicate by exaggerating the specious importance of a particular,
perhaps dubiously relevant, verbal formulation. It is against this
trend that Torraca and Bosco react in their commentaries; equally
unconvinced is Mario Fubini, who, in the course of an excellent
stylistic analysis of *Paradiso* XXXIII, makes trenchant comments that
challenge the very principle of the search for *riscontri*. He argues that
it is inevitably misguided, because the prayer should not be detached
from its narrative context in the *Commedia* and compared with texts
arranged according to non-poetic conventions or designed by authors
with, apparently, very different aims in view.[43]

Fubini denies altogether the value of textual comparison between
the fictional Bernard's prayer and the historical Bernard's writings;

---

[42] Masseron, *Dante et saint Bernard*, p. 119. Detailed refutation of this claim might start by
pointing out that 'fecundae virginis' and 'vergine madre' are not 'exactly the same' either
semantically, morphologically, or syntactically; and that the idea of fecundity and that of
motherhood, though obviously related, are not identical – the latter being, as it were, the
realization (*in actu*) of the possibilities inherent in the former (*in potentia*). Given that
exactitude is not on offer here, and that the idea of Mary's miraculous virgin motherhood
is universally dwelt on by her medieval devotees, it is hard to accept Masseron's conclusion
that even if the so-called parallel is mere coincidence it would be 'extremely curious'.

[43] Mario Fubini, 'L'ultimo canto del *Paradiso*', in *Il peccato d'Ulisse e altri scritti danteschi* (Milan
and Naples, 1966), pp. 101–36 (p. 109).

and in this he may go too far. But his protest against the forensic approach to *Paradiso* XXXIII only gains in force when read with an eye to some of the more rhapsodic criticism of that canto. It has, in the past, sometimes been the case that determination to establish parallels with Bernard at all costs has led to a narrowness of critical approach quite alien to the spirit of these lines; for, whatever the exact extent of Bernard's (presumed) influence upon him, it would be wholly uncharacteristic of Dante's essentially eclectic practice in the *Commedia* if he were to depend on a single source, however prestigious, for so decisive a nexus of ideas and poetic technique as this 'santa orazione'.

Masseron, however, while unable to exclude altogether the possibility that Dante had recourse to other texts or drew on other sources of inspiration, is still able to fit it into his preconceived structure:

The ideas that Dante developed in the *Commedia*, making of them a kind of apotheosis of the Mother of God, he could have found in other Fathers and Doctors of the Church; and it is, indeed, very probable that, with rare exceptions, he did in fact find them there.

However, it was, in general, from Saint Bernard that he borrowed them ... For reasons that are connected only with art and because he felt that there was a profound affinity between his own genius and that of the abbot of Clairvaux...[44]

The ease with which Masseron shifts from the fatal concession in the first sentence to the obstinate (and unsupported) declaration of faith in the second does serious damage to his argument: the existence of an affinity between Bernard and Dante, which should be the conclusion – and a tentative one at that – of the chain of reasoning, is used here as a major premise, to justify Masseron's view that, even when there is evidence of other possibilities, Bernard of Clairvaux must still have been the *fons et origo* of Dante's thinking about Mary. This too is unnecessarily narrow. In what follows I shall argue that there are certainly some celebrated passages in Bernard's work that may have struck a chord in Dante; that there are, however, other factors that need to be taken into account if the Bernard–Dante relationship is to be properly evaluated; and that any more restrictive approach does a disservice to text and reader alike.

[44] Masseron, *Dante et saint Bernard*, pp. 109–10.

In order to evaluate the previously identified textual *riscontri* between Bernard's Marian writings and *Paradiso*, XXXIII. 1–39, it will be convenient to follow Cavedoni's practice of studying the 'orazione' *terzina* by *terzina*, and occasionally phrase by phrase – especially at the opening, where the syntactic structure (a series of complimentary phrases addressed to the Virgin and set in apposition, with only sequential links to each other) forms a kind of mosaic of verbal elements that can readily be examined in turn. It need be no surprise, moreover, that the most thought-provoking material turns out to be connected with the prayer's first seven *terzine*, defined above as the doxology in which the several aspects of Dante's commitment to Mary – personal devotion, exemplary function, and regal status – are fused. The remaining, supplicatory lines (22–39) are largely devoid of doctrinal statement, functioning rather as an example of the practical application, within the particular narrative circumstances of the poem, of the dogma expounded in lines 1–21.

*Vergine madre*: Masseron's enthusiastic attempt to link this title with the beginning of Bernard's sermon *De aquaeductu* ('fecundae virginis') has been noted, and rejected, above. Cavedoni supplies a list of occurrences in Bernard's writings, which is followed by Vallone; and the idea does, as mentioned above, occur elsewhere in Dante's works.[45] But the paradoxical combination of virginity and motherhood is so fundamental to the Christian view of Mary that it would be literally astounding if any Christian writer in the Middle Ages failed to mention it. It is found in scores of medieval theologians (Cavedoni gives a short list of Bernard's predecessors, which barely scratches the surface), and contemporary hymnody is also rich in such locutions as 'virgo mater', 'parens virgo', and so on.[46]

*Figlia del tuo figlio*: Neither of Cavedoni's references to Bernard, which seem not to have been supplemented by later scholars, is especially convincing.[47] One, from an apocryphal sermon, describes Mary as 'summa summi mater filii' ('highest mother of the highest son'); the other, from an authentic work, refers to Mary's prerogative 'quod Filium unum eundemque cum Patre meruit habere communem' ('that she deserved to have one and the same Son in common with the Father') – which, if anything, seems more relevant to the similar passage ('nos quoque eundem patrem et filium...') in

---

[45] Cavedoni, *L'orazione*, pp. 142–3; Vallone, 'La Preghiera', p. 96.
[46] See, for example, *Analecta hymnica medii aevi* (*AHMA*), II. 36 (p. 165); IV. 58 (p. 42); IX. 79 (p. 63); and X. 145 (p. 110).          [47] Cavedoni, *L'orazione*, pp. 144–5.

Dante's letter to the Italian cardinals (*Ep.*, XI. 3).[48] Cavedoni's *riscontri* from other authors, all of which are of the pattern 'mother of the father' ('pariens parentem', 'patris parens', 'genitrix genitoris', 'patris sui mater et filia') are equally unhelpful. It is not a mere quibble to suggest that this idea is something rather different from that encapsulated in the Dantean phrase 'figlia del tuo figlio'. The idea of mutual dependence implicit in the daughterhood of Mary and the sonhood of Christ is not the same as that of mutual procreation found in the image of Mary as mother of Christ the father. Dante's lapidary formulation has an entirely separate range of connotations.

But, although it seems to have no source in Bernard, it is not original to Dante: the epithet 'daughter of the son' is applied to Mary, albeit infrequently, in medieval hymnody. There she is saluted as 'nata nati', 'nati nata', 'nati filia'; and the idea can take more elaborate verbal form: 'placa nobis, o beata / patrem, natum, parens, nata' ('placate for us, blessed one / the father, as his mother, the son, as his daughter'); 'parit natum nati nata' ('the daughter of the son gives birth to the son'); 'patris mater et nati filia' ('mother of the father and daughter of the son'). Hymns containing these and similar expressions are found in widely scattered regions of Europe, and the likely conclusion is that the concept of Mary as daughter of her own son, though not a staple of Marian devotion, was known in the late Middle Ages, and reached Dante via other channels than those that lead to Bernard.[49]

*Umile e alta più che creatura*: Mary's humility is at the core of her exemplary role for both Bernard and Dante (as it is, indeed, from the Gospel account of the Annunciation onwards), and the oxymoronic combination of that humility with her exaltation as Mother of God is dwelt on by Bernard in a passage that forms one of Cavedoni's more persuasive parallels: 'O si scires quantum tua humilitas Altissimo placeat, quanta te apud ipsum sublimitas maneat! ('If you [Mary] but knew how much your humility pleases the Most High, how exalted you are in his sight!').[50] Vallone adds two suggestions at this point: one, which is not immediately convincing, from Bernard's first

---

[48] Bernard, *Sermo in Annuntiatione Beatae Mariae Virginis*, II. 2; see *Opera*, V (1968), 31; *PL*, 183, col. 391.

[49] See *AHMA*, VIII. 89 (p. 73); IX. 69 (p. 56); IX. 87 (p. 71); XV, *Salutationes BVM* (p. 68); XX. 302 (p. 213); XXXII. 74 (p. 108); LIV. 233 (p. 370); LIV. 276 (p. 417); LIV. 281 (p. 426).

[50] Cavedoni, *L'orazione*, pp. 145–6, quoting Bernard, *In laudibus Virginis Matris*, III. 10; see *Opera*, IV (1966), 42–3; *PL*, 183, col. 76.

sermon *In laudibus Virginis Matris* ('Pulchra permixtio virginitatis et
humilitatis: nec mediocriter placet Deo illa anima' – 'A beautiful
admixture of virginity and humility; nor does that soul give only
middling pleasure to God'); the other, perhaps more suggestive,
from another Marian sermon ('Nec humilitas tanta minuit magnani-
mitatem, nec magnanimitas tanta humilitatem' – 'Nor does such
humility diminish her greatness, nor such greatness her humility').[51]

Again, the idea is found in many other Marian writers: Cavedoni
gives a particularly interesting quotation from Richard of St Victor,
and the concept also occurs in some of the minor thirteenth-century
Franciscans. One of the most intriguing instances comes in Ubertino
da Casale's *Arbor vite crucifixe Jesu*, a work that may very well have
found itself on Dante's bookshelf at some point:

Nonne videtis quanta charitatis dilatatione mens huius virginis ampliatur?
Numquid etiam non attenditis quod thalamus eius virtutis vacat nitore?
Videtis stupendius quod in tanta virtutum plenitudine ipsa videtur
humilitatis abyssus.[52]

But, of course, the idea also has deep Biblical roots, in Mary's
words to Elisabeth that form the universally familiar prayer known as
the *Magnificat*: 'For he hath regarded the low estate of his
handmaiden: for, behold, from henceforth all generations shall call
me blessed. For he that is mighty hath done to me great things' (Luke
1. 48–9).

Finally, 'plus quam creatura' is a standard formula in describing
Mary's exaltation in Latin hymnody, and, indeed, the combination
of her humility and her sublimity is also a hymnodic *topos*.[53]

*Termine fisso d'etterno consiglio*: Cavedoni points out the occurrence
of 'eterno consiglio' in Dante's *Convivio* (IV. v. 1); and for this line also
his *riscontri* are plausible enough to have been adopted by several
commentators, including Vallone and the habitually circumspect
Petrocchi.[54] Especially significant is this use of 'consilium' in

[51] Vallone, 'La Preghiera', pp. 96–7, quoting Bernard, *Sermo in dominica infra octavam
Assumptionis*, 13; *Opera*, v (1968), 272.
[52] Ubertino da Casale, *Arbor vite crucifixe Jesu*, I. vii.
[53] For 'plus quam creatura', see *AHMA*, xv. 123 (p. 150); xvII, *In sanctificatione BVM* (p. 22).
For the humility/exaltation *topos*, see *AHMA*, x. 132 (p. 102); xxxII. 10 (p. 21); and Guido
of Bazoches, 'Dei matris cantibus', in *The Hundred Best Latin Hymns* (*HBLH*), edited by
J. S. Phillimore (London, 1926), p. 107.
[54] Cavedoni, *L'orazione*, pp. 146–9; Vallone, 'La Preghiera', pp. 97–8; Petrocchi, 'Dante e la
mistica', p. 229.

Bernard's sermon *In nativitate Virginis* (*De aquaeductu*): 'Intuere, o homo, consilium Dei, agnosce consilium sapientiae, consilium pietatis ... redempturus humanum genus, pretium universum contulit in Mariam' ('Hear, o man, the intention of God, recognize the intention of wisdom, the intention of holiness ... He will redeem the human race, he has found the reward of all in Mary').[55]

As for the underlying idea, that Mary had been pre-ordained from all eternity to fulfil her role in the scheme of human salvation, that is a familiar feature of medieval Mariology, to which, for example, numerous hymns refer. In these, such phrasing is used of Mary as 'quam elegit ab aeterno rector aetherorum' ('she whom the lord of the heavens chose from all eternity'); 'ordinata ab aeterno' ('ordained from eternity'); 'quam elegit sibi pater priusquam mundum statuit' ('she whom the father chose for himself before he created the world'); 'praeelecta ipsius gratia ante saecularia tempora' ('chosen by his grace before the beginning of time'); 'electa ante saecula' ('chosen before time'); and 'a dilecto praeelecta' ('chosen by the beloved'). Devotees had long since been prepared to apply to Mary such Biblical texts as Proverbs 8. 22–3 ('The Lord possessed me in the beginning of his way, before his works of old. I was set up from everlasting, from the beginning, or ever the earth was'); and a glance at the hymnodic instances listed above will reveal that this was well on the way to becoming a cliché by Dante's time.[56] The phrase's elaboration through the addition of 'termine fisso' seems, however, to be unprecedented.

*Tu se' colei che l'umana natura / nobilitasti sì, che'l suo fattore / non disdegnò di farsi sua fattura*: No really compelling parallel between Bernard's work and these lines has yet been brought to light. The 'creator/creature' antithesis, which Cavedoni and Vallone attribute to Peter Damian's *Oratio* LXI,[57] was a *topos* in hymnody by the early Trecento: there are two particularly interesting occurrences in this area that have previously gone unremarked. One, in an anonymous

---

[55] Bernard, *Opera*, v (1968), 278; *PL*, 183, cols. 440–1.

[56] See *AHMA*, I. 56 (p. 94); I. 185 (p. 170); II. 72 (p. 61); IV. 75 (p. 50); v. 15 (p. 57); v. 16 (p. 59); v. 19 (p. 67); x. 145 (p. 110); XII. 64 (p. 46); LIV. 197 (p. 307). The author of this last example, Adam of St Victor, also calls Mary 'ab aeterno vas provisum' ('a vessel chosen from all eternity') in his 'Salve mater salvatoris'; see *The Oxford Book of Medieval Latin Verse*, pp. 232–4.

[57] Cavedoni, *L'orazione*, pp. 149–50; Vallone, 'La Preghiera', p. 98. For the *factor/factura* antithesis, see also *AHMA*, III. 2 (p. 22); XI. 90 (p. 57); and 'Cantet omnis creatura', *OBMLV*, pp. 441–2.

Italian hymn, brings together in a single stanza several ideas familiar to readers of *Paradiso* XXXIII:

> Virgo carne, virgo mente,
> virgo mater es repente,
> virgo paris filium.
> Nulla talis genitura
> qua creator fit factura:
> altum hoc consilium.[58]

The other also has some relevance to *Paradiso*, as it describes the transforming effect of the Incarnation on human nature:

> En antiqua carnis jura
> mutat nova genitura
> et dum factor fit factura
> suum perdit ius natura.[59]

*Nel ventre tuo si raccese l'amore, / per lo cui caldo ne l'etterna pace / così è germinato questo fiore*: Cavedoni traces this astounding aggregation of metaphors to Bernard's sermon *In Adventu*, II: 'Virginis alveus floruit, sic inviolata integra et casta Mariae viscera, tamquam pascua aeterni viroris florem protulerunt' ('A virgin womb has flowered, the inviolate, whole and chaste bowels of Mary, like pastures of eternal greenness, have put forth their flower'). He is followed by a number of critics, including Sapegno, who describes the image as 'modellata sullo schema di analoghe espressioni dei mistici'.[60] This more general attribution seems to come nearer the truth. The verbal resemblance between Bernard's phrasing and Dante's is far from close: in particular, the Bernardine passage lacks the duality of the *Paradiso* image, which is based on heat as well as flowering. In addition, Bernard uses 'alveus' rather than 'venter' (the direct cognate of Dante's 'ventre'), and 'proferre' rather than 'germinare' – the only word the two extracts actually have in common, in fact, is 'flos'/'fiore'.

---

[58] 'Sponsa Dei, virgo mitis', *HBLH*, p. 154: 'A virgin in flesh, a virgin in mind, / Virgin, you suddenly become a mother, / Virgin, you bear a son. / Never before was such a birth / by which the creator becomes a creature: / this was a lofty plan.'

[59] *AHMA*, xv. 15 (p. 57): 'See how the old laws of flesh / are changed by this new birth / and as the creator becomes a creature / nature loses its power.'

[60] Cavedoni, *L'orazione*, pp. 150–2; Sapegno, *'Divina Commedia'* (Milan and Naples, 1957), p. 1184.

There may well be a variety of sources for these lines: the Biblical account of Christ's conception in Mary's womb and Elisabeth's salutation of her (later to become the *Ave Maria*), with its image of germination ('blessed is the fruit of thy womb', Luke 1. 42); or numerous medieval hymns, perhaps beginning with St Ambrose's famous *Veni redemptor* ('Alvus tumescit virginis' – 'The womb of a virgin has swollen'), which may have been a source for Bernard himself.[61] None of these forerunners, however, even approaches the metaphorical complexity of the lines from *Paradiso*, or their marvellous poetic power; and their verbal texture also seems to be owed chiefly to Dante *poeta* himself.

*Qui se' a noi meridïana face / di caritate, e giuso, intra' mortali, / se' di speranza fontana vivace*: Erich Auerbach claims that the imagery of this *terzina* is based on that of Bernard's sermon *In Cantica canticorum*, XXXIII; while Cavedoni and his epigones quote the second of Bernard's sermons *In Assumptione*: 'Processit ergo gloriosa virgo, cuius lampas ardentissima ipsis quoque angelis miraculo fuit' ('Therefore the glorious virgin has gone forth, she whose brightly burning lamp was a miracle to the very angels themselves').[62] Auerbach's reference is linked to the fact that in his exegesis of Song of Songs 1. 7 ('Tell me, O thou whom my soul lovest, where thou feedest, where thou makest thy flock to rest at noon'), Bernard expands at length on the symbolic meaning of 'meridies' ('noon'). But it is not easy to relate this use of midday imagery to Mary – to whom, on the other hand, it is unmistakably applied by Dante. In Bernard's sermon, the 'true midday' is Christ, and he later exclaims, addressing Christ himself, 'Vultus tuus meridies est' ('Your face is noon'). Cavedoni's suggestion is initially more plausible, but here the imagery has the 'lampas' (equivalent, presumably, to *Paradiso*'s 'face') without the 'meridies'/'meridïana' element. Here again, in fact, we have only a partial resemblance in Bernard to a complex Dantean image, which in itself suggests that whatever texts Dante may have had in mind at this point have undergone profound transformation while being turned into his poetry.

Seeing this insufficiency in the quoted parallels, Masseron (followed by Petrocchi) draws attention to Bernard's phrase 'lucem quippe meridianam' ('the light of noon, in fact') in the sermon *In*

---

[61] See *HBLH*, p. 10.
[62] Auerbach, 'Dante's Prayer', p. 142; Cavedoni, *L'orazione*, pp. 152–4; Vallone, 'La Preghiera', p. 99.

*nativitate Virginis.*[63] He also connects the opposition between Heaven and earth in *Paradiso*, XXXIII. 10–11 ('*Qui* se' a noi ... e *giuso*, intra ' mortali') with the opening paragraph of Bernard's sermon, where a similar contrast is developed:

> Fecundae Virginis amplectitur caelum presentiam, terra memoriam veneratur. Sic nimirum totius boni illic exhibitio, hic recordatio invenitur: ibi satietas, hic tenuis quaedam libatio primitiarum; ibi res, et hic nomen.[64]

This certainly cannot be excluded as a potential *riscontro*, but again the real resemblance is at the level of idea rather than of verbal detail. The contrast between Heaven and earth is obvious and basic in Christian thinking, appearing plainly in as familiar a text as the Lord's Prayer ('on earth, as it is in Heaven'); and Dante has already used it in a Marian context at *Paradiso*, XXIII. 93: 'che là sù vince, come qua giù vinse'. If anything, that phrase, with its genuine contrast between Heaven and earth, past and present, is more pertinent in this situation than *Paradiso*, XXXIII. 10–12, where attention is focused on different, but not contrasting (indeed, simultaneously operative) aspects of Mary's glory. In Bernard, Mary has gone up to Heaven ('ibi res') and left only her name behind ('et hic nomen'); in Dante, she is fully and equally present on both planes ('Qui *se*' a noi ... e giuso ... / *se*' ...'), and what is stressed is not so much the contrast between Heaven and earth as their continuity.

As for the phrase 'lucem quippe meridianam', there is also a Biblical precedent for that, by no means inapplicable to the present case, in the 'meridiana lux' of the Vulgate version of Isaiah 18. 4. Finally, none of these alleged *riscontri* takes into proper account the extension of the midday metaphor in line 11 ('meridïana face / *di caritade*'). Although the phrase is not found in Bernard, there are precedents, once again, in hymnody: there Mary is often called 'fax', and not infrequently 'fax amoris'.[65]

A similar case is that of the image of Mary as 'di speranza fontana vivace'. Mary is described as 'fons' on innumerable occasions in hymnody and liturgy, sometimes in the form, cognate to Dante's phrasing, 'fons vivus'. No example of her being called 'fons spei'

---

[63] Masseron, *Dante et saint Bernard*, p. 119; Petrocchi, 'Dante e la mistica', p. 229.

[64] Bernard, *Opera*, V (1968), 275; *PL*, 183, col. 437: 'Heaven embraces the presence of the fruitful Virgin, Earth venerates her memory. Thus without doubt all the goodness that is hers is on display there, while the memory of it is found here; there is her plenty, here is, as it were, a faint foretaste of her first-fruits; there is the reality, and here the name.'

[65] *AHMA*, XV, *De nominibus BVM* (p. 64); XXXII. 53 (p. 80); XXXII. 81 (p. 117).

('fountain of hope') has come to light, but this may be because it is hard to make the phrase scan in the common metrical schemes of medieval hymns. Certainly the hymnologists connect her intimately with hope: she is 'spes reorum' ('hope of the wicked'), 'spes fidelium' ('hope of the faithful'), 'mundi spes' ('hope of the world'), 'spes salutis' ('hope of salvation'), and so on.[66]

The description of Mary as 'fontana' (*Par.*, XXXIII. 12) leads Giorgio Petrocchi to point to the colloquial title of Bernard's *De aquaeductu* (properly called *In nativitate Virginis*) for that basic image;[67] and this is also the work of Bernard's most clearly evoked by the following six lines of *Paradiso* XXXIII:

> Donna, se' tanto grande e tanto vali,
>     che qual vuol grazia e a te non ricorre
>     sua disïanza vuol volar sanz' ali.
> La tua benignità non pur soccorre
>     a chi domanda, ma molte fïate
>     liberamente al dimandar precorre.          (13–18)

Here, if anywhere, there seems to be a genuine affinity of thought between Bernard and Dante, of the sort in which so many scholars have been so willing to believe. The idea of Mary as the channel of boundless grace flowing down from Heaven is central to *De aquaeductu*, and is here given superbly economical poetic form in *Paradiso*. Commentators are unanimous in referring to *De aquaeductu*, I. 7 ('quia sic est voluntas eius, qui totum nos habere voluit per Mariam' – 'for such is his will, who wanted us to have everything through Mary'), and I. 8 ('Quaeramus gratiam, et per Mariam quaeramus, quia quod quaerit invenit et frustrari non potest' – 'Let us seek grace, and seek it through Mary, for what she seeks she finds, and she cannot be gainsaid'), as well as to Bernard's sermon *In vigiliis Nativitatis Domini*, III. 10: 'quia nihil nos Deus habere voluit, quod per Mariae manus non transiret' (for God did not wish us to have anything that had not passed through the hands of Mary').[68]

So it seems that Bernard and Dante do indeed think alike on this point, and Masseron is particularly eager to elevate this ostensible contact into proof of influence.[69] But there appears to be no real

---

[66] Both usages ('fons' and 'spes') are too common to make exemplification useful.
[67] Petrocchi, 'Dante e la mistica', p. 229.
[68] Cavedoni, *L'orazione*, pp. 154–8; Vallone, 'La Preghiera', pp. 99–100; Bernard, *Opera*, v (1968), 279–80; *PL*, 183, cols. 441–2; and *Opera*, IV (1966), 219; *PL*, 183, col. 100.
[69] Masseron, *Dante et saint Bernard*, pp. 118–24.

affinity between them on the level of expression. The terms in which
Mary is praised in *Paradiso* ('grande', 'tanto vali') are generic
(though the use of 'vali' is a little unusual), and the doctrine of
Mary's mediation is couched in broad terms that have no obvious
point of contact, lexically, with any specific source in Bernard.
Indeed, it might be argued that, if ever Dante intended to pay tribute
to Bernard's influence with unmistakable clarity (other, of course,
than by allotting him his role in *Paradiso* in the first place), this would
have been his chance: for the 'aqueduct' metaphor of Mary's
mediatory activity is so uniquely characteristic of Bernard that a
single allusion to it would probably have sufficed to recall the saint's
Marian writings to the mind of the alert reader (who is, of course, the
reader whom *Paradiso* presupposes – *Par.*, II. 10–15). There is no such
allusion in these lines; and the metaphor that Dante *poeta* does use
('sua disïanza vuol volar sanz' ali'), apart from referring to the
supplicant rather than to Mary, can be traced back to Plautus and
was a *topos* in contemporary Italian lyric poetry.[70] (Masseron, for
once, seems to be on firmer ground when he connects its use with the
fictional Bernard's words at *Paradiso*, XXXII. 145–51.)[71]

All in all, it seems clear that the affinity with *De aquaeductu* exists at
the conceptual level, but the complete lack of verbal similarity
between the two texts must mean that direct contact between Dante
and Bernard on this point can be considered no more than a (distinct)
possibility – despite even Petrocchi's efforts to extend the discussion
by linking *De aquaeductu*, 6 ('totius boni plenitudinem' – 'the fullness
of all good') with *Paradiso*, XXXIII. 21 ('quantunque in creatura è di
bontate').[72] Here too, though the thought is similar, it is also
commonplace, and the expression is again far from identical in the
two texts – though it is at least closer ('boni'/'bontate') than in the
preceding *terzine*. But there is no restraining Masseron's ecstatic
response to *De aquaeductu*: he is certain that the sermon had been 'not
only read, but meditated upon at length' by Dante, and he goes on
to paint a sentimental portrait of the exiled poet wandering around
Ravenna with a manuscript of Bernard's sermon in his hand.[73]
Masseron's 'certitude', alas, is exactly what we do not and cannot
have, either here or anywhere else, when assessing the textual

---

[70] Sapegno, '*Divina Commedia*' (Milan and Naples, 1957), p. 1184; Michele Barbi, *Problemi di critica dantesca: prima serie*, p. 254; Masseron, *Dante et saint Bernard*, p. 123.
[71] Ibid., pp. 123–4.          [72] Petrocchi, 'Dante e la mistica', p. 229.
[73] Masseron, *Dante et saint Bernard*, pp. 118–19.

relationship and possible lines of influence between Bernard's work and Dante's.

Enough has, perhaps, been said by now to show how too narrow a view of Bernardine *riscontri*, used to justify preconceptions rather than to assess a situation objectively, can obscure the complexities of the Bernard–Dante relationship. It is never possible to be certain that a given idea or image in the *Commedia* is derived from Bernard's *opera* when there is no direct textual citation (and there seems to be none); one can at most propound possibilities of greater or lesser force, and some *riscontri*, as indicated above, can be useful adjuncts to such arguments. But it remains helpful not to lose sight of Mario Fubini's warning of the dangers of forensic enquiry into this or any other passage of the *Commedia*. To do justice to Dante's achievement, as well as to the complexity of intertextual relationships in medieval culture, it is as well to take a broad view of influence and its operations, and not to limit our understanding of either the poet's creative scope or the (often mysterious) workings of cultural transmission by adopting, *a priori*, an excessively dogmatic approach.

I have given some examples of other sources that yield material closer to *Paradiso* in expression than some of the Bernardine *riscontri*, but even these are not intended to argue for, let alone to demonstrate, any direct or traceable influence. They merely show that certain intellectual and verbal possibilities were available in the spiritual vocabulary of Dante's culture, as it applied to the Virgin Mary. The extent to which Dante drew directly on that vocabulary, and the identity of the texts or authors to which he was most indebted for guidance or example, remain problematic, and perhaps even, in the end, unknowable. But we always have before us the richest vein of potential evidence: the *Commedia* itself.

The fact that it is Bernard who undertakes the approach to Mary, his self-description as 'fedel Bernardo' and evocation of the ardour that consumes him, the theological depth and poetic efficacy of the words he addresses to her, may all be pointers to the immense significance of this episode in *Paradiso*, and to Dante's sense of Bernard's right to be so crucially involved in it – a sense that may, in turn, derive from his knowledge of the historical Bernard's rhetorical expertise in the area of Marian devotion. But we are compelled, at last, to proceed with caution, by inference and suggestion. There can be no absolute certainty as to which texts of Bernard's Dante had read, or that he had read any of them at all; and to claim that there can is quite as unjustifiable as to deny altogether the possibility – never more than that – that Bernard's work did have some degree of influence on Dante.[74]

Since certainty has to be dispensed with, however reluctantly, it remains important to try to reach at least a more accurate, if less categorical, definition of the Bernard–Dante relationship, based on the kind of broad view advocated above. That will be the concern of the closing pages of this chapter.

The relationship between Bernard's Marian writings and Dante's needs to be seen in the overall context of the development of Marian devotion in the Middle Ages. This was not exclusively the province of theologians and their speculations: Bernard himself would probably have disdained such a title, and much of the Marian writing of the twelfth and later centuries is far from academic in style or intention. Apart from the Biblical accounts and the writings of recognized authorities (including Bernard himself), there exists a mass of related material, in the form of liturgy (as new Marian feasts and devotional practices entered the calendar, so the liturgy expanded to accommodate them), hymns (the number of compositions in the *Analecta hymnica medii aevi* specifically dedicated to Mary runs to several thousand), prayers such as the *Ave Maria* and the *Salve Regina* (the use of which, officially sanctioned in the twelfth century, was soon being propagated on an enormous scale), and collections of pious anecdote (of which the *Legenda aurea* is only the best-known example). Devotion to Mary may also have had consequences in fields of textual production other than the purely religious. Etienne Gilson and M. de Montoliù are among those who have seen it at work in the development of the courtly love tradition, and both ascribe some of the credit for this to the reputation of Bernard of Clairvaux.[75] In short, the spiritual and literary atmosphere of the later Middle Ages, at least in Western Europe, was permeated by devotion to Mary expressed in texts written in her honour.

It seems likely that one result of all this enthusiastic cultural activity was the formulation of a specifically Marian idiolect within

---

[74] Raoul Manselli, in the entry 'Bernardo di Chiaravalle, santo', in the *Enciclopedia dantesca* (I, 601–5), delivers himself of the magisterial opinion that 'l'influenza di B[ernardo] su D[ante] – va detto con molta chiarezza – non è certo di natura dottrinale o, in genere, culturale' (p. 604).

[75] Gilson, 'Saint Bernard et l'amour courtois', in *La Théologie mystique de saint Bernard*, pp. 193–215; M. de Montoliù, 'San Bernardo, la poesìa de los trovadores y la *Divina Comedìa*', *Spanische Forschungen*, Erste Reihe, 12. Band (Münster, 1956), pp. 192–9.

both Latin and the various vernaculars; a common stock of ideas, images, and expressions that all authors on Marian themes more or less unconsciously adopted when they came to write, because this lexicon had become an indispensable part of their intellectual apparatus – the accepted, normative way of writing about Mary. This Marian idiolect is made up, in part, of the scenes from the Biblical version of Mary's life and the Old Testament texts that, through the application of typology, had come to represent Mary, along with the standard metaphors and epithets drawn from those sources; and partly from the accretions that Marian authors and popular devotion had gradually provided to go with the scriptural basis. Over the centuries, and with especial rapidity from the twelfth century onwards, a verbal repertory came into being, on which any Marian writer could hardly avoid drawing for material, and which might be added to by writers possessing particular talent or authority – as Bernard seems to have added the image of the aqueduct. Or a writer might take a neglected or unappealing image from the stock and either transform or establish it by his own authority, as Dante seems to have done with 'figlia del tuo figlio'.

None of this need, necessarily, have depended on conscious act or individual volition. Cultural history lays down patterns of thought and response that become well-nigh impossible for anyone brought up or operative in a particular tradition to transcend, and which can only be detected at a distance, by readers whose alertness to such patterns in other cultures is balanced by their frequent blindness to them in their own. Something of this kind seems to happen among Western writers on Mary between the twelfth and fourteenth centuries – though the process begins much earlier than this, with the first glimmerings of Marian devotion in the early stages of Christian history, and goes on later.

The existence of such an idiolect, unconscious or semi-conscious, with its concomitant habits of thought and conventions of form, would help to explain why the vast mass of medieval Marian literature, so disparate in its social and geographical origins, is yet so homogeneous in its textual nature: hymns from all over Europe, for instance, use the same standard images again and again ('vellus Gedeonis', 'thronus Salomonis', 'flos florum', 'stella maris' and so on). Marian writers discuss the same Biblical episodes, point the same morals, stress the same themes. This, of course, has nothing to do with lack of originality, or even plagiarism, in any modern sense. Much of the time, these authors are not writing for the public or for posterity, but to assist the personal spiritual growth of a few readers in their immediate social situation; and, anyway, originality and plagiarism, as concepts, had little meaning in an age so firmly wedded to the use of *auctores* and, as yet, happily unequipped with a law of intellectual property or authorial copyright. What is at work here is a prevailing tendency in medieval culture, whose representatives are moved by the inherited custom and habit of generations to respond in particular ways, conceptually similar and often textually identical, to the idea of devotion to Mary.

One result of all this is that questions of influence, when not actually reduced to meaninglessness, become much harder to assess than would be the case when dealing with later periods, or with writers seemingly more conscious of their own individuality and prerogatives. If Bernard and Dante were indeed drawing on a common background of Marian language, and if Bernard had come, by Dante's time, to form part of that background himself, it becomes more difficult to argue that Dante was 'influenced' by Bernard in any real sense – unless he actually says so (which would strengthen the argument), or unless his texts can be shown to reflect Bernard's unequivocally (which would make the argument practically ir-refutable). Otherwise Dante might just as well have been influenced by any intermediate author or combination of authors for whom Bernard was also part of the background, or even by texts *about* Bernard rather than by those he wrote or which were attributed to him. It would be unwise to exclude this last possibility: we have already seen that thirteenth-century and later writers whom Dante probably studied, such as Bonaventure and Ubertino da Casale, openly declare their indebtedness to Bernard, and that Bernard's reputation as a Marian writer burgeoned in the thirteenth century, in ways that could not have been justified by strict adherence to the facts supplied by history.

In the end, we have to come back to the texts. Dante may have read Bernard; but we do not know, because the texts do not tell us so. The information gathered here, useful or illuminating though it may be in various ways, still does not amount to proof; though the balance of possibility and probability at times verges on the overwhelming, there always remains, in this case at least, the *Commedia*'s stubborn unwillingness to yield up incontrovertible evidence for its author's reading. And so, perhaps, instead of looking in vain for what the

*Commedia* does not tell us, we should content ourselves with paying closer attention to whatever it is prepared to reveal. We come back to the text, and, in particular, to *Paradiso*, XXXIII. 1–39, one of those moments in reading the poem when the page seems to catch fire before our eyes. From the whole vast corpus of medieval Marian literature, through unimaginable and irrecoverable processes of reading, thinking, and writing, this essence of the traditional language of the Virgin's 'fedeli' has been distilled and given form; and now it is put in the mouth of Bernard of Clairvaux. That simple fact is still the most powerful evidence we have of the debt that Dante felt he owed to Bernard as a writer about Mary.

# CHAPTER 6

# *From* deificari *to* trasumanar? *Dante's* Paradiso *and Bernard's* De diligendo Deo

Rosetta Migliorini Fissi's brief general introduction to Dante's life and works, published in 1979, is outstanding among the many books of its ilk for its combination of substance and concision; and not least among its claims to be better known is its original and fascinating interpretation of *Paradiso*.[1] From the outset, Migliorini Fissi founds her analysis of the third *cantica* on the relationship between Dante's text and the work of Bernard of Clairvaux, which, going beyond the many scholars who have looked for traces of Bernard's presumed influence only in *Paradiso* XXXI–XXXIII, she finds exemplified as early as canto I.[2] For her, the key to understanding Dante-character's experiences in Paradise is the 'pregnante neologismo' *trasumanar* (*Par.*, I. 70), which she identifies as the 'autentico correlativo poetico' of one of the basic concepts of Bernard's mystical theology, *deificatio* (deification).

Returning, in a later article, to the same topic, Migliorini Fissi has also argued that closer attention to Bernard's mystical doctrine among Dantists is called for, in order to redress the balance of a critical history that has tended to see the Bernard–Dante relationship largely in terms of the Mariological question.[3] Her work, then, must be taken into account in the present study, since it constitutes the first thorough-going attempt to develop the perception of Bernard's importance to Dante as a contemplative (which is guaranteed by the text of the *Commedia* – *Par.*, XXXI. 109–11; XXXII. 1) into a theory of his crucially formative significance for the whole theological – and, eventually, mystical – apparatus of *Paradiso*.

Migliorini Fissi herself admits that she is not the first to have made the identification between *deificatio* and 'trasumanar', giving the

---

[1] Rosetta Migliorini Fissi, *Dante* (Florence, 1979).   [2] Ibid., p. 133.
[3] Rosetta Migliorini Fissi, 'La nozione di *deificatio* nel *Paradiso*', *Letture classensi*, 9/10 (1982), 39–72 (p. 42).

credit instead to Alexandre Masseron.[4] In fact even Masseron was not the first to associate the two ideas explicitly: as early as 1911, Evelyn Underhill had remarked that 'the mystic's astonished recognition of a profound change effected in his own personality', as described in the 'temperamental language' of deification, might be compared to 'Dante's sense of a transmuted personality when he first breathed the air of Paradise'.[5] But this comparison occurs as part of a more general discussion of deification, as a theme in the history of mysticism, than that undertaken by Masseron or Migliorini Fissi (and, is, anyway, relegated to a footnote); and it does seem to have been in Masseron's *Dante et saint Bernard* that the first specific juxtaposition of Dante's 'trasumanar' and Bernard's *deificatio* took place.

On closer examination, though, it may be felt that Masseron's introduction of the question – for he can hardly be said to have explored it to any extent – leaves something to be desired. Discussing Bernard's achievements as a contemplative, he quotes extensively from *De diligendo Deo*, and then zeroes in on the use of the verb 'deificari' in chapter x. 28 of that work. Is this not, Masseron asks, 'the same transformation' as that which Dante sought to express in his coinage of 'trasumanar'?[6] But he does not stay for an answer, and there is no further reference to the matter anywhere else in his book. Nor, indeed, does anyone before Migliorini Fissi appear to have taken up the question or attempted a more adequate treatment of it – one that might have asked to what precise extent it is true to say that 'deificari' and 'trasumanar' express 'la même transformation', or indeed whether they do so at all.

Migliorini Fissi's two studies are much more substantial than the fleeting hints dropped by Masseron. Both are copiously documented with apt quotations from the two authors concerned, and together they amount to a highly plausible argument for the existence of a connection between them. Migliorini Fissi's exposition of Bernard's thinking about deification, while heavily – and inescapably – reliant on Etienne Gilson's trail-blazing account, is also admirably coherent.[7]

Briefly, she defines Bernard's *deificatio* as a realignment of the

---

[4] Migliorini Fissi, *Dante*, p. 133.
[5] Evelyn Underhill, *Mysticism* (London, 1911), pp. 415–16.
[6] Masseron, *Dante et saint Bernard*, p. 159.
[7] Gilson, *La Théologie mystique de saint Bernard*.

human will to achieve accord between it and the will of God, through the purgation of *amor sui* (self-love) and *voluntas propria* (self-will). This realignment, begun in response to the unearned initiative of divine grace, consists in an education in the workings of charity; it enables man to escape from the 'region of unlikeness' (*regio dissimilitudinis*) of sin, in which he loses the ethical resemblance to God (*similitudo*) that is the birthright of his creation – though never the metaphysical analogy with God (*imago*) that guarantees the freedom of his will in the first place – and it thus allows that lost resemblance to be restored. The culmination of the whole process comes when the two wills, divine and human, arrive at a condition of perfect harmony expressed in charity; and this is deification, since the double likeness of man to God, in *imago* and *similitudo*, is once more complete – although, of course, man does not and cannot become divine in any existential sense.

Migliorini Fissi relates this definition to various features of Dante's work. The *regio dissimilitudinis* is equated with the 'selva oscura' of *Inferno* I; the disfiguring effect of sin on the human soul is connected with *Paradiso*, VII. 79–81 ('Solo il peccato è quel che la disfranca, / e falla dissimìle al sommo bene, / per che del lume suo poco s'imbianca'); the importance of humanity's capacity for free choice in determining its response to the initiatives of divine grace is linked with *Monarchia*, I. xii. 6 and its 'luogo parallelo' at *Paradiso*, V. 19–24, where the freedom of the will is described by Beatrice as 'lo maggior don che Dio per sua larghezza / fesse creando' (19–20); and, perhaps most interesting of all, the accord of wills, which is the hallmark of *deificatio* in Bernard's thought, is seen as the inspiration of Piccarda Donati's discourse in *Paradiso* III, with its celebrated declaration that, for the blessed, ''n la sua volontade è nostra pace' (85). All this stems from, and depends on, Migliorini Fissi's initial identification of 'trasumanar' as the 'autentico correlativo poetico' of Bernardine *deificatio*; and the validity of that identification will thus be the basic question addressed in this chapter. In order to provide some background for the enquiry, however, it will be necessary to turn to the history of deification itself, and to establish Bernard's – and Dante's – place in it.

The history of deification in medieval Christian thought is at once that of a concept and that of a lexicon. In other words, the formulation of a body of doctrine about deification did not proceed at an equal rate with the development of a vocabulary capable of giving adequate expression to that doctrine's nuances and ramifications. At any given time, there were likely to be some writers who tackled the theme without using the technical language generally considered appropriate to their subject, while others were busily adapting the language itself for use in other theological contexts. Even in the twelfth century, when thinking about mystical experience and attempts to subject it to a definitive taxonomy flourished as never before (at least among Western Christians), *deificari* and the words associated with it were neither the most commonly employed nor the most precise terms available; and among later writers, Thomas Aquinas was by no means alone in avoiding their use whenever possible. For such reasons as these, the history of deification language often needs to be treated as distinct from that of the concept itself, although, of course, the two are never wholly separable.

The position is further complicated by the cultural divergence among those who thought and wrote about deification. The subject was of major importance in the Greek Church from its earliest days, and a large body of writing on it grew up in the Eastern Mediterranean region, especially in churches connected with Alexandria. However, declining familiarity with Greek culture in the West, especially after the language was replaced by Latin in the liturgy, meant that later writers on deification in the Latin Church were, at best, imperfectly acquainted with the work of their Greek-speaking predecessors, and had to depend very largely on such translations as became haphazardly available for their knowledge of this older and deeper-rooted tradition. As a result, Greek and Latin thinking about deification developed at different rates and along substantially different lines, and although there was a certain amount of export of Greek ideas (especially in Latin versions of such key authors as pseudo-Dionysius and Maximus Confessor), the time-lag between formulation in Greek and absorption into the thought and, still more, the vocabulary of the Latin Church was often enormous.

Latin traditions regarding deification thus have to be taken, to some extent at least, as a separate issue. In the particular case of Bernard of Clairvaux, the chief obstacle to the assimilation of Greek thinking on his part was the fact that he himself knew no Greek, and was therefore denied immediate access to Eastern Christian texts; but that alone does not put an end to the question. Latin translations of some Greek authors were certainly available to him in the library at Clairvaux, and the Greek theological tradition continued to be generally influential in the West during the twelfth century, even if, necessarily, it was mostly mediated through translators and expositors.[8] The history of Eastern thinking about deification, and of the language used to express it, thus remains an essential prolegomenon to any account of later developments in the West.[9]

Deification language seems to have made its first appearance in Greek in the writings of Clement of Alexandria (c. 150–c. 215), though movement towards the definition of a vocabulary specifically associated with the concept is discernible in his near-contemporary Theophilus of Antioch.[10] Neither Clement nor Theophilus, however, can claim credit for having been the first to conceive deification as an idea. The primitive elements of the doctrine can be traced back as far as Ignatius of Antioch (c. 35–c. 107), and can also be detected in a variety of first- and second-century theologians, including Justin Martyr and Tatian. As might be expected, at this stage the doctrine is rudimentary and even incoherent, lacking as it does a systematically expressive vocabulary. Irenaeus (c. 130–c. 200) seems to have been the first to codify an existing body of teaching on the subject, but his approach is marked by its sedulous avoidance of linguistic innovation. Clement, in contrast, steps willingly outside the bounds of such traditional vocabulary as already existed, and begins, above all, to use the verb *theopoiein* to mean 'to cause to partake of the divine nature'.

But there remains an ambiguity in Clement's use of deification terminology: it seems to refer both to the future state of the Christian afterlife (deification as salvation, the climax of a process that leads the believer from paganism to faith, from faith to *gnosis*, and from gnosis to charity), and to the possibility that the soul might already be able to achieve some kind of peak of perfection in this earthly life. It is primarily in the former sense, of deification as immortalizing the

---

[8] Leclercq, *Bernard of Clairvaux and the Cistercian Spirit*, pp. 25–6.

[9] In what follows, I have relied chiefly on M. Lot-Borodine, 'La doctrine de la déification dans l'Eglise grecque jusqu'au xie siècle', *Revue de l'Histoire des Religions*, 105 (1932), 5–43, 106 (1932), 525–74, and 107 (1933), 8–55; the article 'Divinisation' in the *Dictionnaire de spiritualité* (*DS*), iii (1957), cols. 1370–459; Jaroslav Pelikan, *The Emergence of the Catholic Tradition (100–600)*, volume i of *The Christian Tradition: A History of the Development of Doctrine* (Chicago and London, 1971); and Bernard McGinn, *The Foundations of Mysticism: Origins to the Fifth Century*, volume i of *The Presence of God: A History of Western Christian Mysticism* (New York, 1992).

[10] For the first- and second-century theologians, see *DS*, iii, cols. 1377–8. For Clement, see *DS*, iii, col. 138; Pelikan, *Emergence*, p. 155; McGinn, *Foundations*, p. 107; and G. W. Butterworth, 'The Deification of Man in Clement of Alexandria', *Journal of Theological Studies*, 17 (1916), 157–69.

Christian after bodily death, that the earliest thinkers seem to have understood the idea: as the product of the healing forgiveness brought to the sinner by Jesus the Saviour.[11] But for Clement the problem of deification is also intimately bound up with the scope of human activity in this life, and, in particular, with the true meaning of the Incarnation of Christ, for 'the Logos of God had become man so that you might learn from a man how a man may become God'.[12] It is this ultimately mystical, rather than eschatological, understanding of deification, predicated on the possibility of a transformation through contact with the divine that need not be postponed until after death, that helps to found the tradition that leads to Bernard and Dante.

Clement's thought was taken up and elaborated by Origen (c. 185–254), who sought to relate deification more closely to a textual basis in Scripture, to link it more firmly with the question of the Incarnation (for, as Jaroslav Pelikan neatly puts it, 'the church could not specify what it meant to promise that man would become divine until it had specified what it meant to confess that Christ had always been divine'),[13] and to stress it as the restoration of a condition of originary perfection lost by humanity through Adam's fall. This scriptural grounding was to give the new doctrine greater stability and increase its appeal, to the extent that by the time of Athanasius (c. 296–373), both its broad delineation and some of its technical lexicon were beginning to find widespread acceptance as an axiomatic basis for argument.

Athanasius was to be one of the key figures in the expansion of deification doctrine, and his influence remained perceptible in both Greek and Latin thought.[14] One text in particular (cited, incidentally, by at least one modern editor of Bernard's *De diligendo Deo*) elegantly encapsulates the intellectual synthesis that Athanasius was able to bring about: 'The Word became man that we might become gods; he became visible in his body that we might have an idea of the Father invisible; he endured the cruelty of man, that we might share his immortality'.[15] In this passage from the work significantly known

---

[11] Butterworth, 'Deification', pp. 161–2; Pelikan, *Emergence*, pp. 154–5.

[12] Clement, *Protrepticus*, I. viii. 4; quoted by Pelikan, *Emergence*, p. 155, and McGinn, *Foundations*, p. 107.

[13] Pelikan, *Emergence*, p. 155; see also *DS*, III, cols. 1379–80; McGinn, *Foundations*, 128–9.

[14] For Athanasius, see *DS*, III, cols. 1380–1; Pelikan, *Emergence*, p. 206.

[15] Athanasius, *De incarnatione Verbi*, LIV. 3; quoted in *Select Treatises of St Bernard of Clairvaux*, edited by Barton R. V. Mills and Watkin Williams (Cambridge, 1926), p. 50n.

in Latin as *De incarnatione Verbi*, the first, basic statement clearly owes much to the tradition derived from Clement of Alexandria, while the second and third equally clearly reflect the two possible approaches to deification, as a grace acting on us in this life and as a condition of immortality in the afterlife. What Athanasius has done is link them into a chain of mutually dependent propositions, rather than leaving them as unconnected (and potentially contradictory) responses to the idea of the human capacity to become, in whatever sense, divine.

After Athanasius, and thanks to his authority, both the concept and the language of deification began to occur in a wide variety of authors, many of whom made notable individual contributions to the tradition's growth in the Greek Church. To a significant degree, however, they tended to follow in the footsteps of the early Alexandrian Fathers, whose writings were to remain the classic exposition of the subject at least until the sixth century. Basil (c. 330–379), for example, develops the Athanasian position, while scrupulously avoiding the use of such deification language as could not already be found in the Bible.[16] Gregory of Nazianzus (329–389), on the other hand, uses deification language freely, basing much of it on his reading in Neoplatonist philosophy.[17] In his turn, Gregory of Nyssa (c. 330–c. 395) reacts against Neoplatonist influence, apparently because of its tendency towards pantheism, and follows his brother Basil in avoiding non-Biblical language.[18]

Gregory is, in fact, at some pains to stress the width of the gulf that separates the human from the divine nature, even though we possess the image of God at the heart of our being. In this he shows himself to be aware of the greatest difficulty inherent in the existence of a doctrine of deification within a monotheistic religion: that of asserting that a human being can be 'deified' in any meaningful way, when there is but one God, who is humanity's creator, and who alone is truly divine. (This difficulty was eventually to be dealt with by distinguishing between the proper and analogous sense of any quality predicated of God, so that the sense in which God must be said to be 'divine' could clearly be seen to differ from that in which man might be – but this was long after the fourth century.) In his emphasis on the *diastema* (distance) between God and man, even when the latter was 'deified', Gregory was evidently more alert than many of his

---

[16] *DS*, III, cols. 1381–2.   [17] Ibid.   [18] Ibid., cols. 1382–3.

contemporaries to the potential theological dangers lurking beneath the surface of the developing concept of deification.

Partly in response to such fears, associated as they were with the powerful and steadily growing influence of Neoplatonist thought, some fourth-century theologians began to make a defensive move in the direction of greater stress on the specifically Christian elements of deification. John Chrysostom (c. 347–407) centred his argument on the 'deifying' function of the Eucharist, and followed Basil and Gregory of Nyssa in eschewing non-Biblical deification language as far as possible.[19] The most successful synthesis between this approach and that of the Cappadocian Fathers, which led back to Athanasius, was the work of Cyril of Alexandria (who died in 444). Nevertheless, even Cyril steered clear of using deification language in his writings, preferring the conceptual language of filiation as his expression of the relationship between the individual and God.[20]

Cyril may be taken as marking a term in the development of deification doctrine in the Greek Church. He was among the last to look back directly to the Athanasian synthesis, and also to hold out against the increasing domination of Neoplatonist modes of thinking. The early sixth century saw the composition of the texts wrongly but durably attributed to Dionysius the Areopagite (who 'clave unto' St Paul, Acts 17. 34); and with their appearance (first recorded in 533) the course of thinking about deification was perceptibly and irrevocably altered.[21] Pseudo-Dionysius – whether 'he' was an individual or a collective *auctor* – deliberately aimed at an essentially mystical fusion of Christian theology and Neoplatonist philosophy; and thus, as far as deification is concerned, his writings contrasted sharply with the sacramentally based, theological interpretations of John Chrysostom and his sympathizers. Instead he took up the Neoplatonist hints of Gregory of Nazianzus, collated them with the philosophical schemes of, in particular, Iamblichus and Proclus, and thence derived a theory of deification whose basis in mystical experience and formative inheritance from Neoplatonism were undeniable.

This radical shift in emphasis was accompanied by – indeed, embodied in – a change in terminology. The older term *theopoiesis*,

[19] Ibid., col. 1383.        [20] Ibid., cols. 1383–5; Pelikan, *Emergence*, pp. 233–4.
[21] *DS*, III, cols. 1385–6; Lot-Borodine, 'Doctrine' (1932), 15–17; McGinn, *Foundations*, pp. 178–9. *Pseudo-Dionysius*: *The Complete Works*, edited and translated by Paul Rorem and others (New York, 1987), is superbly edited and has much useful introductory material.

whose linguistic antecedents, in this context, stretched all the way back to Clement of Alexandria, was discarded, making way for *theosis*, a word found in Gregory of Nazianzus but clearly enhanced, in pseudo-Dionysius's eyes, by its use in Proclus. Henceforth, deification was almost invariably to be seen, in the Greek Church, from a mystical rather than a strictly theological perspective – and thus as essentially indescribable in human language; and its exact definition, always problematic, was, as a result, to become and remain irrecoverably elusive.

The importance of all this in the present context is that pseudo-Dionysius and his explicators (chief among them Maximus Confessor), through the Latin translations made in the ninth century by John Scotus Erigena, marked the point at which the Greek tradition of deification began to enter the mainstream of Christian thinking in the West, and to provide solid support for the tentative efforts at definition, via fragile verbal coinages, that earlier centuries had produced. It was the prolific seventh-century author Maximus, through his various sets of *scholia* on pseudo-Dionysius and in his own *Ambigua*, who constructed the definitive exegetical synthesis of the *soi-disant* Areopagite and his precursors – and his version was further refined by John Damascene (c. 675–c. 749) – but thereafter the Greek tradition ceases to be important for the development of deification doctrine in the West. The infusion of new ideas from pseudo-Dionysian sources provided the impetus for developments there that took no account of what continued to happen in the East (where thinking about deification remained productive and influential at least as far as Gregory Palamas in the fourteenth century).[22]

Theories of deification were thus being devised and elaborated simultaneously in the Latin and Greek Churches; but, for the reasons outlined above, opportunities for exchange and cross-fertilization were limited. The result was that deification acquired different theological resonances in the West. Indeed, it is fair to say that there was always less interest in the topic in the Latin Church than in the Greek: fewer Western writers discussed it, and those who did usually spent less time on it than did their Greek-speaking counterparts.

Furthermore, at the heart of the Latin approach to deification was

[22] For Maximus and John Damascene, see *DS*, III, cols. 1387–8; Lot-Borodine, 'Doctrine', 17; Jaroslav Pelikan, *The Spirit of Eastern Christendom (600–1700)*, volume II of *The Christian Tradition: A History of the Development of Doctrine* (Chicago and London, 1974), pp. 10–16 (on Maximus), 259–60 (on Symeon the New Theologian), and 267–8 (on Gregory Palamas).

an emphasis on a basically human morality, the practice of which would lead, with the aid of grace, to a state of sanctity identifiable as deification. This was clearly distinct from – because more limited in scope than – the Greek idea of restored resemblance to God and eventual absorption into the divine, which was to be achieved through the sacraments in their function as the literal embodiment of the hypostatic union in the person of Christ. Greek thought had traditionally stressed the mysterious and gratuitous nature of deification; Latin thought, in general, had approached it with the assumption that it was a matter less mysterious than simply practical. Where the Greek tradition accentuated the mystery in which the Word became flesh in order to restore man's lost divine image, Latin writers on deification highlighted the redeeming work of Christ, which enables humanity to recover, in this life, the objective condition of sanctity forfeited by Adam.[23]

The linguistic history of deification among Latin writers is no more straightforward than the corresponding history in Greek. It was perfectly possible to write about deification in Latin without exploiting the technical language represented by the group of words etymologically related to the basic verb *deificari*, as several of the authors discussed below (most obviously Thomas Aquinas) will illustrate. But it will be useful here to concentrate on *deificari* and its cognates, because theirs is the language characteristic of Bernard of Clairvaux's most extensive treatment of the subject, and thus that which, according to Migliorini Fissi's hypothesis, might be expected to have been influential on Dante.

The earliest usage of deification language in Latin, at least among Christian writers (pagan usage, where polytheistic religions offered far more scope and a broader semantic range for it, being a separate issue), seems to have been in the *Apologeticus* of Tertullian (c. 160–c. 225).[24] He uses the adjectival form *deificus* to mean 'divinizing', and applies it to God. The same form appears in one of the letters of Cyprian (d. 258), though there it seems to mean no more than 'divine'.[25] From the beginning, then, deification language in Latin was susceptible of a range of related meanings. It never became a commonplace in patristic literature: even the *Thesaurus linguae latinae*

---

[23] *DS*, III, col. 1389.  [24] Tertullian, *Apologeticus*, 11; *Patrologia latina* (*PL*), 1, col. 335.

[25] Cyprian, *Epistulae*, LII. 2; in *Opera*, edited by Wilhelm Hartel, Corpus Scriptorum Ecclesiasticorum Latinorum, III/1 (Vienna, 1868), p. 618: 'deificam et ecclesiasticam disciplinam'.

manages to amass no more than a score of instances.[26] But, even from
a small sample, it is still possible to identify at least three main clusters
of ideas expressed by the use of *deificari* and its cognates.

The first of these is characterized by the transitive use of the verb
*deificare* in the simple sense of 'to deify', to proclaim the divinity of a
person or object, as the pagan Romans had deified their emperors.
Indeed, it is precisely in the context of pagan history that this usage
occurs most often, as in a commentary on Paul's Epistle to the
Romans attributed to St Ambrose,[27] or in the *Historia tripartita* of
Cassiodorus (c. 485–c. 580).[28] In the same passage, Cassiodorus also
uses the passive verb *deificari* in a way that illustrates the second set of
meanings attached to deification language, that connected with the
controversy over the relationship of humanity and divinity in the
person of Christ. This, as we have seen, was one of the main
theological arenas in which deification language was developed and
tested by Greek thinkers as well. Its use in this debate is highly
specialized, and differs somewhat from its more general application
to the spiritual life of the individual Christian. It appears in fifth-
century writers involved in polemics around the Nestorian heresy,
such as pseudo-Marius Mercator[29] and pseudo-Arnobius;[30] and also,
outside the purely controversial context but still in a discussion of the
dual nature of Christ, in a sermon of Augustine's.[31]

But the most important, as well as the most common, use of
deification language is in the sense identifiable in Athanasius, and
before him in Clement of Alexandria: that of man being or becoming
in some way a partaker of the divine nature. This can be applied to
some of the human attributes of Christ (though not to his essential
nature), as it was, in the late fourth century, by pseudo-Rufinus.[32]
More often, however, it is applied to the individual Christian in his
(and perhaps, by extension, her) relations with God. Even within
these outlines, numerous variations in approach and emphasis remain
possible.

The most important thinker about deification in the early centuries

---

[26] *Thesaurus Linguae Latinae* (Leipzig, 1900– ), v/1, fasc. 2 (1910), cols. 403–4.

[27] Pseudo-Ambrose, *Commentarium in Epistolam ad Romanos*, 1. 24; *PL*, 17, col. 59.

[28] Cassiodorus, *Historia tripartita*, vii. 2; *PL*, 69, cols. 1066–7.

[29] Pseudo-Marius Mercator, *Translationes Epistularum Nestorii in causa Pelagiana scriptarum*, 1 ('ad Caelestinum papam'), 3; *PL*, 48, col. 177.

[30] Pseudo-Arnobius, *Conflictus de deo trino et uno*, ii. 14; *PL*, 53, cols. 292–3.

[31] Augustine, *Sermo* cxxvi, 14; *PL*, 38, col. 704.

[32] Pseudo-Rufinus, Commentary on Psalm 51. 11; *PL*, 21, col. 856.

of the Latin Church was Augustine: his teaching towers over his own
age and endures as an inescapable influence on all subsequent
thinking in this domain. Indeed, it may be that the apparently
definitive nature of Augustine's formulations inhibited, or at least
retarded, further enquiry into deification in the Western Church,
and helps to explain why it never became as central a doctrine there
as it did in the East. After Augustine, most Latin writers restate or
rework his version of deification theology, rather than extending its
boundaries significantly. While this is not entirely true of Bernard,
even his profound indebtedness to Augustine's thinking needs to be
acknowledged from the outset.

A good working definition of the basic Augustinian teaching on
deification may be taken from this gloss on verse 6 of Psalm 81
(Vulgate numeration), which actually occurs in his commentary on
Psalm 49. 1. Here he grapples with the inherent ambiguity of the
wording in a way that was, for many later theologians, to define
conclusively the relationship of human and divine participation in
the experience of deification:

Videte in eodem psalmo quibus dicat: Ego dixi, Dii estis, et filii Excelsi
omnes ... Manifestum est ergo, quia homines dixit deos, ex gratia sua
deificatos, non de substantia sua natos. Ille enim justificat, qui per
semetipsum non ex alio justus est; et ille deificat, qui per seipsum non
alterius participatione Deus est. Qui autem justificat, ipse deificat, quia
justificando filios Dei facit ... Si filii Dei facti sumus, et dii facti sumus: sed
hoc gratiae est adoptantis, non naturae generantis. Unicus enim Dei Filius
Deus et cum Patre unus Deus, Dominus et Salvator noster Jesus Christus, in
principio Verbum et Verbum apud Deum, Verbum Deus. Caeteri qui fiunt
dii, gratia ipsius fiunt, non de substantia ejus nascuntur ut hoc sint quod ille,
sed ut per beneficium perveniant ad eum, et sint cohaeredes Christi.[33]

In this passage Augustine takes extreme care to deflect the dangers
posed by too literal a reading of the text 'Ego dixi, dii estis' ('I have

[33] Augustine, *Enarrationes in Psalmos, ad loc.* Psalm 49. 1; *PL*, 36, col. 565: 'You see in the same
psalm the words in which he says: I have said, you are gods, and all children of the most
High ... It is plain, therefore, that he has called human beings gods, but deified by his grace,
not born of his substance. For he justifies, who through himself and not by virtue of another
is just; and he deifies, who through himself and not by participation in any other is God. Yet
he who justifies, also deifies, because by justifying he makes children of God ... If we have
been made the children of God, we have also been made gods; but this is by the grace of him
who adopts us, not the nature of him who begets us. For there is one and only one son of God,
who is God and one God with the Father, our Lord and Saviour Jesus Christ, the Word in
the beginning and the Word with God, the Word who is God. Others who become gods do
so by his grace; they are not born of his substance so that they may be like him, but so that
through his generosity they may come to him, and be co-heirs with Christ.'

said, Ye are gods'). He insists that deification is a work of grace
operative on man, and not an identity of substance between God and
man ('ex gratia sua deificatos, non de substantia sua natos'); he
declares that the power to justify through grace, which is in effect the
power to deify, belongs to God and God alone ('per semetipsum non
ex alio ... per seipsum non ex alterius participatione'); and he stresses
the second phrase of the Biblical quotation, 'et filii Excelsi omnes'
('and all of you are children of the most High'), arguing that the
divinity conferred in deification is the power to become the children
of God and to be united with him through Christ ('ut per beneficium
perveniant ad eum, et sint cohaeredes Christi').

This power is also, of course, the idea that underlies the opening of
John's Gospel, a text whose presence in Augustine's thinking on this
subject is attested here by the quotation of verse 1 ('in principio
Verbum et Verbum apud Deum, Verbum Deus' – 'In the beginning
was the Word, and the Word was with God, and the Word was
God'). This intertextual allusion, strengthened by the veiled memory
of such texts as John 1. 12 ('But as many as received him, to them
gave he power to become the sons of God [*filios Dei fieri*], even to them
that believe on his name'), confirms that, for Augustine, Christ's role
as mediator of the saving grace that restores fallen man was more
significant than the central Greek conception of the Incarnation as
expressing a form of deified humanity.

Augustine's other uses of deification language are less detailed and
searching than this, but they show him continuing to explore possible
refinements of the idea. In one of his letters he proclaims the need to
retreat from the world in quest of deificatory experience (in terms
that Bernard would not have found uncongenial), while a passing
reference in another commentary on one of the Psalms emphasizes
the magnitude of the grace that makes deification possible.[34]
Augustine further believed – and in this he was to be followed by
nearly all later writers, including Bernard – that the full glory of
deified being could be experienced only by the redeemed soul in
Heaven, after the resurrection of the body.[35] Deification cannot be
fully achieved in this life, for the body is finite, its senses are limited
and doomed to fail, and our knowledge of God must remain restricted
by these ineluctable signs of our physical mortality. Only when these
impediments are removed, therefore, in the life to come, can we hope

[34] Augustine, *Epistula* x(to Nebridius), 2; *PL*, 33, col. 74; *Enarrationes in Psalmos, ad loc.* Psalm
117. 16; *PL*, 37, col. 1498.    [35] Augustine, *Sermo* CLXVI, 4; *PL*, 38, col. 909.

to enjoy deification, and thus truly adhere to the nature of God. This is accepted by the Augustine of *Sermo* CLXVI, by the Bernard of *De diligendo Deo*, x. 29, and, I shall argue, by Dante in his definition of 'trasumanar'. But Augustine also believed that some progress towards deification was still possible in this life; for him, as for Bernard, the imitation of God, the doing of his will and the according with it of man's own will are the means by which we may become disposed to receive the necessary grace.[36]

This sketch of the development of deification language and doctrine in the early Church has of necessity, up to now, been divided both linguistically and culturally: on the one hand the tradition of the Greek Fathers, stemming from Clement and Athanasius, on the other the Latin tradition, which reaches its apogee of thought and expression in Augustine. After a long period without noteworthy innovation – though the doctrine is clearly essential to such as Leo the Great (d. 461), who, interestingly, altogether avoids using deification language as such, despite his obvious debt to Augustine[37] – a turning-point was reached in the ninth century. The decisive factor, for the development of deification doctrine in general and for Bernard's understanding of it in particular, was the marriage of the Greek and Latin traditions brought about by John Scotus Erigena's translations of pseudo-Dionysius and Maximus Confessor (which are conveniently collected in volume 122 of the *Patrologia latina*). For the first time, these Greek writers, whose works treated deification in exhaustive detail, were available to thinkers brought up on Augustine in the Latin West. Although their impact was limited at first (though other aspects of pseudo-Dionysius's thinking, such as his angelology, were taken up swiftly and enthusiastically), they seem to have provoked a particularly warm response in the twelfth century, not least in Bernard of Clairvaux.

No major treatise on deification appeared in the two or three centuries after the completion of Erigena's translations; but some monastic authors of the eleventh and twelfth centuries began to consider the subject, in ways that show the influence of both patristic (specifically, Augustinian) tradition and the new teaching from the East. These monks – a sizeable group that includes Anselm, Peter the Venerable, and Rupert of Deutz – conceive of deification in a basically Athanasian sense, as a participation in the divine nature

---

[36] Augustine, *De civitate Dei*, XIX. 23; *PL*, 41, col. 653.   [37] *DS*, III, cols. 1397–8.

brought about by the action of grace, and use deification language liberally, though always in contexts sanctioned by patristic precedent.[38] However, in none of these authors did deification itself (or contemplative mysticism in general) occupy the central place that it did in Bernard of Clairvaux's theological scheme; nor did any of them, as individuals, enjoy even remotely similar authority. Along with his younger contemporaries and admirers William of St Thierry and Richard of St Victor, it is Bernard who stands at the heart of the flowering of interest in deification in the twelfth century.

Etienne Gilson has sought to prove that the *Ambigua* of Maximus Confessor, in Erigena's translation, was a shaping influence on Bernard's best-known statement of the nature of deification (*De diligendo Deo*, x. 28), to the point where certain expressive metaphors for the process passed almost intact from one text to the other.[39] His detailed exposition makes a convincing case for this view; but it is still vital, when analysing Bernard's thought, to proceed cautiously, if only because of the subtleties of terminology characteristic of Maximus's writing (and faithfully rendered by his translator). As Gilson makes clear, *deificatio*, for Maximus, is the *result* of an approach to God inspired by grace, not the approach itself. The soul moves towards God in an ecstatic transport, called by Maximus *excessus*, which purges it of the excrescences of self and establishes its true nature in relation to God, by restoring its lost likeness to its creator. But *excessus* itself cannot be perfected in this life; at best it can achieve an ineffable participation in the divine nature that still falls short of complete involvement, remaining firmly on the level of analogy or assimilation. The soul thus becomes God-*like*, though always essentially human. This, in Gilson's account, is Maximus' conception of *deificatio*.[40] I shall argue below that this distinction between preparation and achievement, process and product, may be useful in relating Dante's 'trasumanar' to Bernard's idea of deification.

That idea has been extensively studied by scholars as expert as Gilson himself and Jean Leclercq, and their work, much of it now several decades old, still provides the best commentary currently available on this aspect of Bernard's thought.[41] A few remarks on the subject may still, however, be useful here.

---

[38] Ibid., cols. 1399–405.   [39] Gilson, *Théologie mystique*, pp. 38–42.
[40] Ibid., p. 41.
[41] Of Leclercq's many pertinent writings on Bernard, see especially *Saint Bernard mystique* (Bruges, 1948).

Bernard is very sparing in his use of deification language. Apart from a few adjectival uses ('deificata', 'deifica'), where the specific gravity of the words seems not to be very great, the only instance is the occurrence of the infinitive 'deificari' in *De diligendo Deo*, x. 28, where it appears in an extended discussion of the process through which man is lifted towards God by the action of divine love on the soul:

O amor sanctus et castus! O dulcis et suavis affectio! O pura et defaecata intentio voluntatis, eo certe defaecatior et purior, quo in ea de proprio nil iam admixtum relinquitur, eo suavior et dulcior, quo totum divinum est quod sentitur! Sic affici, deificari est. Quomodo stilla aquae modica, multo infusa vino, deficere a se tota videtur, dum et saporem vini induit et colorem, et quomodo ferrum ignitum et candens igni simillimum fit, pristina propriaque exutum forma, et quomodo solis luce perfusus aer in eadem transformatur luminis claritatem, adeo ut non tam illuminatus quam ipsum lumen esse videatur, sic omnem tunc in sanctis humanam affectionem quodam ineffabili modo necesse erit a semetipsa liquescere, atque in Dei penitus transfundi voluntatem.[42]

The chapter from which this passage is extracted describes the fourth and last of the stages identified by Bernard in the soul's movement towards God, that in which man loves himself for God's sake alone. But this stage is not easy of access, nor does it last long even if achieved in this life (as Bernard neatly puts it elsewhere, such experiences come, if at all, 'rara hora, parva mora', 'rarely and briefly').[43] Mortal man is scarcely capable, in fact, of withdrawing himself sufficiently from this world, and its pleasures and concerns, to enjoy for more than an instant the deifying vision ('deifica visio', *De diligendo Deo*, iv. 12) of God. This is made powerfully clear in the passage immediately preceding the one quoted above:

Te enim quodammodo perdere, tamquam qui non sis, et omnino non sentire teipsum, et a temetipso exinaniri, et paene annullari, caelestis est

---

[42] Bernard, *De diligendo Deo*, x. 28; *Opera*, III (1963), 143; *PL*, 182, col. 991: 'O holy and chaste love! O sweet and pleasant affection! O pure and cleanly intention of the will, certainly the more pure and cleanly because nothing of its own now remains mixed in with it, the more pleasant and sweet because everything that is felt in it is divine! To enjoy this feeling is to be deified. Just as a tiny drop of water, mixed with a lot of wine, seems completely to dissipate, when it takes on the taste and colour of the wine; and as heated, molten iron becomes like fire itself, putting off its original and specific form; and as the air, shot through with the light of the sun, is transformed into the brightness of that light, so that it seems not so much to be lit up as to become light itself; so then, in the saints, every human inclination will of necessity begin to alter its very nature, in some unspeakable way, and will be completely fused with the will of God.'

[43] Bernard, *In Cantica canticorum*, XXIII. 15; *Opera*, I, 148; *PL*, 183, col. 892.

conversationis, non humanae affectionis. Et si quidem e mortalibus quispiam ad illud raptim interdum, ut dictum est, et ad momentum admittitur, subito invidet saeculum nequam, perturbat diei malitia, corpus mortis aggravat, sollicitat carnis necessitas, defectus corruptionis non sustinet, quodque his violentius est, fraterna revocat caritas.[44]

From these key passages, then, it is clear that Bernard conceives of deification as an experience properly belonging not to this life but to that to come ('caelestis est conversationis, non humanae affectionis'); the transformations that he envisages, and to which he gives such cogent metaphorical expression (even though two of his images, the sun-drenched air and the molten iron, are taken directly from Erigena's version of Maximus), will be operative in the future on the souls of the blessed, rather than being readily available in the here and now ('sic omnem *tunc in sanctis* humanam affectionem ... necesse *erit* a semetipsa liquescere').

But it may still be possible to enjoy deification in this life, fleetingly and fragmentarily, if one strives to bring one's own will into accord with God's, thereby making the essential response to his generous and undeserved offer of grace. Whether in this life or the next, this is the kernel of Bernard's doctrine of deification: the accord of wills. It does not require the negation or the abolition of the human will, nor the abject surrender of its faculties to divine power; for the will is a vital aspect of human nature – helps, indeed, to define what it is to be human – and it must be preserved in its autonomy if the whole scheme of grace and free will, central to the Christian concept of humanity in its relationship with God, is not to be fatally devalued. So the deified human will retains its existential independence, but is perfectly and indistinguishably aligned, in every respect, with its divine counterpart. Their exact correspondence with this difficult idea is what gives the images of *De diligendo Deo*, x. 28 such remarkable resonance: for the water seems to be absorbed into the wine, yet in reality retains its own nature; molten iron seems to become fire, yet

---

[44] Bernard, *De diligendo Deo*, x. 27; *Opera*, III (1963), 142; *PL*, 182, col. 990: 'For to lose yourself in some way, as if you were not, and to feel your own existence in no way at all, and to depart from your own being entirely, and almost to be annihilated, belongs to the experience of Heaven, not to the nature of humanity. And if any mortal whatever is caught up like this in the meantime, as has been said, and admitted to that experience for a moment, at once the wicked world begins to envy him, the evil of the day to disturb him, the body of death to weigh down on him, the needs of the flesh to pester him; the weakness of corruption cannot sustain him, and, what is more powerful than all these, fraternal charity calls him back.'

remains iron in essence despite the alteration of its form; and the air shot through by the sun's rays appears itself to become light, while all the time remaining, essentially, air.[45]

Clearly, then, deification involves, above all, transformation, and transformation in the strictest sense: for it is the form of human nature, the *way* in which a human being is human, that undergoes change, while the essence of that nature, the *fact* that a human being is human, remains unaltered. Human will ('intentio voluntatis') is purged of what is its own ('de proprio nil iam admixtum relinquitur'), but this is achieved by realigning it, through the action of love, so as to conform with God's will, so that there is no longer anything of the human being's that is not also God's ('totum divinum est quod sentitur'). But what belongs to human beings continues to belong to them, and certainly does not cease to exist; throughout, an individual's humanity remains the essence of what he (or she) is. This is also made clear in one of Bernard's sermons, where the individual's human substance and 'affectio' are also at issue: 'Absorpta videtur in deitatem humanitas, non quod mutata sit substantia, sed affectio deificata.'[46]

Bernard speaks elsewhere of the transformation involved in the soul's assimilation to God, but nowhere with such fervour or such depth of meaning. The necessity for the realignment of human nature is also asserted, for instance, on two occasions in the sermons *In Cantica canticorum*. In both cases the key word is *transformari* ('to be transformed'). 'Nescio enim qua vicinitate naturae, cum semel revelata facie gloriam Dei speculari anima poterit, mox illi se conformari necesse est atque in eamdem imaginem transformari', runs one passage from sermon LXIX;[47] and a related extract from sermon LXII shows still more plainly the core of Bernard's thinking (as well, incidentally, as the informing presence of St Paul):

Etenim revelata facie speculantes, in eamdem imaginem transformamur de claritate in claritatem, tamquam a Domini Spiritu. Transformamur cum

---

[45] Bernard, *De diligendo Deo*, x. 28 (see n. 42 above). The borrowings from Maximus Confessor are identified by Gilson, *Théologie mystique*, p. 40.

[46] Bernard, *Sermo in dominica infra octavam Assumptionis*, 1; *Opera*, v (1968), 262; *PL*, 183, col. 429: 'Humanity appears absorbed into deity, not that its substance has been changed, but that its inclinations have been deified.'

[47] Bernard, *In Cantica canticorum*, LXIX. 7; *Opera*, II (1958), 206; *PL*, 183, col. 1116: 'By I know not what affinity of their natures, when once the soul has been able to behold the glory of God face to face, it soon finds it necessary to begin to resemble that face and be transformed into that same image.'

conformamur. Absit autem ut in maiestatis gloria, et non magis in voluntatis modestia, Dei ab homine conformitas praesumatur.[48]

These, though, are only sketches, in comparison with the sustained exaltation of *De diligendo Deo*, x. 28. There Bernard expounds his doctrine of deification in a way that potently unites spiritual fervour with intellectual rigour. Yet, for all Bernard's eloquent intelligence, there is still a point beyond which he cannot go. When he seeks to explain the transformations involved in deification by using imagery, he seems to succeed brilliantly; and yet the action of love on the human will, inspired by grace, still takes place 'quodam ineffabili modo' ('in some indescribable fashion').[49] Even Bernard cannot find the words to render the totality of the ineffable experience that is deification. Just as human beings cannot perfectly enjoy deification in this life, because of the limitations imposed by their mortality, so they cannot effectively communicate it, even if they have attained some transitory experience of it, because of the limitations inherent in their language. Like Dante with 'trasumanar', Bernard ultimately finds it impossible to convey the meaning of deification '*per verba*'.

Bernard's thought had a lasting effect on many later twelfth- and early thirteenth-century theologians and contemplatives, and not only on those who might be expected to have felt an instinctive sympathy with him because of their membership of the Cistercian Order. This influence was to wane somewhat with the increasing ascendancy of scholastic ways of thinking (and writing), but Bernard the *auctor* never dropped entirely from view, least of all in the areas that, as we have seen, posterity came to associate most closely with him: devotion to Mary and contemplative mysticism. Within the Cistercian Order itself, of course, his prestige remained unrivalled: every Cistercian thinker of the twelfth century is deeply marked by acquaintance with his writings (and, in some cases, with him personally), and some, such as Gilbert of Hoyland, continuator of the interrupted series of sermons *In Cantica canticorum*, deliberately set out to develop those aspects of the master's work that he had left unfinished or insufficiently polished.

---

[48] Bernard, *In Cantica canticorum*, LXII. 5; *Opera*, II (1958), 158; *PL*, 183, col. 1078: 'For when we see him face to face, we are transformed into that same image, from brightness into brightness, as if by the spirit of the Lord. We are transformed as we are made to resemble. Let it, however, be only in the modesty of the will, and not in the glory of majesty, that the resemblance of mankind to God be thought to consist.'

[49] On ineffability in the Bernardine and twelfth-century contexts, see Manuela Colombo, *Dai mistici a Dante: il linguaggio dell'ineffabilità* (Florence, 1987).

But such Cistercian devotion to Bernard's memory did not imply that members of the Order were unable to bring their own emphases or reinterpretations to their chosen themes; and, in the case of deification doctrine, certain independent nuances are discernible in the work even of those most intimately connected with Bernard himself. William of St Thierry, for instance, shows the influence of pseudo-Dionysius much more markedly than does his teacher, and draws the marrow of his concept of 'theophany' from that source.[50] Another author much affected by Bernard (though not himself a Cistercian), Richard of St Victor, arrives at a definition of *deificatio* that, despite the similarity of idea, is not strictly identifiable with Bernard's own:

In hoc statu dum mens a seipsa alienatur, dum in illud divini arcani secretarium rapitur, dum ab illo divini amoris incendio undique circumdatur, intime penetratur, usquequaque inflammatur seipsam penitus exuit, divinum quemdam affectum induit, et inspectae pulchritudini configurata tota in aliam gloriam transit.[51]

Though there are things here that recall Bernard – notably the stress on utter transformation ('tota in aliam gloriam transit') – the whole atmosphere is different: more violent in its imagery ('alienatur', 'rapitur', 'incendio undique circumdatur', 'penetratur', 'inflammatur'), and, perhaps because of this very verbal intensity, less sharply defined. In particular, the importance of the realignment of the human will through love is absent from Richard's depiction of the process. Moreover, this passage is a description of the *third* of the four stages of growth in divine love that Richard identifies: his fourfold categorization is different from Bernard's, in which deification occurs, if at all, as part of the fourth and final stage.

Richard has, in fact, a subtle and highly developed theology of contemplation, and examines its effects on the soul in some detail in several of his works. Its importance to him is obvious from the alternative (and more formal) titles of his most famous writings: that of the treatise often called *Benjamin minor* is *De praeparatione animae ad*

---

[50] *DS*, III, cols. 1408–11.
[51] Richard of St Victor, *De IV gradibus violentae caritatis*, 38. See *Über die Gewalt der Liebe: Ihre vier Stufen*, edited and translated by Margot Schmidt (Munich, Paderborn and Vienna, 1969), pp. 60–2; *PL*, 196, col. 1221: 'In this state, while the mind is detached from itself, while it is caught up into that chamber of divine secrecy, while by that fire of divine love it is surrounded on all sides and intimately penetrated, it becomes so thoroughly inflamed that it almost puts its own self aside, takes on a certain divine inclination, and, totally remodelling itself on the beauty it has seen, crosses over into another glory.'

*contemplationem*, that of *Benjamin major*, *De gratia contemplandi*. In both works, though more fully in the latter – as their alternative titles imply – Richard studies and defines the mechanism of the soul's approach to God in contemplation. He uses, throughout, a characteristic lexicon of his own, which does not include the cognates of *deificari*, his preferred term being, in the tradition of Maximus Confessor as rendered by Erigena, *excessus*.

Greater stress on the crucial role of the will is to be found in a well-known formula, devised by William of St Thierry but often attributed (as it is, for example, by Bonaventure) to Bernard: 'Voluntas crescit in amorem, amor in caritatem et caritas in sapientiam.'[52] For William, as for Bernard, the return to God is made possible by the action of grace on the will, which moves the individual to love God for himself, and so to restore the divine resemblance forfeited through sin. Here, in his immediate circle, Bernard's influence is naturally at its strongest. But it is not confined to that circle, nor indeed to the Cistercian Order.

The major Franciscan writers on deification, as on so much else, in the thirteenth century were Alexander of Hales and Bonaventure. Bernard's thinking about the subject seems to have made little impression on Alexander, who devised a coherent theory of his own, which was to influence not only Bonaventure and his fellow-Franciscans but also, through Alexander's rudimentary presentation of the concept of *participatio*, Thomas Aquinas.[53] (Traces of the concept, as well as the use of the word itself, can be found, however, as far back as Augustine, and also occur in Erigena's translation of Maximus Confessor's *Ambigua*.)[54] For Alexander, divine grace instils in the soul a quality that makes it pleasing to God, and, eventually, what makes it pleasing to God makes it 'deiformis' ('God-like'); the soul is thus restored to resemblance with God and, purified, illumined, and perfected, it can be assimilated to the Trinity.

Bonaventure, in turn, takes up the word 'deiformis', and establishes a terminology in which God's 'condescensio' inspires the granting of grace to the soul, leading to the soul's 'reversus' towards God, the restoration of its 'habitus deiformis', and its ultimate

---

[52] 'The will grows into love, love into charity and charity into wisdom.' Quoted in Bonaventure's commentary on Book III of Peter Lombard's *Sententiae*, d. 27, a. 1, q. 3, fund. 1, as 'Bernardus de amore Dei capitulo secundo' ('Bernard in the second chapter on the love of God'): Bonaventure, *Opera omnia*, 10 vols (Ad Claras Aquas, 1882–1902), III (1887), 596. The work referred to is actually William's *De natura et dignitate amoris*; *PL*, 184, col. 382.

[53] *DS*, III, cols. 1415–16.     [54] Gilson, *Théologie mystique*, pp. 40–1.

assimilation.[55] Bonaventure's lexical inventiveness may, to some extent, be the sign of his declaration of theological independence from Bernard and the Cistercian tradition: though, as we have seen (chapter 2), he quotes Bernard frequently in his writings, only a few of those many quotations relate to deification – and most of those few in fact attribute texts of William of St Thierry's to Bernard.[56] On the whole the quotations evoke neither dissent nor even much comment from Bonaventure, and it may therefore be surmised that he, like many of his scholastic contemporaries and successors, was willing to accept Bernard's account without bothering to challenge or even to explore it thoroughly.

The same is not true of Thomas Aquinas, sceptical as ever in his estimation of the merits of Bernard's thinking. It was impossible that, in the construction of a theological edifice as imposing as the *Summa theologiae*, he should fail to touch on the points that had exercised Bernard; but it is not surprising that he should have chosen to do so in ways that differ both lexically and conceptually from the solutions adopted by his Cistercian predecessor.

Aquinas' use of deification language in the *Summa theologiae* is as sparing as Bernard's own; and not all the instances are even connected with *deificatio* in the mystical Bernardine sense, belonging rather to the field of Christology.[57] At one point in the *Pars tertia*, while engaged in a discussion of Christ's bodily nature, Aquinas distinguishes between the deified flesh's possible loss or retention of its own properties in a way that shows his awareness of the fundamental ambiguity, in a monotheistic framework, of the idea of any man's becoming God;[58] and elsewhere, again discussing the views expressed by Gregory of Nazianzus and John Damascene on the dual nature of Christ's person, Aquinas quotes some of their translators' uses of deification language, and comments laconically: 'idem autem est fieri Deum quod deificari' ('then becoming God and being deified are the same thing').[59]

In both these cases, then, Aquinas' deification language is used in

---

[55] *DS*, III, cols. 1416–21.

[56] For Bonaventure and Bernard in general, see J. G. Bougerol, 'Saint Bonaventure et saint Bernard', *Antonianum*, 46 (1971), 3–79, and pp. 31–2 above; for Bonaventure and William, see J. G. Bougerol, 'Saint Bonaventure et Guillaume de Saint-Thierry', *Antonianum*, 46 (1971), 298–321.

[57] See *A Lexicon of St Thomas Aquinas*, edited by Roy J. Deferrari and M. Inviolata Barry (New York, 1948), s.v. *deificare*.

[58] Thomas Aquinas, *Summa theologiae* (*ST*), (Rome, 1962), IIIa. 2. 1 ad 3 (p. 1872).

[59] *ST*, IIIa. 16. 7 (p. 1954).

the specialized context of the dispute over the dual nature of Christ, a practice that, as we have seen, goes back (in Latin) at least to the Nestorian controversies of the fifth century. But, in the *Summa theologiae*'s only other instance of this terminology, Aquinas arrives at an idea that is, albeit distantly, related to Bernard's concept of deification: 'Sic enim necesse est quod solus Deus deificet, communicando consortium divinae naturae per quandam similitudinis participationem' ('thus it is necessary that only God should deify, bestowing involvement in the divine nature through a certain participation in likeness').[60]

Here, Aquinas combines a standard term from deification language ('deificet', in the transitive sense of a power to deify), with verbal niceties of his own. The stress on grace as coming from God alone is, of course, a familiar element of the tradition; but the idea of sharing in the divine nature ('communicando consortium divinae naturae') through an analogical participation that is neither identity of substance nor equality of standing ('per quandam similitudinis participationem') is especially characteristic of Aquinas' thinking about deification, and the word *participatio* seems, indeed, to have been one of his favourite devices for the avoidance of more straightforward deification language. The use of *similitudo* also connects Aquinas with the tradition of *deificatio* as such: the implication that we are to share in divinity only through resemblance to God, since we can never become God as he is God, is, as noted above, fundamental in Bernard and many other writers in his tradition.

This, however, is only a professorial aside, compared with the close examination of the vision of God *per essentiam* that occupies much of *quaestio* 12 of the *Pars prima* of the *Summa*. There Aquinas considers, in some depth, the whole question of the soul's approach to God and the possibility of enjoying, in life, the final vision of him that Bernard – and others – thought could be achieved, albeit imperfectly and by a few, in *deificatio*. Aquinas commits himself to no such conclusion here. He uses none of the standard terminology of the subject, seems to exclude the possibility of reaching even a fragmentary vision of the divine in this life (*art.* 11), and, above all, declines to consider the action of love on the human will to realign it with God's will and thus make possible the restored union of God and God-like man. This

---

[60] *ST*, IaIIae. 112. 1 (p. 1068).

accord, central to Bernardine *deificatio*, is missing from Aquinas' treatment here, which is cast entirely in terms of the vision of God by the *intellectus creatus* ('created intellect'), achieved not by the action of grace-inspired love on the human will, but by that of the *lumen gloriae* ('light of glory') – still inspired by grace – on the intellect:

Dicendum ergo quod ad videndum Dei essentiam requiritur aliqua similitudo ex parte visivae potentiae, scilicet lumen gloriae, confortans intellectum ad videndum Deum: de quo dicitur in Psalmo: in lumine tuo videbimus lumen. Non autem per aliquam similitudinem creatam Dei essentia videri potest, quae ipsam divinam essentiam repraesentet ut in se est.[61]

It would, however, be misleading to concentrate on this *quaestio* alone, or to conclude that the doctrine of deification is unimportant in Aquinas' thought simply because its usual terminology is almost completely absent from his writings. Aquinas has, in fact, a strongly developed sense of the possibility of humanity assimilating to God in this life, though it differs from Bernard's on several points and stands, indeed, at a slight angle to the course of previous thinking about deification in the Western Church.

First, as is clear from *Summa theologiae*, 1a. 12, especially articles 4 ('Whether any created intellect can see the divine essence through its own natural powers') and 5 ('Whether the created intellect needs any created light in order to see the essence of God'), Aquinas conceives assimilation to God, and thus participation in his nature, more in terms of knowledge than of love. This intellectualist approach can be detected as far back in theological history as the early Greek Fathers Clement and Origen, but it contrasts very obviously, in the late medieval West, with the stress on love and the will typical of the more mystical (in whatever sense) post-Dionysian tradition – of which Bernard, of course, is such a notable exemplar.

Second, Aquinas prefers to use less unequivocal terminology when dealing with the subject. As we have seen, he uses cognates of *deificari* very rarely; more typical of him is the vocabulary of participation used, for example, in considering 'whether grace and virtue are the same'.[62] Here he concludes that virtue acquired through human action belongs to the order by which man is man; but that infused

---

[61] *ST*, 1a. 12. 1 (p. 51): 'It must therefore be said that, to see the essence of God, some likeness is required on the part of the visual power, namely the light of glory, which will strengthen the intellect for the sight of God: of which it is said in the psalm: in your light we shall see light. Not, indeed, through any created likeness can the essence of God be seen, which would represent the divine essence as in itself it is.'   [62] *ST*, 1a. 110. 3 (p. 1062).

virtue relates human beings to a higher nature, which shares in the divine ('ad naturam divinam participatam'). According to the extent of our adherence to this higher nature, 'we may be said to be reborn as children of God' ('dicimur regenerari in filios Dei').

It is clear from this article alone that any conclusion based solely on *ST*, 1a. 12, from which it appears that the *lumen gratiae* is not, in this life, a means of sharing in the divine nature, will be gravely unbalanced. The relationship between *participatio* and the divine *caritas* to which humanity aspires is explored further at *ST*, 11a11ae. 24. 2, where Aquinas gives a sketch of the essentials of deification, but deliberately, it appears, employs a specific terminology not historically connected with the doctrine:

Respondeo dicendum quod, sicut dictum est, caritas est amicitia quaedam hominis ad Deum fundata super communicationem beatitudinis aeternae. Haec autem communicatio non est secundum bona naturalia, sed secundum dona gratuita: quia, ut dicitur Rom. 6, gratia Dei vita aeterna. Unde et ipsa caritas facultatem naturae excedit. Quod autem excedit naturae facultatem non potest esse neque naturale neque per potentias naturales acquisitum: quia effectus naturalis non transcendit suam causam. Unde caritas non potest neque naturaliter nobis inesse, neque per vires naturales est acquisita, sed per infusionem Spiritus Sancti, qui est amor Patris et Filii, cuius participatio in nobis est ipsa caritas creata.[63]

In this account, then, grace ('communicatio beatitudinis aeternae'), freely given ('secundum dona gratuita'), transforms the soul ('ipsa caritas facultatem naturae excedit'), and, through the action of the Holy Spirit ('per infusionem Spiritus Sancti'), makes possible a sharing ('participatio') in the divine nature. Evidently this is much closer to a definition of deification than anything in *ST*, 1a. 12. Moreover, the stress on the concord of human and divine wills, missing from both these *articuli*, is not, in fact, unfamiliar to Aquinas: 'voluntas ordinatur in illum finem et quantum ad motum intentionis, in ipsum tendentem sicut in id quod est possibile consequi, quod pertinet ad spem: et quantum ad unionem quandam spiritualem, per

---

[63] *ST*, 11a11ae. 24. 2 (p. 1189): 'I reply that it must be said that, as already stated, charity is a certain friendship between the human being and God, founded on a sharing of eternal beatitude. This sharing, however, is achieved not through natural goods, but according to a gift of grace: for, as is said in Romans 6, the grace of God is eternal life. Wherefore this charity also exceeds the bounds of nature. That, however, which exceeds the bounds of nature can be neither natural nor acquired through natural potentialities: because a natural effect cannot transcend its cause. Wherefore charity can neither inhere in us naturally, nor be acquired by natural powers, but only through an infusion of the Holy Spirit, which is the love of the Father and the Son, whose sharing with us is that created charity.'

quam quodammodo transformatur in illum finem, quod fit per caritatem'.[64] Finally, the idea that the will's action is at the basis of the human being's love for God emerges as part of Aquinas' teaching on *caritas* itself.[65]

Aquinas' most thoroughgoing treatment of the possibility of deification in this life, however, forms the *quaestio De raptu* (*ST*, пaпae. 175). Here he concedes straight away that elevation to the presence of God through the action of grace is both possible and fitting for human beings:

Ad secundum dicendum quod ad modum et dignitatem hominis pertinet quod ad divina elevetur, ex hoc ipso quod homo factus est ad imaginem Dei. Et quia bonum divinum in infinitum excedit humanam facultatem, indiget homo ut supernaturaliter ad illud bonum capessendum adiuvetur: quod fit per quodcumque beneficium gratiae. Unde quod sic elevetur mens a Deo per raptum, non est contra naturam, sed supra facultatem naturae.[66]

In the rest of this *quaestio*, as elsewhere in the *Summa theologiae*, Aquinas avoids deification language as such, dwelling instead on the etymology and significance of the term *raptus*, distinguishing it from contemplation in general and *excessus* in particular, and discussing the traditional Biblical exemplars of this kind of experience, Paul and Moses. Of special interest, for its possible connection with Dante's 'trasumanar', is Aquinas's summing-up of the characteristics of Pauline *raptus*:

Ad secundum dicendum quod divina essentia videri ab intellectu creato non potest nisi per lumen gloriae, de quo dicitur in Psalmo: In lumine tuo videbimus lumen. Quod tamen dupliciter participari potest. Uno modo, per modum formae immanentis: et sic beatos facit sanctos in patria. Alio modo, per modum cuiusdam passionis transeuntis: sicut dictum est de lumine prophetiae. Et hoc modo lumen illud fuit in Paulo, quando raptus fuit ... Et ideo talis raptus aliquo modo ad prophetiam pertinet.[67]

[64] *ST*, пaпae. 62. 3 (p. 808): 'The will is ordained to that end both as concerns the movement of intention, tending towards it as towards that which it is possible may be brought about – and this has to do with hope; and as concerns a certain spiritual union, through which, in some way, it is transformed into that end, which is done through charity.'

[65] *ST*, пaпae. 23. 2 (pp. 1183–4).

[66] *ST*, пaпae. 175. 1 ad 2 (p. 1768): 'To the second it must be said that it befits both the nature and the dignity of mankind that it be lifted to the divine, from that fact alone that mankind is made in God's image. And because divine goodness infinitely exceeds human capacities, human beings need supernatural help if they are to reach that goodness: which is done through some kind of gift of grace. Wherefore the fact that the mind is lifted to God in *raptus* is not against nature, but beyond the limits of nature.'

[67] *ST*, пaпae. 175. 3. ad 2 (p. 1770): 'To the second it must be said that the divine essence can only be seen by the created intellect through the light of glory, of which is said in the psalm: in your light we shall see light. Which participation can, however, be brought about in two

This text, in my view, is of the greatest importance in underpinning the vital distinction, to which we shall return below, between the condition of Dante *personaggio* and that of the souls he meets in Paradise. They enjoy, now and forever, the vision of God 'per modum formae immanentis', for such is the nature of their beatified existence; while Dante, who must return to life on earth, sees God only 'per modum cuiusdam passionis transeuntis'. But we know – because the poem tells us so – that when Dante does return to earth, he will give voice to a prophecy of his own, which will, of course, take the form of the *Commedia*; and despite his explicit denial that he is comparable with Paul (*Inf.*, II. 32), for him too his prophecy stems from, and is inseparably linked with, his vision of God in *raptus*.

The suggestive parallels do not end there. Aquinas goes on, in *art*. 4, to consider first whether the vision of God is possible 'sine abstractione a sensibus' ('without detachment from the senses'), concluding that it is not, and then to explain why Paul found it impossible to recall or recount the totality of his experience. The relevant portion of this article is illuminating indeed, when set against the 'ineffability *topos*' of *Paradiso*:

Ad tertium dicendum quod Paulus, postquam cessavit videre Deum per essentiam, memor fuit illorum quae in illa visione cognoverat, per aliquas species intelligibiles habitualiter ex hoc in eius intellectu relictas, sicut etiam, abeunte sensibili, remanent aliquae impressiones in anima: quas postea convertens ad phantasmata, memorabatur. Unde nec totam illam cognitionem aut cogitare poterat, aut verbis exprimere.[68]

Here again Aquinas is not saying anything new about deification: the inevitable incommunicability of mystical experience is assumed in Christian tradition from the beginning, finding its Biblical foundation in the 'unspeakable words, which it is not lawful for a man to utter', heard by St Paul (2 Corinthians 12. 4). But that is just the point. Contrary to the impression created by the near-total absence of deification language from the *Summa theologiae* (or indeed

ways. One, in the manner of an immanent form: and this is what makes the saints blessed in their homeland. The other, in the manner of a transient sensory experience: as is said of the light of prophecy. And in this way that light was in Paul, when he was carried up … And so this *raptus* is in some way connected with prophecy.'

[68] *ST*, папае. 175. 4. ad 3 (p. 1171): 'To the third it must be said that Paul, after he ceased to see God in essence, remembered the things that he had known in that vision, through certain intelligible images that remained in his intellect, as is normal; just as, in the absence of a tangible object, certain impressions of it remain in the mind: which it afterwards, converting them into mental phenomena, remembers. Wherefore he could neither mentally retain, nor express in words, the whole of that knowledge.'

any of his other works), Aquinas definitely belongs to – more, is a central figure in – the mainstream of the Western Church's thinking about mystical experience in general and deification in particular. In fact, all the essentials of Dante-character's climactic experience in *Paradiso* could be gleaned from an attentive reading of the relevant parts of the *Summa theologiae*, chief among them IIaIIae. 175; and, to the extent that it is legitimate to equate that experience specifically with the concept of deification, it is certainly possible to argue that Dante *poeta* need not have looked beyond Aquinas for theological grounding for this part of his narrative.[69]

Conversely, it must be admitted that neither Aquinas nor any other source in the deification tradition seems to have supplied Dante with the technical vocabulary he employs for the evocation of his character's adventures in mysticism: neither Aquinas' *raptus* nor Bernard's *deificari* nor Maximus Confessor's (Latinized) *excessus* has left any verbal traces in the text of *Paradiso*. The contention that behind Dante stands a long and complex history of thinking about humanity's power to become divine – one that may, in part or as a whole, have affected the course of Dante's own thinking – must be tempered by the acknowledgement that when he, as poet, comes to render the experience for which tradition offered him so many and such authoritative precedents, he does so in terms, both conceptual and lexical, that are resoundingly his own.

At least since Jacopo della Lana in the 1320s, commentators on the *Commedia* have been intrigued by the neologism 'trasumanar' that Dante uses at *Paradiso*, I. 70; and their interest has only been heightened by the narrative voice's refusal to provide a concrete definition of the term – or rather, its assertion that no such definition is possible: 'trasumanar significar *per verba* / non si porìa'. Modern commentators, no less alive than their medieval counterparts to the challenge posed by a word with no connotations beyond those provided by its presence here in *Paradiso*, have generally disregarded the warning implicit in Dante's text, and have offered definitions more or less akin to the canonical rendering of Scartazzini: 'Trasumanar: divenire più che umano, passare dall'umano al divino'.[70] Similar phrasing can be found in such of Scartazzini's late nineteenth-century contemporaries as Poletto ('passare al di là dell'umano, senza di che non è possibile vedere Iddio') and Casini

---

[69] On Dante and *raptus*, see Kenelm Foster, *The Two Dantes* (London, 1977), pp. 70–2.

[70] Scartazzini, '*Divina Commedia*' (Leipzig, 1874–90), III, 15.

('il passaggio dallo stato umano allo stato divino'); while more recent commentators coin terser formulas still: Chimenz's 'divenire di natura superiore all'umana', Sapegno's 'innalzarsi oltre i limiti dell'umano', Bosco and Reggio's 'oltrepassare i limiti della natura umana'.[71]

What all these definitions have in common is that the human being is their referent and the human condition their point of departure: in them the 'transhumanized' individual has become more than human, has, in fact, left his humanness altogether behind and (at least for the nineteenth-century commentators) become divine. (The twentieth-century definitions stress the abandonment of humanity, but seem to lose the sense of where the process of 'trasumanar' is tending.) Moreover, all these definitions are, in effect, simple translations of Dante's word, based on its etymology: *tras* + *uman*[o], with the infinitive ending *-ar*. None attempts to explain what the word, as a semantic unit, might actually mean, in the context of the poem's narrative and the poet's intention, or to engage seriously with the provocative suggestion that its 'significar' is somehow ultimately unsayable. Yet the medieval commentators, however tentatively, do precisely this.

Jacopo della Lana (followed at a distance by Pietro Alighieri) immediately makes the fundamental connection with contemplation, and, by implication, with the insufficiency of merely human powers to undertake contemplative activity: 'Or qui vuole mostrare Dante come per la visione di Beatrice ello trasumanò, cioè che ello diventò più abile e disposto a contemplare che non può dare la spezia di sua natura umana'.[72] But even he, identifying 'trasumanar' as a kind of higher degree in contemplative studies, inclines to limit the term's significance by underestimating the profundity of the change of state that it implies.

Francesco da Buti, on the other hand, highlights the change, at the expense of the fuller understanding shown by Lana: 'trasumanar, cioè passare dall'umanità a più alto grado, che non può essere se none Iddio: imperò che nulla natura è più nobile dell'umana se non la divina'.[73] But Buti also sets 'trasumanar' firmly in the context of transformation suggested by the Glaucus allusion in the preceding

---

[71] Poletto, *'Divina Commedia'*, III, 18; Casini/Barbi, *'Divina Commedia'*, p. 693; Chimenz, *Divina Commedia*, p. 628; Sapegno, *'Divina Commedia'* (1957), p. 788; Bosco and Reggio, *'Divina Commedia'*, III, 17.

[72] Lana, *Commento*, III, 23; Pietro, *Commentarium*, pp. 550–1.        [73] Buti, *Commento*, III, 24.

lines (of which more below): 'E questo esemplo àe indutto l'autore, a dimostrare com'elli fu trasformato, secondo l'anima, dell'umanità alla divinità'.[74] Buti goes on to support his argument with lengthy quotations from Boethius's 'libro della Filosofica Consolatione', and finally to draw the threads together in a subtle, if at times dubiously relevant, analysis that is very much his own:

[L']esemplo dato dimostra che trasumanare è montare dall'umanità alla divinità, siccome Glauco di pescatore diventò iddio marino gustando l'erba che avea quella virtù, così l'anima umana gustando le cose divine diventa divina. In questa fizione à volsuto dimostrare l'autore nostro in sè come li santi omini che sono nel mondo si trasumanano per grazia, stando in vita contemplativa che sono quanto a l'anima risplendenti come è lo Sole nel cospetto di Dio; e così per opposito si dè intendere che li omini scelerati che sono rifiutati da Dio si disumanano e diventano bestie varie, secondo vari vizi, come dice ancora Boezio nel predetto luogo nel libro terzo, e diventano sozzi e oscuri quanto all'anima, come è lo dimonio, stando in questa vita.[75]

The last part of the second sentence here certainly owes more to Boethius than to Dante, at least if *Paradiso* 1 is still meant to be the focal point of Buti's attention (though there may, of course, be a vestigial reminiscence of *Inferno* 1 behind the reference to 'bestie varie'); but his interpretation of 'trasumanar' is of immense interest, both for its recognition of the action of grace ('per grazia') and for its stress on contemplation as an activity befitting this world ('li santo omini che sono *nel mondo*'). (The negative counterpart of 'trasumanar', the 'disumanar' undergone by the wicked, is also seen by Buti as belonging to this world: 'diventano sozzi e oscuri quanto all'anima … stando in questa vita'.) Both these elements clearly connect Buti's understanding of 'trasumanar' with the tradition of contemplative mysticism as such, giving the etymologically based definition a more specific theological charge, and going beyond Lana's basic recognition that 'trasumanar' simply enables Dante *personaggio* to be a better contemplative.

As so often, however, it is left to Benvenuto da Imola to supply the fullest and most learned explication of word and concept alike:

Hic poeta superextollit hanc suam mirabilem transmutationem, quae non potest sermone explicari, nec dari alteri intelligi; et ad huius literae satis obscurae declarationem est primo praesupponendum, quod nullum animal in rerum natura tantum recedit et elongatur a natura sua, quantum homo in bonum et in malum. Homo enim de sui natura est perfectissimus

[74] Ibid.　　　　　[75] Ibid.

animalium, et perfectissimum corpus hominis invenitur proportionatum coelo et mundo; ideo solus homo, ut inquit Hermes, est nexus Dei et mundi, eo quod intellectum divinum in se habet, per quem aliquando elevatur supra mundum; unde homo perseverans in culmine mentis trahit ad se corpus et mundum, quia anima nata est principari corpori et mundo, et naturalis ordo est quod anima contineat corpus ne dissolvatur: sic nunc poeta noster per contemplationem stans in terra erat in caelo; fortunam negligebat et vivens erat in paradiso ... Modo ad propositum dicit Dantes, quod non potest nunc referre verbaliter, sed exemplariter tantum, suam intrinsecam occultam transmutationem, de hoc se excusans; unde dicit: *trasumanar*, idest, quomodo homo fiat plusquam homo, vel aliud quam homo.[76]

This long passage is, first of all, a further illustration of the Trecento commentaries' perennial eclecticism (which, be it said, is truer to the spirit of their text than the ideological straitjackets preferred by too many modern interpreters): where Buti chooses Boethius as the presiding genius of the concept of 'trasumanar', Benvenuto begins from the hermetic tradition, and gives a markedly Neoplatonic twist to the contemplation which he sees Dante *personaggio* as being engaged in at this point. But he is also careful to relate the experience to the mainstream of Christian mysticism: the 'nexus Dei et mundi' is able to achieve his transhumanized state in this life ('stans in terra erat in caelo'), and, moreover, he does so in a way explicitly sanctioned by the authority of Christian tradition: '*a cui grazia serba esperienza* [*sic*], idest illi, cui divina gratia concedet experiri hoc, sicut autor experiebatur nunc, et sicut multi magni doctores theologi experti fuerunt ante eum in vita'.[77] No other

---

[76] Benvenuto, *Comentum*, IV, 317–18: 'Here the poet praises that amazing transformation of his, which cannot be explained in words, nor given to any other to understand; and for the elucidation of this sufficiently obscure passage it must first of all be presupposed that no animal in the universe is as far distant and withdrawn from its nature as is man in good and evil. For man, by his nature, is the most perfect of animals, and the most perfect human body is found to be that which is proportioned to heaven and earth; so that only man, as Hermes says, is the nexus of God and the world, by the fact of his having in him a divine intellect, through which he can sometimes be lifted up above the world; wherefore a man who dwells at the peak of his mind draws body and world to himself, because his soul is born to govern body and world, and the natural order is that the soul should restrain the body lest it destroy itself: thus now our poet, through contemplation, though standing on earth was in Heaven; he disregarded his destiny and, living, was in Paradise ... Well to the point Dante says that his secret inner transformation cannot now be recounted in words, but only by example, and he excuses himself for this, saying 'trasumanar', that is, the way in which a human being becomes more than human, or something other than human...'

[77] Ibid., IV, 318: 'that is, to him, to whom divine grace allows this experience, as our author is experiencing it now, and as many great and expert men, learned in theology, who preceded him in life, have experienced it.'

medieval commentator takes such pains to relate the description of Dante-character's experience to that of earlier mystical *auctores*.

Benvenuto also recognizes both the profundity and the mysteriousness of the concept of 'trasumanar', in the effective economy of his phrase 'suam intrinsecam occultam transmutationem'. But the most pertinent detail of his analysis, from our point of view, does not appear until he comes to gloss lines 73–5 of *Paradiso* I ('S'i' era sol di me quel che creasti / novellamente, amor che'l ciel governi, / tu'l sai, che col tuo lume mi levasti'):

[*N*]*ovellamente*, idest, de praesenti in ista mea novella ascensione: ita recte dicebat Paulus loquens de raptu suo ad coelum sive in corpore, sive extra corpus etc. Et hic nota quod autor non immerito fingit se non recordari suae mirabilis transmutationis, quoniam, ut bene ait Augustinus, sicut stilla aquae multo infusa vino deficere in se tota videtur, dum saporem vini induit et colorem; sic hominis affectio quodam ineffabili modo liquescens transfunditur penitus in Dei amorem, et quodam quasi modo oblitus sui per coelestes speras mentaliter scandens ad aeternum Regem perduci festinat, mente iam ebria suavitate gratiae infusae.[78]

What is so interesting about this passage is, of course, that so much of it is owed not to Augustine but to Bernard (*De diligendo Deo*, x. 28): 'Quomodo stilla aquae modica, multo infusa vino, deficere a se tota videtur, dum et saporem vini induit et colorem sic omnem tunc in sanctis humanam affectionem quodam ineffabili modo necesse erit a semetipsa liquescere, atque in Dei penitus transfundi voluntatem.' Benvenuto has, in fact, though seemingly by accident, anticipated by several centuries the argument of Migliorini Fissi that Bernard's *deificatio* is at the root of Dante's *trasumanar*.

Yet there is one small but extremely significant change in what is otherwise a remarkably faithful reproduction of Bernard's text, and one that strikes at the heart of what is characteristically Bernardine in *De diligendo Deo*: the substitution of 'amorem' for 'voluntatem'. The accord of wills, keystone of Bernard's thinking about deification, is edited out of the quotation from *De diligendo Deo*, and replaced by

[78] Ibid., IV, 319: 'that is, at present in this my new ascension: thus Paul rightly said when speaking of his *raptus* to heaven whether in the body or out of it, etc. And note here that the author, not unjustifiably, pretends not to remember his miraculous transmutation, since, as Augustine well says, just as a drop of water mixed with much wine seems to dissipate itself totally, when it takes on the taste and colour of the wine; thus the inclination of mankind in some unspeakable way alters its own nature and is completely fused with the love of God, and, in some way forgetting itself, and mentally ascending through the heavenly spheres, it hastens to be brought into the presence of the eternal King, with a mind now intoxicated with the sweetness of the grace that has been infused into it.'

the much more generic notion of divine love as the destination of the mystical process. This fact alone may have made it easier to misattribute the quotation to Augustine.

The tradition of commentary on 'trasumanar' is, then, reasonably harmonious across the centuries: it signifies a profound change of state in Dante *personaggio*, lifting him from his human predicament towards (or actually to) a state of divinity. The medieval commentators go further than their modern successors in identifying the means through which this change is brought about as the practice of contemplation, which they connect – with emphases that vary according to the nature and extent of their theological interests – with the mystical tradition. It is noteworthy, however, that none of the Trecento commentators makes use of the technical language of deification, in any of its several varieties: their preferred term is always the more general 'contemplazione' or one of its cognates, and even when Benvenuto uses Aquinas' term *raptus* he does so strictly in the context of a quotation from St Paul – which is, of course, where Aquinas himself found it. Not one of them, in short, even comes close to saying: 'trasumanar: cioè deificarsi'. With that in mind, it is time to examine Dante's use of the word more closely.

The occurrence of 'trasumanar' at *Paradiso*, I. 70 is not the earliest sign, in Dante's work, of an interest in the possibility of going beyond the experiential limits normally assigned to humanity. In the *Convivio* Dante had already considered whether a man possessed of every virtue in perfect disposition might not take on, as a consequence, a form of divinity; and, without voicing a definitive conclusion of his own, he had recorded the opinion held by some that it might very well be feasible:

E sono alcuni di tale oppinione che dicono, se tutte le precedenti vertudi s'accordassero sovra la produzione d'un'anima ne la loro ottima disposizione, che tanto discenderebbe in quella de la deitade, che quasi sarebbe un altro Iddio incarnato.[79]

Earlier still, commenting on lines from his 'Le dolci rime d'amor' ('ch'elli son quasi dei / quei ch'han tal grazia fuor di tutti rei / che solo Iddio a l'anima la dona'), Dante had sought to equate the possession of supreme virtue with divinity:

[E] così la vertù è una cosa mista di nobilitade e di passione; ma perché la nobilitade vince in quella, è la vertù dinominata da essa, e appellata

---

[79] Dante, *Convivio*, IV. xxi. 10; edited by Piero Cudini (Milan, 1980), p. 309.

bontade. Poi appresso argomenta per quello che detto è, che nessuno, per poter dire: 'Io sono di cotale schiatta', non dee credere essere con essa, se questi frutti non sono in lui. E rende incontanente ragione, dicendo che quelli che hanno questa *grazia*, cioè questa divina cosa, sono *quasi* come *dei*, sanza macula di vizio; e ciò dare non può se non Iddio solo, appo cui non è scelta di persone, sì come le divine Scritture manifestano.[80]

The most remarkable thing about the perception of divinized humanity articulated in these passages is that it is not conceived at all in religious terms. The *Convivio*'s definition of those who are like gods ('quasi dei') is that they are 'sanza macula di vizio', and, throughout (notwithstanding the reference to 'divine Scritture'), the question is treated from a wholly ethical standpoint: the most perfect human beings are those who have perfect virtue, thanks to which they become like gods. They have undoubtedly gone beyond the limits of normal experience, in possessing virtue to a degree not otherwise encountered in earthly life, but they have thereby become perfected exemplars of a moral ideal, rather than living individuals raised into a new kind of spiritual relationship with God.[81]

This kind of moral deification, if such it may be called, is not without precedent in writers known to Dante. His supremely virtuous deified individual resembles the figure proposed as an ideal in the twelfth-century philosophical poetry of Alan of Lille – a morally perfect being who becomes both man and God, and thus acts as an exemplar for those who remain below in both mind and body:

> Non terre fecem redolens, non materialis
> sed divinus homo nostro molimine terras
> incolat et nostris donet solacia damnis,
> insideat caelis animo, sed corpore terris:
> in terris humanus erit, divinus in astris.
> Sic homo sicque Deus fiet, sic factus uterque
> quod neuter mediaque via tutissimus ibit,
> in quo nostra manus et munera nostra loquantur.[82]

---

[80] Ibid., IV. xx. 3–4; p. 304.

[81] In *Convivio*, III. vii. 6 (p. 168), Dante suggests that, since the scale of being ranges by infinitesimal degrees from the lowest to the highest, there must be some individual 'tanto nobile e di sì alta condizione che quasi non sia altro che angelo'; but this assimilation to the *angelic* condition is clearly not true deification.

[82] Alan of Lille, *Anticlaudianus*, edited by R. Bossuat (Paris, 1955), I. 235–42: 'Not smelling of the grossness of earth, not material / but divine, a man of our dimensions shall inhabit the world / and offer consolation for our sufferings, / in his soul he shall dwell in heaven, but in his body on earth: / in the world he shall be human, but divine among the stars. / Thus he shall be man and thus God, thus made both / and neither, he shall go safest in the middle way, / and in him our hands and our gifts shall speak.'

A similar figure is depicted by Alan's contemporary and fellow philosopher-poet, Bernardus Silvestris:

> Mentem de caelo, corpus trahet ex elementis,
>     ut terras habitet corpore, mente polum.
> Mens, corpus diversa licet iungentur ad unum,
>     ut sacra conplacitum nexio reddat opus.
> Divus erit, terrenus erit, curabit utrumque
>     consiliis mundum, religione deos.
> Naturis poterit sic respondere duabus,
>     et sic principiis congruus esse suis.[83]

What Alan and Bernardus envisage here is evidently a kind of deification ('sic homo sicque Deus fiet'; 'divus erit, terrenus erit'), but it is far indeed from what Bernard of Clairvaux, their contemporary, would have understood by the term. The allegorical setting in which they consider the creation of an ideal human being who will reach, on earth, a pinnacle of intellectual and moral development, thereby becoming a god, is quite unlike anything in Bernard's thought, passionately concerned as that is with the spiritual state of the individual (and far from ideal) Christian believer. Moreover, Bernard would unquestionably have rejected the dichotomy, which the two poets not only tolerate but elevate into a principle, in the idea of a perfect man whose body dwells on earth and partakes of matter while his mind inhabits higher, immaterial regions. Bernard makes no such distinction in his view of 'deified' humanity; indeed, it would be difficult to integrate it with any thoroughly Christian anthropology. For him, the result of the individual's deification is that 'totum divinum est quod sentitur' (*De diligendo Deo*, x. 28): that is, that the whole human being is transformed by experience of the divine, not that it begins to lead a double life as a brute among brutes on earth and a mind among gods in the heavens.

The same is true of Dante, at least in the *Commedia*: the separation between the bodily and mental strata of human existence, acceptable

---

[83] Bernardus Silvestris, *Cosmographia*, II. x. 15–22; edited by Peter Dronke (Leiden, 1978), p. 141: 'He shall take his mind from heaven, his body from the elements, / that he may inhabit the world in his body, and in his mind the sky. / Mind and body, diverse things, shall be joined in one man, / that a holy joining may render a pleasing work. / He shall be divine, he shall be of the world, and he shall take care for both, / for the world in his thinking, in his religion for the gods. / Thus he shall have been able to respond to his two natures, / and thus be in conformity with his origins.'

in philosophical tradition (especially that of Alan and Bernardus'
twelfth-century Platonism) and detectable in the *Convivio*, is there
replaced by a theological approach to the human being as a unique
and indissoluble union of soul (not just mind) and body: a union
validated by the bodily incarnation, suffering, and death of Jesus
Christ. Simply put, a theological understanding of the Incarnation
makes it difficult, if not impossible, to reject or disdain the importance
of the human body, as the locus of all experience of earthly life; and
Dante's concern for the status and dignity of the body, repeatedly
manifest in the *Commedia* (especially in *Inferno* and *Purgatorio*), makes
it clear that by now his earlier interest, in abstract notions of ideal
humanity and its potential for a moral deification that depends on
isolating virtue and mental activity from bodily experience, has been
superseded by the more immediate question of a life in this world and
a relationship with God, whether in deification or not, that can be
achieved in the body and the soul simultaneously. In the *Commedia*,
the body and the life it incarnates are a vehicle for the approach to
God, not an impediment to it; and the poem is thus an urgently
personal work in a sense that does not apply to the *Convivio* or the
allegorical disquisitions of Alan of Lille or Bernardus Silvestris.

There are also, however, two earlier and still more influential
writers whose concepts of moral perfection as a divinizing force may
have found an echo in the *Convivio*: Boethius and Aristotle. In book III
of the former's *De consolatione Philosophiae*, the personification of
Philosophy herself demonstrates to Boethius' complete satisfaction
that supreme beatitude is identical with divinity. To this reassuring
conclusion she adds a corollary:

Nam quoniam beatitudine adeptione fiunt homines beati, beatitudo vero est
ipsa divinitas, divinitatis adeptione beatos fieri manifestum est: sed uti
iustitiae adeptione iusti, sapientiae sapientes fiunt, ita divinitatem adeptos
deos fieri simili ratione necesse est.[84]

Now this may seem to be a merely logical demonstration that by
taking on divinity we become divine, just as by practising justice we
become just, and that, since divinity is identical with beatitude,

---

[84] Boethius, *De consolatione Philosophiae*, III. 10; edited by H. F. Stewart, E. K. Rand, and S. J.
Tester (London, 1973), p. 280: 'For since human beings become blessed by taking on
blessedness, and since blessedness is indeed that divinity, it is plain that by taking on divinity
we become blessed; but, as by taking on justice we become just, or wisdom, wise, thus, by
the same logic, it is necessary that when we take on divinity we become gods.'

'beatos fieri' and 'deos fieri' are also, of necessity, identical. The syllogism is unexceptionable, but its practical application remains somewhat obscure. In book IV, however, Lady Philosophy returns to her corollary, and continues:

Cum ipsum bonum beatitudo sit, bonos omnes eo ipso quod boni sint fieri beatos liquet. Sed qui beati sint deos esse convenit. Est igitur praemium bonorum quod nullus deterat dies, nullius minuat potestas, nullius fuscet improbitas, deos fieri.[85]

This is the final link in the chain. Since beatitude equals divinity, and being good equals beatitude, therefore being good enables us to become gods: the practice of moral virtue leads to deification (assuming that possessing virtue and practising it are inseparable). Deification thus seems to become, for Boethius, a real possibility in this life, where virtue can certainly be practised, even in the face of time, force, and evil. But this Boethian deification is carried on quite separately from any context of Christian belief (there is, notoriously, nothing in *De consolatione Philosophiae* that unequivocally demonstrates its author's adherence to Christianity), and its vocabulary is not the same as that characteristic of Christian treatment of the subject – though neither of these facts, of course, prevented Boethius from being accepted as a Christian author in the Middle Ages. The phrase 'deos fieri', for instance, is notably less circumspect than any of the forms of deification language current among theologians (though we have seen Aquinas, centuries later, using it as an equivalent to *deificari* in his overview of the Nestorian controversy).

Equally unspecific, though no less resonant, is Aristotle's remark, in the course of an exposition of the contemplative life as happiness in the highest sense, that 'such a life would be too high for man; for it is not in so far as he is man that he will live so, but in so far as something divine is present in him; and by so much as this is superior to our composite nature is its activity superior to that which is the exercise of the other kind of virtue'.[86] Here too there is a hint that the highest form of life on earth can be inspired by contact with 'something divine'; but, again, we are a long way from any orthodox

---

[85] Ibid., IV. 3; p. 332: 'Since that good is blessedness, all the good, by virtue of the fact that they are good, may become blessed. But it is right that those who are blessed become gods. Therefore the reward of the good, which no day can diminish, no power can threaten, no wickedness can darken, is to become gods.'

[86] Aristotle, *Nicomachean Ethics*, x. 7; translated by David Ross, revised by J. L. Ackrill and J. O. Urmson (Oxford, 1980), p. 285.

Christian conception of deification. As far as Dante is concerned, we can perhaps say that texts like these, and the philosophical interpretation of deification that they embody, may well have been absorbed into the intellectual matrix of the *Convivio*, and thus have been filtered through into the *Commedia* as well; but, conversely, that the poem's concerns and its understanding of both humanity and God reflect, at every level, a Christian and theological approach to the questions tackled exclusively with the means of (pagan) philosophy by Aristotle, Boethius, and the twelfth-century Platonists.

This, then, is the background to the use of 'trasumanar' in *Paradiso* 1: an interest in humanity's potential to achieve divinity in this life, which at one time Dante had thought might be attained on the moral plane, through the practice of absolute virtue, but which he had later come to think would be unattainable outside a religious dimension – without the aid of grace, in short. The exploration of that dimension, which is to lift Dante *personaggio*, in both soul and body, to the deifying vision of God *per essentiam*, is the drama of *Paradiso*.

Up to now we have treated 'trasumanar' as an independent semantic unit, untimely ripp'd from its setting in the narrative of *Paradiso* 1. However, since its full meaning must inevitably be dependent, to a large extent, on that very setting (because it is a neologism, and therefore brings along no semantic baggage acquired from usage in other texts), it will be useful now to return to the text of the third *cantica*, and to examine the presence of 'trasumanar' there in a little more detail.

The narrative voice is explaining, at the mid-point of *Paradiso* 1, that Beatrice had fixed her gaze directly on the sun, while Dante-character, unable to bear the force with which its light was searing his human eyes, was gazing, instead, at her:

> Beatrice tutta ne l'etterne rote
>   fissa con li occhi stava; e io in lei
>   le luci fissi, di là sù remote.
> Nel suo aspetto tal dentro mi fei,
>   qual si fé Glauco nel gustar de l'erba
>   che'l fé consorto in mar de li altri dèi.
> Trasumanar significar *per verba*
>   non si poria; però l'essemplo basti
>   a cui esperïenza grazia serba.
> S'i' era sol di me quel che creasti
>   novellamente, amor che'l ciel governi,
>   tu'l sai, che col tuo lume mi levasti.     (64–75)

The episode thus begins on a note of stasis and expectancy ('fissa', 'stava', 'fissi') that is soon to be resolved by a change as profound as it is imperceptible and inexplicable. (As Beatrice explains a few lines later (88–90): 'Tu stesso ti fai grosso / col falso imaginar, sì che non vedi / ciò che vedresti se l'avessi scosso'; Dante has neither understood nor even noticed what has happened to him.) And this, indeed, is the first and most obvious thing that must be said about 'trasumanar' in its narrative context: it expresses a change of state. Dante transhumanized is not what he was before. This is, in fact, only the first of a whole series of neologisms minted in *Paradiso* in the attempt to convey the startling, almost literally unthinkable novelty of the experience that the *cantica* depicts, an experience so transcendental as to pass beyond the existing boundaries of human speech.

Thus the progress of Dante-character's steadily deepening perception of the nature of heavenly reality is summed up in the new verb 'imparadisare', while the evolving relationships he enjoys with Beatrice, with God, and, not least, with himself, are rendered in the still more daring coinages 'inleiare', 'inluiare', 'inmiare', 'intuare', and 'indiare'.[87] So 'trasumanar' too instantly conveys the idea of a transformation, to a condition not readily imaginable within the limits of terrestrial vocabulary. But, as Charles Singleton has observed, it is also, crucially, a verb of motion.[88] The changes that Dante *personaggio* undergoes in Heaven are not only interior or spiritual: he is still a traveller, still journeying from 'place' to 'place' (to give the immaterial spheres of Heaven a convenient spatial relationship). As Dante rises, in the body, through the heavens towards God, 'trasumanar' comes to include the meaning 'to travel beyond the confines of the human world', in a concretely physical sense.

This sense is reinforced by the use, elsewhere in *Paradiso*, of equally concrete images that depict Dante's movement from sphere to sphere. In *Paradiso* v, for instance, passing from the sphere of the Moon to that of Mercury, the traveller is compared to a speeding arrow, a 'saetta che nel segno / percuote pria che sia la corda queta', while in canto II he is drawn ever upwards by a thirst: 'la concreata

---

[87] *Paradiso*, XXVIII. 3; XXII. 127; IX. 73; IX. 81; and IV. 28 (used of an angel rather than of Dante-character). See Brenda D. Schildgen, 'Dante's Neologisms in the *Paradiso* and the Latin Rhetorical Tradition', *Dante Studies*, 107 (1989), 101–19.

[88] Singleton, '*Divine Comedy*', III, part 2, p. 18.

e perpetüa sete / del deïforme regno'.[89] But these essentially physical connotations of 'trasumanar' do not detract from its equally powerful connotations of imperceptible and inexpressible mystery. Other transitions from sphere to sphere are themselves mysterious, and, like the initial movement implicit in 'trasumanar', go unperceived and uncomprehended by their protagonist: 'io non m'accorsi del salire in ella'; 'ma del salire / non m'accors'io'.[90] The movement of 'trasumanar' is both literal and metaphorical, both physical and metaphysical.

'Trasumanar' is thus the beginning of a process of movement and growth that will continue throughout *Paradiso*, taking Dante *personaggio* from the fixing of his eyes on Beatrice (1. 65–6) to the fixing of his mind on God: 'Così la mente mia, tutta sospesa, / mirava fissa, immobile e attenta, / e sempre di mirar faceasi accesa' (XXXIII. 97–9). But before it even takes place, and before the narrator can warn us of the impossibility of expressing it verbally, the text attempts to draw an explanatory parallel between Dante-character's position, as he gazes at Beatrice, and that of the mythological fisherman Glaucus (1. 67–9). It is my contention that this single *terzina* has frequently been misunderstood in the past, and that a reading that is more attentive to both its placing in *Paradiso* and its intertextual background may clarify its own significance as much as that of 'trasumanar'.

The Glaucus story is found, of course, in Ovid's *Metamorphoses*, and recounts how the Boeotian fisherman of that name was transformed into a god after he ate a certain magic herb, and then ('for some reason', remarks one understandably baffled lexicographer), leaped into the sea.[91] The tale clearly appeals to all the medieval commentators on *Paradiso* 1, who retell it with varying degrees of gusto, and conclude that the point of the allusion here is that Dante-character is turned into a kind of god by contemplating Beatrice, just as Glaucus was after his maritime picnic. The fullest explanation, predictably, is Benvenuto da Imola's:

[N]am Glaucus piscator figuraliter est poeta Dantes, qui diu fuerat piscatus in aqua inferni et purgatorii, et tandem pervenerat ad pratum virens, ubi nunquam fuerat alius poeta, scilicet ad paradisum deliciarum, et ibi tamquam piscator bonus posuerat homines captos sermone suo, qui facti

---

[89] *Paradiso*, v. 91; II. 19.   [90] *Paradiso*, VIII. 13; X. 34–5.
[91] See the *Oxford Classical Dictionary*, edited by N. G. L. Hammond and H. H. Scullard, second edition (Oxford, 1970), p. 468.

avidi, gustata nova herba, idest doctrina, quae hucusque fuerat inviolata et intacta, intraverunt mare; et ipse novus Glaucus relicta terra more Glauci factus est primo semideus, et plene et perfecte lotus dulci aqua fluviorum paradisi deliciarum factus est deus in magno mari paradisi cum aliis beatis mutata forma primae naturae et vitae.[92]

Benvenuto's carefully worked-out identification, with its clear connection between deification ('factus est deus') and 'trasumanar' ('mutata forma primae naturae et vitae'), might well have been grist for Migliorini Fissi's mill; and it has continued to exert some influence on those many twentieth-century critics who see the Glaucus allusion as, in some way, defining the nature of Dante's transformation. These include Singleton and, especially, Sapegno, who dwells on the lines in the *Metamorphoses* (XIII. 945–6) that best lend themselves to support of this interpretation: 'cum subito trepidare intus praecordia sensi / alteriusque rapi naturae pectus amore'.[93] This is certainly justifiable, to the extent that these lines do indeed describe a profound transformation in a human individual; but it is quite another matter to argue that this transformation is identical with, or even closely analogous to, that of Dante *personaggio*.

The whole atmosphere of the Glaucus story – the miraculous outward transformation (*Met.*, XIII. 960–5) into a pagan deity – is, in fact, decisively different from that of the (equally miraculous) *inner* transformation ('tal dentro mi fei') of the Christian Dante; and even the potential analogy between the two is diluted by Glaucus' overt rejection of the human world ('repetenda ... numquam / terra, vale!' – 'farewell, dry land where I shall never walk again!', XIII. 947–8), which sits strangely with the emphasis on humanness and the duty to return to the mortal world that are characteristic of Dante in

---

[92] Benvenuto, *Comentum*, IV, 317: 'For Glaucus the fisherman is, figuratively speaking, the poet Dante, who for a long time had fished in the waters of Hell and Purgatory, and at last had come to a green meadow, where no other poet had ever been, that is, to the Earthly Paradise; and there, like a good fisherman, he had placed the people captured with his words, who, made greedy, having tasted that new herb (that is, doctrine), which up till now had remained untouched and untasted, entered the sea; and he, a new Glaucus, having left the shore, in the manner of Glaucus was first transformed into a demigod, and then, when fully and perfectly washed in the sweet water of the rivers of the Earthly Paradise, was made a god in the great ocean of Paradise with the other blessed, having changed the form of his first nature and life...'

[93] Singleton, '*Divine Comedy*', III, part 2, pp. 17–18; Sapegno, '*Divina Commedia*' (1957), p. 788. The text of *Metamorphoses* is quoted from *P. Ovidius Nasonis: Metamorphoseon libri XV*, edited by B. A. Van Proosdij (Leiden, 1982). The lines quoted by Sapegno might be translated 'when suddenly I felt the inmost fibres of my being tremble, and my heart was seized by desire for a different world'.

Paradise. Furthermore, Glaucus after his transformation is wholly divine ('"Non ego prodigium nec sum fera belua, virgo, / sed deus" inquit "aquae, nec maius in aequore Proteus / ius habet"', – '"I am not a monster, nor a savage beast, maiden, but a god", he said, "of the waters, nor does Proteus have greater authority in the sea than I do"', XIII. 917–19), which Dante can never be: his retention of the essence of his humanity is guaranteed, not least by the etymological unpicking of the very word 'trasumanar', where the human element remains as firmly at the centre of the word as it must at the centre of Dante's transmogrified being. The parallel between Glaucus and Dante is, at best, not in what they become but in the manner of their becoming – not in deification, in short, but in transformation.

Those who limit their interpretation of the Glaucus allusion to its role as an image of transformation, let alone those who identify Glaucus's transformation too closely with Dante-character's, are not listening closely enough, either to Dante or to Ovid. The text of *Paradiso*, in fact, itself makes clear just why Glaucus is mentioned at this point: 'Trasumanar significare *per verba* / non si poria; però l'essemplo basti' (I. 70–1). The central point about 'trasumanar' is its ineffability; and the relevance of the Glaucus story here is that it too describes a transformation that is ultimately ineffable. Only in this respect are the situations of Dante *personaggio* and Glaucus truly identical. After describing his leap into the sea, the narrating Glaucus adds:

> Hactenus acta tibi possum memoranda referre,
> hactenus haec memini, nec mens mea cetera sensit.
> Quae postquam rediit, alium me corpore toto
> ac fueram nuper, neque eundem mente recepi.[94]    (956–9)

It is, then, not because Glaucus recounts an identical, or even an analogous, experience to his character's that Dante *poeta* cites him here, but precisely because he does not; after his transformation Glaucus's powers of memory and expression fail him, just as do Dante's when he attempts to describe 'trasumanar'. The 'essemplo' thus shows not what it is like to be deified – since that, for Glaucus and Dante, could only mean immeasurably different and even incompatible things – but what it is like to undergo an experience of

---

[94] 'Thus far I can recount to you the deeds that I remember, / thus far I recall these things; but my mind felt nothing more. / When afterwards it returned to me, I was different in my whole body / from what I had been, nor was I the same in my mind.'

transformation and then be unable to recall or recount it exactly. To interpret Glaucus as an image of the ineffability of mystical experience and the limitations of human perception might, perhaps, assist in a re-evaluation of Dante's concept of 'trasumanar'.[95]

What, then, is left of Migliorini Fissi's correlation of Bernard's *deificatio* and Dante's 'trasumanar'? We have seen that deification has a long and tortuous conceptual history in both philosophy and theology, and that none of the key texts in that history, not even Bernard's, seems to have left tangible traces in Dante's writing; we have seen that the text of *Paradiso* I does not itself point unequivocally to the depiction of an experience strictly identifiable as deification, since even the Glaucus allusion seems to have other, more powerfully functional, connotations. And yet that text most certainly does describe a process connected with contemplative mysticism.

The signs are unmistakable: the moment of fixity and repose with which the episode begins (64–6); the concentration and absorption into an Other achieved by Dante *personaggio* (67–9); the experience's ineffability (70–1); the acknowledgement that anyone who is to share the experience will do so through the action of grace (71–2); the uncertainty as to whether only the soul, or body and soul together, are involved – clearly modelled on the Pauline precedent of 2 Corinthians 12. 3 (73–4); and the invocation of divine love (74) as agent of the transformation, achieved through the uplifting effect of its light (74–5). All these will easily be recognized as elements in the mainstream Christian tradition of mystical experience; but none of them is specific to deification as such, or to any *auctor* in particular. 'Trasumanar' is an unutterably profound transformation of Dante's human condition, and therefore a mystical experience of some kind; but that does not necessarily make it a correlative of deification, or tie it specifically to Bernard.

'Trasumanar' is, in fact, only the *beginning* of a protracted and arduous education in mystical experience and spiritual growth, which Dante *personaggio* is required to undergo in Paradise. The Dante who is transhumanized at *Paradiso*, I. 70 is being made ready

---

[95] Rudolf Palgen, 'Il mito di Glauco nella *Divina Commedia*', *Convivium*, 25 (1957), 400–12, argues that the Glaucus reference 'rappresenta "moralmente" una deificazione' (p. 402), and distinguishes this from Pauline *raptus*. He does not mention ineffability. For another excellent reading of Glaucus, closer to my own in spirit (but which I saw only after completing this chapter), see Kevin Brownlee, 'Pauline Vision and Ovidian Speech in *Paradiso* I', in *The Poetry of Allusion: Virgil and Ovid in Dante's 'Commedia'*, edited by Rachel Jacoff and Jeffrey T. Schnapp (Stanford, 1991), pp. 202–13.

to embark on that course, but he most certainly has not yet completed it; and this fact alone is fatal to the correlation of *deificatio* and 'trasumanar'. If Dante had indeed been brought to the peak of mystical experience in the act of 'trasumanar', he might have been expected to begin immediately to share to the full the attributes of the blessed souls whom he encounters in Heaven; and this is clearly not the case. They are still, and remain until Dante reaches his climactic vision of God, possessed of more knowledge about their beatified existence than he – hence his questions, their exposition of doctrine, their right to examine him for orthodoxy of belief – and the simplest but most vital difference between Dante *personaggio* and them is that they have died in the body, and thus already entered on the eternal enjoyment of a bliss that for Dante, still living and destined to return to the world, can only be transitory.

In the terms of Aquinas' *quaestio De raptu*, quoted above, the blessed perceive God 'per modum formae immanentis' – that is, they are deified, since they participate directly and immanently in the divine – while Dante can only do so 'per modum cuiusdam passionis transeuntis'. The two are not the same. And Dante-character himself makes this plain in *Paradiso* III, where he admits to Piccarda Donati that he does not and cannot comprehend the appearance of the blessed, which is so different from what he had been led to expect:

> Ond' io a lei: 'Ne' mirabili aspetti
> vostri risplende non so che divino
> che vi trasmuta da' primi concetti:
> però non fui a rimembrar festino;
> ma or m'aiuta ciò che tu mi dici,
> sì che raffigurar m'è più latino.      (58–63)

The blessed, then, have about them a 'non so che divino' that provokes wonder ('mirabili') in Dante; a mysterious quality that, like mystical experience itself, inhibits his powers of memory and perception (61–3), and which he himself – even after being trans-humanized – clearly does not possess or even understand. (This questioning wonderment of Dante's, as a motif, runs through the whole third canto of *Paradiso*: see also 37–41, 64–6, and 94–6.) He has not, then, arrived at the state of beatitude enjoyed by Piccarda; he has, at most, set out on his journey towards it. 'Trasumanar' was the initiation, the rite of passage, the passport that made the journey possible; by transforming Dante's humanity beyond recognition it made him ready for – eventual – contact with the divine. But that contact only takes place in the very last lines of the poem (*Par.*, XXXIII. 142–5):

> A l'alta fantasia qui mancò possa;
> ma già volgeva il mio disio e'l *velle*,
> sì come rota ch'igualmente è mossa,
> l'amor che move il sole e l'altre stelle.

Here, at last, divine love acts on Dante-character's will, to bring it into accord with God's; here, for the first time, imagination loses its power, and language fails; here – and not before – Dante is deified. And this deification is one that Bernard of Clairvaux would have recognized, since it depends precisely on that accord of human and divine wills that is the hallmark of deification in his thought.

Migliorini Fissi is quite right to point out, however, that such accord is also the basis of Piccarda Donati's definition of the condition of the blessed in *Paradiso* III.[96] Though she tends to overstate her case (whatever else it may be, Bernard's influence in these lines is not 'chiarissimo'), it is hard to deny that she draws a very thought-provoking parallel between Piccarda's speech and Bernard's doctrine of *deificatio*. Here, above all, and more clearly than anywhere else in the *Commedia* – before the final lines – is the requisite stress on the accord of wills brought about by the action of divine love:

> 'Frate, la nostra volontà quïeta
> virtù di carità, che fa volerne
> sol quel ch'avemo, e d'altro non ci asseta.
> Se disïassimo esser più superne,
> foran discordi li nostri disiri
> dal voler di colui che qui ne cerne;
> che vedrai non capere in questi giri,
> s'essere in carità è qui *necesse*,
> e se la sua natura ben rimiri.
> Anzi è formale ad esto beato *esse*
> tenersi dentro a la divina voglia,
> per ch'una fansi nostre voglie stesse;
> sì che, come noi sem di soglia in soglia
> per questo regno, a tutto il regno piace
> com' a lo re che 'n suo voler ne 'nvoglia.
> E 'n la sua volontade è nostra pace.                    (70–85)

This stunningly beautiful essay in poetic theology, with its insistent but subtly varied wordplay on the key idea of will ('volontà',

---

[96] Migliorini Fissi, *Dante*, pp. 135–6.

'volerne', 'disïassimo', 'disiri', 'voler', 'voglia', 'voglie', ''nvoglia', 'volontade'), beyond question anticipates the description of Dante-character's own experience in *Paradiso* xxxiii, where the 'disïo' characteristic of his (and Piccarda's, iii. 73–4) humanity is finally aligned with the '*velle*' (the Latinized 'volontà', 'voler', 'volontade') proper to God. Piccarda is describing what she has, and what Dante will soon have for himself. But he does not have it yet.

Transhumanized Dante and deified Piccarda are not on the same level of existence: they will become so, briefly, when Dante attains his vision of God 'per modum cuiusdam passionis transeuntis' at the end of *Paradiso* xxxiii, and they will be so eternally when Dante dies and enters on the vision 'per modum formae immanentis', as Piccarda herself has already done; but for the time being they are not. The great gulf of Dante's mortality is still fixed between them. And so, even if Bernard's influence on these lines were indeed 'chiarissimo', as Migliorini Fissi would have it, it still would not follow that his *deificatio* finds its 'autentico correlativo poetico' in Dante's 'trasu-manar'.

Etienne Gilson provides a definition of Bernard's *deificatio* on which it would be hard to improve:

The mystical union integrally respects this real distinction between the Divine substance and the human substance, between the will of God and the will of man; it is neither a confusion of the two substances in general, nor a confusion of the substances of the two wills in particular; but it is their perfect accord, the coincidence of two willings. Two distinct spiritual substances – two substances even *infinitely* distinct – two wills no less distinct as far as concerns the existential order, but in which intention and object coincide to such an extent that the one is a perfect image of the other, there we have the mystical union and unity as St Bernard conceived them.[97]

This 'coincidence of two willings' is unquestionably achieved in *Paradiso*, at xxxiii. 143, but not, I would suggest, at i. 70. 'Trasumanar' is no more than the change of state that makes the movement towards God possible. It is an experience, indeed, that might well be related, rather than to *deificatio*, to another term typical of Bernard's mystical writing, *excessus*. Here is Gilson's definition:

A generic term signifying, in a general way, any exceeding of the limits of a state in order to attain another. To free oneself of one's passions is already an *excessus*. However, the word takes on a mystical sense only when it indicates

---

[97] Gilson, *Théologie mystique*, p. 146; quoted from the translation by Downes, p. 123.

the passage from a normal human state, even were this attained by the aid of grace, to a state that is more than human.[98]

'The passage from a normal human state ... to a state that is more than human': does this not, by now, sound somewhat familiar? Might it not serve equally well, in fact, as a definition of 'trasumanar'? But, alas for all those who have posited Bernard of Clairvaux's thinking about deification as the principal influence on Dante at this point, this is a definition of *excessus*, not of *deificatio*; and the difficulties involved in identifying even an attenuated Bernardine influence in this context do not end there. As Gilson himself makes clear, *excessus* is a massively generic term, found very frequently in Christian writers; and there is no particular slant to Bernard's usage that would enable it to be distinguished from that of any other mystical *auctor*. Indeed, as we have seen, if there is a late medieval writer of whom the term may properly be said to be characteristic, it is Richard of St Victor; and even so eminent a Bernard scholar as Jean Leclercq has been willing to admit that some of Richard's writings (along with Bonaventure's *Itinerarium mentis in Deum*) may have been at least as strongly influential on *Paradiso* (especially canto XXXIII) as any of Bernard's.[99]

All this might seem to invalidate Migliorini Fissi's hypothesis; or, at the very least, to throw a cup or two of cold water over it. Certainly, as far as the correlation with 'trasumanar' is concerned, she does seem to have misunderstood the nature and relationship of the two terms: if anything, it is in the distinction between, rather than the assimilation of, their meanings that the key to their relationship is to be found. But her suggestion of a direct influence on the Piccarda episode – and thus, by extension, on the definition of the situation of the blessed as a group, since that, in theological terms, is what Piccarda undertakes – is potentially more stimulating. For if the state of the blessed is indeed identifiable as *deificatio* in the Bernardine sense, and if it may thus be surmised (though not, I think, proved) that contact with the historical Bernard's work played a part in determining the conceptual boundaries of Dante's thinking about that state, then we may have, perhaps, another clue to Bernard's problematic presence in the *Commedia*, and to the significance of his

[98] Gilson, p. 132n.; quoted from Downes, p. 237.
[99] Jean Leclercq, François Vandenbroucke, and Louis Bouyer, *The Spirituality of the Middle Ages* (London, 1968), p. 366. On Bonaventure's *Itinerarium* and *Paradiso* XXXIII, see Hagman, 'Dante's Vision of God'.

role as a character within it. Given these premises, Dante *personaggio* can be seen to aspire, throughout the poem, to reach a condition of Bernardine *deificatio*; and that might help to explain just why, when he does so, it should be through the intervention and under the auspices of Bernard of Clairvaux himself – rather than, as might have been anticipated by the even the most careful reader, in the company of Beatrice.

Here too appears not the assimilation of 'trasumanar' and *deificatio* but the distinction between them: the former is connected with Beatrice, who accompanies Dante at the moment of his trans-humanization, and gradually educates him thereafter in the implications and responsibilities that arise from it; the latter is associated with Bernard, who prepares Dante for, obtains on his behalf, and finally presides over, the deifying vision that ends the journey of both *personaggio* and reader – and whose theological basis is laid in the historical Bernard's own writings.

Once again, however, as in the case of Bernard the Mariologist, the most compelling evidence for Dante's appreciation of those writings is found not in extraneous textual citation, but in the integration of this aspect of Bernard's cultural achievement into the fabric of his speech and actions in the *Commedia*. The poem tells us that Bernard is a contemplative; the poem depicts a contemplative experience that has parallels in Bernard's own work; the poem sets this whole episode under the seal of Bernard himself. It is left to the reader to make the connections. So once again, at the end of our prolonged excursion through the history and meaning of *deificatio*, we find ourselves – as it is right that we should – face to face with the text of the *Commedia*; but the journey will have been worthwhile if it has left us even a little better equipped to listen to what the poem itself has to say.

# CHAPTER 7

# *Eloquence – and its limits*

Much has been made, in the course of this book, of the importance of eloquence in the presentation of Bernard of Clairvaux as a character in Dante's *Commedia*: and it has been tacitly assumed, throughout, that the possession and use of oratorical powers are seen by Dante *poeta* as unequivocally good in themselves, and that they form, outside the fictional context of the poem, some part of the artistic and intellectual ideal to which he, as poet, seeks to aspire. It may be useful, however, as a brief conclusion to my argument, first to refine the former of these ideas and then to take issue with challenges to the latter; and also, finally, to consider how – in *Paradiso* especially – the practice of eloquence and the appreciation of its virtues co-exist, more or less uneasily, with a clear consciousness of its limitations.

For if, as I believe, Bernard's role in the poem is – at least in part – that of an exemplar of eloquence, and if his position in the narrative (as the last individual encountered by Dante-character, and as spokesman for the celestial multitude) might seem to encourage the view that his linguistic skills, and their exemplary function, enjoy some particular prestige or sanction associated with his proximity to God and with the divinely ordained mission he undertakes on Dante's behalf, it must none the less be conceded that the last word in the *Commedia* is not, after all, his; and that, moreover, the poem's final canto, both before and, even more, after Bernard ceases to speak (*Par.*, XXXIII. 39), poses a challenge to the resources of eloquence that, it seems, cannot be met easily, adequately, or perhaps even at all, by any form of human language. This problem, though focused with unique acuity in *Paradiso* XXXIII, can plausibly be seen to subtend the entire third *cantica*, and to have weighty consequences for our reading(s) of it.

The centrality of eloquence in the Dantean scheme of things can scarcely be better demonstrated than by pointing out that without it

Dante-character's journey would never have taken place; that, in a word, he would never have been saved.[1] The passage that makes this plain is tucked away in Virgil's explanation, in *Inferno* II, of the circumstances in which he was commissioned by Beatrice to come to the aid of her errant admirer. Virgil quotes directly the terms in which Beatrice made her appeal to him:

> 'O anima cortese mantoana,
>    di cui la fama ancor nel mondo dura,
>    e durerà quanto'l mondo lontana,
> l'amico mio, e non de la ventura,
>    ne la diserta piaggia è impedito
>    sì nel cammin, che vòlt' è per paura;
> e temo che non sia già sì smarrito,
>    ch'io mi sia tardi al soccorso levata,
>    per quel ch'i' ho di lui nel cielo udito.
> Or movi, e con la tua parola ornata
>    e con ciò c'ha mestieri al suo campare,
>    l'aiuta sì ch'i' ne sia consolata.'          (58–69)

The indispensable element in this project for Dante's rescue is clearly the fact that Virgil both possesses, and knows how to use, a 'parola ornata' (67). This alone, in contrast with the much more generic 'ciò c'ha mestieri al suo campare' (68), is specified as the means by which Dante will be helped and Beatrice consoled; and it is essential to note that Virgil's word is designated as 'ornata' – not just any old word, however charged with salvific meaning, but a word (or, more precisely, a language – synecdoche is clearly at work here) that is recognizably embellished with the devices whose presence and operation are normally seen, by speakers and hearers, as constituting eloquence. Virgil is not just to speak the rescuing word, but to pay attention to the aesthetic and intellectual implications of its usage; and the efficacy of his speech is manifestly dependent, at least to some degree, on the elegance and persuasiveness of its formulation.

Dante-character's initial recognition of his mysterious interlocutor as 'quella fonte / che spandi di parlar sì largo fiume' (*Inf.*, I. 79–80)

---

[1] I return to the issues sketched in what follows (not without some degree of overlap, both conceptual and verbal), in an article entitled 'Dante and the Authority of Poetic Language', forthcoming in *Dante: Contemporary Perspectives*, edited by Amilcare A. Iannucci (Toronto, 1993).

is thus retrospectively justified, as we see that for Beatrice too – and hence, no doubt, for the whole hierarchy of heavenly ladies that leads from Beatrice herself backwards and upwards towards God – this is the immediately relevant aspect of Virgil's historical personality, the one that best equips him to become Dante's rescuer, guide, and mentor in Hell and Purgatory. Entrusting Dante's spiritual well-being, at least for the first two-thirds of his journey, to a user of 'parola ornata', a possessor of eloquence, helps to ensure the eventual success of the enterprise; and, consequently, it is under the auspices of another possessor of eloquence, Bernard, that the journey comes to an end.

The narrative progression through the poem is thus, among other things, a movement from one 'parola ornata' to another – from Virgil's eloquence to Bernard's, and thus, generically, from poetry to preaching (*Paradiso* xxxii) and prayer (*Paradiso*, xxxiii. 1–39) – as well as from the pagan word that offers worldly fame ('lo bello stilo che m'ha fatto onore', *Inf.*, i. 87) to the Christian word that offers eternal bliss. The former, however, grounds the process that leads to the latter; and, at both ends of the journey, the functional importance of the word and its usage is paramount.

Three significant caveats need, however, to be entered at this point: the first regarding a word, the second a character, and the third the narrative structure of *Inferno* itself.

Virgil's is not the only word (or language) in *Inferno* distinguished by the epithet 'ornata'. It recurs in canto xviii, as part of the retelling of the sinful exploits of Jason, who appears there in the *bolgia* of the seducers:

> Ello passò per l'isola di Lenno
> poi che l'ardite femmine spietate
> tutti li maschi loro a morte dienno.
> Ivi con segni e con parole ornate
> Isifile ingannò, la giovinetta
> che prima avea tutte l'altre ingannate. (88–93)

It will instantly be apparent that Jason's 'parole ornate' are morally quite different from Virgil's 'parola ornata': instead of rescuing they betray, instead of embodying the truth they act as a vehicle of deceit. Their ornamental quality is clearly specious, employed to conceal Jason's malicious and self-seeking intent; eloquence has become the means of procuring another's harm. The situation is, in fact, the exact reverse of that in which Virgil's eloquence comes to Dante-character's rescue; and yet the terms in which eloquence is evoked, in these two diametrically opposed cases, are (save in respect of grammatical number) identical. At the very least, this extract from *Inferno* XVIII offers sound reasons for hesitating before arriving at the conclusion that 'ornata' in the *Commedia* is necessarily a term of praise, or that eloquence itself, for Dante *poeta*, is necessarily a positive value. The issue is more complex than that.

The second caveat involves the acknowledgement that, even in the case of Virgil, eloquence is not constantly and uniformly operative as a principle governing his choice and use of words – it has limits. The earliest decisive proof of this comes in the dramatic episode of Virgil's and Dante's (physical and mental) bafflement when confronted by the hostility of the devils who inhabit the city of Dis (*Inf.*, VIII. 67 – IX. 105). Faced with the devils' refusal to admit the travellers to their infernal fortress – which takes the unmistakably concrete form of slamming its gates in Virgil's face (VIII. 115–17) – Dante's guide, to whom the text has only just referred as 'mar di tutto 'l senno' (VIII. 7), finds himself, in a painful paradox, paralysed both intellectually and linguistically, knowing neither what to do nor, more significantly, what to say:

> Attento si fermò com'om ch'ascolta;
>     ché l'occhio nol potea menare a lunga
>     per l'aere nero e per la nebbia folta.
> 'Pur a noi converrà vincer la punga',
>     cominciò el, 'se non... Tal ne s'offerse.
>     Oh quanto tarda a me ch'altri qui giunga!'     (IX. 4–9)

The interrupted sentence (7–8) gives the game away. Virgil embarks on the verbal expression of an idea; finds it misconceived, erroneous, or at least inappropriate to his responsibilities in this situation (since he comes perilously close, with the words 'se non', to admitting that the divine assistance promised to Dante may not, after all, be available); and breaks off abruptly, to begin again on an entirely different tack. This verbal clumsiness is more than merely inelegant; it is also fatally unsuccessful in its aim, which is to reassure Virgil's timid protégé that all will still be well. Dante *personaggio* realizes, thanks to Virgil's maladroit use of language, that he is attempting to conceal something (his own perplexity); and, because Virgil's words have failed to convey a precise meaning – have not, that is, been used effectively – Dante ends up fearing that the something concealed may turn out to be considerably worse than it really is:

> I' vidi ben sì com' ei ricoperse
>   lo cominciar con l'altro che poi venne,
>   che fur parole a le prime diverse;
> ma nondimen paura il suo dir dienne,
>   perch' io traeva la parola tronca
>   forse a peggior sentenza che non tenne.          (10–15)

Virgil's momentary loss of eloquence, issuing in a 'parola tronca' that neutralizes his more characteristic 'parola ornata', has consequences that bring him and Dante-character to the brink of disaster, enmeshing them in a net of mental and verbal impotence whose moral gravity is figured immediately thereafter in the threatening appearance of Medusa (ix. 52–60), and from which they can only be released by the direct intervention of divine authority in the form of the angelic envoy who is 'da ciel messo' (ix. 64–105). Even though it is Virgil who protects Dante against the Gorgon (58–60), and even though he will soon recover his intellectual and linguistic equipoise (to retain it through many subsequent adventures), the damage is already done. The moment of paralysis outside the gates of Dis has laid bare the limitations of Virgil's eloquence, and shown that when the pagan 'parola' will not suffice, its divine counterpart becomes indispensable. The angel's speech to the devils instantly succeeds where Virgil's had failed (91–9), and the text makes clear that the newfound confidence with which Dante and Virgil advance into the city of Dis is owed entirely to the example of celestial eloquence:

> Poi si rivolse per la strada lorda,
>   e non fé motto a noi, ma fé sembiante
>   d'omo cui altra cura stringa e morda
> che quella di colui che li è davante;
>   e noi movemmo i piedi inver' la terra,
>   sicuri appresso le parole sante.          (100–5)

So Virgil's 'parola ornata' cannot, it seems, always be relied on to guide Dante, or preserve him from the threat of harm; it carries within itself the capacity to fail, to become 'tronca'. Language in the mouth of a pagan, even one as literarily distinguished and morally admirable as Virgil, cannot fulfil the conditions under which alone it can take on the form of ideal eloquence, because it does not rest on a foundation of divinely guaranteed meaning. The thematic development of the *Commedia*, as a result, will turn out to be one in which the poem undertakes a quest for an infallible 'parola', a word in which the believer can repose complete confidence that it will hold meaning, express truth, and possess protective power; and I would argue that such a word is found, above all, in the discourse of Bernard of Clairvaux – a discourse which, like that of the angelic envoy of *Inferno* IX, but like no other body of speech in the *Commedia*, is explicitly designated as consisting of 'parole sante' (*Inf.*, IX. 105; *Par.*, XXXII. 3).

This epithet, indeed, can be seen as vital in the definition of the *Commedia*'s ideal of eloquence; and this brings us to the third of our caveats. For, as we have seen in the case of Jason (*Inferno* XVIII), the moral validity of eloquence is not assumed in Dante's scheme; it is affected by the intentions of the speaker and, in the bluntly narrative terms of the poem's fiction, by the speaker's location in the realms of the afterlife. The word spoken by the denizens of Hell may be 'ornata' – at times to a dazzling degree – but it cannot be holy, and it may not, quite simply, be true. This defect, visible even in the speech of a Virgil – as described above – debars infernal eloquence from attaining the moral status of its purgatorial or paradisiacal equivalent; in the *Commedia*, true eloquence is the eloquence of the true.

*Inferno* is rich in instances of eloquent speakers whose verbal felicity reveals itself as no more than the tangible realization of their moral and intellectual failings. One need only think of the honeyed self-justification of Francesca da Rimini, the intricate but sterile word-play of Pier della Vigna, the lofty yet vapid rhetoric of Brunetto Latini, or, most pointed of all, the scathingly ironic image of Ulysses, first quoting his own inspiring exhortation to his crew and then, with odious self-satisfaction and false modesty, congratulating himself on the efficacy of the 'orazion picciola' that persuaded them to their (and, of course, his) doom:

> 'O frati,' dissi, 'che per cento milia
> perigli siete giunti a l'occidente,
> a questa tanta picciola vigilia
> d'i nostri sensi ch'è del rimanente
> non vogliate negar l'esperïenza,
> di retro al sol, del mondo sanza gente.
> Considerate la vostra semenza:
> fatti non fosti a viver come bruti,

> ma per seguir virtute e canoscenza.'
> Li miei compagni fec'io sì aguti,
>   con questa orazion picciola, al cammino,
>   che a pena poscia li avrei ritenuti;
> e volta nostra poppa nel mattino,
>   de' remi facemmo ali al folle volo,
>   sempre acquistando dal lato mancino. (*Inf.*, XXVI. 112–26)

The oratorical polish and emotive power of Ulysses' 'orazion', taken by itself, are extraordinary and undeniable, and have been recognized by readers from Benvenuto da Imola to Primo Levi;[2] but in their double context – their original delivery to Ulysses's crew and their later narration to Virgil and Dante – his words can be seen to be cruelly deceptive, the product of an eloquence turned against itself, and, more important, against the divine will that ought to be its only guiding principle. Ulysses' 'orazion' is the reverse of 'santa'; his eloquence serves falsehood, not truth.

This is enough to disqualify it from any possibility of being exemplary, just as eloquence itself, as a concept or practice unmodified by particular circumstances, must be so disqualified. What preoccupies Dante *poeta*, and what is to become the object of the *Commedia*'s linguistic quest, is, instead, an eloquence that shall be both efficacious and true, and thus fully accord with the prescriptions of the God who is himself the Word (John 1. 1–12). Mere ability to manipulate words in pleasing and meaningful patterns – 'parola ornata' – will not suffice; for although the speaker of such words may be a Virgil, he may also be a Jason or, worse, a Ulysses. Instead, eloquence must be governed by divine authority, and sanctioned by divine precedent; it must become sacred. And this is the ideal of eloquence to which the poem truly aspires: the 'orazion picciola' of *Inferno* XXVI must become the 'santa orazione' of *Paradiso* XXXII, the eloquent falsity of a Ulysses must be redeemed into the eloquent veracity of a Bernard. Then and then alone will it be possible for a human being to speak the word that is both 'ornata' and 'santa', both eloquent and true – the word that saves.

The moral evaluation of eloquence in the *Commedia* thus requires close attention to the identity, situation, and presumed intentions of

---

[2] Benvenuto (*Comentum*, II, 290) refers to the 'effectum mirabile istius pulcerrimae persuasionis' ('the amazing effect of this most beautiful piece of persuasion'); Levi makes the speech the basis for a moving episode ('Il canto di Ulisse') in his *Se questo è un uomo* (Turin, 1947).

the speaker; and, in consequence, it seems logical enough to look for exemplars of (sacred) eloquence, or statements of such eloquence as an ideal, in *Paradiso*, where every speaker deals in truth, and their words are placed visibly, directly, and necessarily at the service of God. From that choice it follows that the speaker who appears, in narrative terms, closest to God himself, and who takes upon himself the role of expositor of the nature of the highest echelons of Heaven, might plausibly be proposed as the poem's most powerful exponent of eloquence. The rest of this book has attempted to make a case for seeing Bernard of Clairvaux in precisely this light. But the very idea of Bernard (or any other character) as an 'exemplar' of eloquence, which brings with it the notion that eloquence (at least the morally acceptable kind) is somehow to be practised or imitated outside the immediate context of the poem – presumably by readers, in their own dealings in words – raises the question of how far the standards of verbal usage apparently propounded in the *Commedia* are actually attributable to Dante himself *as poet*; that is, how far the eloquence of the characters in the poem is not only the product of, but also a commentary on, the eloquence of Dante *poeta*.

This is thorny territory indeed, especially in the last decade of the twentieth century, when scepticism about the power of words to mean anything at all (least of all whatever they appear to mean) has become alarmingly widespread among readers and critics, and when belief in eloquence as a positive good is arguably much less common than suspicion of it as a potential evil. One result of this growing reluctance to attribute referential capacity or argumentative co-herence to any use of language – but especially to uses characterized by a high degree of formal organization and/or substantive, even absolutist, claims to intellectual comprehensiveness or ethical uni-versality – has been the emergence, in Dante studies, of the belief that Dante himself was our soulmate and precursor in this regard; that, in short, the linguistic scepticism and distrust of intellectual authority characteristic of the modern (or rather post-modern) age are anticipated in, not to say shared by, the *Commedia*, and that Dante himself, as poet, simply does not believe in his own poem's ostensible aspirations.[3]

---

[3] Here, and in what follows, I am thinking more of recent (and to some extent still ill-defined) tendencies in criticism than of individual critics, and I hope it will be clear that my ruthlessly compressed and paraphrased formulations are not to be understood as representing any one scholar's viewpoint or approach. A recent book that does, however, seem to encapsulate the

The *Commedia*'s claim to truth, in this view, is inevitably undermined by its own status as fiction – which is to say, as a lie. From here it is but a step to the suggestion that Dante *poeta* is not only aware of, but positively rejoices in, this inescapable contradiction; and, in consequence, that the poem's real destination is not truth but falsehood, not coherence but chaos, not the eloquence of speech but the meaninglessness of silence. By this criterion, the *Commedia*'s manifest diversity and vivacity of poetic language are not signs of its success but the reverse, since, even with his linguistic resources stretched to the utmost, Dante-poet still cannot achieve a fully realized representation of what purports to be the matter of his poem. His language can never be adequate to its aims; and even a partial accomplishment of those aims, partaking as it must of some degree, however tiny, of imperfection, is still to be sternly stigmatized as failure. Dante *poeta*, though, is seen as having anticipated this conclusion, and, indeed, as having so designed his text as not only to have taken it into account but to have made it the poem's principal message – in so far as the concept of a poem's having a 'message' retains any meaning in the context of this argument – to the reader.

Prominent among the evidence that might help to support this hypothesis is the series of narratorial interventions and exclamations in *Paradiso* that proclaim, quite overtly, the inadequacy of Dante's (or any human) language effectively to convey the reality of what it is seeking to describe. This collection of passages – which, taken together, are usually recognized in critical jargon as constituting Dante's 'ineffability *topos*' – is extensive and consistent enough to have been perceived as one of the more important bodies of metapoetical reflection in Dante's work; and its presence, which begins at the very moment of Dante-character's entry into Paradise (as discussed in the previous chapter), does seem to take an axe to the very roots of Dante's ostensible project, since it offers the reader a constantly nagging reminder that what he or she is encountering here is an image, pretending to be a reality but, necessarily, failing in the attempt. And yet the attempt is made; *Paradiso* is written (and, sometimes, read); and the reader who remains unimpressed by the extent of Dante's success in creating a plausible representation in words of what he, as a Christian, held (and what the text itself declares) to be the fundamentally unrepresentable, is one who might

tendencies I have in mind, in an especially pure and concentrated form, is Jeremy Tambling, *Dante and Difference: Writing in the 'Commedia'* (Cambridge, 1988).

justifiably be accused of invoking standards of linguistic operation
that are so impossibly demanding as to be meaningless.

This, indeed, is precisely the point: that the attempt to write
*Paradiso* be made, even in the teeth of its own impossibility, and of
Dante-poet's consciousness of that impossibility. It is surely more
satisfactory – at the very least, more objectively congruent with the
norms of Dante's individual and collective culture – to interpret the
very existence of *Paradiso* as an assertion, even a celebration, of the
innate power of language, its potential to undertake an expressive
enterprise as daring, but also as rewarding, as the representation to a
human audience of an experience of the divine, than it is to see it as
a text forever gloomily and pointlessly harping on its own repre-
sentational inadequacy. And the validity of *Paradiso*'s assertion of the
worth of language is not negated, it seems to me, by the recognition
– given voice in the 'ineffability *topos*' – that, however far language
may go, it can never go far enough. Imperfection is inherent in the
human condition; yet it does not make life unlivable, or words
unsayable. Acceptance that limits are set to the range of human
language is an obligatory corollary of the – fundamentally Christian
– belief that limits are set to every form of human activity and every
moment of every human life – that, in the Adamic terms of *Paradiso*,
XXVI. 117, there is always a 'segno' that humanity must not (and
cannot, because it is human) 'trapassar'.

Dante *poeta* is Ulysses' spiritual kinsman in the audacity of his
(poetic) voyage, but the relationship ends when it comes to respecting
the conditions placed on that voyage by a higher – divine – power.
Linguistically, the poet travels as far and as fast as he can, and
delights in the experience; but he accepts that it must come to an end,
and an end that falls short of what he as poet, and indeed as believer,
might desire. The attempt becomes its own justification; the linguistic
journey, not its arrival at silence, is what matters.[4]

The absolutism of the demand that Dante's language fully embody
the experience that it sets out to describe, the refusal to allow it any
validity on the basis of its (inevitable) failure, and, above all, the
attribution to Dante himself of the same self-conscious scepticism that
pervades late twentieth-century readings of this kind, are all the fruit
of a theologically deracinated criticism that has lost touch with the

---

[4] A version of the Dante *poeta*–Ulysses relationship diametrically opposed to my own, fruitful
disagreement with which inspires these remarks, is offered by Giuliana Carugati, *Dalla
menzogna al silenzio. La scrittura mistica della 'Commedia' di Dante* (Bologna, 1991), pp. 89–112.

conception of humanity – and thus of language – as essentially fallen. Absolutist readers demand that Dante write not about God, nor even like God, but as God; which is a demand to which no Christian author could possibly respond. Human use of words must fall short of perfection, since every other aspect of human existence does so, and has done since Adam and Eve's disobedience 'brought death into the world, and all our woe'; but it is profoundly contrary to the spirit of both Dante's theological beliefs and his linguistic theory (to which his writings bear ample witness) to suggest that this inherent lack of perfection instantly consigns every use of human language to the category of perfection's polar opposite. Words cannot do everything; but they can do much, and, in the mouth of a skilled and morally pristine speaker – a Bernard of Clairvaux, for instance, – they can come infinitesimally close to the plenitude of meaning, beauty, and referential power that, in the last analysis, is reserved for the Word that is God.[5]

The 'ineffability *topos*' in *Paradiso* is, then, a necessary acknowledgement of the limits of eloquence, but not a shamefaced confession of its failure. The recognition of *Paradiso*'s ultimate insufficiency in no way precludes it from serving also as a celebration of words, through words. Indeed, the *cantica*'s informing tension, between the desire to probe language's boundaries and the knowledge that those boundaries are firmly established by an unchallengeable authority, is, finally, creative: the poetic exhilaration generated by pushing language to its limits is not diluted by – in fact, it depends on – defining the existence of those limits.

Moreover, if *Paradiso* abounds in avowals of ineffability, it abounds also in neologisms. New words, that is, created to express the (formerly) inexpressible, and thus to redraw the boundaries of language, giving practical proof that ineffability can be counteracted or even diminished. Every time Dante *poeta* coins a neologism, he wins, and celebrates, a victory over silence and meaninglessness. The poetry of *Paradiso* is, in general, exultant rather than diffident about its own claims to mean, to refer, and to express; and when those claims are made in the name of God and for the communication of his will – as they are in the speeches of Bernard of Clairvaux in *Paradiso*

[5] A lucid account of the relationship between Dante's '*verbum*' and God's, and of the *Commedia*'s 'subordination to the Bible' is presented by Zygmunt G. Barański, 'Dante's (Anti-)Rhetoric: Notes on the Poetics of the *Commedia*', in *Moving in Measure: Essays in honour of Brian Moloney*, edited by Judith Bryce and Doug Thompson (Hull, 1989), 1–14 (p. 10).

XXXI–XXXIII – the result is the forging of a truly sacred eloquence, charged to the fullest possible extent with expressive, truth-bearing power, that functions not only as a defining characteristic of certain individuals within the fiction of the *Commedia*, but as an exemplary principle for both poet and reader in the life of the world.

# Bibliography

Alan of Lille, *Anticlaudianus*, edited by R. Bossuat (Paris, 1955).

Albertus Magnus, *Opera omnia*, edited by B. Geyer and others (Münster, 1951– ).

Alexander of Hales, *Quaestiones disputatae antequam esset frater* (Ad Claras Aquas, 1960).

*Summa theologica*, 4 vols. (Ad Claras Aquas, 1924–47).

*Analecta hymnica medii aevi (AHMA)*, edited by Guido Maria Dreves, Clemens Blume, and H. M. Bannister, 58 vols. (Leipzig, 1886–1922).

Anderson, William, *Dante the Maker* (London, 1980).

Aristotle, *Nicomachean Ethics*, translated by David Ross, revised by J. L. Ackrill and J. O. Urmson (Oxford, 1980).

Arnald of Bonneval, *De laudibus Beatae Mariae Virginis*, in *Patrologia latina*, 189, cols. 1725–34.

Auden, W. H., *Collected Poems*, edited by Edward Mendelson (London, 1976).

Auerbach, Erich, 'Dante's Prayer to the Virgin and Earlier Eulogies', in *Gesammelte Aufsätze zur romanischen Philologie* (Berne and Munich, 1967), pp. 123–44; originally in *Romance Philology*, 3 (1949–50), 1–26.

Augustine, *De civitate Dei*, in *Patrologia latina*, 41, cols. 13–804.

*Enarrationes in Psalmos*, in *Patrologia latina*, 36.

*Epistula* x, in *Patrologia latina*, 33, cols. 73–4.

*Sermo* cxxvi, in *Patrologia latina*, 38, cols. 698–705.

*Sermo* clxvi, in *Patrologia latina*, 38, cols. 907–9.

Austen, Jane, *'Northanger Abbey' and 'Persuasion'*, edited by John Davie (London, 1971).

Aversano, Mario, 'San Bernardo e Dante', *L'Alighieri*, 29 (1988), no. 1, 37–45.

*San Bernardo e Dante: teologia e poesia della conversione* (Salerno, 1990).

Barański, Zygmunt G., 'Dante's (Anti-)Rhetoric: Notes on the Poetics of the *Commedia*', in *Moving in Measure: Essays in honour of Brian Moloney*, edited by Judith Bryce and Doug Thompson (Hull, 1989), 1–14.

Barbi, Michele, *Problemi di critica dantesca: prima serie* (Florence, 1934).

*Problemi di critica dantesca: seconda serie* (Florence, 1941).

Barré, Henri, 'Saint Bernard docteur marial', in *Saint Bernard théologien*

(*Actes du congrès de Dijon*, 15–19 *septembre* 1953), *Analecta Sacri Ordinis Cisterciensis*, 9 (1953), fascicules 3–4, pp. 92–113.

Bellomo, Saverio, 'Primi appunti sull'*Ottimo commento* dantesco', *Giornale storico della letteratura italiana*, 157 (1980), 533–40.

*Benedicti Regula*, edited by Rudolf Hanslik, Corpus Scriptorum Ecclesiasticorum Latinorum, 75 (Vienna, 1960).

Benvenuto da Imola, *Comentum super Dantis Aldigherii Comediam*, edited by G. F. Lacaita, 5 vols. (Florence, 1887).

Bergin, Thomas Goddard, 'Lectura Dantis: *Inferno* v', *Lectura Dantis*, 1 (1987), 5–24.

Bernard of Clairvaux, *Sancti Bernardi Opera*, edited by Jean Leclercq, H. Rochais, and C. Talbot (Rome, 1957– ).

*Select Treatises of St Bernard of Clairvaux*, edited by Barton R. V. Mills and Watkin Williams (Cambridge, 1926).

Bernardus Silvestris, *Cosmographia*, edited by Peter Dronke (Leiden, 1978).

*Bibliographie générale de l'Ordre cistercien*, 'Saint Bernard', edited by H. Rochais and E. Manning, 12 fascicules *hors série* (Brussels, 1979–82).

Blum, Rudolf, *La biblioteca della Badia fiorentina e i codici di A. Corbinelli* (Vatican City, 1951).

Boccaccio, Giovanni, *Esposizioni sopra la 'Comedia' di Dante*, edited by Giorgio Padoan (Verona, 1965).

Boethius, *De consolatione Philosophiae*, edited by H. F. Stewart, E. K. Rand, and S. J. Tester (London, 1973).

Boitani, Piero, 'The Sibyl's leaves: Reading *Paradiso* XXXIII', in *The Tragic and the Sublime in Medieval Literature* (Cambridge, 1988), pp. 223–49.

Bonaventure, *Opera omnia*, 10 vols. (Ad Claras Aquas, 1882–1902).

Boninus Mombritius, *Sanctuarium seu vitae sanctorum*, edited by 'duo monachi solesmenses', 2 vols. (Paris, 1910).

Botterill, Steven, 'Dante and the Authority of Poetic Language', in *Dante: Contemporary Perspectives*, edited by Amilcare A. Iannucci (Toronto, forthcoming).

'Doctrine, Doubt and Certainty: *Paradiso* XXXII. 40–84', *Italian Studies*, 42 (1987), 20–36.

'Life after Beatrice: Bernard of Clairvaux in *Paradiso* XXXI', *Texas Studies in Literature and Language*, 32 (1990), 120–36.

'"Quae non licet homini loqui": The Ineffability of Mystical Experience in *Paradiso* I and the Epistle to Can Grande', *Modern Language Review*, 83 (1988), 332–41.

'The Trecento Commentaries on Dante's *Commedia*', in vol. II of *The Cambridge History of Literary Criticism*, edited by Alastair Minnis (Cambridge, forthcoming).

Bougerol, J. G., 'Saint Bonaventure et Guillaume de Saint-Thierry', *Antonianum*, 46 (1971), 298–321.

'Saint Bonaventure et saint Bernard', *Antonianum*, 46 (1971), 3–79.

Bozzoli, A., 'Due paragrafi sul prologo della *Divina Commedia*', *Aevum*, 41 (1967), 518–29.

Bredero, A. H., 'Etudes sur la *Vita Prima* de saint Bernard', *Analecta Sacri Ordinis Cisterciensis*, 17 (1961), 3–72, 215–60; 18 (1962), 3–59.

Brownlee, Kevin, 'Pauline Vision and Ovidian Speech in *Paradiso* 1', in *The Poetry of Allusion: Virgil and Ovid in Dante's 'Commedia'*, edited by Rachel Jacoff and Jeffrey T. Schnapp (Stanford, 1991), pp. 202–13.

Burr, David, *Olivi and Franciscan Poverty: The Origins of the 'Usus Pauper' Controversy* (Philadelphia, 1989).

Busnelli, Giovanni, *Il concetto e l'ordine del 'Paradiso' dantesco*, 2 vols. (Città di Castello, 1911–12).

Buti, Francesco da, *Commento di Francesco da Buti sopra la 'Divina Comedia' di Dante Allighieri*, edited by Crescentino Giannini, 3 vols. (Pisa, 1858–62).

Butler, A. J., *The Paradise of Dante* (London, 1885).

Butterworth, G. W., 'The Deification of Man in Clement of Alexandria', *Journal of Theological Studies*, 17 (1916), 157–69.

Caesarius of Heisterbach, *Dialogus miraculorum*, edited by Josephus Strange, 2 vols. (Cologne, 1851).

Calinescu, Matei, *Rereading* (New Haven and London, 1993)

Cambon, Glauco, 'Dante's Noble Sinners: Abstract Examples or Living Characters?', in *Dante's Craft: Studies in Language and Style* (Minneapolis, 1969), pp. 67–79.

Carugati, Giuliana, *Dalla menzogna al silenzio. La scrittura mistica della 'Commedia' di Dante* (Bologna, 1991).

Cassiodorus, *Historia tripartita*, in *Patrologia latina*, 69, cols. 879–1214.

Cavazzuti, Giuseppe, 'Nel tempio del suo voto (*Paradiso* XXXI)', in *Letture dantesche* (Modena, 1957), pp. 213–35.

Cavedoni, Celestino, *L'orazione di san Bernardo alla beatissima Vergine nell'ultimo canto del 'Paradiso' di Dante esposta co' riscontri di quel santo padre e d'altri*, in *Raffronti tra gli autori biblici e sacri e la 'Divina Commedia'*, edited by Rocco Murari (Città di Castello, 1896).

Celletti, Maria Chiara, 'Iconografia', s.v. 'Bernardo di Chiaravalle', in *Bibliotheca sanctorum*, 12 vols. (Rome, 1961–9), III (1963), cols. 37–41.

*Cento meditazioni di S. Bonaventura sulla vita di Gesù Cristo: volgarizzamento antico toscano*, edited by Bartolommeo Sorio (Rome, 1847).

Chatillon, J., 'L'Influence de saint Bernard sur la pensée scolastique au XIIe et au XIIIe siècle', in *Saint Bernard théologien* (Dijon, 1953; *Analecta Sacri Ordinis Cisterciensis*, 9, 1953, fascicules 3–4), pp. 268–88.

Chaucer, Geoffrey, *The Works of Geoffrey Chaucer*, edited by F. N. Robinson, 2nd edition (Oxford, 1966).

Chiappelli, Alessandro, *Il canto XXXI del 'Paradiso'* (Florence, 1904).

Chiari, Alberto, 'Il canto XXXI del *Paradiso*', *Ateneo Veneto*, fascicolo speciale (1965), 327–50.

*Chiose sopra Dante: testo inedito* ['Falso Boccaccio'], edited by Lord Vernon (Florence, 1846).

Colombo, Manuela, *Dai mistici a Dante: il linguaggio dell'ineffabilità* (Florence, 1987).

Conrad of Saxony, *Speculum beatae Mariae Virginis* (Ad Claras Aquas, 1904).

Croce, Benedetto, *Poesia antica e moderna*, 2nd edition (Bari, 1943).

Cyprian, *Opera*, edited by Wilhelm Hartel, Corpus Scriptorum Ecclesiasticorum Latinorum, III/1 (Vienna, 1868).

Dante Alighieri, *Convivio*, edited by Piero Cudini (Milan, 1980).

La '*Divina Commedia*', edited by Umberto Bosco and Giovanni Reggio, 3 vols. (Florence, 1979).

La '*Divina Commedia*', edited by Tommaso Casini, revised by S. A. Barbi, 3 vols. (Florence, 1955–9).

La '*Divina Commedia*' edited by Siro A. Chimenz (Turin, 1966).

Die '*Göttliche Komödie*': *Kommentar*, edited by Hermann Gmelin, 3 vols. (Stuttgart, 1954–7).

La '*Commedia*' di Dante Alighieri [with the commentary of Cristoforo Landino] (Venice, 1491).

La '*Commedia*' secondo l'antica vulgata, edited by Giorgio Petrocchi, 4 vols. (Milan, 1966–7).

La '*Divina Commedia*', edited by Giacomo Poletto, 3 vols. (Rome, 1894).

La '*Divina Commedia*', edited by Manfredi Porena, 3 vols. (Bologna, 1953).

La '*Divina Commedia*', edited by Vittorio Rossi and Salvatore Frascino, 3 vols. (Rome, 1948).

La '*Divina Commedia*', edited by Natalino Sapegno (Milan and Naples, 1957).

La '*Divina Commedia*', edited by Natalino Sapegno, 3 vols. (Florence, 1978; first edition, 1955).

La '*Divina Commedia*', edited by G. A. Scartazzini, 4 vols. (Leipzig, 1874–90); revised by Giuseppe Vandelli, 4 vols. (Milan, 1922).

The '*Divine Comedy*', translated with a commentary by Charles S. Singleton, 3 vols. (Princeton, 1971–5).

La '*Divina Commedia*', edited by Francesco Torraca (Milan, 1920; first edition, 1905).

Davis, Charles T., 'Education in Dante's Florence', *Speculum*, 40 (1965), 415–35 (revised and reprinted in *Dante's Italy and Other Essays*, Philadelphia, 1984, pp. 137–65).

'The Early Collection of Books of S. Croce in Florence', *Proceedings of the American Philosophical Society*, 107 (1963), 399–414.

'The Florentine *Studia* and Dante's "Library"', in *The 'Divine Comedy' and the Encyclopedia of Arts and Sciences*, edited by Giuseppe Di Scipio and Aldo Scaglione (Amsterdam and Philadelphia, 1988), pp. 339–66.

Di Pino, Guido, 'Canto XXXII', in *Letture dantesche: 'Paradiso'*, edited by Giovanni Getto (Florence, 1961), pp. 655–72.

Di Scipio, G. C., *The Symbolic Rose in Dante's 'Paradiso'* (Ravenna, 1984).

*Dictionnaire de spiritualité (DS)*, edited by Marcel Viller and others (Paris, 1932– ).

*Dictionnaire de théologie catholique*, edited by A. Vacant, E. Mangenot, and E. Amann, 15 vols. (Paris, 1923–50).

Doglio, Maria Luisa, 'L'"officio di dottore". *Institutio ed exempla* nel canto XXXII del *Paradiso*', *Giornale storico della letteratura italiana*, 156 (1989), 321–39.

Dronke, Peter, *Dante and Medieval Latin Traditions* (Cambridge, 1986).

Dunbar, Helen Flanders, *Symbolism in Medieval Thought and its Consummation in the 'Divine Comedy'* (New Haven, 1929).

*Enchiridion symbolorum*, edited by Heinrich Denzinger and Adolf Schönmetzer, 32nd edition (Barcelona, 1963).

*Enciclopedia dantesca*, edited by Umberto Bosco and others, 6 vols. (Rome, 1970–9).

Esposito, Enzo, 'Il canto dell'ultima visione (*Paradiso* XXXIII)', *Letture classensi*, 7 (1979), 13–26.

*Excellentissimi et sanctissimi viri domini Alberti Magni episcopi Ratisponensis ordinis praedicatorum in evangelium Missus est Gabriel angelus* (Milan, 1488).

Fallani, Giovanni, *Il canto XXXI del 'Paradiso'* (Rome, 1957).

Fornaciari, Raffaello, *Il canto XXXII del 'Paradiso'* (Florence, 1904).

Foster, Kenelm, *The Two Dantes* (London, 1977).

Freund, Elizabeth, *The Return of the Reader: Reader-Response Criticism* (London and New York, 1987).

Fubini, Mario, 'L'ultimo canto del *Paradiso*', in *Il peccato d'Ulisse e altri scritti danteschi* (Milan and Naples, 1966), pp. 101–36.

*Critica e poesia* (Bari, 1956).

Gabrieli, Francesco, *Il canto XXXI del 'Paradiso'* (Turin, 1965).

Gadamer, Hans-Georg, *The Relevance of the Beautiful and Other Essays*, edited by Robert Bernasconi (Cambridge, 1986).

*Wahrheit und Methode* (Tübingen, 1960; 2nd edition, 1965).

Gardner, Edmund G., *Dante and the Mystics* (London, 1913).

*The Book of St Bernard on the Love of God* (London, 1916).

Gilson, Etienne, *La Théologie mystique de saint Bernard* (Paris, 1947; first edition, 1932).

*The Mystical Theology of Saint Bernard*, translated by A. H. C. Downes, second edition (London, 1955).

Graef, Hilda, *Mary: A History of Doctrine and Devotion*, 2 vols. (London, 1963–5).

Gualberto de Marzo, Antonio, *Studi filosofici, morali, estetici, storici, politici e filologici su la 'Divina Commedia'*, 3 vols. (Florence, 1864–82).

Gualterus Cancellarius and Bartholomaeus de Bononia, OFM, *Quaestiones ineditae de Assumptione BVM*, edited by A. Deneffe and H. Weisweiler, 2nd edition (Münster, 1952).

Guardini, Romano, 'Bernhard von Clairvaux in Dantes *Göttlicher Komödie*', in *Unterscheidung des Christlichen: Gesammelte Studien 1923–1963* (Mainz, 1963), pp. 558–68.

Guido da Pisa, *Expositiones et Glose super Comediam Dantis*, edited by Vincenzo Cioffari (Albany, NY, 1974).

Gutiérrez, David, 'La biblioteca di Santo Spirito di Firenze nella metà del secolo XV', *Analecta Augustiniana*, 25 (1962), 5–88.

Hagman, Edward, 'Dante's Vision of God: The End of the *Itinerarium Mentis*', *Dante Studies*, 106 (1988), 1–20.

Hall, Ralph G., and Madison U. Sowell, '*Cursus* in the Can Grande Epistle: A Forger Shows his Hand?', *Lectura Dantis*, 5 (1989), 89–104.

Hirsch, E. D., Jr, *Validity in Interpretation* (New Haven and London, 1967).

Holub, Robert C., *Reception Theory: A Critical Introduction* (London and New York, 1984).

Hopkins, Gerard Manley, *The Oxford Authors: Gerard Manley Hopkins*, edited by Catherine Phillips (Oxford, 1986).

*The Hundred Best Latin Hymns*, edited by J. S. Phillimore (London, 1926).

Jacobus a Voragine, *Legenda aurea*, edited by Th. Graesse (Dresden, 1890; photographic reprint, Osnabrück, 1969).

Jannaco, Carmine, 'Il canto xxxi del *Paradiso*', *Letture classensi*, 1 (1966), 109–20.

Jenaro-MacLennan, L., *The Trecento Commentaries on the 'Divina Commedia' and the Epistle to Cangrande* (Oxford, 1974).

Joachim of Fiore, *Expositio in Apocalipsim* (Venice, 1527).

    *Liber concordie novi ac veteris testamenti* (Venice, 1519).

    *Liber figurarum*, edited by Luigi Tondelli, Marjorie Reeves, and Beatrice Hirsch-Reich (Turin, 1953).

    *Psalterium decem chordarum* (Venice, 1527).

    *Tractatus de vita sancti Benedicti*, edited by Cipriano Baraút, *Analecta Sacra Tarraconiensia*, 24 (1951), 33–122.

John of Salisbury, *Historia pontificalis*, edited by Reginald L. Poole (Oxford, 1927).

Kaftal, George, *Iconography of the Saints in Tuscan Painting* (Florence, 1952).

Kelly, Henry Ansgar, *Tragedy and Comedy from Dante to Pseudo-Dante* (Berkeley and Los Angeles, 1989).

Lami, Giovanni, *Sanctae ecclesiae Florentinae monumenta etc.* (Florence, 1758).

Lana, Jacopo della, *La 'Comedia' di Dante degli Allagherii col 'Commento' di Jacopo della Lana bolognese*, edited by Luciano Scarabelli, 3 vols. (Bologna, 1866).

Lawless, George, *Augustine of Hippo and his Monastic Rule* (Oxford, 1987).

Leclercq, Jean, 'Les Sermons sur les Cantiques ont-ils été prononcés?', in *Recueil d'études sur saint Bernard et ses écrits*, 3 vols. (Rome, 1962–9), I, 193–212.

    'Pour l'iconographie de saint Bernard', *Analecta Sacri Ordinis Cisterciensis*, 9 (1953), fascicule 1, 40–5, 226–8.

    *Bernard of Clairvaux and the Cistercian Spirit*, translated by Claire Lavoie (Kalamazoo, 1976; originally *Saint Bernard et l'esprit cistercien*, Paris, 1966).

    *Jean de Paris et l'ecclésiologie du XIIIe siècle* (Paris, 1942).

    *Saint Bernard mystique* (Bruges, 1948).

Leclercq, Jean, François Vandenbroucke, and Louis Bouyer, *The Spirituality of the Middle Ages* (London, 1968).
Lekai, Louis J., *The Cistercians: Ideals and Reality* (Kent, USA, 1977).
Levi, Primo, *Se questo è un uomo* (Turin, 1947).
*A Lexicon of St Thomas Aquinas*, edited by Roy J. Deferrari and M. Inviolata Barry (New York, 1948).
Longen, Eugene, 'The Grammar of Apotheosis: *Paradiso* XXXIII', *Dante Studies*, 93 (1975), 209–14.
Lot-Borodine, M., 'La doctrine de la déification dans l'Eglise grecque jusqu'au XIe siècle', *Revue de l'Histoire des Religions*, 105 (1932), 5–43, 106 (1932), 525–74, and 107 (1933), 8–55.
Luddy, Ailbé J., *Life and Teaching of St Bernard* (Dublin, 1927).
Maclean, Ian, 'Reading and Interpretation', in *Modern Literary Theory: A Comparative Introduction*, edited by Ann Jefferson and David Robey, 2nd edition (London, 1986), pp. 122–44.
Maggini, Francesco, 'Il canto XXXI del *Paradiso*', in *Letture dantesche: 'Paradiso'*, edited by Giovanni Getto (Florence, 1961), pp. 641–51.
Manselli, Raoul, 'Dante e l'"Ecclesia Spiritualis"', in *Dante e Roma* (Florence, 1965), pp. 115–35.
*La 'Lectura super Apocalipsim' di Pietro di Giovanni Olivi* (Rome, 1955).
Masseron, Alexandre, *Dante et saint Bernard* (Paris, 1953).
Matthew of Aquasparta, *De anima*, edited by A. J. Gondras (Paris, 1961).
*De anima beata* (Florence, 1959).
*De beata Maria virgine*, edited by C. Piana (Florence, 1962).
*De Christo* (Ad Claras Aquas, 1914).
*De gratia*, edited by V. Doucet (Ad Claras Aquas, 1935).
*De productione rerum et de providentia*, edited by G. Gal (Florence, 1956).
*Quaestiones de fide et de cognitione* (Ad Claras Aquas, 1903).
McGinn, Bernard, *The Foundations of Mysticism: Origins to the Fifth Century*, volume I of *The Presence of God: A History of Western Christian Mysticism* (New York, 1992).
McNair, Philip, 'Dante's Vision of God: An Exposition of *Paradiso* XXXIII', in *Essays in Honour of John Humphreys Whitfield*, edited by H. C. Davis and others (London, 1975), pp. 13–29.
Migliorini Fissi, Rosetta, 'La nozione di *deificatio* nel *Paradiso*', *Letture classensi*, 9/10 (1982), 39–72.
*Dante* (Florence, 1979).
Mohrmann, Christine, 'Observations sur la langue et le style de St Bernard', in Bernard, *Opera*, II (1958), ix–xxxiii.
Montanari, Fausto, 'Il canto XXXII del *Paradiso*', *Nuove letture dantesche*, 7 (1974), 255–63.
Montoliù, M. de, 'San Bernardo, la poesìa de los trovadores y la *Divina Comedìa*', *Spanische Forschungen*, Erste Reihe, 12. Band (Münster, 1956), pp. 192–9.
Moore, Edward, *Studies in Dante*, edited by Colin Hardie, 4 vols. (Oxford, 1968; original edition, 1896–1917).

Nardi, Bruno, 'I bambini nella candida rosa dei beati', *Studi danteschi*, 20 (1937), 41–58.

Orlandi, Stefano, *La biblioteca di S. Maria Novella in Firenze dal sec. XIV al sec. XIX* (Florence, 1952).

*L'Ottimo commento della 'Divina Commedia': testo inedito d'un contemporaneo di Dante*, edited by Alessandro Torri (Pisa, 1827–9).

*The Oxford Book of Medieval Latin Verse*, 2nd edition, edited by F. J. E. Raby (Oxford, 1959).

*The Oxford Classical Dictionary*, edited by N. G. L. Hammond and H. H. Scullard, 2nd edition (Oxford, 1970).

*The Oxford Dictionary of the Christian Church*, edited by F. L. Cross, 2nd edition (Oxford, 1974).

Ovid, *P. Ovidius Nasonis: Metamorphoseon libri XV*, edited by B. A. Van Proosdij (Leiden, 1982).

Palgen, Rudolf, 'Il mito di Glauco nella *Divina Commedia*', *Convivium*, 25 (1957), 400–12.

Paolazzi, Carlo, 'Nozione di "comedìa" e tradizione retorica nella dantesca *Epistola a Cangrande*', in *Dante e la 'Comedìa' nel Trecento* (Milan, 1989), pp. 3–110.

*Patrologia latina*, edited by J.-P. Migne (Paris, 1844–91).

Pelikan, Jaroslav, *The Emergence of the Catholic Tradition (100–600)*, volume I of *The Christian Tradition: A History of the Development of Doctrine* (Chicago and London, 1971).

   *The Spirit of Eastern Christendom (600–1700)*, volume II of *The Christian Tradition: A History of the Development of Doctrine* (Chicago and London, 1974).

Penco, Gregorio, *Storia del monachesimo in Italia* (Rome, 1961).

Pennington, M. B., 'The Influence of Bernard of Clairvaux on Thomas Aquinas', *Studia Monastica*, 16 (1974), 281–91.

Pérez, Paolo, *I sette cerchi del 'Purgatorio' di Dante: saggio di studi* (Verona, 1867).

Pernicone, Vincenzo, *Il canto XXXII del 'Paradiso'* (Turin, 1965).

Pertile, Lino, '*Paradiso*, XXXIII: l'estremo oltraggio', *Filologia e critica*, 6 (1981), 1–21.

Petrocchi, Giorgio, 'Dante e la mistica di san Bernardo', in *Letteratura e critica: studi in onore di Natalino Sapegno*, edited by Walter Binni and others, 4 vols. (Rome, 1974), I, 213–29.

   'Il canto XXXI del *Paradiso*', *Nuove letture dantesche*, 7 (1974), 235–53.

   'Sulla composizione e data delle *Meditationes Vitae Christi*', *Convivium*, Sept.–Oct. 1952, 757–78.

   *Vita di Dante* (Bari, 1983).

Petrus de Natalibus, *Catalogus sanctorum* (Venice, 1506).

Piccolomini, E., 'Inventario della libreria Medicea privata compilata nel 1495', *Archivio storico italiano*, third series, 20 (1874), 51–94.

Pietro Alighieri, *Il 'Commentarium' di Pietro Alighieri nelle redazioni*

*Ashburnhamiana e Ottoboniana*, edited by Roberto della Vedova and Maria Teresa Silvotti (Florence, 1978).

*Petri Allegherii super Dantis ipsius genitoris Comoediam Commentarium*, edited by Vincenzo Nannucci (Florence, 1846).

Pietro di Giovanni Olivi, *Peter Olivi's Rule Commentary*, edited by David Flood (Wiesbaden, 1972).

*Quaestiones in secundum librum Sententiarum*, edited by B. Jansen, 3 vols. (Ad Claras Aquas, 1922–26).

*Quaestiones quatuor de Domina*, edited by Domenico Pacetti (Florence, 1954).

*Quodlibeta* (Venice, c. 1510).

Pisanti, Tommaso, 'Il canto XXXII e la poesia del *Paradiso*', in *Filologia e critica dantesca: studi offerti a Aldo Vallone* (Florence, 1989), pp. 329–50.

Pseudo-Ambrose, *Commentarium in Epistolam ad Romanos*, in *Patrologia latina*, 17, cols. 47–192.

Pseudo-Arnobius, *Conflictus de deo trino et uno*, in *Patrologia latina*, 53, cols. 239–322.

Pseudo-Dionysius the Areopagite, *Pseudo-Dionysius: The Complete Works*, edited and translated by Paul Rorem and others (New York, 1987).

Pseudo-Marius Mercator, *Translationes Epistularum Nestorii in causa Pelagiana scriptarum*, in *Patrologia latina*, 48, cols. 173–84.

Pseudo-Rufinus, Commentary on Psalm 51, in *Patrologia latina*, 21, cols. 854–6.

Quarré, Pierre, 'L'Iconographie de saint Bernard à Clairvaux et les origines de la *vera effigies*', in *Mélanges saint Bernard* (Dijon, 1953), pp. 342–9.

Richard of St Victor, *De IV gradibus violentae caritatis*, in *Über die Gewalt der Liebe: Ihre vier Stufen*, edited and translated by Margot Schmidt (Munich, Paderborn and Vienna, 1969).

Robert of Basevorn, *Forma praedicandi*, in Th. M. Charland, *Artes praedicandi: contribution à l'histoire de la rhétorique au Moyen Age* (Paris and Ottawa, 1936), pp. 231–323.

Roffarè, Francesco T., 'Canto XXXI', in *Lectura Dantis Scaligera: 'Paradiso'* (Florence, 1968), pp. 1097–134.

Roustang, François, 'On Reading Again', in *The Limits of Theory*, edited by Thomas M. Kavanagh (Stanford, 1989), pp. 121–38.

Russi, Antonio, 'Canto XXXII', in *Lectura Dantis Scaligera: 'Paradiso'* (Florence, 1968), pp. 1135–90.

Sandkühler, Bruno, 'Die Kommentare zur *Commedia* bis zur Mitte des 15. Jahrhunderts', in *Die italienische Literatur im Zeitalter Dantes und am Übergang vom Mittelalter zur Renaissance* (*Grundriß der romanischen Literaturen des Mittelalters*, x/1), edited by August Buck (Heidelberg, 1987), pp. 166–208.

*Die frühen Dantekommentare und ihr Verhältnis zur mittelalterlichen Kommentartradition* (Munich, 1967).

Sayers, Dorothy L., 'The Beatrician Vision in Dante and Other Poets', *Nottingham Medieval Studies*, 2 (1958), 3–23.

Schildgen, Brenda D., 'Dante's Neologisms in the *Paradiso* and the Latin Rhetorical Tradition', *Dante Studies*, 107 (1989), 101–19.

Scott James, Bruno, *St Bernard of Clairvaux : An Essay in Biography* (London, 1957).

Serravalle, Giovanni Bertoldi da, *Fratris Johannis de Serravalle translatio et comentum totius libri Dantis Aldigherii, cum textu italico Fratris Bartholomaei a Colle*, edited by Marcellino da Civezza and Teofilo Domenichelli (Prato, 1891).

Sisinni, Francesco, 'Il canto di San Bernardo', *L'Alighieri*, 25 (1984), no. 2, 18–31.

Southern, R. W., *Robert Grosseteste : The Growth of an English Mind in Medieval Europe* (Oxford, 1986).

Stefanini, Ruggiero, 'Spunti di esegesi dantesca : due contrappassi (*Inf.* VI e XIX) e due *cruces* (*Purg.* XXVII. 81 e *Par.* XXXII. 139)', in *Forma e parola : studi in memoria di Fredi Chiappelli*, edited by Dennis J. Dutschke, Pier Massimo Forni, and others (Rome, 1992), pp. 45–65.

'Talice da Ricaldone, Stefano', *La 'Commedia' di Dante Alighieri col commento inedito di Stefano Talice da Ricaldone*, edited by Vincenzo Promis and Carlo Negroni, 3 vols. (Milan, 1888).

Tambling, Jeremy, *Dante and Difference : Writing in the 'Commedia'* (Cambridge, 1988).

Tertullian, *Apologeticus*, in *Patrologia latina*, 1, cols. 257–536.

*Thesaurus linguae latinae* (Leipzig, 1900– ).

Thomas Aquinas, *D. Thomae de Aquino doctoris angelici sermones* etc. (Rome, 1571).

*Summa theologiae* ('Editio Paulina'), (Rome, 1962).

Toynbee, Paget, *A Dictionary of Proper Names and Notable Matters in the Works of Dante*, revised by Charles S. Singleton (Oxford, 1968).

Ubertino da Casale, *Arbor vite crucifixe Jesu* (Venice, 1485).

Underhill, Evelyn, *Mysticism* (London, 1911).

Vacandard, Elphège, *Vie de saint Bernard, Abbé de Clairvaux*, 2 vols. (Paris, 1895).

Vaccari, Alberto, 'Le *Meditazioni della vita di Cristo* in volgare', in *Scritti di erudizione e di filologia, I : Filologia biblica e patristica* (Rome, 1952), pp. 341–78.

Valli, Luigi, *Il canto XXXI del 'Paradiso'* (Rome, 1914).

Vallone, Aldo, 'Ancora del "Veltro" e della preghiera di san Bernardo', in *La critica dantesca nel Settecento e altri saggi danteschi* (Florence, 1961).

'La Preghiera', in *Studi su Dante medievale* (Florence, 1965), pp. 83–109.

*Storia della critica dantesca dal XIV al XX secolo* (Padua, 1981).

Vandelli, Giuseppe, 'Una nuova redazione dell'*Ottimo*', *Studi danteschi*, 14 (1930), 93–174.

Williams, Watkin Wynn, *St Bernard of Clairvaux* (Manchester, 1935; second edition, 1953).

Wilmart, André, *Auteurs spirituels et textes dévots du Moyen Age latin* (Paris, 1971; original edition, 1932).

# Index

Characters in the *Commedia* and persons of the Trinity have been omitted from this index, as have the editors of primary texts (other than the *Commedia* itself) and collective volumes.

Abelard, Peter, 27, 90, 173
Adam of St Victor, 183n.
*Ad clericos de conversione* (Bernard of Clairvaux), 25
*Ad fratres de Monte Dei* (pseudo-Bernard), 39, 44, 132n.
*Aeneid* (Virgil), 134
Alan of Auxerre, 22
Alan of Lille, 227–9
Albert the Great, 28–9, 40, 41, 57
Alexander III, Pope, 58, 139
Alexander of Hales, 32–3, 34, 40, 214
Alighieri, Jacopo, 120
Alighieri, Pietro, 119n, 120, 121, 125–6, 131–4, 135, 136, 147, 222
*Ambigua* (Maximus Confessor), 202, 208
Ambrose, St, 185
Anacletus, anti-Pope, 173
*Analecta hymnica medii aevi*, 47–8, 180n., 181n., 182n., 183n., 184n., 186n., 190
Anderson, William, 79n.
'Anonimo Fiorentino' (*Commedia* commentary), 131
Anselm, 144, 207
Anthony, St, 138
*Anticlaudianus* (Alan of Lille), 227–8
Apollonio, Mario, 152n.
*Apologeticus* (Tertullian), 203
*Apologia ad Guillelmum* (Bernard of Clairvaux), 26, 57, 123–4
Aquinas, Thomas, 28, 29–30, 32, 33, 40, 41, 48, 57, 58, 97, 101n., 124, 131, 147, 197, 203, 214–21, 226, 230, 237
*Arbor vite crucifixe Jesu* (Ubertino da Casale), 39–40, 182
Aristotle, 57, 58, 229
Arnald of Bonneval, 21, 22, 126–7
Athanasius, 199–201, 207

Auden, W. H., 26
Auerbach, Erich, 163–4, 177, 185
Augustine, St, 32, 33, 39, 40, 57, 58, 125–6, 131, 138, 144, 147, 148, 204, 205–7, 225–6
*Ave Maria*, 156, 159, 190
Aversano, Mario, 176n.

Balzac, Honoré de, 18n.
de' Bambaglioli, Graziolo, 119n.
Barański, Zygmunt G., 252n.
Barbi, Michele, 105n., 137n., 188n.
Barré, Henri, 166
Basil, St, 200, 201
Bellomo, Saverio, 119n.
Benedict, St, 138
*Benjamin major* (Richard of St Victor), 214
*Benjamin minor* (Richard of St Victor), 213–14
Benvenuto da Imola, 107n., 120, 121, 135, 137–47, 150n., 223–6, 233–4, 248
Bergin, Thomas Goddard, 149n.
Bernardus Silvestris, 228–9
Bertoldi da Serravalle, Giovanni, 121, 137–8, 145–7, 150n.
Bible, 16, 29, 31, 35, 42–3, 44, 45, 48, 58, 62–3, 70, 91, 93–4, 122, 124, 132, 134, 155–6, 165, 168–9, 182, 183, 185–6, 190, 200, 201, 204, 205–6, 219–20, 226, 248
Blum, Rudolf, 56
Boccaccio, Giovanni, 5, 7, 120, 135
Boethius, 32, 131, 223, 224, 229–31
Boitani, Piero, 109n.
Bonaventure, St, 31–2, 33, 34, 40, 41, 97, 101n., 157, 192, 214–15, 240
Boniface VIII, Pope, 31
Boninus Mombritius, 26

Bosco, Umberto, 67n., 177–8, 222
Botterill, Steven, 72n., 82n., 89n., 97n.,
    99n., 101n., 112n., 121n., 148n., 243n.
Bougerol, J. G., 31, 32n., 215n.
Bozzoli, A., 176n.
Bredero, A. H., 23
Brownlee, Kevin, 236n.
Burr, David, 38n.
Busnelli, Giovanni, 150n.
Buti, Francesco da, 119n., 121, 125, 135–7,
    139, 145, 150n., 151, 174, 175, 222–3,
    224
Butler, A. J., 71n.
Butterworth, G. W., 198n.

Caesarius of Heisterbach, 24–5
Calinescu, Matei, 2n.
Calò, Pietro, 25
Cambon, Glauco, 149n.
*Can Grande, Letter to* (Dante?), 82n., 148–9,
    158
*Cardinalibus ytalicis*, letter (Dante), 152,
    180–1
Carugati, Giuliana, 251n.
Casini, Tommaso, 125, 177n., 222
Cassiodorus, 204
Cauli, Giovanni de', 42–5
Cavazzuti, Giuseppe, 66n.
Cavedoni, Celestino, 175–8, 180–7
Celletti, Maria Chiara, 51
Chatillon, J., 27, 31
Chaucer, Geoffrey, 108
Chiappelli, Alessandro, 66n.
Chiari, Alberto, 66n.
Chimenz, Siro A., 222
Cicero, 57
Cistercian Order:
    and manuscripts of Bernard's works, 61
    Dante as a would-be Cistercian, 128–30
    in Florence, 56
    in Italy, 62–3
    view of Bernard, 21–8, 48, 63, 212–13
Clement of Alexandria, 198–9, 200, 202,
    207, 217
Colombo, Manuela, 212n.
*Commentarium in Epistolam ad Romanos*
    (pseudo-Ambrose), 204
*Conflictus de deo trino et uno* (pseudo-
    Arnobius), 204n.
Conrad of Saxony, 34, 40
*Convivio* (Dante), 152, 182, 226–7, 229
*Cosmographia* (Bernardus Silvestris), 228
Croce, Benedetto, 87, 108, 163–4
Cyprian, 203
Cyril of Alexandria, 201

Dartmouth Dante Project, 119n.
Davis, Charles T., 58n.
*De anima* (Matthew of Aquasparta), 33n.
*De anima beata* (Matthew of Aquasparta),
    33n.
'*De aquaeductu*' (*Sermo in nativitate Virginis*)
    (Bernard of Clairvaux), 169, 180, 183,
    185–6, 187–8
'*De baptismo*' (Bernard of Clairvaux), 26,
    33n., 99, 100
*De beata Maria virgine* (Matthew of
    Aquasparta), 34
*De bono* (Albert the Great), 29
*De Christo* (Matthew of Aquasparta), 33n.
*De civitate Dei* (Augustine), 207n.
*Declamationes ex Bernardo*, 132n.
*De consideratione* (Bernard of Clairvaux), 26,
    29, 30–1, 32, 33, 34, 36–7, 38n., 39,
    40n., 50, 56, 57, 140, 143, 148
*De consolatione Philosophiae* (Boethius), 223,
    229–30
*De contemplatione* (Richard of St Victor), 148
Decretals, 132n.
*De diligendo Deo* (Bernard of Clairvaux), 29,
    32, 33, 176n., 195, 199, 207, 209–12,
    225, 228
*De duodecim stellis* (pseudo-Bernard), 176
*De gradibus humilitatis et superbiae* (Bernard of
    Clairvaux), 25, 29, 33n., 57, 176
*De gratia* (Matthew of Aquasparta), 33n.
*De gratia contemplandi* (Richard of St Victor),
    214
*De gratia et libero arbitrio* (Bernard of
    Clairvaux), 25, 32, 33, 39, 57, 100
*De humanitate Jesu Christi domini nostri*
    (Thomas Aquinas), 30
*De incarnatione Verbi* (Athanasius), 199–200
*De lamentatione Beatae Mariae Virginis*
    (pseudo-Bernard), 144
*De laudibus beatae Mariae* (Arnald of
    Bonneval), 126–7
*De laudibus nove militie* (Bernard of
    Clairvaux), 44n., 57
*De monarchia* (Dante), 152, 196
*De potestate regia et papali* (John of Paris),
    30–1
*De praecepto et dispensatione* (Bernard of
    Clairvaux), 26, 29, 32, 33, 38n., 39, 50
*De praeparatione animae ad contemplationem*
    (Richard of St Victor), 213–14
*De productione rerum et de providentia* (Matthew
    of Aquasparta), 33n.
*De psalmo 'Qui habitat'* (Bernard of
    Clairvaux), 26, 39, 44n.
*De quantitate animae* (Augustine), 148

*De IV gradibus violentae caritatis* (Richard of St Victor), 213n.
De Sanctis, Francesco, 149n.
'*De tribus osculis*' (Bernard of Clairvaux), 58
*De veritate* (Thomas Aquinas), 30
*De vulgari eloquentia* (Dante), 92
*Dialogus miraculorum* (Caesarius of Heisterbach), 24–5
*Dicta Bernardi*, 57
Di Pino, Guido, 86n., 106n.
Di Scipio, G. C., 88n.
Doglio, Maria Luisa, 86n.
Dominican Order:
  in Florence, 56
  view of Bernard, 28–31, 58
Dronke, Peter, 148n.
*Dulcis Jesu memoria*, 49
Dunbar, Helen Flanders, 112n.

*Enarrationes in Psalmos* (Augustine), 205–6
*Epistolae* (Bernard of Clairvaux), 29, 32, 33, 34, 39, 56, 58, 140, 166, 172–4
*Epistolae* (Dante), 148, 152, 158, 180–1
*Epistulae* (Augustine), 206n.
*Epistulae* (Cyprian), 203n.
Esposito, Enzo, 109
Eugenius III, Pope, 31, 36, 140
*Exempla Bernardi*, 57
*Exordium magnum cisterciense*, 22
*Expositio in Apocalipsim* (Joachim of Fiore), 35, 37
*Expositio super regulam fratrum minorum* (Pietro di Giovanni Olivi), 38n.

Fallani, Giovanni, 66n.
'Falso Boccaccio', 121, 135, 139n.
Fischer, Columban, 42n.
Fish, Stanley, 2n.
Fishacre, Richard, 31
Flaubert, Gustave, 17
Florence:
  libraries at, in Dante's time, 55–9
    Badia, 56
    Santa Croce, 56, 58–9
    Santa Maria Novella, 56, 57–8, 59
    Santo Spirito, 56–7, 59
  manuscripts of Bernard's works at, 60–1
  at Santa Croce, 60
*Forma praedicandi* (Robert of Basevorn), 40
Fornaciari, Raffaello, 86n., 106n.
Foster, Kenelm, 221n.
Francis of Assisi, 138–9
Franciscan Order:
  and deification, 214–15

in Florence, 56
view of Bernard, 31–40, 58
Frascino, Salvatore, 87n.
Frederick II, Emperor, 138
Freund, Elizabeth, 2n.
Frugoni, Arsenio, 34n.
Fubini, Mario, 106n., 178–9, 189

Gabrieli, Francesco, 66n.
Gadamer, Hans-Georg, 8
Gardner, Edmund G., 176n.
Geoffrey (Gaufridus) of Auxerre, 22, 50–2, 58
Gilbert of Hoyland, 212
Giles of Rome, 57
Gilson, Etienne, 79n., 190, 195, 208, 211n., 214n., 239–40
Gmelin, Hermann, 150n.
Graef, Hilda, 166
Graves, Robert, 17n.
Gregory I (the Great), Pope, 32, 33, 40, 57, 131, 147
Gregory of Nazianzus, 200–2, 215
Gregory of Nyssa, 200–1
Gregory Palamas, 202
Grosseteste, Robert, 33
Gualberto de Marzo, Antonio, 125
Gualterus Cancellarius, 126
Guardini, Romano, 150n.
Guerric of Igny, 27
Guido da Pisa, 119n.
Guido of Bazoches, 182n.
Gutiérrez, David, 56n.

Hagman, Edward, 109n., 240n.
Hall, Ralph G., 148n.
Hirsch, E. D., Jr, 7, 8
*Historia pontificalis* (John of Salisbury), 40
*Historia tripartita* (Cassiodorus), 204
Holub, Robert C., 2n.
Hopkins, Gerard Manley, 150
Hugh of St Victor, 26, 27, 58, 99

Iamblichus, 201
Ignatius of Antioch, 198
*Il Vangelo secondo Matteo* (Pasolini), 158
*In Adventu* (Bernard of Clairvaux), 184
*In Annuntiatione Beatae Mariae Virginis* (Bernard of Clairvaux), 181n.
*In Assumptione Beatae Mariae Virginis* (Bernard of Clairvaux), 170–2, 185
*In Cantica canticorum* (Bernard of Clairvaux), 26, 29, 32, 33–4, 39, 40n., 44, 51, 53, 56, 57, 144n., 167, 185, 209n., 211–12

*In dedicatione ecclesiae* (Bernard of Clairvaux), 132n.
*In dominica infra octavam Assumptionis* (Bernard of Clairvaux), 182n., 211n.
*Ineffabilis Deus* (Pius IX), 173
*Inferno* (Dante), 2, 7, 15, 64, 65, 79, 109, 122, 124, 154–5, 165, 176, 196, 220, 223, 229, 243–8
*In festo Pentecoste* (Bernard of Clairvaux), 132n.
*In laudibus Virginis Matris* (Bernard of Clairvaux), 26, 32, 53, 77, 127, 166–8, 181–2
*In nativitate Virginis, see ' De aquaeductu'*
*In purificatione Beatae Mariae Virginis* (Bernard of Clairvaux), 166
*In vigiliis Domini* (Bernard of Clairvaux), 187
Irenaeus, 198
Isaac of Stella, 27
Iser, Wolfgang, 2n.
Isidore of Seville, 131
*Itinerarium mentis in Deum* (Bonaventure), 240

Jacobus a Voragine, 25, 57
Jannaco, Carmine, 66n.
Jauss, Hans-Robert, 2n.
Jenaro-MacLennan, L., 121n.
Jerome, St, 32, 33, 39, 57, 131, 147
Joachim of Fiore, 35–8, 40, 41
John Chrysostom, St, 201
John Damascene, St, 33, 202, 215
John of Paris, 30–1, 33, 40, 41
John of Salisbury, 40
John Scotus Erigena, 202, 207, 208, 210, 214
Justin Martyr, 198
Juvenal, 134

Kaftal, George, 52–3
Kelly, Henry Ansgar, 148n.
Kilwardby, Robert, 31
Knights Templar, Order of, 44n., 79n.

Lacaita, G. F., 137
Lactation of the Virgin, 24, 51, 53–4
Lana, Jacopo della, 119n., 121, 122–31, 135, 139, 142, 146, 147, 150, 221, 222–3
Landino, Cristoforo, 5, 125, 146
Leclercq, Jean, 21n., 30n., 31n., 50, 91n., 167n., 198n., 208, 240
*Legenda aurea* (Jacobus a Voragine), 25, 48, 58, 147, 173, 190
*Legendae de sanctis* (Pietro Calò), 25–6

Lekai, Louis J., 62n.
Leo the Great (Pope St Leo I), 207
Levi, Primo, 248
*Liber concordiae novi ac veteris testamenti* (Joachim of Fiore), 35, 36–7
*Liber de compassione Beatae Mariae Virginis* (pseudo-Bernard), 144
*Liber figurarum* (Joachim of Fiore), 38
Lombard, Peter, 27, 32, 214n.
Longen, Eugene, 109n.
Lot-Borodine, M., 198n., 201n., 202n.
Luddy, Ailbé J., 24n.

Mabillon, Jean, 54n.
Maclean, Ian, 2n.
*Madame Bovary* (Gustave Flaubert), 17
Maggini, Francesco, 66n.
Manselli, Raoul, 38n., 190n.
manuscripts:
  of Bernard's works in Italy, 59–62
  of the *Vita prima* in Italy, 23–4
Manzoni, Alessandro, 18n.
*Mariale* (pseudo-Albert the Great), 28
Mary (the Virgin), 34, 39–40, 44, 45, 48, 50, 51, 53–4, 77, 81, 124, 126, 148–93
Masseron, Alexandre, 155, 168n., 174, 175n., 177–80, 195
Matthew of Aquasparta, 33–4, 40
Maximus Confessor, 197, 202, 207, 208, 210, 211n., 214, 221
Mazzoni, Francesco, 137n.
McGinn, Bernard, 198n., 201n.
McNair, Philip, 150n.
*Meditationes passionis Christi*, 43
*Meditationes piissimae* (pseudo-Bernard), 132, 133, 136
*Meditationes vitae Christi* (Giovanni de' Cauli), 42–7
*Meditazioni della vita di Cristo*, 43–7, 48, 136
*Metamorphoses* (Ovid), 233–6
Migliorini Fissi, Rosetta, 194–6, 203, 225, 234, 236, 238–9
Mohrmann, Christine, 169
*Monarchia* (Dante), *see De monarchia*
Montanari, Fausto, 86n.
de Montoliù, M., 190
Moore, Edward, 150n.
*Mystical Theology* (pseudo-Dionysius the Areopagite):
  Albert the Great's commentary on, 29

Nardi, Bruno, 88n.
*Nicomachean Ethics* (Aristotle), 230
*Northanger Abbey* (Jane Austen), 64

Olivi, Pietro di Giovanni, 38–9, 41
Onder, Lucia, 96n.
Origen, 199, 217
*Originalia Bernardi*, 57
Orlandi, Stefano, 57n.
*Ottimo commento* (Andrea Lancia), 119n., 131
Ovid, 233–6

Palgen, Rudolf, 236n.
Paolazzi, Carlo, 148n.
*Paradiso* (Dante), 2, 5, 9, 13–17,
    18–21, 37–8, 49, 52, 64–115, 119,
    121–2, 123–7, 128, 130, 131–4, 135–7,
    138–9, 140, 141–4, 145, 146, 149, 150,
    151–4, 155, 157, 159, 160–5, 171–2,
    173–4, 176–90, 193, 194, 196, 220–1,
    223, 225, 231–41, 242, 244, 247–53
Pasolini, Pier Paolo, 158
Paul, St, 40, 81–2, 122, 201, 211, 226
Pelikan, Jaroslav, 198n., 199, 202n.
Penco, Gregorio, 62–3
Pennington, M. B., 30n.
Pérez, Paolo, 157
Pernicone, Vincenzo, 86n., 87
Pertile, Lino, 109n.
Peter Damian, 183
Peter the Venerable, 207
Petrocchi, Giorgio, 3, 42n., 43, 59n., 66n.,
    90n., 150n., 174–5, 177, 182, 187–8
Philippe le Bel, king of France, 31
Piccolomini, E., 56
Pisanti, Tommaso, 86n., 106n.
*Planctus Mariae* (pseudo-Bernard), 58, 144
Plautus, 188
Poletto, Giacomo, 125, 176, 221–2
Porena, Manfredi, 49n.
Proclus, 201–2
*Protrepticus* (Clement of Alexandria), 199n.
*Psalterium decem chordarum* (Joachim of
    Fiore), 35, 37
pseudo-Ambrose, 204
pseudo-Arnobius, 204
pseudo-Dionysius (the Areopagite), 197,
    201–2, 207
pseudo-Marius Mercator, 204
pseudo-Rufinus, 204
*Purgatorio* (Dante), 65, 68, 78–9, 114, 132,
    139, 140, 146, 155–60, 229

*Quaestiones de Assumptione* (Gualterus
    Cancellarius), 126
*Quaestiones de fide et de cognitione* (Matthew of
    Aquasparta), 33n.
*Quaestiones disputatae antequam esset frater*
    (Alexander of Hales), 33n.

*Quaestiones in secundum librum Sententiarum*
    (Pietro di Giovanni Olvi), 38n.
*Quaestiones quatuor de Domina* (Pietro di
    Giovanni Olivi), 38
Quarré, Pierre, 51–2
*Quodlibeta* (Pietro di Giovanni Olivi), 38n.

Reggio, Giovanni, 67n., 177n., 222
Richard of St Victor, 148, 182, 208, 213–14,
    240
Robert of Basevorn, 40, 41
Roffarè, Francesco T., 66n.
Rossi, Vittorio, 87n.
Roustang, François, 2n.
Rules, monastic:
    Cistercian, 124
    of St Benedict, 123, 124n.
    of St Augustine, 123–4
Rupert of Deutz, 207
Russi, Antonio, 86n., 88n., 106n.
Russo, Vittorio, 137n.

*Salve Regina*, 49, 156, 190
*Sanctuarium* (Boninus Mombritius), 26
Sandkühler, Bruno, 120n., 121n.
Sapegno, Natalino, 49n., 67n., 80, 87, 175,
    177, 184, 188n., 222, 234
*Satires* (Juvenal), 134
Sayers, Dorothy L., 66n.
Scartazzini, G. A., 78n., 106n., 112n., 125,
    221
Schildgen, Brenda D., 232n.
Scott James, Bruno, 24n.
Seneca, 33
*Sermones* (Augustine), 204
    *Sermo* cxxvi, 204n.
    *Sermo* clxvi, 206n., 207
*Sermones de diversis* (Bernard of Clairvaux),
    32, 58, 166, 176
*Sermones de sanctis* (Bernard of Clairvaux), 32
*Sermones de tempore* (Bernard of Clairvaux),
    32, 44n., 166, 167
    *In Adventu*, 184
    *In Annuntiatione Beatae Mariae Virginis*,
        181n.
    *In Assumptione Beatae Mariae Virginis*,
        170–2, 185
    *In dedicatione ecclesiae*, 132n.
    *In dominica infra octavam Assumptionis*,
        182n., 211n.
    *In festo Pentecoste*, 132n.
    *In nativitate Virginis* ('*De aquaeductu*'), 169,
        180, 183, 185–6, 187–8
    *In purificatione Beatae Mariae Virginis*, 166
    *In vigiliis Nativitatis Domini*, 187

Serravalle, Giovanni da, *see* Bertoldi da
    Serravalle, Giovanni
Siger of Brabant, 31, 40, 41
Singleton, Charles S., 150n., 232, 234
Sisinni, Francesco, 66n.
Southern, Sir Richard, 33
Sowell, Madison U., 148n.
*Speculum beatae Mariae Virginis* (Conrad of
    Saxony), 34, 157
Spiritual Franciscans, 34–40
Stefanini, Ruggiero, 105n.
*Summa contra Gentiles* (Thomas Aquinas), 124
*Summa theologiae* (Thomas Aquinas), 30, 124,
    215–21, 237
*Summa theologica* (Alexander of Hales), 32
*Super Isaiam* (Albert the Great), 29
*Super 'Missus est'* (Bernard of Clairvaux),
    *see In laudibus Virginis Matris*
Symeon the New Theologian, 202n.

Talice da Ricaldone, Stefano, 137
    *Commedia* commentary (wrongly
    attributed to), 121, 137n., 138–41
Tambling, Jeremy, 250n.
Tatian, 198
Tertullian, 203
Theophilus of Antioch, 198
Torraca, Francesco, 176–8
Toynbee, Paget, 71n., 157

*Tractatus de vita Sancti Benedicti* (Joachim of
    Fiore), 35–6
*Translationes Epistularum Nestorii in causa
    Pelagiana scriptarum* (pseudo-Marius
    Mercator), 204n.

Ubertino da Casale, 38–40, 41, 182, 192
*Unam sanctam* (Boniface VIII), 31
Underhill, Evelyn, 195

Vacandard, Elphège, 24n.
Vaccari, Alberto, 43n.
Valli, Luigi, 66n.
Vallone, Aldo, 121n., 165n., 177–8
Vandelli, Giuseppe, 78n., 106n., 119n.
*Veni redemptor* (Ambrose), 185
Verdi, Giuseppe, 108
Vidal, Gore, 17n.
Villani, Filippo, 149
Viscardi, Antonio, 79n.
*Vita nuova* (Dante), 78, 79, 152, 154, 158–9
*Vita prima* (of St Bernard), 21–5, 26, 36, 37,
    50, 51, 58, 138, 147, 173
*Vita secunda* (of St Bernard), 22, 24

William of St Thierry, 21, 22, 25, 208,
    213–15
Williams, Watkin Wynn, 24n.
Wilmart, André, 144

# CAMBRIDGE STUDIES IN MEDIEVAL LITERATURE

### TITLES PUBLISHED

1 *Dante's 'Inferno': Difficulty and dead poetry*, by Robin Kirkpatrick
2 *Dante and Difference: Writing in the 'Commedia'*, by Jeremy Tambling
3 *Troubadors and Irony*, by Simon Gaunt
4 *'Piers Plowman' and the New Anticlericalism*, by Wendy Scase
5 *The 'Cantar de mio Cid': Poetic creation in its economic and social contexts*, by Joseph Duggan
6 *The Medieval Greek Romance*, by Roderick Beaton
7 *Reformist Apocalypticism and 'Piers Plowman'*, by Kathryn Kerby-Fulton
8 *Dante and the Medieval Other World*, by Alison Morgan

9 *The Theatre of Medieval Europe: New research in early drama*, edited by Eckehard Simon

10 *The Book of Memory: A study of memory in medieval culture*, by Mary J. Carruthers

11 *Rhetoric, Hermeneutics and Translation in the Middle Ages: Academic traditions and vernacular texts*, by Rita Copeland

12 *The Arthurian Romances of Chrétien de Troyes: Once and future fictions*, by Donald Maddox

13 *Richard Rolle and the Invention of Authority*, by Nicholas Watson

14 *Dreaming in the Middle Ages*, by Steven F. Kruger

15 *Chaucer and the Tradition of the 'Roman Antique'*, by Barbara Nolan

16 *The 'Romance of the Rose' and its Medieval Readers: Interpretation, reception, manuscript transmission*, by Sylvia Huot

17 *Women and Literature in Britain, 1150–1500*, edited by Carol M. Meale

18 *Ideas and Forms of Tragedy from Aristotle to the Middle Ages*, by Henry Ansgar Kelly

19 *The Making of Textual Culture: Grammatica and literary theory, 350–1100*, by Martin Irvine

20 *Narrative Authority, and Power: The medieval exemplum and the Chaucerian tradition*, by Larry Scanlon

21 *Medieval Dutch Literature in its European Context*, edited by Erik Kooper

22 *Dante and the Mystical Tradition: Bernard of Clairvaux in the 'Commedia'*, by Steven Botterill